CW00867550

Debating *Orientalism*

Also by Ziad Elmarsafy

SUFISM IN THE CONTEMPORARY ARABIC NOVEL

THE ENLIGHTENMENT QUR'AN
The Politics of Translation and the Construction of Islam

FREEDOM, SLAVERY AND ABSOLUTISM
Corneille, Pascal, Racine

THE HISTRIONIC SENSIBILITY
Theatricality and Identity from Corneille to Rousseau

Also by David Attwell

J. M. COETZEE
South Africa and the Politics of Writing

REWRITING MODERNITY
Studies in Black South African Literary History

J. M. COETZEE
DOUBLING THE POINT
Essays and Interviews (*editor*)

BURY ME AT THE MARKETPLACE, ES'KIA MPHAHLELE AND COMPANY,
LETTERS 1943–2006 (*ed. with N. Chabani Manganyi*)

THE CAMBRIDGE HISTORY OF SOUTH AFRICAN LITERATURE
(*ed. with Derek Attridge*)

Debating *Orientalism*

Edited by

Ziad Elmarsafy
Reader, Department of English and Related Literature,
University of York, UK

Anna Bernard
Lecturer, Department of English and Comparative Literature,
King's College London, UK

and

David Attwell
Professor of Modern Literature, Department of English and Related Literature,
University of York, UK

palgrave
macmillan

Selection and editorial matter © Ziad Elmarsafy, Anna Bernard, David Attwell 2013
Individual chapters © Respective authors 2013

All rights reserved. No reproduction, copy or transmission of this publication may be made without written permission.

No portion of this publication may be reproduced, copied or transmitted save with written permission or in accordance with the provisions of the Copyright, Designs and Patents Act 1988, or under the terms of any licence permitting limited copying issued by the Copyright Licensing Agency, Saffron House, 6–10 Kirby Street, London EC1N 8TS.

Any person who does any unauthorized act in relation to this publication may be liable to criminal prosecution and civil claims for damages.

The authors have asserted their rights to be identified as the authors of this work in accordance with the Copyright, Designs and Patents Act 1988.

First published 2013 by
PALGRAVE MACMILLAN

Palgrave Macmillan in the UK is an imprint of Macmillan Publishers Limited, registered in England, company number 785998, of Houndmills, Basingstoke, Hampshire RG21 6XS.

Palgrave Macmillan in the US is a division of St Martin's Press LLC, 175 Fifth Avenue, New York, NY 10010.

Palgrave Macmillan is the global academic imprint of the above companies and has companies and representatives throughout the world.

Palgrave® and Macmillan® are registered trademarks in the United States, the United Kingdom, Europe and other countries.

ISBN 978–0–230–30352–2

This book is printed on paper suitable for recycling and made from fully managed and sustained forest sources. Logging, pulping and manufacturing processes are expected to conform to the environmental regulations of the country of origin.

A catalogue record for this book is available from the British Library.

A catalog record for this book is available from the Library of Congress.

Contents

Figures

Acknowledgements

We would like to thank the people at the University of York who helped us mark the thirtieth anniversary of the publication of *Orientalism* in 2008, thereby setting in motion the debates that made this book possible: the Department of English and Related Literature, the Centre for Modern Studies, the Institute for the Public Understanding of the Past, Trevor Sheldon and the Forum for the Enhancement of Learning and Teaching (FELT). We would also like to thank the Roberts Fund and F. R. Leavis Fund for their generous and timely support.

Our efforts were aided and abetted by numerous collaborators and interlocutors, including Jane Elliott, Donna Landry, Gerald MacLean, Rebecca MacKenzie, Stuart Murray, Nicola Robinson, Caroline Rooney, Helen Weinstein and Patrick Williams. Paula Kennedy and Ben Doyle at Palgrave Macmillan were a constant source of patient guidance. Our deepest and warmest thanks to them all.

Finally, we hereby gratefully acknowledge permission granted by the Palmach Photo Gallery to reproduce the photographs in Yonatan Mendel's piece here.

Note on Transliteration: We have generally followed the *IJMES* system for transliterating Arabic. Some of the better-known names are transliterated according to the more widespread form (hence Sadik Jalal al-ʿAzm rather than Ṣādiq Jalāl al-ʿAẓm).

Contributors

Moneera Al-Ghadeer received her PhD in comparative literature from the University of California, Berkeley, and is now Head of the Department of English Literature and Linguistics at Qatar University. Her publications include *Desert Voices: Bedouin Women's Poetry from Saudi Arabia* (2009). She is currently finishing two books, *Zoopoetics and the Politics of the Nonhuman in Arabic Literature* and *The Anxiety of the Foreign*.

David Attwell is Professor of Modern Literature at the University of York. A world-renowned expert on Coetzee, his publications include *J. M. Coetzee: South Africa and the Politics of Writing* (1993) and *Rewriting Modernity: Studies in Black South African Literary History* (2006). With Derek Attridge, he is co-editor of *The Cambridge History of South African Literature* (2012).

Anna Bernard is Lecturer in English and Comparative Literature at King's College London. Her publications include essays on Israel/Palestine and 'third-world literature,' the Israeli–Palestinian conflict in metropolitan popular culture and transnational genres of partition literature. She is completing a book on contemporary Palestinian and Israeli world writing.

Ziad Elmarsafy is a reader in the Department of English and Related Literature at the University of York. He is the author of *The Enlightenment Qur'an: The Politics of Translation and the Construction of Islam* (2009) and *Sufism in the Contemporary Arabic Novel* (2012).

Peter Gran is Professor of History at Temple University, where he specializes in Contemporary Arabic Studies and Comparative Third-World History. His publications include *Islamic Roots of Capitalism: Egypt 1760–1840* (1979), *Beyond Eurocentrism: A New View of Modern World History* (1996) and *The Rise of the Rich* (2008).

Joanna de Groot is a senior lecturer in the Department of History at the University of York. Her publications include *Religion, Culture and Politics in Iran: From the Qajars to Khomeini* (2007) and, with Mary Maynard, *Doing Things Differently? Women's Studies in the 1990s* (1993).

Nicholas Harrison is Professor of French Studies and Postcolonial Literature at King's College London. His publications include *Postcolonial Criticism: History, Theory and the Work of Fiction* (2003), and, as editor, *The Idea of the Literary* (*Paragraph*, July 2005) and *Gillo Pontecorvo's Battle of Algiers, 40 Years On* (*Interventions*, November 2007).

Robert Irwin is a publisher and writer of both fiction and non-fiction. His works of non-fiction include *The Arabian Nights: A Companion* (1994), *Islamic Art* (1997), *Night and Horses and the Desert: An Anthology of Classical Arabic Literature* (1999), *The Alhambra* (2004), *For Lust of Knowing: The Orientalists and Their Enemies* (2006), *Camel* (2010) and *Memoirs of a Dervish* (2011). A Fellow of the Royal Society of Literature, the Royal Asiatic Society and the Society of Antiquaries, he is also a consulting editor at the *Times Literary Supplement* and a senior research associate of the History Department of the School of Oriental and African Studies, London University.

Donna Landry is Professor of English and Director of the Centre for Studies in the Long Eighteenth Century at the University of Kent. Her publications include *Noble Brutes: How Eastern Horses Transformed English Culture* (2008) and *The Invention of the Countryside: Hunting, Walking, and Ecology in English Literature, 1671–1831* (2001).

Yonatan Mendel is a postdoctoral researcher in the Department of Politics and Government at Ben-Gurion University of the Negev. His PhD dissertation (2012) deals with the securitization of Arabic studies in Israel, and his current research deals with Zionist publications in Arabic in the pre-state period. Mendel used to work as a journalist, and currently contributes to the *London Review of Books*.

Mishka Sinha is currently a Fellow-Elect at the Program Zukunftsphilologie, Forum Transregionale Studien, Berlin. She obtained an MPhil from Oxford and her PhD from Cambridge. Her doctoral work analysed the history of Sanskrit in Britain and America, from 1832 to 1939. Her research interests include transcolonial interactions in interwar London, histories of spiritualism and the self in the Victorian and Modern periods, and the intellectual history of empire.

Robert Spencer is Lecturer in Postcolonial Literatures and Cultures at the University of Manchester. His research interests include postcolonial and especially African fiction and poetry, postcolonial theory and the work of Edward Said. He is the author of *Cosmopolitan Criticism and Postcolonial Literature* (2011). It seeks to show how, as a crucial aspect of their appeal and utility, postcolonial literary texts can inculcate the aptitudes of cosmopolitan citizenship.

Andrea Teti is Lecturer in International Relations and Middle East Politics at the University of Aberdeen, and a senior fellow at the Brussels-based European Centre for International Affairs. His research focuses primarily on political theory and Mediterranean politics. He has published on both Egypt and Italy, as well as on a range of theoretical issues, including democratization theory, constructivism, post-structuralism, European democracy promotion and leftist opposition groups in Egypt.

Nicholas Tromans is a senior lecturer at Kingston University, London. He is the author of *David Wilkie: The People's Painter* (2007), *Richard Dadd: The Artist and the Asylum* (2011) and *Hope: The Life and Times of a Victorian Icon* (2011). He was the curator and catalogue editor of the Tate Britain exhibition *The Lure of the East: British Orientalist Painting*, which toured to Istanbul and Sharjah in 2008–09.

1
Orientalism: Legacies of a Performance

Ziad Elmarsafy and Anna Bernard

Books, as Catullus reminds us, have fates of their own. Our concern is with the fate of one book, Edward Said's *Orientalism*. To many, this seminal work is an enduring touchstone, a founding text of the field of postcolonial studies and a book that continues to influence debates in literary and cultural studies, Middle Eastern studies, anthropology, art history, history and politics. To others, however, *Orientalism* has serious failings, not least in blaming the wrong people – namely, Orientalists – for the crimes of European imperialism. Thirty-five years after its first edition, popular and academic reactions to *Orientalism* continue to run the gamut from enthusiasm to apoplexy. Yet few assessments of this work ask the 'so what?' question, addressing the book's contemporary relevance without lionizing or demonizing its author. This is our aim in *Debating Orientalism*. Bridging the gap between intellectual history and political engagement, the contributors to this volume interrogate *Orientalism*'s legacy with a view to moving the debate about this text beyond the Manichean limitations within which it has all too often been imprisoned. Too much ink has been spilled on what *Orientalism* got right or wrong – especially in its historical and political registers – and too little on taking stock of its impact and building on that to appraise its significance to current debates in multiple fields. This book seeks to consider *Orientalism*'s implications with a little less feeling, though no less commitment to understanding the value and political effects of engaged scholarship.

Orientalism's influence came above all from its decisive linking of politics with the humanities, a position that was to have revelatory effects for humanities scholars. If it is still an obligatory point of reference today, that is partly because the political and intellectual climate to which it responded is little changed,[1] but it is also because

Orientalism made it all but impossible to write about colonialism and culture, intellectuals and institutions or the representation of non-European 'difference' without at least acknowledging its claims.[2] This volume takes *Orientalism* as a springboard, seeking to recreate the rush of excitement it sparked when it was first published. We are interested in what *Orientalism* has come to mean as it has travelled across disciplines and historical periods, and in the kinds of thinking it has enabled and, in some cases, suppressed, especially in relation to contemporary understandings of the Arab and Islamic world. Has the book become 'a spectacular and depressing instance of traveling theory,' as Timothy Brennan has argued, used to authorize an identity politics that equates cultural location with epistemological and political position?[3] Or have its peregrinations given us something to celebrate, in the decisive changes in academic work that have made cultural production and practice inseparable from its political circumstances?

Orientalism caused polemics even before its publication, as witness Said's bitter private exchange with Syrian philosopher Sadik Jalal al-ʿAzm that spilled over into a very public three-way argument between Said, al-ʿAzm and the Syrian poet Adūnīs.[4] In the intervening decades, the book has been attacked, defended, rebutted and restituted with no apparent end. These debates have been marked by recurring points of dissent, to the extent that it has become difficult to say anything new about this text. Depending on what one reads, *Orientalism* is a Foucauldian book, or it is a challenge to Foucault; it made possible a textualist and dehistoricizing postcolonial studies, or it set out very different points of theoretical and political allegiance; it essentialized the West in much the same way that it accused Orientalists of doing, or it emphasized the agency of individual thinkers and writers and the fundamental imbalance of power between Western and Eastern sites of knowledge production in the modern period.[5] Each of these assessments is passionately argued and just as passionately refuted, as much in recent years as in the 1980s and 1990s. Ali Behdad, writing in 2010, praises *Orientalism* for 'rigorously interrogating the ideological underpinnings of familiar scientific and artistic representations of otherness in modern European thought.'[6] Daniel Martin Varisco, three years earlier, dismisses the text on almost exactly the same grounds: 'Said's amateurish and ahistorical essentializing of an Orientalism-as-textualized discourse from Aeschylus to Bernard Lewis has polemical force, but only at the expense of methodological precision and rhetorical consistency.'[7] But even its critics return to it again and again: *Orientalism* is a text, as Varisco concedes, that 'engages even the reader it enrages.'[8]

While *Orientalism* was explicitly framed, in the final chapter 'Orientalism Now,' as a response to American foreign policy, in the last decade the global 'war on terror' has brought a new degree of urgency and controversy to its claims. The book has been taken up as a means of challenging the murderous indifference of American military intervention (see Landry and Al-Ghadeer, this volume), at the same time that it has been excoriated for its apparent condoning of anti-American violence (see Spencer's discussion of Ibn Warraq, Kramer and Irwin, this volume). These more recent assessments indicate one of the key reasons that *Orientalism* continues to attract attention, since the idea of a 'clash of civilizations' between the Arab-Islamic world and the metropolitan West remains alarmingly current. *Orientalism* is accused of fuelling a 'politics of resentment,' in al-ʿAzm's phrase,[9] forever pitting West against East. Yet for other contemporary readers, like Stephen Morton, the book makes it possible for us to name the discourse of terror as an instance of present-day colonial discourse, one that is used to obscure the geopolitical contexts of particular forms of non-state violence.[10]

It is not just *Orientalism*'s subject matter that gives it its continuing prominence, however, but also its methodology and style. Aijaz Ahmad, in his infamous attack on Said in *In Theory*, suggests caustically (with perhaps a hint of begrudging admiration) that although the book's references were drawn from comparative literature and philology, the book was as bewildering to literary critics as it was to Middle East scholars. The former were asked to read their customary objects of study as documents of 'the Orientalist archive, which they had thought was none of their business'; the latter scholar found himself 'with no possibility of defending himself on what he had defined as his home ground.'[11] Even Ahmad admits that this authoritative interdisciplinarity was 'electrifying, because the book did serve to open up, despite its blunders, spaces of oppositional work in both' fields.[12] But what Ahmad calls the book's 'narrative amplitude'[13] describes something more profound than bringing the tools of close reading to bear on ideas normally associated with political history or area studies. The book's sheer breadth of reference gave its readers a sense of glimpsing a kind of historical totality, in keeping with a method Said would later describe in his autobiography as 'making connections between disparate books and ideas with considerable ease ... [I would] look out over a sea of details, spotting patterns, phrases, word clusters, which I imagined as stretching out interconnectedly without limit.'[14] Said's 'intellectual generalism'[15] was of course greatly inspired by Erich Auerbach's *Mimesis* (see Spencer,

this volume), which may help to account for *Orientalism*'s stature, especially in postcolonial studies, as the *Mimesis* of its time. Not all of Said's
readers were persuaded by this display of erudition (see Irwin, this volume), but many humanities scholars found in *Orientalism* a suggestive
model for trying to grasp the full 'imaginative geography' of colonial
and neocolonial forms of rule across and within a wide array of contexts
and periods.[16] It is not just that Said 'violat[ed] disciplinary borders and
transgress[ed] authoritative historical frontiers,' as an influential assessment has it[17]; it is that he found an eclectic (if arguably inconsistent)[18]
means of knitting these disciplines and histories together.

This is not to offer an unequivocal endorsement of this method and
its legacy, for the embrace of *Orientalism* has proved, in some ways, more
problematic than its rejection. 'Orientalism' quickly became 'a code-
word for virtually any kind of Othering process,'[19] through which the
specificity of Said's readings of individual texts became the grounds for
indiscriminate assertions about the primacy of discourse in any form
of cultural encounter. Nicholas Dirks recalls Said's dismay at realizing
that many anthropologists had taken the text as an invitation to priv-
ilege representation over all other subjects of enquiry, 'repeating the
political delusions of philosophical and literary theories and preoccupations that stressed meaning and interpretation over the clamorous
demands of politics and history.'[20] Said's interlocutors are divided on
the question of whether this mode of reception stems from a fundamental misreading of the book – 'an *Orientalism* that Said did not write'[21] –
or from the contradictions in its positioning and methodology, which
allowed its readers to selectively emphasize the moments in which Said
claims that no 'true' representation is possible, or that there is no 'real'
Orient, over the moments in which he defended the responsible and
self-critical production of knowledge.[22] Part of the aim of this collection
is to enable a return to the notions of textual and historical specificity
that *Orientalism* demonstrated with characteristic verve. Many of our
contributors point the way toward what Graham Huggan calls a 'relocal-
ized' (and rehistoricized) Orientalism, even as they express reservations
about some of its more sweeping appropriations.[23]

Among Orientalism's many articulations, its status as performance
deserves special mention. We use the term 'performance' as Said himself
did, taking his cue from a complex genealogy involving the legendary
pianist Glenn Gould, R. P. Blackmur (who taught Said at Princeton) and
Richard Poirier (the man Said called 'America's finest literary critic'[24] and
the dedicatee of *Humanism and Democratic Criticism*). 'Performance' is a
loaded term for Said: where others might detect dissimulation, Said saw

an approach to authenticity. Said admired Blackmur's 'back-and-forth restlessness' that transformed criticism 'from the mere explication, to the *performance*, of literature.'[25] He repeatedly used the phrase 'bringing literature to performance' to describe a core element of his critical and intellectual project, namely taking a text through a philological close reading that unfolds its discourses and animates its silences to bring out its situated worldliness.[26] In his foreword to the 1992 edition of Poirier's *The Performing Self*, Said saw in the 'performing ethic' a laudable rejection of fixed identity and completeness as bases for critical authority. Instead, via Poirier, Said urges us to let go of the idea that 'words and objects are in stable contact with each other,' of literature as a 'magistrate's court or a closely guarded fiefdom,' and of professional expressions of piety, awe and particularity as acceptable substitutes for 'real identity, real particularity, which in fact have to be forged and re-forged constantly.'[27] Poirier himself emphasizes the point that literature is not, and cannot be, 'a world elsewhere,' adding that 'no book can, for very long, separate itself from this world; it can only try to do so, through magnificent exertions of style lasting only for the length of the exertion.'[28] Although Said was at the farthest possible remove from wanting to separate himself, or his books, from the world, the phrase 'magnificent exertion of style' might usefully describe his performance – as critical mode and as intervention – in *Orientalism*.

For Said, moreover, performance is an activity that entails responsibility 'for those voices dominated, displaced or silenced by the textuality of texts.'[29] That responsibility became, as is well known, the story of Said's life: giving voice to those that he considered silenced by the 'systems of forces institutionalized by the reigning culture,' in the Middle East and elsewhere. So important is performance for Said that it is the first quality he lists in describing the critic's activity during the course of his 1976 interview with *Diacritics*: 'We need to acknowledge that criticism is a very complex act: it involves performance, cognition, intuition, style, ritual, and charlatanry of course.'[30] As he strives to perform, the critic/reader must 'decreate' and reorder the material at hand to liberate the voices of the silenced.[31] Of course, the terms 'decreation' and 'reordering' might also very usefully describe the things that Said does with the traditional understanding of Orientalism, now undone and re-arranged to look much less objective and neutral than before, more domineering over and oppressive of those it claims to represent. Along with decreation and reordering, we might add 'invention' as the final term in the critical triad informed by the performing ethic. In a late piece on Glenn Gould whose title could have served as a good description of

Said himself – 'The Virtuoso as Intellectual' – Said invokes Cicero and Vico to conflate the musical and rhetorical meaning of invention, now understood as *inventio*, finding or discovering. Between Bach's outstanding command of the *ars combinatoria* that yielded his near-miraculous musical compositions, and Gould's eccentric re-working and revelation of those aspects of Bach's inventiveness that themselves constitute a major re-discovery of Bach's oeuvre, Said sees a powerful instance of invention as a form of 'creative repetition and reliving.'[32] This energetic capacity for (re-)discovery should, Said argues, be part of every critical project. The attitude of the critic should be 'frankly inventive, in the traditional rhetorical sense of *inventio* so fruitfully employed by Vico, which means finding and exposing things that otherwise lie hidden beneath piety, heedlessness or routine.'[33] Attending to performance enables invention, including the *inventio* or unearthing of the Orient that lies hidden beneath those texts that set out to represent it.

In truth, our emphasis on *Orientalism*'s style is not entirely new. Robert Irwin's negative account of *Orientalism* describes its virtues as follows:

> On the whole, though, the qualities of *Orientalism* are those of a good novel. It is exciting, packed with lots of sinister villains, as well as an outnumbered band of goodies, and the picture that it presents of the world is richly imagined, but essentially fictional.[34]

Wit and talk of essences aside, when a novelist calls a book a 'good novel' the moment is worthy of attention. Similarly, the 'fictional' quality of *Orientalism* does not mean that it can simply be dismissed on that count. Indeed, the participation of ostensibly non-fictional, truth-telling genres in literary modes of conduct has been one of the mainstays of literary theory and criticism for the past four decades. The Nietzschean moment, in which truth is recognized as a 'mobile army of metaphors, metonyms and anthropomorphisms,' played a decisive role in the sort of writing that went on around the time of the composition of *Orientalism*.[35] Said invokes Nietzsche's phrase to call attention to the play of representational forces in the constitution of Orientalism, whereby to Western minds 'the Orient was a word which later accrued to it a wide field of meanings, associations, and connotations, and that these did not necessarily refer to the real Orient but to the field surrounding the word.'[36] But we might also consider *Orientalism* as a text that deploys mobile armies of tropes, figures and ideas, under Said's formidable command, to perform the task of the critic, making it a text to which wide fields of meanings, associations and connotations would later accrue. And while we might agree with the many criticisms and corrections that take stock of the gaps between *Orientalism* and 'the real Orient,' we might also explore the truth contained in this very rhetorical text, in much the same way that we turn to art and literature in search of truths that cannot be found because they cannot be expressed elsewhere.

To detail those truths is not our aim here; all we want to do is suggest a different way of reading this most influential of books. Numerous other perspectives are put forward in the chapters that follow, all bearing witness to the fact that, even when Said's putative errors are removed, there remains something particularly valuable about *Orientalism* as an intervention. This thing of value is not only an argument that rotates around the colonial–postcolonial axis – in and of itself the claim for the implication of Orientalists in the European imperial enterprise would not be especially original, since it was put forward years before Said by Anouar Abd el-Malek, Talal Asad and others.[37] *Orientalism* goes beyond that, making a case for the 'literariness' of the misconstrued Orient, and with it a major claim about the power of the work of art.[38] The discourse on art's ability to communicate ideas is not itself necessarily devoid of art or its techniques: hence the value of *Orientalism* as an artful and artistic performance. Furthermore, the claim that art and literature hide as much as they show, and that much can be learned from attending to what they hide, remains a vital part of Said's lesson.

One of the truths told by Said's performance is, of course, that of the peoples of the Middle East, and how it came to be that their occupation by Western powers was deemed desirable in the name of reason, culture and art rather than as an exercise of imperial power. This is the sort of thinking that led to the appalling misrepresentation of the Palestinian cause during (and after) the years in which Said was working on *Orientalism*. In this respect, *Orientalism* remains a very autobiographical book, and an important forerunner of Said's memoir, *Out of Place*. How is it, Said seems to be asking, that the same democratic American public that opposed the Vietnam War and fought for civil rights could unquestioningly support the state of Israel despite the injustice done to the Palestinian people? What does that public not see or hear, and what representational dynamics made these false claims acceptable? How do the dispossession, occultation and suffering of entire populations become banal? How does it come about that parts of the globe are misrepresented as being so dysfunctional as to require occupation and imperial domination? Said answers the question allegorically in *Orientalism* (and to a degree in the two books that he published alongside it, *Covering Islam* and *The Question of Palestine*): the many discourses that circulate about the Orient in *Orientalism* are a major part of what makes these things possible. Once normalized, these discourses legitimize that which cannot be legitimized otherwise, operating as a Nietzschean army of tropes that aims to make force seem just and violence seem necessary. Past that point, erroneous stereotypes and false beliefs become so routinely and deeply embedded that only the hard work of the critic can undo their nefarious effects. Needless to say, the degree to which this discursive and rhetorical history really does originate with Aeschylus and meanders through medieval and early modern European representations of Islam is debatable. But the collusion between various intellectuals, 'experts' and imperial power during the twentieth and twenty-first centuries, together with the disastrous results of the military, rather than merely verbal or discursive, dealings with the Middle East, are not in dispute. It is here that Said's performance is at its most convincing; it is here that figurative and literal are most successfully joined. And it is this conjunction that might have repaid careful reading at the turn of the twenty-first century by state leaders and decision-makers prosecuting other wars in the Middle East and Afghanistan. That, though, is another story.

*   *   *

In view of Said's commitments to justice and the Middle East, it is perhaps inevitable that most of the chapters in this volume coalesce around this topic. The arrangement reflects, very roughly, the order of magnitude of the context, from the very broad to the more specific, from the discursive framework that surrounds the ideas set out in *Orientalism* to more particular disciplinary and theoretical interrogations.

The first contribution comes from one of the earliest reviewers of *Orientalism*, Peter Gran.[39] Gran returns to Said's text to assess its impact on the study of world history and Middle Eastern history in particular over three decades after its publication. Gran details the institutional history surrounding the publication and reception of *Orientalism* to show how Said's work continues to oblige scholars in those areas to rethink their post-Hegelian 'Rise of the West' framework. Gran surveys, *inter alia*, the rise of postmodernism as a part of neo-liberal culture that accompanied the resurgence of a traditional Orientalist outlook toward the Middle East after the Iranian Revolution of 1979. The net effect of this resurgence, Gran argues, is the isolation of the Middle East from 'the wider multi-culturalist fabric of the late twentieth century.' Gran proceeds to evaluate three recent works written with explicit reference to *Orientalism* to illustrate a curious phenomenon, whereby those scholars who take an anti-Said line (like Robert Irwin) end up sounding rather Saidian, while those who set out to write histories that agree with the basic tenets of *Orientalism* end up producing arguments that oppose it. He concludes with a searing indictment of the failure of historians to produce a metanarrative of world history that dispenses with categories such as 'the West' and 'the Orient.'

Robert Irwin, one of Said's best-known critics, uses historical and biographical detail to plead against Said's presentation of Flaubert in *Orientalism*. Irwin's piece is striking for the degree to which it gets inside the mind of the novelist, taking individual moments and scenes from his travels in Egypt with Maxime du Camp and demonstrating their transformation by Flaubert's creative interventions. That said, Irwin cautions against the facile assumption that travel to the Orient *ipso facto* produces Orientalist texts: in Flaubert's case, the most important result of the voyage to Egypt was *Madame Bovary*. Irwin also takes issue with Said's reading of Flaubert's relationship with the people he met in Egypt, notably Kuchuk Hanem, as well as his interpretation of *Salammbô*. Far from being a location associated with danger, excitement and sexual mystery, the Orient was very often the locus of ennui. In closing, Irwin reminds the reader that there are key political dimensions associated with travel to the Middle East in the nineteenth century that deserve closer scrutiny, chief among them being the travellers' age and class.

The collection then moves to examine iterations of Orientalism at particular historical moments, beginning with Donna Landry's discussion of representations of the Orient that predate those addressed in *Orientalism*. Landry challenges Ahmad's critique of Orientalism as an 'uninterrupted history of narcissistic discourse'[40] by arguing that Orientalism may be understood as a broad cultural paradigm that is differently articulated in specific historical and geographical contexts. For Landry, Said's understanding of Orientalism as a machine for constructing the 'Orient' is relevant not only to our present moment (especially the representation of Palestine and the Palestinians), but also to the early modern period, when the wealth and power of the Ottoman Empire inspired the 'imperial envy' of its European observers. Instead of the confident authority of the nineteenth-century English writers, these writers evince what Landry calls a proto-Orientalism, aspirationally imperialist but shot through with a sense of inferiority to the Ottomans, which produced aggressive representations of Ottoman barbarism as well as admiring accounts of Ottoman civility. Landry cautions against the contemporary scholarly tendency to exaggerate instances of English–Turkish rapprochement in this period, but she also suggests that the Ottoman *millet* system, with its official policy of toleration of non-Muslims and cultural autonomy for minorities, can inspire our thinking about more cosmopolitan modes of social organization in the present.

Mishka Sinha addresses another historical locus of Orientalism by examining the rise of Sanskrit studies in the nineteenth-century American academy. This development in some ways prefigures the contemporary forms of American Orientalism that several of our contributors address, but it complicates conventional understandings of their genealogy. Sinha argues that Said's effort to trace a straight line from British imperial attitudes toward the Middle East and Islam to post-war American foreign policy leads him to overlook this earlier phase of American Orientalism, which was associated with India rather than the Middle East, and derived primarily from a German Orientalist tradition, not from Britain or France. She sees the formation of this field as crucial to the American academy's drive to assert its intellectual independence from Europe. William Dwight Whitney, who held the first Chair in Sanskrit at Yale, was a key figure in the production of a new idea of the American university with comparative philology at the heart of its curriculum, built on the 'scientific' study of the foundational language of Sanskrit. This form of American Orientalism was not used to rule over the 'Orient,' but rather to assert an American intellectual exceptionalism, using Sanskrit instrumentally as a means of producing a uniquely American field of knowledge. Sinha's account thus helps to flesh out the institutional lineage of American area studies, showing that it is indeed bound up with European imperial history, but in ways that extend and exceed Said's analysis.

Yonatan Mendel addresses a third historical location of Orientalism that is especially salient with respect to Said: the fusion of military power and knowledge in the history of the mistaʿaravim unit of the Palmach, a unit composed of Arabic-speaking Jews recruited specifically for military and security operations in Palestine and the surrounding countries. The history of the mistaʿaravim provides an excellent example of the ways in which knowledge of the Arab world immediately translated into a strategic, military and imperial advantage. Furthermore, the configuration and training of the unit adds further weight to the persistence of essentialist mythologies surrounding the Orient, and the violent use to which these mythologies are put. No less violent, however, is the seemingly constant re-arrangement of selves and identities that made the operation of the mistaʿaravim unit possible: recruits were required to 'de-Arabize' themselves, the better to distinguish their identity from that of the Palestinian Arabs. Needless to say this process was a vital part of the greater project of building, and consolidating, a Zionist Jewish image that differed completely from its Arab counterpart. Mendel thus substantiates the Orientalist contours of the Zionist project.

Continuing in this mode, Moneera Al-Ghadeer responds to the American Orientalism of our contemporary moment, noting the shift from the representation of the 'Orient' as a site of aesthetic value in the nineteenth-century texts Said discussed to the current depiction of the Middle East as a site of savagery and spectacular violence. She proposes the notion of the 'cannibalistic spectacle' as a means of understanding the violence visited on Muslim and Arab male bodies by American soldiers waging the 'war on terror,' with particular reference to the photographs of the interrogations at Abu Ghraib. The exposure, disfigurement, sexual degradation and assault, and in some cases actual physical consumption of the prisoners' bodies became a form of transgressive communal ritual, through which American troops sought to alleviate their fear of the 'foreign' body by assimilating it as the 'same.' She suggests, drawing on the work of Derrida and Irigaray, that such graphic acts of physical and discursive violence might be countered by the notion of an 'anticannibal ethics.' Such an ethics would resist the 'figurative cannibalism' of the repression or denial of these atrocities by making it possible to mourn them, insisting on the impossibility of integration through consumption and on an ethics of non-appropriative reciprocity.

The chapters in the final part of the book address some of the disciplinary formations that continue to take *Orientalism* as a key point of reference, drawing out the possibilities for future enquiry that Said's work suggests. Andrea Teti addresses the theoretical consequences of *Orientalism* by re-situating the relationship between Said and Foucault. Instead of focusing on the early Foucault and the question of his 'influence' on Said, or of the latter's appropriation of some of his theoretical claims, Teti maps the dominant structures of the *History of Sexuality* onto those of *Orientalism*. The parallels between Said's analysis of Orientalism as discourse and Foucault's arguments about a 'regime of truth' reveal the operation of the former as a confessional mechanism that connects 'Normal Self' (the West) to 'Deviant Other' (the Orient). This in turn enables an exploration of the ways in which Orientalist discourses are deployed in what Teti calls 'the contemporary politics of truth.' Teti thus provides a theoretical basis both for a new perspective on the formation of subjectivities and, more urgently, for a Saidian theory of resistance, thereby reversing the many claims that *Orientalism* is lacking on that score.

In a more anti-Foucauldian register, Robert Spencer challenges the assumption, ironically shared by postcolonial scholars and some of Said's most vocal critics, that *Orientalism* argues that it is impossible for scholars in the 'West' to produce true knowledge about the 'East.' Instead, Spencer reads *Orientalism* as a profoundly humanist text, with humanism understood as a continuous self-consciousness and self-criticism of one's own methodology and practice. He points to Said's praise for 'Orientalist' scholars like Clifford Geertz, Maxime Rodinson and Jacques Berque, whom he saw as capable of freeing themselves from Orientalist ways of thinking, and of course his admiration for Auerbach, whose work demonstrated a means of drawing general conclusions from particular examples while remaining scrupulously aware of one's own biases and limitations. Said's own scholarship hardly sought to avoid representation: instead, he worked throughout his career to create and circulate knowledge about the Palestinians, the Arabs and the Middle East. Spencer presents this defence of Said as a challenge to the recent backlash against *Orientalism*. He takes Ibn Warraq and Martin Kramer to task for their openly partisan attack on Said's 'anti-American' scholarship, and he questions Robert Irwin's focus on Said's errors in *Orientalism* at the expense of an engagement with his central insights. Spencer charges these critics with seeking to close down debate about *how* to generate knowledge, and with substituting an unquestioning faith in the disinterestedness of scholarship for Said's careful attention to the political circumstances of its production.

Nicholas Tromans' chapter takes a related approach, contrasting *Orientalism*'s influence in the field of art history with a more nuanced idea of the visual's potential that emerges in Said's later work. In *Orientalism*, the image marks the point of exhaustion of the particularities of language and argument, giving way to an all-encompassing imperial 'vision.' The book's legacy for theories of the visual persists in the notion of the image as a vehicle for racial stereotypes (especially images of 'the Arab'), and in its figuring of the 'gaze' as an instrument of imperial control. In Said's later work, however, he showed that images could also contest static and circumscribed ways of knowing: in *After the Last Sky*, for instance, he used Jean Mohr's photographs of Palestinian individuals to challenge metropolitan narratives of 'Arabs' en masse. Tromans argues that art historians have neglected the activist dimension of Said's later engagements with the image, after having largely abandoned *Orientalism*'s insights in favour of an emphasis on the 'complexity' of East–West interaction. He suggests that the political urgency of *Orientalism*'s critique might be reclaimed through attention to the history of Western denigrations of non-Western visual competence, or to the history of Western ownership and control of technologies of representation.

Joanna de Groot addresses *Orientalism*'s legacy for the field of gender studies, noting its enduring paradox: that even though Said is frequently criticized for neglecting questions of gender, his paradigm has been widely taken up by scholars of gender and sexuality. She extends her analysis through attention to two particular cases: first, the career of the nineteenth-century Ottoman painter Osman Hamdi Bey, and second, contemporary debates around female practices of 'veiling.' In each case, de Groot argues, an empirical analysis doubly informed by the critical tools of gender and Orientalism makes it possible to evaluate highly complex interactions of cultural and material phenomena. De Groot's case studies are linked by the central position that gender and domestic reform occupy in discourses of modernization, with a particular emphasis on gendered dress codes. Hamdi Bey's portraiture reframed gendered tropes of European Orientalist painting, using representations of male and female forms of traditional and European dress as a means of envisioning a distinctly Ottoman modernity. Similarly, contemporary discourses around veiling betray its extraordinary polyvalence and elasticity. Rather than affirming a dichotomy where veiling is traditional and unveiling is modern, contemporary veiling practices respond to a complex set of associations with veiling as a decolonizing practice, as a response to discrimination in Europe and as a form of self-expression and individual agency. De Groot contends that it is only through an intersectional gendered and cross-cultural analysis that such historical complexities can be unravelled and understood.

Finally, Nicholas Harrison argues that *Orientalism*'s enormous impact stemmed from its insistence that humanities scholarship could itself have an 'impact' on the world outside of academia. This idea has become newly topical in British universities, where academic research is now formally assessed on these grounds. Harrison argues that although Said's legacy might seem to provide an exemplary instance of 'impact,' the example he set for other literary scholars is unclear. Said's oeuvre is marked by a sharp distinction between literary criticism and political advocacy, and his own writing on the work of the intellectual betrays an ambivalence about the social value of academic work; indeed, at times he seemed to suggest that intellectuals' 'impact' can come only from their commitments beyond academia. Against this rather bleak assessment of academic practice, however, Harrison points to the moments in *Orientalism* which ascribe an independent value to the work of writers like Nerval and Flaubert. He contends that this cautious assertion of the distinctiveness of the aesthetic takes fuller shape in Said's music criticism, where Said articulates a notion of artistic value that cannot be easily assimilated to political concerns. It becomes more powerful still in his late descriptions of the classroom as a place apart, and of teaching – especially the teaching of literature – as a key form of political and social praxis in its own right. Our collection thus ends with a decisive reminder of the reasons behind the enduring interest of Said's *Orientalism*, and its ability not only to provoke lively (and sometimes hostile) debate, but also to remind us of why our activities both within and without the academy still matter.

Notes

1. Joseph Massad, 'Affiliating with Edward Said,' in *Edward Said: A Legacy of Emancipation and Representation*, eds. Adel Iskandar and Hakem Rustom, 33–49 (Berkeley, CA and London: University of California Press, 2010), 27–8.
2. This is a frequent observation in assessments of the book's impact. See, among others, Nicholas Dirks, 'Edward Said and Anthropology,' in Iskandar and Rustom (2010), 86; James P. Rice, 'In the Wake of Orientalism,' *Comparative Literature Studies* 37, no. 2 (2000), 223.
3. Timothy Brennan, 'The Illusion of a Future: "Orientalism" as Traveling Theory,' *Critical Inquiry* 26, no. 3 (2000), 558–9.
4. The story is narrated in Sadik Jalal al-ʿAzm, *Dhihniyat al-Taḥrīm: Salman Rushdie wa Ḥaqīqat al-Adab* (Damascus: Dār al-Madā, 2007), 63–70. Al-ʿAzm's critique of *Orientalism* is found in pp. 13–62. The first part of this critique was published in English as 'Orientalism and Orientalism in Reverse,' in the socialist revolutionary journal *Khamsin* 8 (1981), 5–26, and reprinted in *Forbidden Agendas: Intolerance and Defiance in the Middle East*, ed. Jon Rothschild (London: Saqi, 1984), 349–76. Al-ʿAzm's reading of *Orientalism* matters not only because of its aftermath, but also because it was and remains one of the very few Arabic engagements with *Orientalism*.
5. For a summary of these debates that challenges the idea that *Orientalism* is a Foucauldian text and marks Said's distance from the identity politics that came to dominate postcolonial studies, see Brennan, 'The Illusion of a Future' and his subsequent revisions of the argument in *Wars of Position* (New York: Columbia University Press, 2006), 93–125, as well as 'The Critic and the Public: Edward Said and World Literature,' in Iskandar and Rustom 2010, 102–20. Brennan makes a case for Said's emphasis on the agency of individual scholars: 'the biographical methodology of *Orientalism* [...] is a deliberate construct, put there to highlight the historical stakes involved in the careers of named individuals who have made something by force of will

and by rhetorical skill' (2000, 581). For a contrasting view, see Andrea Teti's contribution to this volume.

6. Ali Behdad, 'Orientalism Matters,' *Modern Fiction Studies* 56, no. 4 (2010), 709.

7. Daniel Martin Varisco, *Reading Orientalism: Said and the Unsaid* (Seattle, WA: University of Washington Press, 2007), 22.

8. Varisco, *Reading Orientalism*, 10.

9. Sadik Jalal al-ʿAzm, 'Orientalism, Occidentalism, and Islam: Keynote Address to "Orientalism and Fundamentalism in Islamic and Judaic Critique: A Conference Honoring Sadik al-Azm,"' *Comparative Studies of South Asia, Africa and the Middle East* 30, no. 1 (2010), 7.

10. Stephen Morton, 'Terrorism, Orientalism, and Imperialism,' *Wasafiri* 22, no. 2 (2007), 36–7.

11. Aijaz Ahmad, *In Theory: Classes, Nations, Literatures* (1992) (London: Verso, 2008), 176, original emphasis.

12. Ahmad, *In Theory*, 177.

13. Ahmad, *In Theory*, 173.

14. Edward W. Said, *Out of Place* (London: Vintage, 2000), 165. Said is speaking here of his precocious adolescent intellect, rather than the process of writing *Orientalism*, but the recollection seems distinctly coloured by his later methods.

15. Brennan, 'The Illusion of a Future,' 578.

16. Said, 'Orientalism Reconsidered' (1985), in *Reflections on Exile and Other Essays* (Cambridge, MA: Harvard University Press, 2000), 199.

17. Gyan Prakash, 'Orientalism Now,' *History and Theory* 34, no. 3 (1995), 201.

18. The charge of methodological and philosophical inconsistency is one of the most frequent criticisms of *Orientalism*. For a recent assessment of the evidence and effects of the text's oscillation between Foucauldian discourse analysis and its commitment to humanism, see Neil Lazarus, *The Postcolonial Unconscious* (Cambridge: Cambridge University Press, 2011), 184–97.

19. Graham Huggan, '(Not) Reading Orientalism,' *Research in African Literatures* 36, no. 3 (2005), 125–6.

20. Dirks, 'Edward Said and Anthropology,' 88–9.

21. Brennan, 'The Illusion of a Future,' 567.

22. See Lazarus, *The Postcolonial Unconscious*, 184–8, 195–6.

23. Huggan, '(Not) Reading Orientalism,' 126, original emphasis.

24. As recalled by Mariam Said in her foreword to Said's *On Late Style: Music and Literature against the Grain* (London: Bloomsbury, 2006), viii–ix.

25. Said, 'The Horizon of R. P. Blackmur' (1986), in *Reflections on Exile*, 252.

26. This phrase occurs, among other places, in 'Sense and Sensibility' (1967) in *Reflections on Exile*, 17; *The World, the Text and the Critic* (Cambridge, MA: Harvard University Press, 1983), 53; *Humanism and Democratic Criticism* (Basingstoke and New York: Palgrave Macmillan, 2004), 66; and Moustafa Bayoumi and Andrew Rubin, 'An Interview with Edward W. Said,' in *The Edward Said Reader*, 419–44 (New York: Vintage, 2000), 424. Blackmur uses the phrase to foreground a reading that brings out the classical form underlying the novel, with specific reference to the tragic core in what he called the 'loose and baggy monsters of Henry James' (*The Ambassadors, The Golden*

Bowl and *The Wings of the Dove*), based on the conviction that 'in the novel [...] what is called technical or executive form has as its final purpose to bring into being – to bring into performance, for the writer and for the reader – an instance of the feeling of what life is about.' *The Lion and the Honeycomb: Essays in Solicitude and Critique* (London: Methuen, 1956), 268. Criticism thereby becomes 'the work we do to bring into the performance of our own language the underlying classic form in which they [the Muses] speak' (288). Said clearly brings a deeply committed social and critical dimension to Blackmur's lesson.

27. Richard Poirier, *The Performing Self: Compositions and Decompositions in the Languages of Contemporary Life*, Foreword by Edward W. Said (New Brunswick, NJ: Rutgers University Press, 1992), xii.

28. Poirier, *Performing Self*, 68.

29. *The World, the Text and the Critic*, 53. Said was, of course, a performer in the more quotidian senses of the word: a professional-class pianist who preferred the world of ideas to the concert hall, a master lecturer and eloquent speaker. Many of Said's spontaneous performances – some outrageous, some hilarious, all memorable – are narrated in H. Aram Veeser, *Edward Said: The Charisma of Criticism* (New York and London: Routledge, 2010).

30. Said, 'Interview,' *Diacritics* 6, no. 3 (Autumn 1976), 32.

31. The terms 'decreation' and 'reorder' occur in one of Said's early readings of Foucault: 'the reader must be involved in a process simultaneously entailing disordering, decreation, and reordering.' 'Michel Foucault as an Intellectual Imagination,' *boundary 2* 1, no. 1 (1972), 8. In a long footnote attached to this sentence, Said cites with approval other proponents of the 'creative dissociation' that goes into critical reading, including Richard Poirier, author of *The Performing Self*. Said also quotes a passage from Lévi-Strauss's *Tristes tropiques* that could apply to Said himself as he makes his way through the material that would eventually constitute *Orientalism*: 'Like a brush-fire, my mind burns its way into territory which may sometimes prove unexplored; sometimes these excursions prove fertile, and I snatch at a harvest or two, leaving devastation behind me' ('Michel Foucault,' 31). In historical terms, the significance of this essay inheres in the fact that its crystallization in Said's mind seems to have taken place around the same time as what would later become *Orientalism*. See William Spanos's account of how he invited Said to submit the article for the inaugural issue of *boundary 2* in *The Legacy of Edward W. Said* (Urbana, IL and Chicago: University of Illinois Press, 2009), 198.

32. Said, *On Late Style*, 128.

33. *The World, the Text and the Critic*, 53.

34. Robert Irwin, *For Lust of Knowing: The Orientalists and Their Enemies* (London: Allen Lane, 2006), 309.

35. Nietzsche's phrase comes from his essay 'On Truth and Lie in an Extra-Moral Sense' and is quoted in *Orientalism*, 203. William Spanos traces the passage of this idea via Foucault to Said in *The Legacy of Edward Said*, 92–5. Said returns to this moment in Nietzsche repeatedly: we find it in his theoretical formulations on beginnings, in his reading of Conrad and his call for a renewed philology. See *Beginnings: Intention and Method* (1975) (London:

Granta, 1997), 38–40; 'Conrad and Nietzsche' (1976), in *Reflections on Exile*, 72–3, and *Humanism and Democratic Criticism*, 58.

36. *Orientalism*, 203.
37. On the place of Said's *Orientalism* in the history of the critique of Western accounts of the Middle East, see Peter Gran's contribution to this volume.
38. Needless to say such claims are not without their complications, as witness Nicholas Harrison's work on the operation of literariness in the Said canon. See his ' "A Roomy Place Full of Possibility": Said's *Orientalism* and the Literary,' in *Edward Said and the Literary, Political and Social World*, ed. Ranjan Ghosh (New York and London: Routledge, 2009), 3–18, as well as the chapter contributed to this volume.
39. See his thoughtful review of *Orientalism* in the *Journal of the American Oriental Society* 100, no. 3 (July–October 1980), 328–31.
40. Ahmad, *In Theory*, 180–1.

2
Orientalism's Contribution to World History and Middle Eastern History 35 Years Later

Peter Gran

Since the nineteenth century, the dominant metanarrative in the university has been the one constructed from Hegel's notion of the rise of the West, complete with a stagnant Orient and a people without history. Edward Said's *Orientalism* (1978) argued that one major part of this triad, namely that of the Orient, lacked credibility, that it would not exist as a scientific concept apart from the context of colonialism and imperialism. While neither fully digested much less accepted by most of his readers, his argument has nonetheless had a continuing impact throughout the academy.

As this collection and others demonstrate, some evidence of Said's influence can be found in nearly all disciplines to one extent or another. In certain fields his contribution has, however, been considerably more influential than in others. In world history and Middle Eastern history, Said's work was so influential it brought on a crisis, one which is still with us today.

From a survey of Said's impact on those two fields comes the central claim of this chapter; namely that while the academy as a whole may be implicated in Said's writing, it is in these two fields especially that Said obliges the researcher to confront his criticism of Hegel most directly and, doubtless, to realize the illogic of continuing to use phrases like 'the Rise of the West' and 'the Orient.' To show this, the chapter begins with a brief survey of these fields and of the impact of Said's work on them; it then turns to consider three recent works, which brings the account of Said's continuing influence in these fields up to date.

Said's *Orientalism* and the Crisis in World History and Middle Eastern History

To test the larger hypothesis laid out here would involve a consideration of the role Said has played in many different fields and a demonstration, through a process of elimination, of how some of these fields were more affected by Said's work than others. This is beyond the scope of this chapter. What is undertaken here is the more feasible test of the more limited hypothesis that, in both world history and Middle Eastern history, Said's work brought on and contributed to long-lasting crises. To do this, one must move from general observations about Said and Hegel's theory of history to the more specific consideration of the trajectories of knowledge production in these fields and of how Said's work intersects with them. Moreover, one must take note of Said's continuing participation in debates about these subjects from the 1978 publication of *Orientalism* up until his death in 2003. Several major political developments in this period, among them the Iranian Revolution, must be mentioned as well, as they influenced how the book was received in these fields.

For world historians, Said's *Orientalism* appeared on the scene at a crucial juncture in terms of the trajectory of the field.[1] The Western civilization course, which had been the standard at least since the First World War was at that point in decline and in fact was just about on the way out. By the end of the 1970s, many historians were looking forward to being able to offer a more world historical orientation than they had been able to theretofore. Said's work appeared to be a justification to do just that. The old Western civilization course with its rise-of-the-West approach would no longer suffice; something would have to be added to it. Students, it was said, hated it, as did many of the instructors. I recall hearing at the time different explanations for why teaching Western civilization was becoming so difficult. A colleague in sociology claimed that there was too much downward mobility in Western society to keep on emphasizing the idea of the rise of the West any more. Someone else claimed the Western civilization model was too assimilationist. For that individual, the idea of the rise of the West was not so appealing. There were groups, and I suspect this individual may have belonged to one of them, which clearly did not want to be assimilated and made into Westerners, be it to rise or fall.[2]

In 1982, there emerged the World History Association (WHA), an association whose charge was to make world history multicultural in order to have it conform to the realities of the US and of the world in the age of globalization. The big question for the WHA, and no doubt for the foundations which were giving it seed money, as well as the Air Force Academy which was always conspicuously present at its conferences, was, would a multicultural history course serve as an adequate replacement for the Western civilization course? Would it foster the same collective identity, the same sense of hegemonism? Thirty years' experience suggests that it would not. Multiculturalism served some purposes but the older concept of 'the Orient' left over from the Western civilization course was still needed. Thus, despite the appeal of Edward Said's critique of the concept of the Orient, it was never abandoned but rather it kept on being updated, most recently to fit the age of terrorism. As of 2008, one can thus be multicultural but still stereotype Muslims in the so-called Orient as having a hybrid modernity, all the while still singing the praises of Edward Said.

This is not to suggest that overall the WHA was unsuccessful in its attempts to reform the prevailing approach to world history – quite the contrary. Various ideas, quite revisionist in their own way, gained acceptance and sometimes even prominence among historians thanks to the WHA. Among these one might list, the idea that Africans had a precolonial history apart from Europe, or the idea that the East Asian part of the Orient, past or present, was neither stagnant nor 'Oriental.' The acceptance of such ideas leads one to wonder how it is that Africa and East Asia managed to escape the Hegelian model to a certain degree, but the Middle East has not?[3]

Still, as one looks at the WHA today, one has the impression that, despite its achievements, some of the initial excitement has worn off. There is even a sense of having become stalled. Toppling the 'Rise of the West' paradigm requires more than simply making a few piecemeal adjustments in line with the general growth in knowledge. Rather, what it requires is a real alternative, and such an alternative has not yet been effectively promulgated. For all its virtues, multiculturalism speaks to coverage and culture rather than to power and history. It thus leaves Hegel's narrative of power and history intact. So it is that today that the textbook may cover more than before; it may even introduce new ideas and controversies. It is far more advanced than was the old Western civilization text which simply chronicled some names and dates from European history. Today, even new students are not infrequently introduced to the problem of Eurocentrism, and when they are, Edward Said is likely to be mentioned by name; his book *Orientalism* is sometimes assigned as a course requirement even if the course as a whole is built around the rise of the West.

Let us turn now to the situation in Middle Eastern history. What is it that has changed since 1978? My impression is that here, too, at least on the level of the general book, not very much has changed. While the quantity and variety of technical publications has grown immeasurably, we still tend to find in Middle Eastern studies today on the level of the general book what Said found in the 1970s: a polarity of the West and the Orient. To illustrate this let us take one example of a general work, one which has had unquestioned influence over the 35 years under consideration. Rafael Patai's *The Arab Mind*, first published in 1973, has been republished several times since, most recently in 2007.[4] While it is technically a work in social science it is widely used by historians. Many outside of the academy have read it as well. It thus scarcely seems necessary to justify its choice here or for that matter even to go through its grab-bag of Western world/Arab world binary oppositions in any detail. Suffice to say that, for Patai, race, culture and behaviour all bear a one-to-one relationship to each other. In the past decade or so, not only has it often been referred to in academic circles but in the mass media as well. More recently, it came to light that it was being used as well as a training manual in the US Army, whose soldiers were being taught 'applied Orientalism' to facilitate the occupation of Iraq.

Now, this raises an interesting question: what will happen to this book and its paradigm if applied Orientalism drawn from books such as Patai's is perceived to be responsible for the US's failure in Iraq, or to be more precise if the Pentagon comes to think that, given assumptions picked up from this book those engaged in the war fundamentally misunderstood what they were doing and that this explained their setback? In such a case, would the US Army demand another paradigm for understanding the Middle East?[5]

Take for example Abu Ghraib (Abū Ghurayb) as an example of one such setback. Abu Ghraib was, of course, a public relations disaster. This was the Pentagon's first reaction. Perhaps this is the way the Pentagon will continue to look at it but perhaps not. Perhaps some of the military leaders will see it as not just a public relations disaster but as a failed experiment at gaining information based on using Orientalism. Will the curriculum in the war colleges change and Orientalism be put aside?

To sum up, the continuing importance of Edward Said's *Orientalism* for the fields of world history and the Middle East today lies in the persistence of the concept of the Orient as a part of the academic metanarrative of history. Said exposed the non-scientific quality of this concept and showed the wider ramifications of using it. Lacking, however, an alternative to put in its place, his criticism remained on an external level. Given this lack of an alternative to put in its place, world historians and Middle Eastern historians read his book, acknowledge his criticism but then perforce ignore it. This explains in part how old-style books such as Patai's *The Arab Mind* live on.[6]

Another irony: although the name of Edward Said has long been synonymous with the critique of Orientalism, Said for his part never claimed to and certainly could not have claimed to have invented it. The critique of Orientalism already existed. It had arisen many years before out of the anti-colonial struggle of the Third World. What Said did was to take and modify pieces of that older critique and insert them in the Western academy. Shortly after he did that by publishing *Orientalism*, the critique of Orientalism itself underwent a considerable change. The older forms of critique all but disappear to be replaced by newer forms, forms we associate today with postcolonial discourse. When this happened, Said held his own; many others did not. Many of the writers from the *Review of Middle East Studies* (ROMES) group and from those writing for *Khamsin*, all critics of Orientalism as Said himself was, simply disappeared.

What brought about this change was obviously more than simply the end of colonialism, although that was important. No doubt more important was the neo-liberal revolution in world capitalism, and in its wake events in the Middle East such as the Iranian Revolution. These developments taken together affected the general cultural direction across the world. Thus, for example, with the coming of the neo-liberal phase of capitalism, one finds a general decline of interest in nation states and their histories and in their place a rise of interest in religions and civilizations. What speeded up this process of intellectual change in the particular case of Middle Eastern history was doubtless the series of events beginning in 1979 in Iran. In that interval, there was the Iranian Revolution followed by the Hostage Crisis, the latter extending on into 1981. Following these events, not only did postcolonial discourse take off rather rapidly, but so too did traditional Orientalism, the two increasingly coalescing as time went on: the study of culture on the rise; the study of nation states on the decline. This was the beginning of what we now call neo-Orientalism, that curious mixture of multiculturalism, Orientalism and critique.[7] For some, one could thus say 1981 was a moment of rejuvenation. Some of the traditional Orientalist institutions, such as Princeton University's Center for Near Eastern Studies, for example, got a new lease on life. They began to hold large government-sponsored conferences explaining the Iranian Revolution in terms of Islam. Under such conditions, what little remained of the older more secular criticism of Orientalism was forced to go in other directions. At this point in the early 1980s, Said himself turned from a critique of the Orientalism of scholarship to a critique of the Orientalism of the media.[8] He soon became a leading figure in this postcolonial discourse.

By the mid-1980s, under the aegis of postcolonial discourse, the concept of the Orient had been reformulated. It now implied hybridity. The Middle East was now modern. Its modernity was a mix of universal Western secular culture and Middle Eastern religious culture. Other changes in the preoccupations of Middle East studies were apparent as well. Concerns with economic development and political rights were replaced with concerns for human rights and civil society. There was a particular interest in spreading democracy. The US government was moving toward democracy promotion. At this point, Said decided to involve himself more deeply in Palestinian politics; postcolonial discourse was not a final resting place for him.

As the 1980s progressed, postcolonial discourse began to gain the upper hand over the older forms of liberalism, eventually going on the offensive against them. A debate arose in the university about the need for area studies programmes in the age of globalization, the 'future of area studies' debate. If you know about Islam and Islamic culture, do you need to study particular countries? For some this was a question of re-defining American priorities, but for a growing number of others it was a question about knowledge or epistemology. In this debate, Orientalists defending area studies were pitted against the proponents of postcolonial discourse, the latter preferring to emphasize the global flow of migrants, commodities and capital over the specificities of particular countries. As the debate over area studies went on, somehow its outcome came to hinge on what one needs to know to understand Islam. For those no longer drawn to area studies, the question of what is Islam was resolved in terms of Islamic law. Thus, for example, a good number of those drawn to postcolonial discourse, who appeared to be winning the debate, came to prefer the study of Islamic law in general over Islamic law as a part of specific national histories or Islamic law as *Madhāhib* or Islamic law as a part of some larger more complicated Islamic Habitus. Thus in 1996 arose the *Journal of Islamic Law and Culture* to 'foster a deeper understanding of law and public policy.' And, for better or worse, from the mid-1980s, it was the rare postgraduate student in the US who attempted to study a particular Middle Eastern country in terms of its own dynamics on any extended basis. Most seemed to become Middle East experts, putatively capable of explaining how the Middle

East related to the West and what the policy implications of that relationship were.

Similarly, from the mid-1980s onwards, one could observe that travel literature written by the Victorians – work which Said had ridiculed in *Orientalism* – was actually making a comeback, not simply as light reading but as a source for understanding the Middle East. A few years after that ASTENE (the Association for the Study of Travel in Egypt and the Near East), an organization dedicated to reviving this work, was founded at the universities of Durham and Oxford.[9] Today, this travel literature is very much in vogue as it seems to fit with the new liberal writing on tourism.

Finally, there was an equally important but qualitatively different development that started in this period, one that helps to explain both the changing reception of *Orientalism* as a particular work but more broadly put, the changing nature of academic culture as it shifted from the older development studies liberalism of the Walter Rostow era to the new liberalism of Foucault, Said and Anthony Giddens.

What I am referring to is the change in graduate education dating from that period. There was in that period, in many disciplines including history, a considerable shift in power relations in graduate education that affected knowledge production. By this point, quite a few professors no longer tried to teach the traditional canon, nor did they expect the traditional PhD based on it. They no longer seemed to believe in it but they did not know what to put in its place. So it was that students became junior colleagues. They designed their own educational fields and learned what they chose to. The stated rationale for this was that the premium now was not so much on old-style foundationalist graduate education which was logocentric but on riding the latest wave of literary and cultural theory. In such a context, a professor could serve as a student's senior colleague but not much more.[10]

I don't mean to overstate what was transpiring. While some embraced Said's *Orientalism* and the idea that knowledge was in one sense or another an expression of the ebb and flow of power relations, others did not see it that way at all. In fact, many scholars, scholars one could term classical liberals such as Bernard Lewis, opposed Said and what he represented. And among those scholars, one finds the beginnings of a counter-attack against *Orientalism* and against other books like it. These attacks grew louder and more insistent as the decade progressed. Said tried to defend his position in a couple of articles and published interviews, but I do not think he put his best foot forward. To be more precise, I would suggest that perhaps he unnecessarily brought various problems on himself by the way he tried to defend himself. For example, he claimed to be concerned with science but he failed to define what he meant by science. He stated in several places, notably in 'Orientalism Reconsidered' that positivist knowledge of the sort based on observing, naming and accumulating was not something he wanted to deal with.[11] But surely he did want to deal with science and positivist knowledge in some sense, especially in his discussions of Palestine. So, around the issue of science, some murkiness remained. In justifying the omission of the subject of German Orientalism from his own account of Orientalism, a point on which he was much criticized, all Said said in his own defence was that this criticism was superficial and trivial, and that there was no point in responding to it.[12] While this was for him doubtless simply an example of positivism, it was a place where a good deal of the contention entered. Without holding Said to the requirement of producing a systematic study of the field, one is still entitled to ask: if one writes about French and British Orientalism, then why not German Orientalism? The three developed together. Germany gave the field of Orientalism one of its main techniques, that of philology. This was the technique of studying later texts by basing oneself on the meanings of words found in well-known works which had come earlier. Philology was thought by most scholars to be useful in Arabic language studies, at least for the period prior to the impact of the West in the nineteenth century (the impact of the West having been to muddy the waters). At that point, languages such as Arabic drifted toward some kind of hybrid modernism. *The Encyclopedia of Islam*, *The Index Islamicus* and Karl Brockelman's *History of Arabic Literature* are prominent examples of philologically based Orientalist scholarship. And few, even among the critics of Orientalism, doubt the usefulness of these works. For Said, however, this fetishizing of philology as an approach to language, as he termed it, underscored the archaic and static nature of Orientalists' understanding of Arabic and Arab culture. And, indeed if one looks in the first edition of the *Encyclopedia of Islam* one might find an entry on some institution which would begin with a discussion of the Arabic name of an institution and how it was derived from an Aramaic root in some previous millennium. For Said, this proved that to the Orientalist, Arabic was born a dead language and so it remained until the coming of the Europeans who gave it life.

And no doubt he had a point, but not to the extent, one would think, of throwing out Arabic philology altogether. He was, of course, correct to argue that knowledge, in general, and language, in particular, are radically driven by context as well as by angle of observation. And that this means that there is no one stable basis of knowledge about language of the sort one associates with the *Encyclopedia of Islam*, but that applies to all knowledge, even to the hard sciences. In attacking Arabic philology as he did in *Orientalism*, Said was exaggerating the limitations of positivism in general and not simply of positivism in philology. But Said did not see it this way, at least when he wrote *Orientalism* and then when he wrote this article.

The Middle East as we know it, Said argued in 'Orientalism Reconsidered,' is quite complicated and eternally in flux (92). No one who sets out to interpret it can stand 'at some Archimedean Point outside the flux' (93). His point of reference here is Shakespeare criticism. What one finds, he says, are 'communities of interpretation and not what Orientalists think one finds, namely the thing in itself.' This then is how Said wants to be understood, more as a philosopher of power and knowledge than as a critic of Western writing on the Middle East. As a philosopher of power and knowledge, Said insists that one only really understands Orientalism as a field from understanding its conceptual vocabulary, in particular the term Orient itself, not from understanding all its minutiae. The word, 'Orient' is a human production. As a result, it has a certain meaning. This meaning is related to who gives it its meaning. Orientalists thus are a part of the knowledge they produce. If they resist this insight, this then is something to be studied. At this point in 'Orientalism Reconsidered,' Said generalizes a bit, more than he did in the original book, noting similarities between the work he was engaged in and the scholarship in women's studies, black studies and other such fields (91). To maintain as some of his critics did that modern knowledge production has nothing to do with modern policy is patently false. To clinch this point, he quoted (99) a professor at Hebrew University on how knowledge of Arabic studies produced in his university served the Israeli Occupation of the West Bank.

By the 1980s as we noted, Said was increasingly concerned with the media image of the Middle East. What interested him in those later years was how the media reproduced the same Orientalist worldview as the text did. This, he finally concluded, was predictable. No one in particular was to blame. For someone to be more objective and overcome distortions brought on by Orientalism in the media image would be a huge task. Indeed, one could not get very far without changing some of the reality which gives the Orientalist image its credibility. The rather pathetic attempts of the very reactionary petro-dollar regimes to defend their image or defend Islam serve as evidence of this last point (100–1). Hanging up a sign which says, 'Human Rights Organization' on a building is not going to influence the image in the media. So, how can change begin? Here Said's view was that one needed an intellectual who could humanize the elite by weaning it away from totalizing knowledge, Islamic, Arab and so on, which he also called historicism (101–2). The petro-dollar regimes are all historicist in Said's usage, as are the Marxist ones. Indeed, the Marxist theory of the mode of production was a prime example of totalizing knowledge. In place of totalizing knowledge and practices, Said expressed a preference for relativism or 'gnosis' or as he put it for a dissolving and de-centring type of epistemology (90, 102–3). At the same time, he held out some hope at this point in his thinking for the Frankfurt School (103), the trend in Marxism which places some weight on the role of the engaged intellectual bringing about change by humanizing the elite. This was Said's hoped-for solution to the problem of Orientalism either as discourse or as image. And with such ideas one might note on the one hand he found a receptive readership in certain circles in the Anglo-American academy while on the other he stirred up a fair degree of opposition in the Arab world.

Although attractive to the West, it was precisely this idealist and elitist approach to history and change that irritated a number of commentators in Beirut, Jerusalem and Cairo. Among them, one could include the main Arab commentator on Said, the famous Lebanese Marxist theorist Mahdī ʿĀmil. ʿĀmil observed in a book on the subject of Said's *Orientalism* published in 1985 that Said's approach to history allowed for no theory of revolution, no class war, only some incremental humanization of the elite by elite intellectuals.[13] In Gaza or the West Bank, one finds a class structure in place; the views one finds expressed reflect where one is and who one is in this structure. This is what many Middle Eastern intellectuals believe, especially those with a Marxist formation. Said never engaged any of this either as a writer or in practice in his days in Palestinian politics.

To sum up, Said intuited a general problem with the dominant metanarrative of history and stirred people in fields such as world history and Middle Eastern history to take an interest therein. The relevance of *Orientalism* 35 years after its publication thus lies, as I have been suggesting, in the fact that we have still not yet resolved the problem to which he drew our attention. Not surprisingly, writers are still engaging with his work. This is especially apparent in Middle East studies.

Orientalism in Middle East Studies Today

To inquire into *Orientalism* in Middle East studies today, one has to make certain assumptions about the nature of that field beyond simply noting its continuities. I am assuming that Middle East studies today is an example of a field dominated by those supporting postcolonial discourse on the one hand, and on the other by those supporting the classical liberalism of Oriental history and philology. What must be discussed, therefore, are two entirely different receptions of *Orientalism*.

In this last part of the chapter, I look at three recent works written by specialists of the Middle East which share a preoccupation with Said's *Orientalism* and which, when taken together, illustrate the aforementioned tendencies. One of these three is written by a specialist of Arabic literature[14] who claims that *Orientalism* still deserves to be refuted, one by a historian and one by a historical sociologist, who have the opposite view.[15] From a consideration of these three works, one sees not just Said's continuing influence but the long shadow cast by Hegel's model of the rise of the West and stagnation of the Orient.[16]

We begin with Robert Irwin. Irwin is well known not only as a specialist in classical Arabic literature, but as someone who spent much of his career as a journalist at the *Times Literary Supplement*. In 2006, Irwin published *For Lust of Knowing: The Orientalists and Their Enemies*, a book which appeared in the US at the same time as *Dangerous Knowledge; Orientalism and Its Discontents*.[17] He intended it, he said, to be a refutation of Said's *Orientalism*. While his intent is clear, readers are likely to quibble with his use of the term 'refutation' as he was, one finds on closer examination, really only tangentially interested in confronting, much less refuting, Said's arguments. His main concern appears to have been to write his own history of Orientalism; at least, this is what he did. Having done it, Irwin states his contention that Said had no business writing about a subject he was not specialized in and did not know. For Irwin, the subject of Said's *Orientalism* was that of a history of Orientalism. The only acceptable way to write such a book would be to write about it with the same detail and range of coverage as himself. Judged accordingly, Said's book was a work of charlatanry, one which when re-issued failed to correct the errors of detail noted in it, one which in addition made an extreme ideological claim associating Orientalism with Western imperialism. Is it not the case, Irwin asks, that the majority of the famous Orientalists were eccentric individuals, generally marginal in their own times and rarely associated with power structures?[18] Is it not also the case that they were often accused of sympathy for Islam by their contemporaries and not the reverse? Said's view to the contrary, for Irwin their knowledge was not a part of the structures which served colonialism but rather it was their own. Said's correlation of the two is implausible, give or take a handful of exceptions. Irwin then proceeds with some illustrations of this point. As examples of disinterested, eccentric and obscure scholars, he referenced those who made studies of coins in museums, undertook the listing of artefacts and manuscripts or performed other such dull but necessary activities, concluding that this is what Orientalism has mainly been about. Said, he claims, may make assertions about Orientalist imperialism but how credible are they? Can Said tell us when this Orientalist imperialism actually began; was it the Napoleonic invasion of Egypt in 1798, was it earlier, was it later? Said, he seems to be suggesting, has failed to master his subject and doesn't even know where to begin. Perhaps Irwin meant this as a joke, as Said's reputation came from a book entitled *Beginnings*.[19] Perhaps there is a bit of rivalry involved here as Irwin and Said are both literary critics, both concerned with quite similar themes be it that of beginnings or of marginality or even that of truth in literature. This might explain why Irwin unexpectedly appears to have so little patience with Said's inclusion of travel books and the like in his work on Orientalism. This was, Irwin claimed, evidence of Said's confusion as to who the serious scholars were and what they were doing. What difference does it make in a scholarly sense what Flaubert, who was a literary figure and not a scholar, thought about Egypt?

Very near the end of the book (after p. 281), Irwin seems to have second thoughts about what Said was actually doing and about the strategy that he (Irwin) was adopting in trying to refute Said. At that point, he observes that in contrast to his own book, Said's *Orientalism* is not really a history of Oriental studies but a polemic concerning certain aspects of the relation of knowledge and power. But, if this is the case, one wonders why Irwin took what he was doing to be a refutation of Said? Why did Irwin himself not write about knowledge and power if he wanted to refute Said? Here Irwin does not seem so comfortable, his example of the marginal Orientalists notwithstanding, and this may be the explanation. At one point, he asks why doesn't Said write about the Israeli Army, why does he write about Arabists? Why attack me he seems to be saying, I am on your side? And he looks at *Orientalism* this way, that is, not simply as incompetence but as ingratitude.

What one cannot help but observe is that Irwin is quite at home in the colonial tradition of Orientalism, the one which elsewhere he claimed practically did not exist. And, perhaps this would explain how it is that his examples of critics of Orientalism beginning with Said himself are all Middle Easterners. Not all Orientalists would make that claim but all colonialists would. Yet, in proceeding in this fashion Irwin is surely a bit out on a limb. He is ignoring evidence to the contrary, journals, for example, devoted to such criticism, emanating from the scholarly circles of Paris and London, as, for example, the *Review of Middle East Studies* from the Hull Group, *Gazelle Review* and *Khamsin*. To these one might add their American counterparts, *AMESS*, the *Alternative Middle East Studies Newsletter*, *MERIP* and *Critique: Critical Middle East Studies* which began in 1992.

Be that as it may, Irwin devotes a chapter to what he terms the critics of Orientalism and, as noted above, those referenced were or are from the Middle East. He divides the chapter between examples of those who can perhaps be forgiven because they are simply uninformed and those who have had the benefits of a Western education and thus ought to have known better. This explains what might otherwise be the surprising choice of the old-style Syrian belletrist Muhammad Kurdali (Kurd ʿAlī, d. 1953). Kurdali is known as the author of a useful old historical geography of Syria. His foray into anti-Orientalism was for Irwin that of a Syrian writer encountering something new, alien and disagreeable, to wit the writings of Henri Lammens, an Orientalist known for his anti-Islamic bias. I say a surprising choice because elsewhere Irwin himself mentions how unreliable Lammens was as a scholar and at still another place how Orientalists by and large have not been critics of Islam so the association here of anti-Orientalist with anti-Islam is not what the reader was led to expect. On the other hand, when Irwin encounters Abdallah Laroui (ʿAbdallāh al-ʿArwī), a very self-conscious critic of French Orientalism and a Marxist, he is quick to note that Marxism is Western and that Laroui is ungratefully using the tools given him by the West to attack the West.[20] This would apply to Irwin's views of Said as well.

And while Irwin has strong views about the critics of Orientalism, it seems fair to observe that he also has strong views about Orientalists in general. For example, in his chapter on the UK, he refers to the British Orientalists as very rational patricians. However, when he refers to the French Orientalists, he claims they are crazy anti-Semites such as Louis Massignon (220, 225), self-hating Jews such as Maxime Rodinson (255), notoriously unreliable scholars like Henri Lammens (202) or simply eccentrics like Jacques Berque (257). In small doses, I admit that this makes for fairly entertaining reading. Maybe this is Irwin's aim. What is theoretically interesting about all this is that it tends to support the connection Said makes between knowledge and power. This is still the Anglo-American heyday. An Englishman or an American can still write this way about a Frenchman.

Irwin and Said presumably both would assume that Orientalism amounts to Europeans gazing at natives. And they would not be alone

in doing so. Few scholars look at the native as an actor, or as a par-
ticipant in the maintenance of the hegemonic metanarrative of which
Orientalism is a part. This is a complaint made by a number of Arab
thinkers, most notably the Syrian philosopher Sadik al-ʿAzm.[21] In an
article which reportedly annoyed Said, al-ʿAzm pointed out that the
real centre of gravity of Orientalism was probably the Arab world itself,
along with Turkey, and not Europe at all. The biographical dictionaries,
the manuscript and book catalogues, and indeed most of the preoccupation with classical texts were there and not in Europe. In addition,
many of the personnel of the European Middle East studies institutions
came from the Middle East. In the US, this would be very much the case
as well, especially if one looked at Princeton Oriental studies or at the
staff of the Library of Congress. Even the composition of the standard
'European' Orientalist works such as Lane's *Arabic Dictionary* was heavily
dependent on the assistance of an Azharite Shaykh. To sum up this part,
while Irwin is widely regarded as a critic of Said, a defender of positivism
and so on, one could nonetheless read even Irwin as a fellow traveller
of Said's in certain respects. His attraction to the idea of the marginal
as in the marginal Orientalist, his concern with beginnings, his idea of
Orientalism as a Western discourse, point in that direction, as does his
interest in knowledge, authority and power.

Something of an exception to the tendency to ignore the Middle East as a site of Orientalist production is the work of Omnia
El-Shakry, an Egyptian–American historian who teaches at the University of California, Davis, and who is specialized in modern Middle
Eastern history. Her recent book, *The Great Social Laboratory: Subjects of
Knowledge in Colonial and Postcolonial Egypt* (2007), a work which claims
the Saidian heritage, differs from Irwin and Said in this respect.[22] By inte-
grating Egyptians in Egypt into Orientalist knowledge production, as
she does, she is taking a step, as she sees it, toward post-Orientalism.
For our purposes her work shows the continuing vitality of the Saidian
tradition and of postcolonial discourse as it moves to a Middle Eastern
context.

As El-Shakry writes, quoting Said, 'traditional Orientalism sought to
divide, tabulate, index and make generalizations about the Oriental
nature' (14). What is needed now is to examine the local appropriation
by scholars concerned with demography, race, birth control and other
such issues. These scholars, who were Egyptian, she took to be influential nationalists. Their function was to appropriate and adapt European
knowledge. How nationalist they were or how influential they were or
whether what they did can be best characterized as appropriations or

adaptations, however, is hard to know. I say 'hard to know' because the book does not connect these authors or their texts to parliamentary debates or decision-making processes or law systematically enough to make her point. The works referenced are left in her discussion for the most part as accounts of free-standing scholarly productions. Clearly they are appropriations. In what sense, they may also be adaptations, as she also claims, is left open. Indeed, in what sense they even could be adaptations even as 'colonial knowledge' or as representations of cosmopolitanism without upsetting the Hegelian Europe-non-Europe divide is a little hazy. What is clear is that El-Shakry assumed that the trajectory of Egyptian history and the way the Egyptian power structure would use knowledge would come to resemble that of Western Europe once Egypt became independent. However, as her chapter on Abd El-Nasser and the 1952 Revolution suggests this is not what turned out to be the case.

A quote or two about intentions from the beginning of the book, and about achievements from the conclusion makes the author's frustrations clear. 'This study,' El-Shakry writes near the beginning, 'is an exploration of what Gramsci termed the organic relations between state or political society and civil society and in particular of the birth of new parties of dominant groups intended to conserve the assent of the subaltern groups and maintain control over them' (14). This would be Gramsci in a Frankfurt School reading à la Said. The book concludes by the author acknowledging her debt to postcolonial discourse but conveying some frustration that it did not serve her better. The last paragraph, following from a discussion of cyclicalism in Ibn Khaldun and of the idea of man as a herd animal in Nietzsche, raises the question:

> What if we abandon both the calendrical unilineal time of the future and the pathological non-lineal time of the herd and of the symptom. To experience time as cyclical, contrapuntal, filiative or expansive is, perhaps to acknowledge other modes of being that we as a condition of our post-coloniality inhabit inconstantly. (222)

One might accept this but still wonder, if postcolonial discourse did not serve her work, why did she not look elsewhere? Was the fact that Spencer or Malthus or whoever was being commented on evidence simply of the appropriation of European knowledge? Or, could it be more efficiently understood as a somewhat incidental detail within the larger internal discussion about demography in a country in which demography was an already-established subject? I think the latter assumption would have served her purposes better, as it would have established her point about the importance of some of the works she referenced. The Gramscian model she started out with would have worked as well. Of course, there would be a price for using it. If she were to analyse the reception and adaptation of these books in the Egyptian context, she would be questioning the legitimacy of the West/Orient division to which we have been alluding.

Let us now consider another recent book, this one also building on and adapting Said's *Orientalism*, this book less concerned with El-Shakry's praxis of intellectuals and more concerned with the praxis of the state. This is a work by a Columbia University Professor of Historical Sociology, Gil Eyal. His book is called *The Disenchantment of the Orient: Expertise in Arab Affairs and the Israeli State*.[23] It appears to be basically an attempt to explain the surprising rise of the Ashkenazi security officers in 1948 when they could not speak the Arabic language anywhere near as well as the Sephardic Arabists, who had previously dominated the security jobs in the pre-state period, but who were then marginalized following the birth of the state of Israel in 1948.

Eyal approaches the fall of the Sephardic Arabists partly in terms of a kind of Saidian theory and partly in terms of an empirical account of state-building. Why, he asks, when there was no Orient in Mandate Palestine, when instead there were Sephardic middle men who connected the Jewish population to the Arab no-man's lands, did Israel then degenerate into a regular state with an ideology of West and Orient? The explanation he offers, both in a recent article[24] and in his book, revolves around 'the logic of state-building.' After 1948, the new needs of the Israeli state did not include the mediating role of the local Sephardic population for which the Sephardic Arabists had been known. Arabs were now enemies of the state; one studies one's enemies from a distance. To study one's enemies at a distance, however, leads to the production of Orientalists. Eyal is critical of the decision to produce Orientalists, his criticism being of a somewhat scientific sort, not so different from my own criticism of the US Army in Iraq. His most original point seems to be one concerning how an Orient gets made. He spells out in some detail the way in which Israeli knowledge of the Arabs of all kinds gradually became fused into the usual everyday pseudo-expertise about the Orient of the sort we encountered with Rafael Patai, who serves as a kind of culmination of the process.

Eyal's book, however, like El-Shakry's, while certainly interesting on the level of the subjects the authors pursue, disappoints on the level of the analysis for those seeking to achieve a more complete form of post-Orientalism out of the Saidian project. What is missing from Eyal's book as is what is missing from Omnia El Shakry's book: namely, historical analysis. Historical analysis would show that the hegemony strategy of Israel was one of playing race against class. No position of importance in the army or the government or the economy would be lightly given away by the Ashkenazim to the Sephardic community because it would be against the maintenance of the racial hierarchy. In 1948, what took place inside the security forces took place in every other important sphere of Israeli life as well. What Eyal should have argued is that his case study proves what observers have long been saying: that even where members of the Sephardic community were more highly qualified, they were passed over because of this racism. Instead, Eyal writes about the changing needs of the Israeli state as if only the Ashkenazi Jews were capable of coping with changing needs. And, while his idea of the logic of state-building is certainly one that needs to be thought about, it seems unlikely that there is one and only one way to build states or conduct foreign relations. Not all states totally cut themselves off from their neighbours if they had other options, as Israel did. This was a choice at the time. What Eyal shows in effect is that a particular form of state formation may well hinder one's understanding of the other, perhaps producing enemies where none existed.

'From Said's viewpoint,' Eyal goes on to claim,

> Orientalism is a Western discourse, one which invents an imaginary object – the Orient – and depicts it as radically different from the occident...Wrong. The problem with this approach, however, simple and self-evident it may seem, is that it ignores the reality of the boundary itself, the boundary as a result becoming a fine line without any width to it. In fact, actually, the boundary or the no man's land brings hybridity and its own modernity. (7)

Here one thinks of boundary figures such as Albert Hourani or Elie Kedourie. Their work certainly adds something to the idea of the modern. Where Said saw himself as in exile, Eyal saw figures like him as boundary figures. Exile implies being defined as outside of history and as struggling to be heard as with the postcolonial writers, whereas boundary figures are by way of contrast part of history, albeit an ambiguous history.

These points aside, Said's influence on all three of these writers is clear. However different the one is from the other, all make Said their reference point. All three, even Irwin, favour discourse analysis over history. Irwin may have characterized his work as history, but a real history of Orientalism would not have left out Germany nor made derogatory remarks about French scholars. It is in some ways similar to Said's own rather Anglo-centric essay, *The Question of Palestine*, which is not history either.[25]

To sum up, this chapter argued that Said's *Orientalism* after more than 35 years retains some importance for scholars in many fields. As a result of the book and the work based on the book, a much wider readership has come to understand that the idea of the Orient is a problematic one, and they associate this discovery with Said. What underlies this continuing importance of the book is the fact that we still do not have a metanarrative of history which can dispense with categories such as 'the West' and 'the Orient.' The failure of historians to address the problem of metanarrative – and failure does not seem too harsh a word – has led to a certain reaction against history of which postcolonial discourse and other kinds of discourse analyses serve as examples. Within the discipline of history, world historians and Middle Eastern historians bear some special responsibility because in these two fields the weaknesses of the Hegelian paradigm all come to the surface. One can scarcely avoid them, but avoid them these historians do.

Notes

1. Benedikt Stuchtey and Eckhardt Fuchs, eds., *Writing World History 1800–2000* (Oxford: Oxford University Press, 2003); Patrick Manning, *Navigating World History: Historians Create a Global Past* (Basingstoke and New York: Palgrave Macmillan, 2003).
2. Michael Novak, *The Rise of the Unmeltable Ethnics: Politics and Culture in the Seventies* (New York: Palgrave Macmillan, 1972). This contributed to the subsequent multiculturalist movement.
3. More than some others, the *Journal of World History* has done much to introduce and popularize new ideas on these matters. Among other things, it had made the subject of East Asia and especially East Asian penetration into the Indian Ocean the centre of pre-modernity for the world as a whole. This shifted the historiography of pre-modernity off Western Europe of that period.
4. Rafael Patai, *The Arab Mind* (New York: Scribner, 1973).
5. My preference among paradigms is for the one called 'the Rise of the Rich.' Its narrative of power is one emphasizing class and international linkages as opposed to leading countries termed Western or Westernized as one finds in 'the Rise of the West.' One constituent part of 'the Rise of the Rich' is the 'Russian Road.' I take Iraq among other countries to be an example of

'Russian Road.' Peter Gran, *Rise of the Rich: A New View of Modern World History* (Syracuse, NY: Syracuse University Press, 2010), 23–54.

6. For a detailed discussion of Hegel's Orient, see Teshale Tibebu, *Hegel and the Third World: The Making of Eurocentrism in World History* (Syracuse, NY: Syracuse University Press, 2011), 230–96.

7. Edward W. Said, *Covering Islam: How the Media and the Experts Determine How We See the Rest of the World* (New York: Pantheon Books, 1981).

8. Elleke Boehmer, 'East Is East and South Is South: Post-Colonialism as Neo-Orientalism,' in *Edward Said*, ed. Patrick Williams (Thousand Oaks, CA: Sage, 2001), 116–27. The first to introduce the idea of neo-Orientalism as applied to Middle East studies was R. A. Abou-El-Haj, 'Historiography in Western Asia and North African Studies since Sa'id's *Orientalism*,' in *History after the Three Worlds*, eds. Arif Dirlik, Vinay Bahl and Peter Gran (Lanham, MD: Rowman & Littlefield, 2000), 67–84.

9. Association for the Study of Travel in Egypt and the Near East, http://www.astene.org.uk [accessed 1 May 2011].

10. For a dissenting view, Ann Firth and Erika Martens, 'Transforming Supervisors? A Critique of Post-Liberal Approaches to Research Supervision,' *Teaching in Higher Education* 13, no. 3 (2008), 279–89.

11. Edward W. Said, '*Orientalism* Reconsidered,' *Cultural Critique* 1 (1985), 89–107.

12. Said, '*Orientalism* Reconsidered,' 90.

13. Mahdī ʿĀmil, *Marks fī istishrāq Edward Said* (Beirut: Dār al-Farābī, 1985).

14. Robert Irwin, *Dangerous Knowledge: Orientalism and Its Discontents* (Woodstock, NY: Overlook Press, 2006), 3, 281.

15. Omniya el-Shakry, *The Great Social Laboratory: Subjects of Knowledge in Colonial and Postcolonial Egypt* (Stanford, CA: Stanford University Press, 2007), 14, 30, 222; Gil Eyal, *The Disenchantment of the Orient: Expertise in Arab Affairs* (Stanford, CA: Stanford University Press, 2006).

16. Said's attack on the concept of 'the Orient' equally presupposes an attack on Hegel's entire model of history, including his categories of 'the West' and 'people without history.'

17. Irwin's argument that only after making a competent study of a subject is one qualified to write about it might well create problems for him given his penchant to belittle European Orientalists, who most would agree have some claim to be a part of the subject.

18. Here one also thinks of Edward W. Said, *Joseph Conrad and the Fiction of Autobiography* (Cambridge: Harvard University Press, 1966).

19. Edward W. Said, *Beginnings: Intention and Method* (New York: Basic Books, 1975).

20. Muhammad Kurdali, *Khiṭaṭal-Shām* (Beirut: Dār al-ʿIlm lil-Malāyīn, 1969–1971); Abdallah Laroui, *The Crisis of the Arab Intellectual: Traditionalism or Historicism?* (Berkeley, CA and London: University of California Press, 1976).

21. Sadik Jalal al-ʿAzm, 'Orientalism and Orientalism in Reverse,' *Khamsin* 8 (1981), 5–26; Reprinted in Alexander Lyon Macfie, ed., *Orientalism: A Reader* (New York: New York University Press, 2000), 217–38.

22. In my view, the book should be cited as a reference book in Egyptian knowledge production, a field which is up to now very scattered.

23. Eyal's book sheds interesting light both empirically and theoretically on Sephardic history at the time of Israeli independence.
24. Gil Eyal, 'Dangerous Liaisons between Military Intelligence and Middle Eastern Studies in Israel,' *Theory and Society* 31, no. 5 (2002), 653–93.
25. Edward W. Said, *The Question of Palestine* (New York: Vintage Press, 1992).

3
Flaubert's Camel: Said's Animus

Robert Irwin

Camels feature in one of the greatest novels of the nineteenth century, Gustave Flaubert's *Madame Bovary* (1857). In Chapter 6, where the imagery of Emma Bovary's trashily romantic reading is being discussed, we find the following:

> And the sultans with long pipes were there too, swooning in arbours, in the arms of dancing-girls, the djiaours, the Turkish sabres, the Greek fezzes, and, especially, the monochrome landscape of Dithyrambia, which often blend in a single image palm trees and pine trees, tigers to the right, a lion to the left, Tartar minarets on the horizon, Roman ruins in the foreground, then some *camels* [my italics] kneeling; – the whole thing framed by a nicely hygienic virgin forest, with a great perpendicular sunbeam trembling on the water, steel grey, with white-etched signs, here and there for floating swans.[1]

In the above passage Flaubert was fastidiously describing exactly the kind of novel that *Madame Bovary* was not. He could indeed have written a novel featuring giaours, scimitars, palm trees and camels, for just a few years earlier, from 1849 to 1851, he had toured Egypt, Palestine and Greece with a friend. He was certainly very familiar with the camels of Cairo and elsewhere and he wrote home as follows:

> One of the finest things is the camel. I never tire of watching this strange beast that lurches like a turkey and sways its neck like a swan. Its cry is something that I wear myself out trying to imitate – I hope to bring it back with me – but it's hard to reproduce – a rattle with a kind of tremendous gargling as an accompaniment.[2]

He was also fascinated how camel's urine created a glazed paving effect on the sand. Frederick Brown's fine biography describes how Flaubert delighted in the camels of Cairo:

> He was enchanted by urban dromedaries queuing up like ruminant taxi cabs; thrusting their cleft snouts into food stalls; grunting under bundles of faggots as wide as the narrow streets; or in the case of a proud male from the royal stable with feathers on its head, strands of bells around its neck and mirrors on its kneepads, transporting a gorgeous tent.[3]

Unlike most writers Flaubert thought that the camel was beautiful.

Even before he went out to Egypt, camel-riding was the pivotal image of youthful daydreaming about exotic lands. As he put it in *L'Education sentimentale* (published in 1869, but effectively finished in 1845): 'Oh to feel oneself swaying on the back of a camel!' He identified quite strongly with the beast. A year after his return from Egypt, in a letter to his former mistress, Louise Colet, he explained that he cannot change his nature. He is constrained by the gravity of things, 'which makes the polar bear inhabit the icy regions and the camel walk upon the sand.' 'Why the camel?' asked Julian Barnes who commented on this passage in his novel, *Flaubert's Parrot*. Barnes suggests that it is perhaps 'because it is a fine example of the Flaubertian grotesque: it cannot help being serious and comic at the same time,' and Barnes went on to draw attention to the self-comparison Flaubert made between himself and the dromedary, that is that he is hard to get going but once he is involved in some activity, he is hard to stop.[4]

So the possibility of Flaubert choosing to write a novel set in Egypt in which camels featured prominently is one of the might-have-beens of literary history. In 1849 Flaubert, then aged 27, accompanied his friend, the man of letters Maxime du Camp, to Egypt, Palestine and Turkey.[5] It is important to remember that it was not Flaubert the famous novelist who went out East, but Flaubert a young man, unsure of himself and with little to show for his years. As for Du Camp, he was about to make his name as a photographer of Eastern antiquities. The Orientalist painter Marc-Charles-Gabriel Gleyre advised them before they set out. They spent 18 months in the East. Flaubert spent the first four of these months in Egypt brooding over the failure of the first draft of his philosophic fantasy, *La Tentation de Saint Antoine*. Du Camp had been one of those who had told Flaubert that he had written rubbish and that he ought to try something more realistic instead. Though Flaubert was at first depressed and weepy, he loved the sunshine and slowly his mind did turn to something different.

He took copious notes on tiny things, like the aforementioned look of camel urine on the sand. The notes were not for a travel book, or for any specific book. They were taken in order to improve his style. That and only that, Flaubert believed, is what travel should be for. He was working to become a realist. He was thinking about how he should write, but he was not thinking that he should write about Egypt.

Note-taking apart, he was bored. In his *Souvenirs littéraires*, Du Camp observed of Flaubert that from 'our first arrival in Cairo I had noticed that he was listless and bored.'[6] The journey that he had longed for did not satisfy him. Du Camp was busy photographing ancient temples, but in his notes Flaubert wrote, 'the Egyptian temples bore me profoundly. Are they going to become like the churches in Brittany, the waterfalls in the Pyrenees?'[7] A little later he was asking,

> What is it, oh Lord, this permanent lassitude that I drag about with me? It followed me on my travels, and I have brought it home! Demira's tunic was no less completely welded to Hercules' back than boredom to my life! It eats more slowly into it, that's all.[8]

In *L'Education sentimentale*, Flaubert was to write as follows:

> He travelled. He grew to know the sadness of steamboats, the cold awakenings in tents, the dizzying spectacles of landscapes and ruins, the bitterness of friendships cut short. He came home again.[9]

This catches the *tristesse* of travel perfectly.

The role boredom and the accompanying melancholia have played in the culture of Orientalism has received hardly any attention. And here a long digression is desirable. The theme surfaces as early as the seventeenth century as Antiochus in Racine's *Bérénice* declares, 'Dans l'orient désert quel devint mon ennui.'[10] In William Beckford's Orientalist novel, *Vathek* (1786), the caliph of that name is not driven to his atrocities and incest so much by lust or greed, as by boredom. He needs to know everything, 'even sciences that did not exist.'[11] Restlessness, ceaseless questing, the wish to know and experience everything, passion for more than life can offer – these are common characteristics of the Oriental despot as conjured up in the Western imagination. Although a history of Orientalist boredom has yet to be written, more general studies, of course, exist. In *Boredom: The Literary History of a State of Mind*, Patricia

Meyer Spacks has convincingly argued that boredom was an invention of the early modern period, for medieval men and women were, like dogs, never bored and only in eighteenth-century England did the word boredom come to be used for a psychological description.[12] In *Boredom: A Lively History*, Peter Toohey has argued that boredom has been a driving force behind all forms of creativity.[13]

Beckford's Vathek is a type who has precursors in John Hawkesworth's *Almoran and Hamet* (1746), Voltaire's *Zadig* (1748), Samuel Johnson's *Rasselas* (1759) and Frances Sheridan's *Nourjahad* (1767). These Oriental princes are bored, bored with their comfortable state, bored with their pleasures and vices, and restlessly inquiring if there is not something more. We know that Dr Johnson used to suffer from the most horrific fits of boredom and his Orientalist novel, *Rasselas*, can be read as a sustained treatise on the subject. Happy Valley, where Rasselas dwells, grants every desire and, in so doing, makes life extremely boring. What Rasselas desires is to feel desire. In his travels out of Happy Valley with the sage Imlac, he comes to the Pyramids and these he learns were built by an ancient king who was 'compelled to solace, by the erection of a pyramid, the satiety of dominion and tastelessness of pleasures and to amuse the tediousness of declining life, by seeing thousands labouring without end, for no purpose, laid upon another.' In other words, Pharaoh's problem prefigured that of Rasselas, and Rasselas was afflicted with Johnson's boredom.[14]

In the eighteenth century, Orientalist boredom – stifling *ennui* in the seraglios, long drawn-out oriental court rituals and manically restless sultans and shahs – was almost entirely a literary phenomenon. But in the nineteenth century, picturesquely Orientalist boredom would be picked up as a theme by such painters as Gérôme, Lecomte de Nouy and, arguably, John Frederick Lewis. Some critics, including Rana Kabbani, Alain Grosrichard and Linda Nochlin, have written about the strong erotic content of Orientalist painting in that period, yet the boredom, whether restless or complacent, is more obvious. Consider all those paintings of bored odalisques playing with pets, smoking hookahs or cigarettes, passing time in claustrophobic hammams, or lounging by the feet of no less bored-looking sultans and pashas. Then there are the Nubian palace guards propping up doorposts and the Cairene shopkeepers reposing on *mastabas* – and the caravans of pilgrims and merchants tracking across the limitless wastes of Asia and Africa. The despot, Sardanapalus, as depicted by Delacroix, is not revelling in the slaughter of his household. Not even this atrocity can stir him. He just looks bored. He is experiencing a premonitory attack of Baudelairean *ennui*.

In 1906 Matisse visited Algeria. At first he was depressed and whole days were spent doing nothing, 'but it has to be said also that the advantage of time spent being bored is that it enables you to penetrate a little into the spirit of the country, quite unconsciously.'[15] It was boring to travel in the Orient. There were long distances to be covered. There were tedious rituals involved in receiving hospitality. There were waits for official written permissions to visit certain regions. Often there were detentions in quarantine centres.[16] It was common for travelling companions to get on each other's nerves and fall out. The Orient has been written about by critics of Orientalism as mysterious, sensuous, threatening, dangerously other and even as a metaphorical woman that Westerners desired to penetrate. Perhaps the Orient was all those things, but often it seems to have been experienced as boring.

Madame Bovary is, among other things, a novel about the sheer boredom (and stupidity) of provincial life.[17] On a trip down the Nile in a *cange*, a long, light-draught houseboat, Flaubert set to thinking hard about writing a novel about Normandy. By the second cataract he had the name of the female protagonist and he was brooding about Emma Bovary. He seems to have thought a lot about boredom and he transferred some of this to his portrait of provincial life in Normandy. It is not the case that, for writers, travelling in the Orient automatically functioned as some kind of sausage machine, into which Oriental experience was poured in at one end and an Orientalist book necessarily came out at the other. Cervantes, set free from captivity in North Africa, went to work on the pastoral *Galatea*, with its purely European setting. Anthony Trollope was in Egypt on Post Office business in 1858 and while there he wrote *Doctor Thorne*, which is set in not very exotic Barsetshire. In 1890 Anton Chekhov travelled from Sakhalin to Singapore, Colombo, Egypt and Constantinople. A few years later (1896) his first play *The Seagull* was produced. There is nothing Oriental in it. Although Ronald Firbank had the idea for *The Flower Beneath the Foot* (1923) in Algiers, he set that novel in Vienna. Daphne Du Maurier wrote *Rebecca* (1938) in Alexandria. As Du Camp wrote of Flaubert, 'amid African landscapes he dreamed of Norman landscapes.'[18]

On his return from Egypt Flaubert worked on *Madame Bovary* and it was first published in the *Revue de Paris* in 1856. So much for the real Flaubert. Now for Edward Said's version of the man. Flaubert, so fastidious in his use of language, was notoriously coarse in other respects. He had animal appetites for food and women which he did not trouble to conceal. Indeed, he regularly boasted in correspondence and conversation about the women he slept with. This is unattractive, and Said obviously found it extremely unattractive. His writing about Flaubert has an animus that should be inappropriate in a literary critic.

Said's discussion of the great writer largely swings round Flaubert's sexual encounter with Kuchuk Hanem.[19] According to Said, 'Her home near the upper reaches of the Nile occupied a place structurally similar to the place where the veil of Tanit – the goddess described as *omnifé-conde* – is concealed in *Salammbô*.'[20] It is not clear what this means, but whatever it does mean, it is based on a straightforward geographical mis-apprehension. Said says that the encounter took place at Wadi Halfa, which is in Sudan, whereas Flaubert's notes are clear and explicit that he met Kuchuk Hanem in Esna in Egypt, some 200 miles to the south of Wadi Halfa.[21] (And, by the way, the upper reaches of the White and Blue Nile are in Uganda and Ethiopia, respectively, a long way up from Wadi Halfa.) And come to that, even if Esna had been at the headwa-ters of the Nile, rather than many hundreds of miles away, in what way would it have been structurally similar to the place where the veil of Tanit was in Salammbô' The veil of Tanit, or the zaïmph of Tanit, the Carthaginian moon goddess, was displayed, not concealed, within the walls of Carthage beneath the Acropolis, surrounded by gardens and courtyards. To touch the veil of Tanit meant death. But neither Flaubert nor Kuchuk Hanem were in danger of dying, unless Said was thinking of *la petite mort*.

It was at Esna, one of the places to which in 1834 Muhammad Ali had exiled the *ghaziyas*, dancing girls who doubled as prostitutes, that Flaubert and Du Camp encountered Kuchuk Hanem ('Little Madame'). Said was under the impression that she was Egyptian, though actu-ally she was Syrian.[22] Flaubert recorded the meeting, her dance and his repeated couplings with her in his private travel notes.[23] Flaubert and Said shared the misapprehension that Kuchuk Hanem was an *almeh* (literally learned woman, but a term applied in the eighteenth and nineteenth centuries to female singers). Now *almehs* were singers, not dancers-cum-prostitutes. If Said had read Edward William Lane's *Manners and Customs of the Modern Egyptians* and its description of the profession of the *almeh*, instead of disparaging a book he clearly had not read, he would have known that.[24] The *almeh* did not display herself at all, but sang from behind a screen, or from another room at wed-dings and other respectable festivities. Consequently the *almehs* were not subject to exile in Upper Egypt. Kuchuk Hanem was a *ghaziya* and Lane (p. 173) had carefully distinguished the *ghaziya* from the *almeh*.[25] So Said's statement about Flaubert's imagination taking off from what he had read about *almehs* in Lane is nonsense. Said claimed that Flaubert had read all about *almeh*s and *khawal*s in Lane's *Manners and Customs*.[26] But he provided no evidence for this and there is none.

In all of Flaubert's Egyptian writings there is just one reference to Lane's book. In a letter to his mother dated 8 March 1850 he recommended to her *An account of modern egyptian customs* (sic) by D[oc]tor (sic) Lane, despite that book being littered with errors and not one that he had read himself.[27] But it was important for Said to insist that Flaubert's experience of Egypt, like those of all typical Orientalists, was textually mediated and hence the inaccurate reference to Lane. It does not seem likely that Said read, rather than glanced at, Lane's *Manners and Customs*.

On the page after the one in which Said refers to Flaubert reading about *almeh*s and *khawal*s, he makes the claim that the Queen of Sheba in Flaubert's *Tentation de Saint Antoine* performed the dance of the bee. The dance of the bee, as performed in nineteenth-century Egypt by the male dancer Hassan al-Bilbeisi, Kuchuk Hanem and doubtless many others, was a kind of striptease in which the dancer, pretending to be harassed by a bee, sheds one garment after another. (Incidentally, Flaubert noted that Hassan al-Bilbeisi was better at it than Kuchuk Hanem.)[28] But Flaubert has the Queen of Sheba boast to St Anthony that she dances *like* a bee. She does not dance a striptease (hardly appropriate behaviour for a queen). Indeed she does not dance at all, unless one counts the fact that, when she walks away from the saint defeated, she went with a dancing step.[29] A person who dances like a bee is different from a person who dances as if he or she has a bee buzzing about in his or her garments. But Said wanted to emphasize that Flaubert's experience of Egypt was, like that of other authors who travelled there, shaped by earlier writings. This would be a just verdict on Nerval's account of Egypt, which was indeed a something of scissors-and-paste job, but surely, if Said had read Flaubert's travel notes carefully, he would have noticed how much they depended on direct observation and not on the recycling of other travel narratives. Why would Flaubert have wanted to read Lane's rather dry ethnographic survey?

Said further comments, 'Kuchuk is a disturbing symbol of fecundity, peculiarly Oriental in her luxuriant and seemingly unbounded sexuality.' And then a few lines later, he comments that 'Kuchuk was doomed to remain barren, corrupting and without issue.'[30] This is surely a case of trying to have it both ways with the barren, fecund woman. And there is no evidence in Flaubert's writings that he thought of this prostitute in either of these ways. There is no sign that he thought of her as a symbol of anything grand or mysterious. She was just someone to satisfy his sexual appetite. But Said, who was determined to give Kuchuk Hanem some kind of literary significance and an almost sacral aura, neglected to refer to Flaubert's letter to Louis Bouilhet (dated 13 March) on the subject, or he might have realized how good, unproblematic and unmysterious a sexual partner she was – 'five rounds of copulation and three of oral sex' in 17 hours. ['A Esneh j'ai un jour tiré 5 coups et gamahuché 3 fois.'] Flaubert continues, 'I say that without circumlocution. I add that it gave me pleasure. Kuchuk Hanem is a very well-known courtesan.'[31] If she was indeed an incarnation of the mysterious, but easily penetrable Orient – some kind of avatar of Salome and Salammbô, Flaubert shows no awareness of it. Instead we get the swank of a cock's man. He boasted about his sex with Kuchuk Hanem in precisely the same way he had boasted in the past and would boast in the future about his sexual encounters with Norman and Parisian prostitutes. He was not alone in this. If one browses through the pages of the Goncourt Journals and their reports of the famous writers' dinners in the Parisian restaurant, Magny, one finds that sexual boasting was part of the regular conversational repertoire of writerly braggadocio.[32] Distasteful, but there it is, or rather was.

It might also be pleaded in mitigation of Flaubert that one should bear in mind his audience. He was not writing for the general public and seeking to persuade them that the Orient was threatening, corrupt, fecund, barren or whatever. He was writing notes to himself and a private letter to a raffish friend. If he was an archetypal Orientalist travel writer, he was one with a very small audience. His travel notes (in an expurgated version) were first published in 1910. Flaubert obviously found Kuchuk Hanem attractive and charming. He wrote that they were 'very affectionate' together and that at the end of it all 'in the morning we said goodbye very calmly.'[33] A little later he wrote to Bouilhet that sex with Kuchuk Hanem reminded him of his brothel nights in Paris.[34] He visited her again on his journey back down the Nile and was sad to finally leave her.[35] Though Said was keen to present Flaubert's encounter with the mysterious Oriental woman as the pivotal moment of his travels in the East, it would seem from a letter of 15 January 1850 to Bouilhet that Flaubert had found an Egyptian boy dancer, Hassan-el-Bilbeisi and his version of 'The Bee' much more erotically seductive.[36] Shortly after watching the boy do his striptease, Flaubert and Du Camp had sex with a couple of prostitutes in Cairo. We know that they were also planning to have sex with the *bardaches*, or young male prostitutes of the Cairo bathhouses, though it is not clear whether they actually did so.[37]

Said claimed that the East was a sexual playground for Flaubert, affording him pleasures he could not find at home.[38] Surely he had not read Flaubert's correspondence with Louise Colet, or Louis Bouilhet, or the Goncourt journals and their accounts of Flaubert's sexual activity in France.[39] If he had, he would surely have realized that there was nothing at all exceptional in Flaubert's encounters with Egyptian prostitutes. And, as noted, in Flaubert's letter to Bouilhet detailing his sex with Kuchuk Hanem, he explicitly compares the experience of lying beside her to similar previous experiences in Parisian brothels.

The literary critic also failed to note what has struck Frederick Brown, the biographer, and that is the detached precision of the writing regarding the meeting with Kuchuk:

> 'She wore a tarboosh surmounted by a convex gold disc in the middle of which was set an imitation emerald,' wrote Flaubert, who registered every detail of her person, noting for example, how the blue tassel of her hat 'caressed' her shoulder and that one incisor needed dental care. Her bracelet is made of two thin gold rods twisted around each other, her necklace consists of three strands of hollow gold beads. Her earrings are gold discs, convex, with gold beads around the rim. A line of blue writing is tattooed on her right arm.[40]

This is indeed a writer in training, a writer who perhaps was using Egypt as a kind of gymnasium for his warm-up exercises. Flaubert was learning how to write Madame Bovary: 'No lyricism, no reflections, the personality of the author absent. It won't be fun to read.'[41]

In *Orientalism*, Said denounced French travellers in Egypt for allowing their responses to the country to be mediated by Orientalist texts.[42] As a comment on Gerard de Nerval's *Voyage en Orient*, this would be fair enough. He used the writings of Silvestre de Sacy, Chateaubriand and Edward William Lane to plump up his journalism and his fantastic inventions. But Flaubert was guilty of no such thing. When Flaubert took a rest from direct observation, he read Homer's *Odyssey* instead. Additionally, Du Camp once recorded Flaubert sitting in the ruins of Philae and reading *Le Gerfaut*, a fashionable novel by Charles de Bernard.[43] Moreover, Flaubert did not have to meet Kuchuk Hanem in order to come up with idea of a femme fatale. Femmes fatales were a dime a dozen in nineteenth-century French fiction (in the writings of Théophile Gautier and others) and Flaubert had already conjured up two in earlier writings, in *Un parfum à sentir* and in *La Tentation de Saint Antoine*.[44]

According to Said, Flaubert wrote, 'Inscriptions and birddroppings are the only two things in Egypt that give any indication of life.'[45] This would be damning if true. But, in the original French, what he wrote was 'les inscriptions et les merdes d'oiseaux, voilà les deux seules choses sur les ruines d'Égypte qui indiquent la vie,' which is unexceptionable. Said who only quotes Flaubert's Egyptian writings via the translations in Steegmuller's brief book, *Flaubert in Egypt*, did not reproduce Steegmuller's translation in full, where one finds the words 'in the ruins of Egypt.'[46] Flaubert was not disparaging all Egypt as lifeless: he was commenting on the ruins and how they were defaced by tourist graffiti and bird droppings. On the other hand, it was perhaps because Said relied so exclusively on the Egyptian material provided by Steegmuller that he did not realize how disparaging Flaubert had been about Palestine, writing 'Jerusalem strikes me as a fortified charnel-house; old religions are silently rotting away in there, you tread on turds and all you can see are ruins: it is immensely sad.'[47]

It seems clear that Said's French was pretty good. Why then did he not refer directly to the published letters and the notebooks, rather than cite Steegmuller's selected translations? I think that the numerous errors here and elsewhere and the undue reliance on a single skimpily selective source are due to the extraordinary haste and consequent carelessness with which *Orientalism* was written, as well as the publisher's failure to provide a decent copy editor.[48] His need to make all his material conform to a predetermined thesis may have been a further factor.

Said made the following claim: 'In all of his novels Flaubert associates the Orient with the escapism of sexual fantasy.'[49] It is, of course true that in *L'Éducation sentimentale* Frédéric has an erotic fantasy in a harem setting, but that surely is necessarily a feature of Frederic's weak, sentimental and unrealizable fantasies.[50] Flaubert was tacitly satirizing precisely the sort of Orientalism that Said so disliked. Anyway, 'all' Flaubert's novels is hyperbole. All his novels? Not *Madame Bovary*, nor *Bouvard et Pécuchet*.

Turning now to Said's account of *Salammbô*: 'Less a woman than a display of impressive but verbally inexpressive femininity, Kuchuk is the prototype of Flaubert's Salammbô and Salomé.'[51] But what exactly are the parallels between Kuchuk Hanem and Salammbô beyond the fact that they were both women who lived in North Africa whom Flaubert wrote about? Salammbô was an aristocrat and a woman passionately in love. Kuchuk Hanem was neither. Yes, Kuchuk had no French and therefore did not speak to Flaubert, but it simply will not do to present Salammbô as verbally inexpressive. In the novel she speaks frequently, eloquently and at length. Her eloquence enraptured crowds. Mattho was practically dumb before her. Hence my suspicion that Said had not actually read this novel. (By the way, though Kuchuk Hanem resembles Salome in that they both do dances, Salome, who indeed does not get to say a single line in Flaubert's short story, is, as we shall see, not a particularly important character in that story.) So with regard to Said's claim that Flaubert valorized Oriental women and that Kuchuk Hanem was the prototype, sometimes it is best not to detect hidden connections where there are none.

Said asserts that *Salammbô* was one of the textual children of Napoleon's expedition to Egypt and that the book derived its strength from European mastery of the Orient.[52] But *Salammbô* was published in 1862, when France had no colonial presence in the Middle East. It is certainly possible that the novel might have derived its strength from the French presence in Algeria from 1830 onwards, and it would be interesting to see how that argument might run, but, in general, Said chose not to discuss the French presence in North Africa. And if we are to read *Salammbô* as an Orientalist novel, which lot are the Orientals? The Carthaginians? Or the polyglot army of mercenaries besieging the Carthaginians? The one seems as decadent as the other.

(Though Flaubert, who prided himself on the accuracy of his historical research, put camels in *Salammbô*, this was one of quite a few historical and archaeological mistakes. There had been camels in North Africa prior to the rise of Carthage and there would be again after the fall of Carthage, but at the time of the revolt of the mercenaries against Carthage there were no camels in Tunisia.)[53]

A. J. Krailsheimer in his introduction to a translation of *Salammbô* remarks that 'Flaubert's lifelong obsession with *ennui*, cosmic tedium, lies heavy on this book, and because he is dealing with a civilization and a city destroyed beyond recall there is no hope of progress, implicit or explicit, to redeem the decaying memory of the past.'[54] One can go further and suggest that in writing about a decaying and doomed empire, Flaubert was writing about Carthage, but thinking about Second Empire France.[55] Flaubert, who had no substantial criticisms of the khedivial regime in Egypt, had a great deal of contempt for his own bourgeois France. In *Salammbô* he described a soulless commercial Carthaginian culture that was indifferent to art or intellect. As the biographer Geoffrey Wall has observed of another of Flaubert's works, *La Tentation de Saint Antoine*, this was designed as 'a great escape from all the railways, the umbrellas, the frock coats and the newspapers to which the more prosperous citizens of the nineteenth century were so inexplicably attached.'[56] Lisa Lowe and Anne Green have both suggested that the violence and turbulence of Salammbô's Carthage was modelled on the French working-class revolts of 1848, which is an interesting idea, though hard to prove.[57] Rather than looking to Egypt as the key source of inspiration for Salammbô, it makes sense to look to London and the Great Exhibition of 1851. Flaubert visited it and took careful notes on all the exotica he saw displayed there. As Frederick Brown has observed, the 'Indian and Chinese pavilions yielded detail for future reference on musical instruments, women's attire, the palanquins and silver brocaded harness of elephants.'[58] For many people, though not of course for Flaubert, the Great Exhibition was indeed their first exposure to the exotic. Exhibitions like those in London in 1851, in Paris in 1899 and Chicago in 1893 brought Oriental artefacts and even peoples almost to the doorsteps of people who were too unadventurous or too poor to travel to distant parts.[59]

Rana Kabbani, a commentator whose criticisms of the evils of Orientalism have paralleled those of Said, has presented Flaubert's portrait of Salome in a short story entitled 'Hérodias' as part of some kind of vendetta with the Orient.[60] But, as the title may suggest, the story is mostly about Herodias and her husband, Herod. Salome's dance takes up just two pages of the story. Salome is really an instrument, not a protagonist. When Flaubert gave a reading of 'Hérodias,' Edmond Goncourt commented that 'the whole thing struck me as a playful exercise in Romantic archaeology.'[61] As the above discussion of *Salammbô* may suggest, Flaubert's chief vendetta was not against the Orient or the Arabs, but against the French bourgeoisie. A few days before he died he wrote to his niece, 'For the past two weeks I have been gripped by the longing to see a palm tree standing against the blue sky, and to hear a stork clacking its beak at the top of a minaret.'[62] It is an odd way for an alleged hatred of the Middle East to be expressed. But I guess that, when the dying man longed for the palm tree and the blue sky, he was yearning for the young man he was when he first saw those things.

Said's cavalier way with French literature may explain why he has no great reputation among French academics and intellectuals. He has not become one of their *maîtres à penser*. His attitude of *nil admirari*, of not allowing any literary merit to fictions set in the Middle East has fostered misreadings of other novels, including those of Scott, Disraeli, James Morier and George Eliot.[63] In the days of F. R. Leavis and William Empson, close reading of literary texts was in fashion. Since the publication of *Orientalism* looser rhetorical strategies for dealing with texts have become popular. And of course the notion that nineteenth-century books on the Orient constitute a genre – a genre that could accommodate Flaubert and Lane and Nerval and Burton – is questionable. Their authors had agendas, yes, but so many agendas.

Two further points remain to be made. Said's approach circumscribed rather than opened out critical horizons. A monocular focus on political subtexts and political motives have occluded other perhaps more important aspects of Orientalist writing. For example importance of social class in Orientalism has been largely ignored. Those who went out to the Orient in the eighteenth and nineteenth centuries and wrote about it tended to come from well-off families – this applies to Volney, Chateaubriand, Lamartine, Doughty, Kinglake, Flaubert, Du Camp and Gertrude Bell among others. It took money to rattle round the Middle East and those who had that money often had patrician or insouciant attitudes to what they saw, whether at home or abroad. They ordered the Arabs about in the same way that they were accustomed to order British artisans, peasants and servants about. Aristocrats dominated the early decades of the Royal Asiatic Society and the Société Asiatique and aristocrats subsidized expensive Orientalist publications.

Second, Westerners travelling in the Middle East for recreation or adventure tended to be young and, since they were young, they were still unsure about what, if anything, would become of them and how their lives would shape out. They were not so much judging the Orient as being judged and tested by it. I am thinking here particularly of Kinglake, Flaubert, Robert Byron and Bell. In his novella *Youth*, Joseph Conrad described both the feeling of adventure and the sense of being tested by the Orient,

> for me all the East is contained in that vision of my youth. It is all in that moment when I opened my young eyes on it. I came upon it from a tussle with the sea – and I was young – and I saw it looking at me. And this is all that is left of it! Only a moment of strength, of romance, of glamour, of youth … A flick of sunshine on a strange shore … [64]

And Gertrude Bell, looking back on her morning rides outside Teheran in the company of a dashing legation secretary, wrote this:

> Life seized us and inspired with a mad sense of revelry. The humming wind and the teeming earth shouted 'Life! Life!' as we rode. Life! Life! The beautiful magnificent! Age was far from us – death far; we had left him enthroned in his barren mountains, with ghostly cities and

outworn faiths to bear him company. For us, the wide plain and limitless world, for us the beauty and freshness of the morning! For us youth and the joy of living![65]

Notes

1. Gustave Flaubert, *Madame Bovary*, trans. Geoffrey Wall (London: Penguin, 1992), 36.
2. Gustave Flaubert, 'Correspondance, I (janvier 1830 à avril 1851)', in *Bibliothèque de la Pléiade*, ed. Jean Bruneau (Paris: Gallimard, 1973), 539; c.f. Julian Barnes, *Flaubert's Parrot* (London: Jonathan Cape, 1984), 54; Robert Irwin, *Camel* (London: Reaktion, 2010), 121–2.
3. Frederick Brown, *Flaubert, A Life* (London: Pimlico, 2007), 242.
4. Barnes, *Flaubert's Parrot*, 54.
5. Francis Steegmuller, ed. and trans., *Flaubert in Egypt* (London: The Bodley Head, 1972).
6. Maxime du Camp, *Literary Recollections* (London: Remington, 1893), 337.
7. Gustave Flaubert, *Voyage en Orient*, ed. Claudine Gothot-Mersch (Paris: Gallimard, 2006), 158; cf. Steegmuller, ed. and trans., *Flaubert in Egypt*, 142.
8. Flaubert, *Voyage*, 172; Steegmuller, ed. and trans., *Flaubert in Egypt*, 151. On Flaubert and boredom more generally, see Guy Sagnes, *L'Ennui dans la littérature française de Flaubert à Laforgue (1848–1884)* (Paris: A. Colin, 1969).
9. Gustave Flaubert, *Sentimental Education*, trans. Robert Baldick (Harmondsworth: Penguin, 1964), 411.
10. Jean Racine, *Bérénice* Act 1, scene 4, l.234.
11. William Beckford, *Vathek and Other Stories*, ed. Malcolm Jack (London: Penguin, 1995), 30.
12. Patricia Meyer Spacks, *Boredom: The Literary History of a State of Mind* (Chicago: University of Chicago Press, 1995).
13. Peter Toohey, *Boredom: A Lively History* (New Haven, CT and London: Yale University Press, 2011).
14. Spacks, *Boredom*, 46–50. See also Ros Ballaster, *Fabulous Orients: Fictions of the East in England 1662–1785* (Oxford: Oxford University Press, 2005), 218–27 for interesting remarks on Western perceptions of China as the 'empire of dulness.'
15. Hilary Spurling, *The Unknown Matisse: A Life of Henri Matisse; The Early Years, 1869–1908* (London: Hamish Hamilton, 1998), 358.
16. Christine Peltre, *L'Atelier du voyage: Les peintres en Orient au XIXe siècle* (Paris: Gallimard, 1995), 39–42.
17. Toohey, *Boredom*, 77–8. More generally, on Flaubert's propensity to boredom and preoccupation with it, see Sagnes, *L'Ennui dans la littérature française*, 166–203.
18. Du Camp, *Literary Recollections*, 338.
19. For a different but highly critical account of Said's version of Flaubert's encounter with Kuchuk Hanem, see Daniel Martin Varisco, *Reading Orientalism: Said and the Unsaid* (Seattle, WA: University of Washington Press, 2007), 158–62.
20. Edward Said, *Orientalism* (London: Routledge and Kegan Paul, 1978), 187.

21. Flaubert, *Voyage*, 131.
22. John Rodenbeck, ''*Awalim*; or The Persistence of Error,' in *Historians in Cairo: Essays in Honor of George Scanlon*, ed. Jill Edwards (Cairo and New York: American University in Cairo Press, 2002), 107.
23. Flaubert, *Voyage*, 131–7.
24. Disparaging references to Lane are frequent in Said's *Orientalism*, but the main discussion is on pages 158–64.
25. Edward William Lane, *An Account of the Manners and Customs of the Modern Egyptians* (1836) (London: Minerva Library, 1890), 173, 325, 463–4; cf. Jason Thompson, *Edward William Lane: The Life of the Pioneering Egyptologist and Orientalist* (London: Haus, 2010), 64–6. For a conclusive account of Said's multiple errors regarding Kuchuk Hanem's location and status, see Rodenbeck, ''*Awalim*,' 115–16.
26. Said, *Orientalism*, 186.
27. Flaubert, *Correspondance*, 597.
28. On Hassan al-Bilbeisi, see below.
29. Gustave Flaubert, *La Tentation de Saint Antoine*, ed. Emile Faguet (London: Dent & Sons; Paris: Crès et Cie, 1913), 34: '*Je pince le lyre, je danse comme une abeille…*'
30. Said, *Orientalism*, 187.
31. Flaubert, *Correspondance*, 605. At the beginning of the notes to his discussion of Flaubert (*Orientalism*, 368, n. 102), Said claimed to have consulted the *Œuvres complètes de Gustave Flaubert*, as well as *Les Lettres de l'Égypte de Gustave Flaubert*. Thereafter, however, he seems to have relied on the condensation of Flaubert's various writings in Egypt provided by Steegmuller and only on Steegmuller. When Steegmuller published his book the full version of Flaubert's travel journal was not available to him.
32. On this particular point, see Geoff Dyer, 'The Goncourt Journals,' in *Working the Room*, ed. Dyer (Edinburgh: Canongate Books, 2010), 200. For the Goncourts on Flaubert's sexual vulgarity, see Brown, *Flaubert*, 384. See also Jacques-Louis Douchin, *La Vie érotique de Flaubert* (Paris: Pauvert, 1984).
33. Flaubert, *Voyage*, 137.
34. Flaubert, *Correspondance*, 607.
35. Flaubert, *Voyage*, 180–1.
36. Flaubert, *Correspondance*, 572.
37. Flaubert, *Correspondance*, 572.
38. Said, *Orientalism*, 190.
39. To get some idea of the range of Flaubert's sexual activities, see the index to Brown's *Flaubert*, s.v. prostitution.
40. Brown, *Flaubert*, 247; Flaubert, *Voyage*, 132.
41. Brown, *Flaubert*, 289.
42. Said, *Orientalism*, 176–7, 179–80.
43. Du Camp, *Literary Recollections*, 338.
44. Mary Orr, 'Flaubert's Egypt: Crucible and Crux for Textual Identity,' in *Travellers in Egypt*, eds. Paul Starkey and Janet Starkey (London: Garnet, 1998), 194.
45. Said, *Orientalism*, 184.
46. Flaubert, *Correspondence*, 633; Steegmuller, *Flaubert in Egypt*, 200.
47. Geoffrey Wall, *Flaubert: A Life* (London: Faber and Faber, 2001), 181.

48. A detailed listing of the factual errors to be found throughout *Orientalism* can be found in Varisco, *Reading Orientalism*.
49. Said, *Orientalism*, 190.
50. Flaubert, *Sentimental Education*, 78.
51. Said, *Orientalism*, 187.
52. Said, *Orientalism*, 87–8.
53. On the complex issue of the chronology of the domestication of the camel in North Africa, see Richard W. Bulliet, *The Camel and the Wheel* (Cambridge, MA: Harvard University Press, 1975), 111–40.
54. A. J. Krailsheimer, 'Introduction,' in Flaubert, *Salammbô*, ed. and tr. Krailsheimer (Harmondsworth: Penguin, 1977), 15.
55. Michael Tilby, 'Flaubert's Place in Literary History,' in *The Cambridge Companion to Flaubert*, ed. Timothy Unwin (Cambridge: Cambridge University Press, 2004), 14.
56. Wall, *Flaubert*, 144.
57. Lisa Lowe, *Critical Terrains: French and British Orientalisms* (Ithaca, NY and London: Cornell University Press, 1991), 9; Anne Green, *Flaubert and the Historical Novel* (Cambridge: Cambridge University Press, 1982), 114.
58. Brown, *Flaubert*, 278; Wall, *Flaubert*, 194; cf. Gustave Flaubert, *Flaubert à l'Exposition de 1851*, ed. and trans. Jean Seznec (Oxford: Clarendon Press, 1951). Flaubert took careful notes on the ornamental picturesque in Chinese and Indian displays.
59. On the Great Exhibition and its Oriental displays, see John M. Mackenzie, *Orientalism: History, Theory and the Arts* (Manchester: Manchester University Press, 1995), 119–20. On the relationship between international exhibitions and Orientalism more generally, see Timothy Mitchell, *Colonising Egypt* (Cambridge: Cambridge University Press, 1988); Zeynep Çelik, 'Speaking Back to Orientalist Discourse at the World's Columbian Exposition,' in *Noble Dreams, Wicked Pleasures: Orientalism in America, 1870–1930*, ed. Holly Edwards (Princeton, NJ: Princeton University Press, 2000), 77–97; Nicky Levell, *Oriental Visions: Exhibitions, Travel and Collecting in the Victorian Age* (London: The Horniman Museum & Gardens, 2000); Roger Benjamin, *Orientalist Aesthetics: Art Colonialism and French North Africa* (Berkeley, CA and London: University of California Press, 2003), 210–19.
60. Rana Kabbani, *Europe's Myths of the Orient: Devise and Rule* (London: Palgrave Macmillan, 1986), 69. For the actual story, see Gustave Flaubert, *Three Tales*, trans. A. J. Krailsheimer (Oxford: Oxford University Press, 1991), 71–105.
61. Edmond de Goncourt, *Pages from the Goncourt Journal*, trans. Robert Baldick (London, 1980), 249.
62. Steegmuller, *Flaubert in Egypt*, 222.
63. On Said's multiple misrepresentations of British novels, see Robert Irwin, 'The Muslim World in British Fictions of the Nineteenth Century,' in *Britain and the Muslim World: Historical Perspectives*, ed. Gerald MacLean (Newcastle: Cambridge Scholars, 2011), 131–42. On Said's misrepresentation of Byron, see Peter Cochran, 'Edward Said's Failure with (Inter Alia) Byron,' in *Byron and Orientalism*, ed. Cochran (Newcastle: Cambridge Scholars, 2006), 183–96. On Said's misreading of Austen's *Mansfield Park*, see Gabrielle D. V. White, *Jane Austen in the Context of Abolition: 'A Fling at the Slave Trade'* (London: Palgrave Macmillan, 2006). On Said's misrepresentation of George Eliot, see

Nancy Henry, *George Eliot and the British Empire* (Cambridge: Cambridge University Press, 2002).

64. Joseph Conrad, *The Nigger of the 'Narcissus'/Youth* (London: Pan Classics, 1976), 177. *Youth* was first published in 1902.
65. Gertrude Bell, *Safar Nameh, Persian Pictures: A Book of Travel* (London: R. Bentley and Son, 1894), 26–7.

4
Said before Said

Donna Landry

Nobody should be allowed to remain innocent of *Orientalism*. More than 30 years after its publication in 1978, the book continues to be indispensable for understanding East–West relations. *Orientalism* has elicited, and withstood, a host of attacks, some more damaging than others. Yet it has transformed academic history writing concerning the Middle East. The field of postcolonial studies and the critique of imperialism within literary and cultural history would be unthinkable without it. The book is not a history of Western Orientalist scholarship. Still less is it a history of the 'East.' Although written during the 1970s, *Orientalism* endures because it retains a powerful purchase on the world we inhabit. What is most troubling about the book's continuing relevance is that despite its sensational exposure of Western errors of perception, representation and policy concerning the Middle East, the discourse of Orientalism, the discursive machine for constructing an Orient, making statements about it, and ruling over it, continues apace. The book has endured, tragically, because its object of critique is so robust; *Orientalism* remains relevant precisely because Orientalism continues to prevail.[1]

I would like to trouble the waters regarding the 'before' and 'after' of Said's own periodization of the Orientalism that most interested him. I am going to suggest that a certain prescience on Said's part has assured the predictive qualities of *Orientalism*, and of another book that is in many ways its companion volume, *The Question of Palestine* (1979). Said's description of Orientalism as a citational system of representation, as a *discourse*, continues to have tremendous explanatory power, even among scholars of the so-called Orient. Dating the origins of his Oxford DPhil to the 'thrill' of reading *Orientalism* as an undergraduate in Jerusalem, Eitan Bar-Yosef ascribes to Said his recognition 'that nothing about my homeland, Israel, would ever seem the same again.'[2] Bar-Yosef finds 'puzzling,' given the foundational importance of Said's work for postcolonial studies, the 'absence of Palestine from postcolonial criticism,' and the 'scant attention' given to 'Britain's imperial ambitions toward Palestine,' gaps which his own work seeks to fill.[3] The Ottoman historian Daniel Goffman concurs that academic, government and media 'condescension' toward the non-European or American world, leading to disciplinary peripheralization, 'has been aptly designated "orientalist" ' by Said.[4] Bruce Masters, another Ottomanist, opines that 'criticism of the abuses of "Orientalism" as an academic discipline by Said, and those influenced by him, has been both thoughtful and substantive,' requiring a heightened degree of self-critical vigilance.[5]

Not only do the discursive features Said maps so powerfully continue to recur on a daily basis in the West's representations of the Middle East, but the paradigm also usefully illuminates, to a certain degree, even Western texts produced before the era of European supremacy. *Orientalism* and *The Question of Palestine* remain required reading for a comparative study of the East and the West, even during the early modern moment of aspirational Western and dominant Eastern empires.

The itinerary of Said's *œuvre* from his early work onwards, in its method, allusiveness and appeal to a common humanity, invites us to return to archives and historical moments, which he himself did not investigate. The Orientalism which principally interested Said is the set of attitudes and practices engendered by British and French imperialism after Bonaparte's invasion of Egypt in 1798 that coalesced in the Sykes–Picot agreement of 1916, the Balfour Declaration of 1917 and the creation of the State of Israel in Palestine in 1948. Said suggests this origin and focus plainly enough, and yet he has often been misunderstood. He did not attempt to write a history of European Orientalist scholarship in all its heterogeneity, but to trace a specific legacy:

> Taking the late eighteenth century as a very roughly defined starting point Orientalism can be discussed and analyzed as the corporate institution for dealing with the Orient – dealing with it by making statements about it, authorizing views of it, describing it, by teaching it, settling it, ruling over it: in short, Orientalism as a Western style for dominating, restructuring, and having authority over the Orient.[6]

Said has written persuasively of his relation to Vico and the importance of a starting point. *Beginnings* (1975), as he indicates in *Orientalism*, was devoted to this question of the necessity of 'formulating a first step, a point of departure, a beginning principle' for every project precisely because 'beginnings have to be made for each project in such a way as to *enable* what follows from them.'[7] Following Vico, Said considers all knowledge to be embodied in the human subjects who produce it. In an interview, Said speaks of finding Vico's notion of 'self-making' – the human subject forming itself 'into a mind and a body, and then into a society' – 'so compelling and so powerful' that it clearly lies 'at the heart of all genuinely powerful and interesting historical visions' (his examples are Marx and Ibn Khaldun).[8]

Said made no secret of his own positioning in *Orientalism*, while arguing that all knowledge is 'positioned.' Without analysing the Sykes–Picot agreement or the Balfour Declaration directly, therefore, Said exemplifies for us the logic of these texts through attention to writing by British politicians such as Arthur James Balfour. In a virtuoso performance, Said reads a 1910 speech on Egypt by Balfour to the House of Commons, showing the dynamics of knowledge and power precisely as they work to constitute Egypt as an object of knowledge for British colonial policy. Closely reading a particular passage, Said shows what we have come to call 'Orientalist' thinking in the service of an imperial vision that would produce the arrogant ambiguities of the Balfour Declaration seven years later:

> Balfour's logic here is interesting, not least for being completely consistent with the premises of his entire speech. England knows Egypt; Egypt is what England knows; England knows that Egypt cannot have self-government; England confirms that by occupying Egypt; for the Egyptians, Egypt is what England has occupied and now governs; foreign occupation therefore becomes 'the very basis' of contemporary Egyptian civilization; Egypt requires, even insists upon, British occupation.[9]

The emphasis upon occupation in Said's unpacking is consistent both with Balfour's logic and with what Said identifies in *Orientalism* as a favoured strategy of imperial power, handed on from France and Britain to America and its client state Israel, and determining military and geopolitical arrangements to this day, not least in Palestine. When Said remarks in 1978 that 'the Orient is at bottom something either to be feared [...] or to be controlled (by pacification, research and development, outright occupation whenever possible),' he was summarizing policy decisions already in place but also predicting with uncanny accuracy the shape of things to come, beyond the Occupied Territories of Palestine to Iraq and Afghanistan.[10] More than 30 years after Said published both *Orientalism* and *The Question of Palestine*, no satisfactory answer to 'the question of Palestine' has been forthcoming.

This lamentable state of affairs may appear to indicate the vitiation of all hope, and intellectual as well as political paralysis, but Said himself never gave up hope. His late work and interviews maintain the view that despite the irreconcilability of Zionist and Palestinian nationalist narratives, some solution is possible. In a 2000 interview, Said commented, 'It is an almost sublime conflict... When you think about it, when you think about Jew and Palestinian not separately, but as part of a symphony, there is something magnificently imposing about it.'[11] Any future vision for Israel and Palestine would have to involve, he suggests, a radical mixing, rather than separatism, sectarianism and chauvinist nationalism. In trying to envisage what he has in mind, Said refers to something he has resolutely avoided investigating in his own work up to this point, with its unitary focus on British and French imperial manoeuvrings. Said admits to Ari Shavit of *Ha'aretz Magazine*: 'I hate to say it, but in a funny sort of way, it worked rather well under the Ottoman Empire, with its *millet* system. What they had then seems a lot more humane than what we have now.'[12]

And what, we might ask, was it that they had that was more 'humane,' more productive for a project of common humanity than rival nationalisms and religious and ethnic absolutisms? Might there have been an Ottoman cosmopolitanism, a toleration or incorporation of difference that appears comparatively humane in the light of hindsight? It is to a revisiting of the Ottoman East, especially in the centuries before 1798, that we now turn.

'Before' Said: Ottomanism

Said's 'corporate institution' for dealing with his Orient, the Islamic Middle East, can be dated, as we have seen, by shorthand reference to Bonaparte's invasion of Egypt in 1798. This event galvanized French and British rivalries as each nation subsequently sought during the nineteenth century to secure Near Eastern imperial and colonial dominion. Empire fever to possess, by carving up, the Ottoman 'Sick Man of Europe,' was brought to the table at the signing of the Sykes–Picot agreement (1916) and the Treaties of Sèvres and Lausanne (1920, 1923). The Treaty of Sèvres 'amounted to the comprehensive death warrant for the Ottoman Empire,' disposing of 'every territory that had belonged to the empire and at least one – Morocco – that never had belonged to it,' as Carter Vaughn Findley comments.[13] If Sèvres assumed 'that the Turkish people were as dead as the empire,' giving away 'most of the future Turkish republic,' Lausanne only granted to the new republic land in Anatolia, leaving the 'punitive' terms of Sèvres, coupled with the ambiguities of the Balfour Declaration of 1917, to determine the fate of 'the Arab lands.'[14]

As Gerald MacLean and Nabil Matar observe in *Britain and the Islamic World*, by the time of the Balfour Declaration in 1917, Britain sought to end 'the Islamic empire of the Ottomans' by establishing in Palestine a British-mandated Jewish 'homeland.' In order to foster the conversion of the Jews, buttressed by efforts to 'transform some eastern Orthodox Arabs into an Anglican congregation,' 'Conversion became an official instrument in the service of empire, and Canterbury an arm of the foreign office.'[15] Fed by a swaggering, staggering confidence that Britain and France were the legitimate inheritors of territorial and administrative responsibility after the dissolution of the Ottoman Empire, these events had been preceded by a long history – in Findley's terms, centuries 'of symbiosis under the banner of a multiethnic Islamic state' to whom the Europeans could never have dictated such terms.[16]

British–French rivalry had been formative for national identity,[17] but should be understood within a more global context of imperial aspiration. If the British took the lead in India, trumping the Portuguese,[18] France had already led the way in Istanbul, first serving as 'Europe's window on the Islamic world,' as Philip Mansel puts it.[19] With the arrival in 1535 of the first French ambassador to the Ottoman Porte, Jean de la Forest, the French had already achieved what the English were struggling with from the late 1570s onwards (with redoubled efforts after 1580, when they first received trading capitulations from the Sublime Porte) – an Ottoman *rapprochement*.[20] Mansel observes that although 'no country had a stronger crusader tradition than France,' the arrival of the first French ambassador in Istanbul in 1535 'marked the beginning of the Franco-Ottoman alliance,' which 'until Bonaparte's invasion of Egypt in 1798, would be the only fixed point in the unending struggle for territory and hegemony between the different powers of Europe.'[21]

The English were thus belated as well as beleaguered in their early dealings with the Ottomans, yet by 1620, London's Levant Company had become the principal European trading partner of the Ottoman Empire. As Bruce McGowan notes, 'Except for the disturbance of England's trade during the English civil wars, from which the Dutch drew some profit, the English were the undisputed leaders in the Levant trade between 1620 and 1683.'[22] By the 1650s, despite its late start, England was forging ahead; it had 'become evident to other European states,' writes Jonathan I. Israel, 'that England possessed outstanding advantages as a colonizing power, and that her Empire might soon outstrip all others.'[23] By the middle of the eighteenth century, Israel concludes, regardless of 'the full-scale armed opposition, at different times, of all of England's main colonial and maritime rivals – the French, Spanish, and Dutch,' Britain had emerged as 'without any doubt the supreme maritime and colonial power and hub of global commerce.'[24] Thus British imperial pre-eminence among European nations arose precociously, and precisely at the same time as her Anglo-Ottoman partnership. Regardless of European clout, however, British relations with the Ottomans were never those of imperial supremacy. Even the 'spectacular expansion in trade,' advises Nicholas Canny, 'which took Englishmen to the African coast, the Levant, Russia, the Indian Ocean, and elsewhere, and which added substantially to the wealth of England because of the opportunities it provided for re-exportation' was not considered 'either imperial or colonial in the seventeenth century.'[25] Canny speculatively attributes this attitude to an absence of 'settlement' – for example, the absence of settler-colonialism in the trading territories of the Levant Company – coupled with a failure on the part of 'English consumers' to 'appreciate the novelty of the means' by which the commodities they craved were being supplied.[26] Contemporary views of the Levant trade as neither imperial or colonial appear quite reasonable in light of the status of the Ottoman Empire as a rival superpower, not a colonizable space.

Thus Said's *Orientalism* requires adaptation and revision for the early modern context. In the light of profound 'Muslim impact' on English commerce and society, Nabil Matar finds it unsurprising that early modern English writers 'did not express either the authority of possessiveness or the security of domination which later gave rise to what Edward Said has termed "Orientalism".'[27] Recognizing that Said focused on the 'post Napoleonic experience of Europe,' Matar opines that it was the beginning of Ottoman 'military and intellectual decline in the eighteenth century' – a cliché not challenged by Matar – that permitted Europeans 'to draw, paint, poeticize and imagine the Muslims the way they liked,' preparing the way for 'orientalist "construction" and for continental and British colonization.'[28] Matar tries to account for the rather more puzzlingly arrogant hostility of some early modern English writers to the Muslim world by connecting these sentiments with the superimposition of New World experiences: 'Whereas in the Americas the natives had been defeated by the European white man, in the dominions of Islam, Britons were humiliated by Muslims'[29] and, in a later book, 'But precisely because the Muslims of the Mediterranean basin were powerful and undominated, English writers turned to super-imposition as an act of psychological compensation and vicarious assurance.'[30]

Richmond Barbour advises that the polarization of Matar's model 'exaggerates the point' of English inferiority.[31] Barbour goes on to stress the limitations of Said's 'confinement,' in *Orientalism*, to a critique of 'a discursive system itself critiqued for taking its own accounts of others as the accounts that matter,'[32] referring us to the Said of *Culture and Imperialism* who acknowledges that what he left out of *Orientalism* was the tradition of resistance that eventuated in decolonization: 'Never was it the case that the imperial encounter pitted an active Western intruder against a supine or inert non-Western native; there was *always* some form of active resistance.'[33] For Barbour, grasping the specificities of the early modern English requires recognizing that there is reason to be sceptical about their self-aggrandizing propaganda. There is something wishful about London theatricalizations of the East: 'The shows of London quickened appetites for exotic exposures, and they probably sharpened personal and corporate resourcefulness. Yet the easeful reach of their geography also fostered premature confidence in England's adequacy to the great world.'[34] For Barbour, what remains crucial is not to dissent from, but to 'advance the spirit of Said's critique,' to 'allow for the full, cultivated humanity of different peoples.'[35]

Like Barbour, literary historians investigating Anglo-Ottoman exchanges have focused primarily on the theatre, including Jonathan Burton, whose chief departure has been to engage with Ottoman history and sources in translation, mindful of Said's contrapuntal reading method in *Culture and Imperialism*, but aware of its limitations for his material.[36] Burton cautions, 'The impulse to seek Muslim responses to European texts is more a product of our one-sided archives than it is of historical circumstances and wrongly assumes that European discourse commanded a response.'[37] Consequently, his book marks a beginning, attending to a few Ottoman sources that show, for example, in exchanges of letters between Elizabeth I and Sultan Murad III, each side modifying traditional rhetoric, mindful of the other's difference.[38] Yet the dominant discursive mode he uncovers is one in which 'whatever version of the Turks was useful for English reasons was often presented as the essential truth about the Turks.'[39]

Why early modern English self-representation should have broadcast such a prematurely inflated sense of agency, when humility was called for, remains a subject of debate. Said himself offered one answer when he proposed that Orientalism's 'detailed logic' was 'governed not simply by empirical reality but by a battery of desires, repressions, and projections.'[40] Something wishful, covetous, emulative often attaches itself to Western representations of the East. Seeking, like Barbour, to advance the spirit of Said's critique, Gerald MacLean has proposed 'imperial envy' as a structure of feeling, in Raymond Williams's terms, that preceded Said's paradigmatic Orientalism. Williams defines structures of feeling as 'meanings and values as they are actively felt and lived, and the relations between them and formal or systematic beliefs,' 'characteristic elements of impulse, restraint, and tone; specifically affective elements of consciousness and relationships: not feeling against thought, but thought as felt and feeling as thought: practical consciousness of a present kind, in a living and inter-relating continuity.'[41] Said himself acknowledges Williams's influence when he writes that he hopes that *Orientalism* might contribute to 'what Raymond Williams has called the "unlearning" of "the inherent dominative mode." '[42] Said has, then, implicitly represented 'Orientalism' as a dominant structure of feeling, against which new and emerging structures of feeling may arise. For MacLean, imperial envy captures the ambivalence of the early modern English discursive stance toward the Ottomans that preceded British imperial Orientalism:

> Where imperial discourses might be expected to produce empowered imperial subjects constituting themselves at the expense of colonized subalterns, the situation proves to be more complex in the case of English views of the Ottomans. Instead of any simple desire for domination, we will find instead a restructuring of desire, knowledge and power: imperial envy.[43]

After all, as MacLean observes, early modern Europeans were dealing with 'an empire that controlled a great deal of Eastern Europe and a third of the known world, not a backward, vulnerable and somehow "orientalised" space waiting to be conquered and controlled.'[44] It is hardly surprising, then, that 'imperial envy' of the Ottomans should have shaped emergent imperial aspirations in England and, later, Britain, or that after the realization of those ambitions, envy 'gives way to an amicable indifference born from a presumed superiority that had, perhaps, always been present.'[45]

Before the fact of British or French mandatory power or territorial possession, then, before either nation has acquired colonial administrative experience in the Islamic Middle East, there are nevertheless intimations of a structure of feeling that could be called 'Orientalist,' aspirationally imperialist, an imagining into being of that positional superiority in advance of 'facts on the ground.' This is not to say that Said's description of post-1798 discourse entirely fits, but rather that in spite of significant differences there are nevertheless enough commonalities for an argument to be made about certain 'pre-emergent,' as Williams might say, or proto-Orientalist strains coming into being, however intermittently and unevenly, during the two-and-a-half centuries before Orientalism-as-such.

Consider these remarks by the eminent non-juring divine Thomas Smith, who served as Levant Company chaplain in Istanbul during the 1660s before returning to take up a fellowship at Magdalen College, Oxford, from whence he published numerous treatises:

> THE *Turks* are justly branded with the character of a Barbarous Nation; which censure does not relate to either the cruelty and severity of their punishments, which their natural fierceness, not otherwise to be restrain'd, renders necessary and essential to their Government; or to want of Discipline, for that in most things is very exact, and agreeable to the Laws and Rules of Polity, which Custom and Experience hath established as the grand support of their Empire; or to want of civil Behavior among themselves, for none can outwardly be more respectful and submissive, especially to their Superiors, in whose power it is to do them a mischief, the fear of which makes them guilty of most base compliances: But to the intolerable Pride and Scorn wherewith they treat all the World besides.[46]

Smith begins by seeming to confirm his readers' prejudices: the Turks are indeed a barbarous nation. But then he disabuses them of the reasons which he imagines they might think justified this label. It is not the Turks' ferocity (for which read their much-feared military prowess), or cruelty (a different legal and criminal-justice system), or ability to dissemble (diplomatic effectiveness), or resistance to social discipline (democratic tendencies), or appeal to an absolute executive authority (absence of oppositional republicanism) that he targets. These are the characteristics that might most likely be anticipated by his readers as signifying Ottoman barbarity. Interestingly, these features point exactly toward socio-political controversies in the post-Civil War, Interregnum, and Restoration period, suggesting a view of Ottoman society tailored to English anxieties. Smith's account climaxes with his revelation that

Turks' barbarity is in fact derived from their sense of superiority: 'intolerable Pride and Scorn' toward 'all the World besides.' What Smith himself finds 'intolerable,' as in not to be tolerated if at all possible, is Ottoman pride and self-confidence. Not only do the Ottomans consider themselves rulers of the known world, with the Sultan the *'padishah,'* a ruler incomparably powerful, above other monarchs, but ordinary 'Turks' seem to have absorbed this sense of cultural superiority, too. In 1678, it is offensive to English sensibilities that another nation should carry themselves with 'Pride and Scorn' for 'all the World besides.' Here, imperial envy takes the form of desire for a hostile take-over, however wishful. A structure of feeling such as Smith's renders the search for early modern instances of cosmopolitan *rapprochement* at the very least problematic.

Yet cosmopolitanism, however elusive, seems firmly on early modernists' agendas, no less than on the agendas of postcolonial critics,[47] requiring ever greater comparativism and revealing disciplinary gaps, not least the failure to engage with Ottoman history. The transatlantic historian Alison Games has recently proposed accounting for a fiscally constrained, militarily weak state's success in producing a 'web of empire,' 1560–1660, by means of the cultural openness of 'English cosmopolitans': 'globetrotters' possessed of 'transoceanic global perspectives' and 'adaptability,' 'men who were often able to encounter those unlike themselves with enthusiasm and curiosity.'[48] 'My approach,' states Games, 'deliberately inverts the trajectory of an older style of imperial history in which Britons were capable of imposing their will on subject people and places, by casting light instead on how places and people far from Europe defined how the English experienced the world and the empire that emerged in their wake.'[49] Collecting everything from 'manuscripts' and 'tacky souvenirs' to 'captives, friends, and experiences,' these men linked 'ties of knowledge and custom and practice' from Virginia to Japan, and from Cairo to the Caribbean; they:

> learned foreign languages, visited synagogues and mosques, befriended Asian and European traders, pursued sexual and romantic relations with indigenous women, fathered children and sometimes shipped them home to England, and sought to understand the cultural mores of an alien land. They pursued avocations as amateur botanists, hosted foreign neighbours for English holiday meals, attended plays, studied foreign music, and fought and sickened and died thousands of miles from home.[50]

This awakening to cosmopolitan openness first occurs, Games opines, when Britons are 'overwhelmed' by the 'cosmopolitan nature' of 'Ottoman cities.'[51] It is curious, then, that when Games's globetrotters insinuate 'themselves into new trading worlds' and master 'a commercial demeanor defined by its style of accommodation and dissimulation,' nothing is said about the originals they must have imitated.[52] Far from 'inverting' the 'trajectory' of an 'older style of imperial history,' Games still places agency firmly in the persons of her English subjects, rather than in the specific 'places and people' they lived with, in however accommodating, sometimes intimate, rather than imperious or belligerent, ways. Committed to keeping New World colonization to the fore, Games measures her global agents against their Spanish, Portuguese and French rivals, without ever noticing the Ottoman age of expansion, although the 'achievements of Columbus and Cortes were eclipsed by their Turkish contemporaries' in the Red Sea, Persian Gulf and Indian Ocean, as Felipe Fernández-Armesto and Giancarlo Casale have shown.[53] Furthermore, when measured 'against the mischief wrought by Spain and Portugal across the Atlantic,' as Caroline Finkel puts it, 'there was no "darker side" to the Ottoman adventure in the Indian Ocean,' but rather the benefits of trade and alliance, surely a more appropriate comparative framework for a historian tracking 'cosmopolitanism.'[54]

Such blind spots suggest how disciplinary boundaries remain a real obstacle to recreating some sense of a vanished world, those 'centuries of symbiosis under the banner of a multiethnic Islamic state.' Yet recent events suggest some of this parochialism is changing: if work by Ottomanists now invokes Said in a critical yet approving way, Said himself was in his last years, however reluctantly – 'I hate to say it, but in a funny sort of way, it worked rather well under the Ottoman Empire' – becoming interested in the lessons to be learned from the Ottoman past.

'After' Said: An Ottoman Cosmopolitanism?

How did Ottoman mechanisms for that 'multiethnic symbiosis' work, and might they provide a means for envisaging cosmopolitan alternatives? Ottoman historians point to the accommodation of Jews and Christians within the *taife* or *millet* system, to which Said alludes.[55] Daniel Goffman explains that Islam developed a doctrine 'not of impartiality but of indulgence,' whereby Christians and Jews, both 'people of the Book,' were allowed to live and worship within the Abode of Islam (*dar al-Islam*) in return for tributary payment of a poll-tax (*cizye*) and 'certain other signs of subjugation': 'This precept enabled Christians and Jews to endure, and even to prosper, under the dominion of this rival faith.'[56] Early modern European expulsion of Jews was met by Ottoman admission of them: the greatest wave of Jewish immigration occurred between 1492 and 1512, in which Sephardim from Spain joined 'Greek-speaking Jews, called Romaniotes, and German Jews, called Ashkenazim, who had also been expelled from their homelands.'[57] 'Ottoman economic policies meant that "for the first time in many centuries, a powerful state offered the Jews full protection".'[58] Jonathan Israel identifies the 1570s, the same decade in which the English began their official turn to the Turks, as a turning point for European Jews. Israel describes the previous century, from 1470 to 1570, as witnessing 'the near destruction of Jewish religion, learning, and life in western and central Europe.'[59] 'The tolerated status of non-Muslims had been codified in Ottoman law since before the reign of Mehmed II'; hence the invitation to many non-Muslims following the conquest of Istanbul in 1453.[60]

Ottoman leniency toward non-Muslims was subject to vicissitudes, especially during the Kadizadeli puritan reforms and Jewish millenarian movements of the seventeenth century,[61] as Caroline Finkel shows, but the enshrining of toleration as official policy was nevertheless radically enlightened by European standards. As a consequence, 'Ottoman Jews subscribed to the idea of "Ottomanism" for longer' than many of their Christian compatriots, many coming to regard 'a homeland within the Ottoman Empire as the best guarantor of their security,' as Finkel puts it.[62] According to Bruce Masters, 'non-Muslim elites in the Arab provinces,' both Jewish and Christian, 'increasingly chose the option of a secular political identity, whether Ottomanism or Arabism, as the empire stumbled into the twentieth century,' thus avoiding the 'paroxysm of ethnic violence' that exploded in Anatolia.[63] Recently, there have been Palestinian efforts – we could include Said's 2000 interview remarks among these – to revive the Ottoman example as a model for peaceful coexistence throughout the whole region, with a minimum of borders.[64] As the Israeli Ottoman historian Gabriel Piterberg rather facetiously observes, 'The Palestinians should be grateful to the Ottomans. Once the empire was dissolved, they were ravished within minutes.'[65]

Recovering such a model of recognized but 'indulged' difference requires reconstructing not only Ottoman civil society but also Ottoman civility. Those astonishingly cosmopolitan cities that so overwhelmed early modern Britons functioned according to certain notions of manners, by means of a powerful state apparatus, but also ideas about what was civilized and what was not. Consider Henry Blount, Oxford wit and member of Gray's Inn, reporting in 1636 his ship-board experience with the Black Sea fleet en route to Rhodes and Alexandria. Blount had set out to study the Ottoman Empire as the pre-eminent polity of the day – 'I was of opinion, that hee who would behold these times in their greatest glory, could not find a better *Scene* then *Turky*' – and to see for himself how a foreign society comported itself – 'whether the *Turkish* way appear absolutely barbarous, as we are given to understand, or rather another kind of civility, different from ours, but no lesse pretending.'[66] Blount, who returned to England eschewing alcohol, and promoting water- and coffee-drinking, was impressed by the 'incredible civilitie' of Ottoman mariners:

> I who had often proved the *Barbarisme* of other Nations at Sea, and above all others, of our owne, supposed my selfe amongst *Beares*, till by experience, I found the contrary; and that not only in ordinary civility, but with so ready service, such a patience, so sweet, and gentle a way, generally through them all, as made me doubt, whether it was a dreame, or reall; if at any time I stood in their way, or encombred their ropes, they would call me with a *Janum*, or *Benum*, termes of most affection.[67]

Keeping their tempers, even when blocked in their labours or tripping over a hapless Englishman tangled among their rigging, the Turkish-speaking mariners are a model of polite forbearance, but also of gentle, even humorous, humanity. With such a spirit of ingrained civility, the 'indulgence' of the foreign enshrined in the *millet* system could, it seems, work pretty well.

When Said comes to describe historic Palestine in the following terms, we should keep in mind this mentality, which preceded but was replaced by nineteenth- and twentieth-century sectarian hostilities:

> In the late tenth century, for example, we find this passage in Arabic:

> Filastin is the westernmost of the provinces of Syria. In its greatest length from Rafh to the boundary of Al Lajjun (Legio) it would take a rider two days to travel over; and the like time to cross the province in its breadth [...] Filastin is watered by the rains and the dew. Its trees and its ploughed lands do not need artificial irrigation; and it is only in Nablus that you find the running waters applied to this purpose. Filastin is the most fertile of the Syrian provinces. Its capital and largest town is Ar Ramlah, but the Holy City (of Jerusalem) comes very near this last in size.

In 1516, Palestine became a province of the Ottoman Empire, but this made it no less fertile, no less Arab or Islamic. A century later the English poet George Sandys spoke of it as '[as] a land of milk and honey; in the midst as it were of the habitable world [...] and no part empty of delight or profit.'[68] Fertile and bountiful, the land is also clearly a land worked by human hands, not bereft of human population; these are ploughed fields; around Nablus there are irrigation systems, invented, maintained. Lyrically evoked as a rich source of all things bucolic which humans could desire, a perfect pastoral, Palestine is also a place of cities, and after 1516, Ottoman cities, with their enshrining of Islamic philanthropy, not only in mosques, but also in schools, hospitals, caravansaries, bath-houses and soup kitchens (one of which in Jerusalem has continued to function to the present day).[69]

And so when Said wrote in *The Question of Palestine* that 'to criticize Zionism now, then, is to criticize not so much an idea or a theory but rather a wall of denials,' a phrase he repeats in the 2000 interview with Ari Shavit,[70] he both predicts the concrete defacements of the 'security wall' and resonantly sketches the destruction of this legacy of civility 'in the midst as it were of the habitable world,' no part of which is 'empty of profit or delight.' Said recommends that 'Palestinians and Israeli Jews' 'sit down and discuss all the issues outstanding between them: rights of immigration, compensation for property lost, and so on, all in the context of a general discussion of future peace.'[71] What is called for is '*Zionist* acceptance of the fact that Jewish national liberation (as it is sometimes called) took place upon the ruins of *another* national existence, not in the abstract,' as well as recognition that 'the question of Palestine is not simply a hermetic debate between Zionists as to how Zionism and Israel are to comport themselves in theory on the land of what once was Palestine, but a vital political matter involving Arabs and Jews, residents in a commonly significant territory.'[72] This advice remains as fundamentally germane to any imaginable solution now as it was in 1979.

In the 2000 interview, Ari Shavit replies to Said's suggestion about the Ottoman *millet* system with a question: 'So, as you see it, the Jews would eventually have a cultural autonomy within a pan-Arab structure?'[73] To which Said responds with a vision inspired at least partly by Ottoman example:

> Pan-Arab or Mediterranean. Why should it not include Cyprus? What I would like is a kind of integration of Jews into the fabric of the larger society, which has an extraordinary staying power despite mutilation

by the nation-state. I think it can be done. There is every reason to go for the larger unit.[74]

In order to demolish the wall of denials and open the borders, neither *Orientalism* nor Ottomanism is without relevance, even now.

Notes

1. Despite denouncing *Orientalism* as 'a work of malignant charlatanry' (4) riddled with 'errors of fact and interpretation' (3), and substituting his own history of the European Orientalist enterprise in all its [heterogeneity] variety and eccentricity, Robert Irwin observes that he has 'no significant disagreements with what Said has written about Palestine, Israel, Kipling's *Kim*, or Glenn Gould's piano playing' (4), and applauds Said's 'advocacy of coexistence and tolerance in a single state,' stating that 'it would be a fine thing if his vision did one day become a reality.' Irwin nevertheless regrets that the single state's 'degree of political practicality' is on a par with 'Shangri-La' (308–9). *For Lust of Knowing: The Orientalists and Their Enemies* (London: Allen Lane, 2006).
2. Eitan Bar-Yosef, *The Holy Land in English Culture 1799–1917: Palestine and the Question of Orientalism*, Oxford English Monographs (Oxford and New York: Clarendon Press and Oxford University Press, 2005), vii.
3. Bar-Yosef, *Holy Land*, 5. Bar-Yosef nevertheless considers Palestine, as the Holy Land already scripturally 'belonging' to English Christians, to be a special case that resists the 'binary logic' of Said's model (7–8).
4. Daniel Goffman, *The Ottoman Empire and Early Modern Europe* (Cambridge and New York: Cambridge University Press, 2002), 5.
5. Bruce Masters, *Christians and Jews in the Ottoman Arab World: The Roots of Sectarianism*, Cambridge Studies in Islamic Civilization (Cambridge and New York: Cambridge University Press, 2001), 2.
6. Edward W. Said, *Orientalism* (1978) (New York: Vintage Books, 2003), 3.
7. Said, *Orientalism*, 15–16, referring to *Beginnings: Intention and Method* (New York: Basic Books, 1975).
8. Said, 'Literary Theory at the Crossroads of Public Life,' in *Power, Politics, and Culture: Interviews with Edward W. Said*, ed. Gauri Viswanathan, 63–93. (London: Bloomsbury, 2005), 78.
9. Said, *Orientalism*, 34.
10. Said, *Orientalism*, 301.
11. Said, 'My Right of Return,' in *Power, Politics, and Culture*, 447.
12. Said, 'My Right of Return,' 455.
13. Carter Vaughn Findley, *Turkey, Islam, Nationalism, and Modernity: A History, 1789–2007* (New Haven, CT and London: Yale University Press, 2010), 218.
14. Findley, *Turkey, Islam*, 219.
15. Gerald MacLean and Nabil Matar, *Britain and the Islamic World, 1558–1713* (Oxford and New York: Oxford University Press, 2011), 197.
16. Findley, *Turkey, Islam*, 211.
17. Linda Colley, *Britons: Forging the Nation, 1707–1837* (London and New Haven, CT: Yale University Press, 1992); Gerald Newman, *The Rise of*

English Nationalism: A Cultural History, 1740–1830 (London: Weidenfeld and Nicolson, 1987).

18. Om Prakash and Manish Chakraborti, *Europeans in Bengal in the Pre-Colonial Period: A Brief History of Their Commercial and Cultural Legacy* (New Delhi: Embassy of the Netherlands, 2008); William Dalrymple, *White Mughals: Love and Betrayal in Eighteenth-Century India* (London: HarperCollins, 2002).

19. Philip Mansel, 'The French Renaissance in Search of the Ottoman Empire,' in *Re-Orienting the Renaissance: Cultural Exchanges with the East*, ed. Gerald MacLean, 96–107. (Basingstoke and New York: Palgrave Macmillan, 2005), 96.

20. MacLean and Matar, *Britain and the Islamic World*, 42–9, 62–3, 77–8, 81–2.

21. Mansel, 'French Renaissance,' 96, 97.

22. Bruce McGowan, *Economic Life in Ottoman Europe: Taxation, Trade, and the Struggle for Land, 1600–1800* (Cambridge: Cambridge University Press, 1981), 21.

23. Jonathan I. Israel, 'The Emerging Empire: The Continental Perspective, 1650–1713,' in *The Origins of Empire: British Overseas Enterprise to the Close of the Seventeenth Century, The Oxford History of the British Empire, Volume I*, ed. Nicholas Canny, 423–44. (Oxford and New York: Oxford University Press, 1998), 423.

24. Israel, 'Emerging Empire,' 423–4.

25. Nicholas Canny, 'The Origins of Empire: An Introduction,' in *Origins of Empire, Oxford History Vol. I*, ed. Canny, 1–33, 4.

26. Canny, 'Origins,' 4.

27. Nabil Matar, *Islam in Britain, 1558–1685* (Cambridge: Cambridge University Press, 1998), 11.

28. Matar, *Islam in Britain*, 11.

29. Matar, *Islam in Britain*, 3–4.

30. Nabil Matar, *Turks, Moors, and Englishmen in the Age of Discovery* (New York: Columbia University Press, 1999), 16.

31. Richmond Barbour, *Before Orientalism: London's Theatre of the East, 1576–1626*, Cambridge Studies in Renaissance Literature and Culture (Cambridge: Cambridge University Press, 2003), 3.

32. Barbour, *Before Orientalism*, 4.

33. Said, *Culture and Imperialism* (New York: Knopf, 1993), xii, quoted in Barbour, *Before Orientalism*, 198, n. 9.

34. Barbour, *Before Orientalism*, 9.

35. Barbour, *Before Orientalism*, 5.

36. Jonathan Burton, *Traffic and Turning: Islam and English Drama, 1579–1624* (Newark, DE: University of Delaware Press, 2005), 39. See also Daniel J. Vitkus, *Turning Turk: English Theatre and the Multicultural Mediterranean*, Early Modern Cultural Studies Series (New York and Basingstoke: Palgrave, 2003); and Matthew Birchwood, *Staging Islam in England: Drama and Culture, 1640–1685*, Studies in Renaissance Literature (Cambridge: D. S. Brewer of Boydell & Brewer, 2007).

37. Burton, *Traffic and Turning*, 39–40.

38. Burton, *Traffic and Turning*, 62–4.

39. Burton, *Traffic and Turning*, 27.

40. Said, *Orientalism*, 8.
41. Raymond Williams, *Marxism and Literature* (Oxford and New York: Oxford University Press, 1977), 132.
42. Said, *Orientalism*, 28.
43. Gerald MacLean, *Looking East: English Writing and the Ottoman Empire before 1800* (Basingstoke and New York: Palgrave Macmillan, 2007), 20.
44. MacLean, *Looking East*, 20.
45. MacLean, *Looking East*, 23.
46. Tho. Smith, B. D. and Fellow of St Mary Magdalen College Oxon, *Remarks upon the Manners, Religion and Government of the Turks* .... (London: Printed for Moses Pitt, at the Angel in St Pauls Church-yard, 1678), 1–2.
47. For excellent work on the problematics of cosmopolitanism, and on Said's exemplary move toward greater 'cosmopolitan solidarity' after *Orientalism*, see Robert Spencer, *Cosmopolitan Criticism and Postcolonial Literature* (Basingstoke and New York: Palgrave Macmillan, 2011), 1–7, 18–39, 163–90. For a reading of the Ottoman Islamic spectre still haunting Europe, and advocacy of a democratic cosmopolitanism requiring a vision of unconditional hospitality, see Meyda Yeğenoğlu, *Islam, Migrancy and Hospitality in Europe* (Basingstoke and New York: Palgrave Macmillan, 2012).
48. Alison Games, *The Web of Empire: English Cosmopolitans in an Age of Expansion, 1560–1660* (Oxford and New York: Oxford University Press, 2008), 7, 9.
49. Games, *Web of Empire*, 10–11.
50. Games, *Web of Empire*, 10.
51. Games, *Web of Empire*, 54.
52. Games, *Web of Empire*, 52.
53. Felipe Fernández-Armesto, *Millennium: A History of Our Last Thousand Years* (1995; London: Black Swan, 1996), 220; quoted in Caroline Finkel, ' "The Treacherous Cleverness of Hindsight": Myths of Ottoman Decay,' in *Re-Orienting* the Renaissance, ed. Gerald MacLean, 148–74. (Basingstoke: Palgrave Macmillan, 2005), 165. The definitive study is now Giancarlo Casale's brilliant *The Ottoman Age of Exploration* (Oxford and New York: Oxford University Press, 2010).
54. Finkel, 'The Treacherous Cleverness,' 168.
55. Colin Imber, *Ebu's-su'ud: The Islamic Legal Tradition* (Edinburgh: Edinburgh University Press, 1997), 6–69.
56. Goffman, *The Ottoman Empire and Early Modern Europe*, 170.
57. Caroline Finkel, *Osman's Dream: The Story of the Ottoman Empire 1300–1923* (London: John Murray, 2005), 88.
58. Benjamin Arbel, *Trading Nations: Jews and Venetians in the Early Modern Eastern Mediterranean* (New York: E. V. Brill, 1995), 176, quoted in Burton, *Traffic*, 201.
59. Burton, *Traffic*, 200, quoting Jonathan Israel, *European Jewry in the Age of Mercantilism* (Oxford: Clarendon Press, 1989), 23; see also David S. Katz, *Jews in the History of England, 1485–1850* (Oxford: Clarendon Press, 1994).
60. Finkel, *Osman's Dream*, 278.
61. Finkel, *Osman's Dream*, 278–81.
62. Finkel, *Osman's Dream*, 533.
63. Masters, *Christians and Jews*, 9.

64. Raja Shehadeh, *A Rift in Time: Travels with My Ottoman Uncle* (London: Profile, 2011).

65. Gabriel Piterberg, private communication to the author.

66. Henry Blount, *A Voyage into the Levant*... (London: Printed by I. L. [John Legatt] for Andrew Crooke, 1636), 4, 5. For the best study of Blount, see Gerald MacLean, *The Rise of Oriental Travel: English Visitors to the Ottoman Empire, 1580–1720* (Houndmills, Basingstoke and New York: Palgrave Macmillan, 2004), 117–76.

67. Blount, *Voyage*, 75.

68. Said, *The Question of Palestine* (New York: Vintage, 1992), 11, quoting Istakhari and Ibn Hankal, in Guy Le Strange, *Palestine under the Moslems: A Description of Syria and the Holy Land from A.D. 650 to 1500 Translated from the Works of the Medieval Arab Geographers* (1890; rpt Beirut: Khayati, 1965), 28, and George Sandys, from Richard Bevis, 'Making the Desert Bloom: An Historical Picture of Pre-Zionist Palestine,' *The Middle East Newsletter* 5, no. 2 (February–March 1971), 4.

69. Amy Singer, *Constructing Ottoman Beneficence: An Imperial Soup Kitchen in Jerusalem* (Albany, NY: State University Press of New York, 2002).

70. Said, *Question of Palestine*, 51, and 'My Right of Return,' 449.

71. Said, *Question of Palestine*, 51–2.

72. Said, *Question of Palestine*, 52.

73. Said, 'My Right of Return,' 455.

74. Said, 'My Right of Return,' 455.

5
Orienting America: Sanskrit and Modern Scholarship in the United States, 1836–94

Mishka Sinha

Introduction

This work explores the history of American Orientalism,[1] in the form of the academic study of Sanskrit in America, in the context of its earliest foundations and its development in the nineteenth century into a discipline of exceptional importance and a field of intense contemporary interest. Although it has received little attention from scholars, Orientalism in America existed as a scholarly subject and a rudimentary disciplinary formation, as well as a means of organizing ideas, from as early as the 1830s. In *Orientalism*, Said acknowledged the founding of the American Oriental Society (AOS) in 1842, but barely alluded to the long history of the scholarly study of the East and the institutionalization of Oriental studies in America from the 1840s until the second half of the twentieth century.[2] The history of Oriental studies in America for Said began with post-war American academic research and contributions to Middle East policy, such as that illustrated by the career of H. A. R. Gibb, a Scottish Orientalist, and Laudian Professor of Arabic at Oxford, who became Richard Jewett Professor of Arabic at Harvard in 1955. This is unsurprising, since Said was concerned with launching a moral critique of an Orientalism whose *telos* lay in post-war and contemporary American politics, which he saw as directly inheriting the British and French Orientalist traditions rooted in their colonial relationships with Islam and the Middle East. Said's particular focus was the intellectual history of a certain kind of Orientalism, whose ontology is primarily entwined with the cultural politics of Orientalism in nineteenth-century France and, to a lesser extent, Britain; as well as its impact on modern political and socio-economic attitudes and policies in the West, especially America, toward the East, specifically the Middle East and Islam. Said's *Orientalism* begins with an account of British Orientalism in India, and uses the immediate connection between Britain's colonial and commercial interests in India and the early Sanskritists, East India Company servants such as Jones and Wilkins, as a starting point for his argument. Yet *Orientalism* is not primarily concerned with Sanskrit or Indology, but rather with Orientalism as a cultural, intellectual and aesthetic means of viewing, analysing and recording the Middle East and Islam. Said noted that Americans would not feel the same about the Orient as the French and British, and to a lesser extent the Germans, and other Europeans. Said argued that this was because Europeans, unlike Americans, 'had a long tradition of . . . Orientalism,' which he described as 'a way of coming to terms with the Orient . . . based on the Orient's special place in European Western experience.'[3] The Orient possessed an imaginative association for Europe, but it had also been 'an integral part of European *material* civilisation.'[4] Said suggested that Americans were more likely to associate the Orient 'with the Far East (China and Japan mainly).'[5] Building upon this representation of European Orientalism, Said posited that 'since World War II, America has dominated the Orient, and approaches it as Britain and France once did.'[6]

I have no quarrel with Said's political critique of American Orientalism, nor do I seek to contradict Said's thesis on the intellectual history of Orientalism insofar as the American inheritance of European attitudes to the Middle East and Islam are concerned. My aim is to challenge some of the assumptions that seem to underlie Said's discussion of American Orientalism, as well as subsequent critical engagements with Said's idea of American Orientalism – as a mainly twentieth-century phenomenon focused on the Middle East and Islam.[7] First, I contend that American Orientalism, in the academic sense, began more than a century before the Second World War. Second, American Orientalism was first most substantially associated with India. Finally, American Orientalism in this older sense is inherited most extensively not from Britain or France, but from Germany. Therefore, I will briefly trace the first phase in the history of Sanskrit in America with a view to recovering a part of nineteenth-century intellectual history that has been largely ignored. Consequently, I seek to open up a new space in which Said's methodology can be constructively employed to offer fresh perspectives on literary and intellectual history.

This chapter will focus on the foundations of Sanskrit in America, and specifically on the establishment of Sanskrit and Oriental studies at Yale and the role of William Dwight Whitney in the development of a 'public understanding' of Sanskrit in America. Through Whitney, Sanskrit became an aspect of the popular consciousness of contemporary culture, which was vitally affected by Victorian debates on language, race, religion and identity. Central to this understanding is the integration of Sanskrit into American university curricula and popular discourses during a period when America was in the process of developing an autonomous intellectual tradition and a new idea of a characteristically American university. My argument is framed within the context of Said's discussion of Orientalism, yet I hope to present a more complex, nuanced history of the American engagement with the Orient.

In general, scholarly discussions of the intellectual and cultural impact of the East on Americans tend to be confined to Emerson, Thoreau and the New England Transcendentalists. Both Edward Said and Raymond Schwab, the historian of Orientalism whom Said greatly admired, noted these influences.[8] However, Said chose not to investigate how nineteenth-century American intellectual and scholarly attitudes to the Orient paved the way for twentieth-century perspectives on the East. Schwab's brief and slightly inaccurate section on the history of nineteenth-century American Orientalism does more justice than Said to the scholars of this extraordinary period. Schwab held that 'the Classical Renaissance immured European man within the confines of a self-sufficient Greco-Latin terrain,' whereas 'this... [Oriental] ... Renaissance deposited the whole world before him.'[9] For Said, among Schwab's 'major theoretical contributions' was that he saw the Orient as a persistently enriching rather than a diminishing and anxiety-ridden influence on Romanticism and nineteenth-century literature. This was also true of America, where the study of Sanskrit provided a wealth of sources for the still-emerging traditions of American philosophy, literature and scholarly research.

In Said's 'Travelling Theory,' which immediately precedes his essay on Schwab and *The Oriental Renaissance*, he framed some of the issues concerning Orientalism as a transcultural theoretical project that were adumbrated both in *Orientalism*, and in his Schwab essay.[10] Said posited a theory of the transmission of ideas that encapsulated the means and manner by which a scholarly field, cultural object and intellectual resource such as Sanskrit, might be transmitted and indigenized within a new context.[11] Said pointed out that it was necessary to 'specify the kind of movements that are possible, in order to ask the crucial question,' whether, 'by virtue of having moved from one place and time to another... a theory in one historical period and national culture becomes altogether different for another period or situation'?[12] The example of American Orientalism illustrates Said's conclusion that 'such movement into a new environment...necessarily involves processes of representation and institutionalization different from those at the point of origin.'[13] Through the metamorphosis effected by its transmission to the West, Sanskrit as a language, literature and a cultural concept, acquired altered associations and significations, including that of an attenuated classicism. The 'Oriental Renaissance' like the European Renaissance brought an identification with antiquity which had modern uses, and bestowed a new cultural authority in its new contexts. As Said explained, 'what German Orientalism had in common with Anglo-French and later American Orientalism was a kind of intellectual *authority* over the Orient'; the same was true for nineteenth-century American Orientalism.[14] The idea of a 'travelling' Orientalism reiterates Orientalism's existence as an idea, or, rather, a collection of ideas, which was not singular, nor consistent, but rather, fungible and fragmented. As Said inferred, 'Orientalism responded more to the culture that produced it than...its putative object,' and it 'borrowed' and was 'informed by' ' "strong" ideas, doctrines and trends ruling' the culture which surrounded it.[15]

The collection, dispensation, and domination of knowledge about India and Sanskrit in America had important parallels with the similar hegemonic treatment of Oriental knowledge by European scholars that Said critiques. One might say about Sanskrit, that if 'the job of displacement was apportioned' so that 'Calcutta provided, London distributed, Paris filtered and generalised,'[16] then beyond the limits of the transcolonial world, in Berlin and Bonn, Tübingen and Leipzig, and across Germany, Sanskrit was institutionalized on a vast scale and transformed into a research industry. From here it was absorbed and transmitted to America, where, in the nascent metropolises and burgeoning university towns of the East, in New York and New Haven, Cambridge and Baltimore, it was reconstituted into a source of intellectual capital to feed newly forged, independent literary, philosophical, aesthetic, theological, philological and political traditions, and a field in which to test and display a modern, independent American scholarly tradition, challenging European dominance.

Even before it acquired territories in 'the Orient', America had a long history of participation in colonial trade and profit in the East. And once the East India Company allowed Christian missionaries in their Indian territories, Americans hastened to send their missionaries to India. America had a long history of maritime trade with India, and goods and materials from India had made their way to American shores. The sea trade excited curiosity about Indian culture while enriching the ports of the Eastern seaboard, culturally and financially contributing to the growing prosperity of New England. The great row of commercial buildings and houses opposite the Boston docks were appropriately named India Wharf, and in Salem a museum was founded to house the curiosities brought by American ships from the East. With the ships also came news of India, its culture and customs, religions and languages, as oral and written accounts from merchants and missionaries, sent in correspondence and published in books brought from Europe and India. Sanskrit translations and studies of the Sanskrit language and literature, in German, French and British works, arrived in America together with the influence of philosophical Idealism and literary Romanticism. A form of Orientalism developed through trade and cultural and intellectual exchange, partly based on old ties with Europe, and partly on American cultural and intellectual ambitions.

Prominent Unitarians in New England with links to the Brahmo Samaj in Calcutta offered a new source of Sanskrit texts, as Unitarian journals published Sanskrit translations by the Brahmo leader, Rammohun Roy, as well as reviews and articles extracted from British journals, which carried studies on India and Sanskrit. Emerson was eager to develop an autonomous intellectual tradition, and urged independence from European influences. India offered a fresh source of intellectual and cultural renewal and an opportunity to challenge European dominance, intellectually as well as materially. Emerson and the Transcendentalists integrated Sanskrit sources into their writings, forging an effective conduit for the transmission of popular Sanskrit in America. Through the continuing impact of Transcendentalism, Sanskrit as an intellectual and cultural resource was assured exceptional traction. However, a separate trajectory of transmission of scholarly Sanskrit had begun in 1842 with the founding of the AOS. One of its earliest members, Edward Elbridge Salisbury, would hold the first Chair in Arabic and Sanskrit in America; his student, William Dwight Whitney, would bring American Sanskrit studies on par with the highest standards of Europe. This is the history with which we are concerned.

Despite the unique features of nineteenth-century American Orientalism there is little existing scholarship on the subject.[17] One reason for this may be that American Orientalism does not provide a simple relation between colonial power and Oriental knowledge. While the same may be said of Germany until the late nineteenth century, America offers further complexities: the controlling image of the Orient was inherited, partly second-hand, from Europe – a relationship which was complicated by America's own colonial past. This kind of fantasizing about the East as a source of raw history to be transplanted and civilized on new soil was similar to the European reduction of the East to an objectified other. In this case, however, the object was not so much a domination of the East by America, as it was to demonstrate the American capacity to dominate their own cultural and historical past and present, impose their own ontological coherence on a fecund and fast-expanding intellectual landscape, and construct a modern, autonomously American intellectual and academic tradition. The second half of the nineteenth century was a moment in the intellectual history of America during which Sanskrit seemed to offer a new means of intellectual and cultural independence from Europe.

The Cultural and Intellectual Context of Sanskrit in America

From the mid-nineteenth century until the Second World War, Sanskrit, as the newest, most crucial branch of philology, was among the most important and exciting areas of humanistic enquiry in America. Carl Darling Buck, Sanskrit Professor at Chicago University, reporting on Sanskrit's significance in the previous century, remarked in 1916 that after William Jones had brought Sanskrit 'to the notice of the Western world,' 'Schlegel had inspired Europe with ... *The Language and Wisdom of the Hindus*,' and 'Bopp had laid the solid foundations of the science of comparative philology,' this new field 'seemed one of the greatest achievements of the age.' 'The Sanskrit language,' Buck reminded his audience of philologists, 'was believed to reflect in all respects the Indo-European parent speech, the Veda to furnish the most faithful picture of primitive religion, the Upanishads to be the last word in philosophy.'[18]

As Darling's address recalled for those listening, from the mid-nineteenth century Sanskrit began to be solidly integrated within the nascent American university system as well as among a broader lay readership. Said, and most postcolonial theorists after him, ignore the history of the institutional incorporation of Sanskrit in the West, and therefore miss the fundamentally dialogic nature of the discourses produced within organizational structures of academic bodies and universities. American intellectual movements, though based on European traditions, were simultaneously tempered by a cultural consciousness based on deeply held religious ideas and philosophical and socio-political perspectives which posited the idea of American 'exceptionalism.' There was a conscious effort to construct a distinctly American intellectual tradition across various fields, exemplified by the formation of American intellectual and scholarly institutions such as the AOS in this period. The impulse to be distinct from Europe was equally present in the development of a uniquely American university. Concomitant with the eagerness to draw from European universities and intellectual resources was a desire to compete with European scholarship. Yet, until the late 1860s, intellectually ambitious Americans found it necessary to travel to Europe to complete their education since there were no opportunities for higher research in America.

When American scholars came to Europe to study they were caught up in the whirlwind of excitement around comparative philology and Sanskrit. As Said recognized, the range of representation of the Orient in the West expanded enormously at the end of the eighteenth century with the emergence of Indo-European philology, 'a new powerful science for viewing the linguistic Orient.' Said reminds us of Foucault's explication of philology, which showed it had come with 'a whole web of related scientific interests.'[19] In conjunction with its imaginative and material uses, Orientalism was for Said an 'enormously systematic *discipline*,' through which European culture was able to 'manage – and even produce – the Orient,' which Said suggested, could best be understood through the Foucauldian idea of 'discourse.'[20] In the context of philology and Oriental studies, it may be understood as a recognition of the means of constituting and controlling knowledge, through the laying bare of the relationship between power and knowledge. In *The Order of Things*, Foucault sought to reveal how 'the organizing models of human perception and knowledge' had 'altered between the Renaissance and the end of the nineteenth-century.'[21] Foucault's models were the disciplines of biology, economics and philology, which he considered essentially constitutive of Western knowledge. Understanding their 'altering presuppositions' would allow 'systematic insights into the ways in which Western culture has structured both its image of the personal self and of reality.'[22] Foucault considered that philology, exemplified by the achievements of Schlegel, Bopp and their contemporaries, which had become marginalized 'on the fringes...of our historical consciousness,' was in fact 'the medium through which the whole mode of being of language [in the West]...had been modified.'[23] As Foucault put it, baldly, 'What changed at the turn of the century...was knowledge itself.'[24] Foucault emphasized the interrelatedness of the disciplines he anatomized, especially the connection between biology and philology. He pointed out that Schlegel had been fully aware that 'the constitution of historicity' in relation to grammar 'took place in accordance' with the model applied in natural science.[25] Schlegel had asserted in *On the Language and Philosophy of the Indians*, his 1808 work seminal to the foundations of Sanskrit studies and Indo-European philology, that the 'comparative grammar of languages' revealed 'as certain a key' of linguistic 'genealogy' as 'the study of comparative anatomy' had done for biology.[26] The comparative study of Indo-European philology pioneered by Bopp, Schlegel and others, had important lessons for the nineteenth-century understanding of linguistic and biological, and therefore historical, cultural and even racial origins. For Said, Foucault's project had clear correlations with Schwab's, and he built his own argument upon their common inferences. Schwab's *La Renaissance orientale*, read both as 'a pre-figuration of' and 'complement to' Foucault's *Les Mots et les choses*, was, for Said, central to the understanding of 'the great transformation in culture' of the late eighteenth and nineteenth centuries.[27] However, Foucault was 'ambiguous' in assigning causes to this shift, while Schwab presented a comprehensive 'case for the-Orient-as-cause.'[28] Schwab had revealed, Said insisted, that philology, in the process of bringing Oriental texts into European consciousness, resulted in the 'arranging and rearranging' of cultural 'identity.'[29] We may infer accordingly that Sanskrit offered Americans fresh perspectives not only on other cultures, but also, vitally, their own.

Writing when disciplinary specialization has made academic fields ever more highly fragmented and contended spaces, it may be necessary to remind ourselves of the interconnectedness of scholarly fields in the nineteenth century. In 1919, Maurice Bloomfield, Professor of Sanskrit and Comparative Philology, Johns Hopkins University (JHU), described the interrelations between philological and scientific knowledge in terms that resonate with Schlegel's and would be recognized by Foucault: 'Comparative philology rejoices in unfolding the history of nations. It has sought to find its laws in the forces of nature, the bodily organization, and external habits of life, the influences of climate.'[30] Bloomfield had declared in 1892: Sanskrit was the seed of comparative philology, and 'the nursery of methods.'[31]

Sanskrit's adoption in American university curricula was closely connected with the development of the American university through innovations in old foundations and the endowment of new ones. American scholars emulated the German philological tradition, built upon a scientific approach to grammar and linguistic analysis. Like their German teachers, they believed that the analysis of Sanskrit grammar and linguistic principles must be based on modern European science, not ancient Indian tradition. Therefore, the Indian grammarians whom British Sanskritists had studied had to be abandoned to re-make Sanskrit as a modern Western scientific discipline. The new American university, taking its cue from the modern German university inaugurated by Wilhelm von Humboldt, would incorporate the scientific method at its core and place philology at the centre of the curriculum. Two pioneering figures in the development of the modern American university system were Charles William Eliot, President of Harvard University from 1869, and Daniel Coit Gilman, who became the first President of JHU in 1876. Eliot revolutionized the Harvard curriculum, transforming a moribund academic system for training clergy into a modern research institution at the forefront of American and international scholarship. Gilman's vision made the newly founded JHU, the first American institution founded as a university, the leader in setting the highest standards for American graduate education and higher research. The influence of German and European philology may be seen in the genealogical lines of early American Sanskrit which crossed and re-crossed the Atlantic: Edward Salisbury studied with Bopp in Berlin, Lassen in Bonn and de Sacy and Burnouf in Paris; Salisbury's student Whitney trained with Bopp and Weber in Berlin, and Roth in Tübingen; Whitney's student Lanman in Tübingen, Berlin and Leipzig.

Eliot and Gilman spent time in Europe, particularly Germany, studying university education. They returned with a keen appreciation of the reforms and innovations taking place in European universities. Yet they were equally convinced of the need to forge a uniquely American institution, taking from, but not blindly emulating European precedents. The strong sense of nationhood that in the course of the nineteenth century came into its own in America demanded a national model for a national culture. Gilman's description of the essential differences between American institutions and their European models reflected the singular virtues that nationalistic Americans most prized in their own society:

There will be among us no control of a central government, as in France and Germany; no historical exemplars, as in England... American ingenuity, independence, indifference to conservative traditions, and love of variety will devise in different places manifold agencies... for the promotion of the higher culture.[32]

Gilman's counterpart at Harvard, Eliot, had similarly stated at the start of his presidency in 1869 that the American university must be 'the slow and natural outgrowth of American social and political habits.'[33]

The changes brought by Eliot and Gilman to Harvard and JHU had commonalities characterizing the salient features of the new American university. Among these the importance of scientific education and the primacy of language were foundational to the incorporation of Sanskrit in their curricula. The scientific method was applicable to all modern subjects, but the science of language was considered essential for the progress of the human sciences. Eliot and Gilman were both firmly committed to the teaching of languages. Eliot's renowned 1891 address on education begins with the importance of languages in the university: 'A university teaches. What does it teach? It *must obviously teach* all the languages in which the greatest literatures which have been preserved were written – Hebrew, Arabic, *Sanskrit*, Greek, Latin, French, Italian, German, Scandinavian, and English.'[34]

Appropriately, the universities that led the transformation of higher education in America – Yale, JHU and Harvard – were the universities at which the first professorships and departments of Sanskrit and Oriental studies were established. Yale had a Professor of Arabic and Sanskrit in 1841 and a separate Professor of Sanskrit by 1854. A department of Sanskrit was established by C. R. Lanman at JHU in 1876, its inaugural year. Sanskrit courses were offered at Harvard from 1872; in 1880 Lanman had become Harvard's first Wales Professor of Sanskrit in the Department of Indo-Iranian Studies. Moreover, all of these institutions were located in the region associated most closely with the foundations of cultural and social change and economic development in nineteenth-century America.

The first known institution of higher education in America to offer Sanskrit classes was a new, relatively uncelebrated public institution then known as the University of the City of New York, now New York University (NYU). In 1836, its timetable included evening courses in Oriental languages: Hebrew, Arabic, Persian and 'Sanscrit.'[35] The instructor for the Sanskrit course was probably Isaac Nordheimer (1809–42), later Professor of German and Oriental Languages.[36] In 1838, Nordheimer wrote a proposal to institute a department of Oriental studies at NYU. Its primary function would be to provide Hebrew instruction, but would also include 'courses for the study of the Chaldee and the Syriac, and likewise for the Arabic, Persian, or Sanscrit.'[37] Nordheimer believed that by pioneering Oriental studies in America, NYU would simultaneously advance to the forefront of humanistic enquiry in America and raise American scholarship in the eyes of the world.[38] Regular courses in Oriental languages would be of practical use to the growing numbers of American missionaries.[39] Unfortunately, by 1842, Nordheimer was dead and hopes of establishing the first Oriental department in America at NYU remained unrealized. The future of American Sanskrit and Oriental studies lay at Yale.

The Age of Whitney[40]

Yale College in New Haven had its own historic connection with the American mercantile tradition, colonial sea-trade and India; a history that clarified old American links with British imperialism. Established in 1701 as the Collegiate School at Saybrook, Connecticut, in 1716 the fledgling institution moved to the more populous and prosperous port town of New Haven. Finding themselves in financial trouble, the administrators approached a former New England resident, Elihu Yale, for aid. Yale was born in New England but entered the service of the East India Company, serving as Governor at Fort St George, Madras, before retiring to Wales as a well-to-do merchant. In 1718 he sent a benefaction including several bales of valuable Madras cotton, the sale of which allowed the college to survive. The college's thanks were registered in its new name, Yale College.[41]

Yale's fourth president, Theodore Dwight Woolsey, initiated the foundation of a future university at New Haven. Woolsey's classical education in Europe had given him an appreciation of 'the high type of continental research' still 'unavailable in America.'[42] In 1847, a year into his presidency, the Yale Department of Philosophy and the Arts was founded, offering seminars across a gamut of disciplines including Sanskrit and philology. Salisbury was introduced to Oriental studies and philology at Yale by Josiah Gibbs, Professor of Sacred Literature, who had studied philology in Europe, and used his linguistic training to aid the defendants in the 1839–40 Amistaad trial. Gibbs was a founding member of the AOS.[43] Like Gibbs, Salisbury came from a wealthy and prominent New England family. In 1836, he interrupted his theological training to study comparative philology in Europe. Salisbury's inheritance and that of his wife helped fund his European studies and the foundations of two Yale professorships, one of which was Whitney's Sanskrit professorship. While in Europe, Salisbury met H. H. Wilson, the first Boden Professor of Sanskrit at Oxford, and wrote that Wilson's 'specialty,' Sanskrit, 'lay at the foundation of the new science of Comparative Philology.'[44] Their meeting left Salisbury with 'a new impression of the reality of the new science.'[45] In 1843, Salisbury inaugurated the first formal academic programme in Oriental studies in America, and by 1845 he was offering graduate courses.

Salisbury returned to Yale from Europe with a rich haul of books and manuscripts, which formed the nucleus of the first important Oriental collection in America. Salisbury's collection greatly benefitted the AOS, founded in New Haven in 1842 as the earliest learned society in America devoted to a particular field of scholarship. The Journal of the AOS was founded in 1843. In their early years, both were indebted to Salisbury's and his student W. D. Whitney's dedicated administration. When few formal academic positions were available in Oriental studies, they offered a forum for scholars who could not have an academic career in Sanskrit to participate in scholarly exchanges and publish their research, extending the boundaries of scholarly Sanskrit beyond individual institutions.

The AOS is the sole representation of nineteenth-century American Orientalism that Said discussed. He commented that at its first annual meeting its president clearly indicated that Americans would study the Orient 'in order to follow the example of the Imperial European powers.' Said concluded from this that 'then as now' the 'framework' of Oriental studies was political as well as scholarly.[46] I have contended that Said's reading of early American Orientalism lacks a sustained and careful consideration of its historical context. While the AOS certainly mimicked its precursors, its concern was more to able to compete with European counterparts and overcome fears of intellectual inferiority, than to prepare by scholarly means for political claims which in the 1840s were in any case unlikely.

Salisbury had two Sanskrit students in the course of his career, both of whom altered the field of American philology. They were James Hadley, later Professor of Greek at Yale, and Whitney. Whitney was born in Northampton, Massachusetts. His father was a banker, and his family well connected among the New England professional, religious and intellectual elite. In 1845, Whitney graduated from Williams College, with a keen interest in natural history and outdoor pursuits. Confined to the house while convalescing after an illness, Whitney discovered Franz Bopp's *Comparative Grammar*. By 1848, having taught himself the basics of Sanskrit and comparative philology, Whitney decided to pursue these subjects at university. Whitney's father's pastor, Rev. George E. Day, suggested Yale, which had then 'the only definite arrangement' yet made in America 'for university work,' and the sole department of Oriental studies.[47] Whitney began his course under Salisbury, but his aptitude for

Sanskrit and philology soon drew him level with his teacher; he required a higher standard of instruction than was available in America. In 1850, Whitney left for Germany to study comparative philology and Sanskrit. He returned to America as the foremost Sanskritist in the country, but there were few opportunities for a career in Sanskrit. The only university position was occupied by Salisbury, who set the course for the future of American Orientalism by resigning the Sanskrit portion of his chair to create a separate 'Professorship of Sanskrit and kindred languages.' The chair was established in 1854 with Whitney as its first incumbent.

On 25 July 1861, Yale became the first university in America to award the PhD degree. The first three PhDs were in physics, philosophy and psychology, and classics. The recipient of the classics PhD, Morris Whiton, took his final examinations in four subjects, including Sanskrit. Between 1859 and 1861, Whiton had 'concentrated his course work in one subject under one instructor, spending two hours weekly studying Sanskrit with the famous specialist William D. Whitney.'[48] That one of the first three PhDs in America was awarded to a Sanskritist reiterates the importance of Sanskrit in the new academic curriculum introduced at Yale and reflects the prominent role of Sanskrit in the development of American higher education.

With Whitney, Sanskrit and philological scholarship in America came of age. In 1869, Gilman, then secretary of the Appointing Board at Yale, wrote an anxious letter to Salisbury to inform him that Whitney had received a tempting offer from President Eliot to take up the well-endowed Professorship of Comparative Philology at Harvard.[49] For those concerned for Yale's progress toward becoming a centre of higher academic research, the loss of Whitney represented a severe setback. Gilman believed philology to be essential to Yale's future as 'a *university*,'[50] and thought Whitney's departure would be 'fatal' to philology and the Department of Philosophy and the Arts as a whole.[51] Salisbury had been instrumental in securing Whitney for Yale in 1854. Gilman hoped that he could persuade Whitney to stay.[52] In 1869, Whitney accepted a new appointment at Yale, to a fully-endowed Professorship of Sanskrit and Comparative Philology founded by Salisbury. Whitney's appointment to the new Edward E. Salisbury Chair was a significant step toward the transformation of Yale from a College to a University, marking its transition from seventeenth-century institution, copied from British and European models, into a modern context which came to define a new international standard for American scholarship and shape the future of American intellectual practice. From 1869, Yale's academic curriculum began to be restructured; the Department of Philosophy and the Arts was re-organized, its facilities thoroughly reviewed. In 1887, Yale College was officially renamed and reconstituted as Yale University.

By the end of Whitney's professorship in 1892–93, Sanskrit was taught within two course categories: Oriental languages and Biblical literature, and ancient languages and linguistics.[53] This reflected the two aspects of Sanskrit as it was received in America, on the one hand a part of the western discovery of Oriental studies – rooted in theological research, on the other a foundational aspect of the modern science of philology. American Sanskritists no longer had to depend on European textbooks. Whitney's 1879 *Sanskrit Grammar* and Lanman's 1884 *Sanskrit Reader* became the standard works to teach students the language in accordance with modern Western scientific methods.[54] However, by the last decades of the century, as Whitney succumbed to an illness that ate away at his legendary physical robustness and zeal for hard work, other institutions began to challenge Yale's dominance in the fields of Sanskrit and philology, and new centres were established at JHU and Harvard by Whitney's student Charles Rockwell Lanman.

The foundations of *universities* at JHU and Harvard were coeval with the establishment of Sanskrit as an essential part of the curriculum offered at these two pioneering institutions. When Gilman was invited to become president of the newly established JHU in Baltimore, he offered Whitney the first professorship at JHU. Whitney refused, although he would present a series of lectures in JHU's inaugural year. In 1876, Gilman appointed Whitney's student, Lanman, as one of JHU's first six Fellows. In 1880, President Eliot convinced Lanman to accept the Professorship of Sanskrit at Harvard, which soon became the new centre for Sanskrit and philology in America. Whitney died in 1894. Through his teaching, research and editorship of the Harvard Oriental Series – among the most important disseminators of original research in Oriental studies anywhere – Lanman would perpetuate Whitney's legacy, by ensuring the growing international recognition of American Oriental scholarship.

Whitney and the Popular Reception of Sanskrit

In his critique of Orientalism as discourse, Said had noted that there was a 'constant...interchange' between the academic and imaginative meanings of Orientalism.[55] American interest in Sanskrit acquired further intensity and resonance through the contexts within which Sanskrit was received, translated and transmitted. American scholars studied Sanskrit because it was understood to be essential to the study of the Indo-European languages, and seminal to the development of comparative philology. The broader public interest in Sanskrit reflected these associations, but also identified Sanskrit with the intellectual brilliance and internationally respected scholarship of Whitney. Whitney's national stature as a scholar gave him a public reputation beyond academic circles. He was America's first professional philologist, and popularly acknowledged as the national expert on language.[56] His fame spread beyond national and disciplinary borders: as Whitney's biographer points out, 'Whitney was one of the few Americans in that era, in any field, to gain a high reputation among scholars in Europe.'[57] He made an immense contribution to 'the science of language,' a field, which, 'was connected with nearly everything in the surrounding intellectual landscape.'[58] Whitney's work helped found American philology and contributed vitally to modern linguistics, influencing the German Neogrammarians, Ferdinand de Saussure, and sociolinguistics.[59] Whitney's linguistic research was presented in public lectures at the Smithsonian and the Lowell Institute, published as *Language and the Study of Language* (1867) and the *Life and Growth of Language* (1875). It addressed a broad educated readership. His Sanskrit publications included the *Atharva Veda Sanhita* (1856), and *Oriental and Linguistic Studies* (1872–74) among others. Whitney's popular fame grew through his editorial involvement in two projects for which he received nation-wide recognition: as co-editor of the fifth, revised edition of *Webster's Dictionary* (1864) and editor-in-chief of the phenomenally successful *Century Dictionary* (1889–91).

Whitney's capacity to extend public knowledge of Sanskrit was particularly effective because of his dual role as a transnational and national figure of scholarly and popular significance. In the 1860s, during the Civil War, Whitney together with the other editors responsible for revising *Webster's Dictionary*, Gilman, Woolsey and Hadley, applied 'their philological expertise to the systematization of a distinctly American national speech, a project with profound political and cultural significance,' representing an unparalleled test for the nationalist uses of philological research.[60] In 1864, at the Smithsonian Institution, Whitney demonstrated his linguistic convictions and nationalist ideals, declaring that, 'in all history no tongue had ever been spoken so nearly alike by all the masses of so great a population as the English now in America.'[61] He was enthusiastically quoted by New England journalists, perhaps as eager to serve the Union's cause. Whitney was becoming a celebrity. In December 1864 and January 1865 he lectured on the history and study of languages at the Lowell Institute in Boston.

The lectures were attended by a broad cross-section of people. One news-paper reported: '[i]n the select class of gifted and studious men who make American scholarship respectable in the eyes of the world, William D. Whitney, Professor of Sanscrit in Yale College, holds an honourable place... He is one of those scholarly and indefatigable truth-seekers in honoring whom our public honors itself.'

In 1870, Whitney won the Bopp Foundation's highly prized annual award in Sanskrit philology for his edition of the *Tāittīriya Prātiśākhya*. American newspapers triumphantly recounted news of the award, reflecting national pride and a growing public interest in philology. The publication of Whitney's *Oriental and Linguistic Studies* in 1872–74, cemented his enviable reputation. Reviewers of the book linked their high opinion of Whitney's scholarship with a valuation of his charac-ter, which reflected the public understanding of what the best kind of American scholarship ought to be. Their adjectives invoked the language of power, authority and puritan, mercantile and nationalistic American values: hard work, sobriety, diligence on the one hand and the energy, virility and independent spirit of a new nation on the other. Whitney possessed, an 'exact and wide acquaintance with... this difficult sub-ject... [and]... a singular mastery... which promise a sure science of language.'[62] Across various publications, reviewers mentioned similar attributes: 'these papers... cannot fail by their own manly, independent spirit, and direct, vigorous style, to tone up the mind of the reader for sharp robust exercise.'[63]

The Victorian absorption in matters of race, religion and language provided an ideological context for Whitney's philological research, and made Whitney's work more relevant to a popular audience.[64] Since comparative philology's roots lay in William Jones' 'discovery' of Sanskrit and his consequent exposure of the relationship between Indo-European tongues, Sanskrit was integral to the scholarly development and popular reception of nineteenth-century philology which became central to Victorian discussions about language, science and religion, the abiding subject of Darwinianism, and troubled debates around the issues of language and race.

In the widely publicized Victorian contests between science and reli-gion, the origins of language became a hotly debated subject, and it was one of the points of contention in Whitney's scholarly quarrel with Friedrich Max Müller in the 1870s. This was the culmination of a prolonged debate over Müller's translations from Sanskrit, the issue of traditional Indian grammar versus scientific European meth-ods, and fundamental differences in linguistic theory. The controversy surrounding Whitney's debate with Müller became a public sensation, as the contest came to be seen as an international jousting match in which Whitney represented not only American linguistics but also American scholarship in general, against a contender who was perceived as not only European but also British. The dispute carried the undertones of an old colonial rivalry. In his analysis of language, Whitney had the support of many scientists, including Darwin, but Müller gained 'popular sympathy.'[65] Whitney defended Darwin against Müller, while Darwin cited Whitney in a revised (1874) edition of the *Descent of Man*.[66] Whitney's association with Darwin and his rivalry with Müller, both international celebrities of the Victorian age, made him a towering public presence and brought him a transatlantic fame unattainable by most Americans of his time.

It was not lost on Whitney's general audience that his area of specialization, the ancient language of a non-Christian people, included the study and explication of an alien religion. Shared linguistic origins also opened up the uncomfortable prospect of a shared cultural and even racial history, and challenged assumptions of Western and Christian superiority. As comparative philology and Oriental studies became more widely known, their cultural, racial and religious connotations demanded attention, and Whitney's *Oriental and Linguistic Studies* offered a focus for such discussions in its reviews. Responses varied from outright rejection of the field on the grounds of its unsavoury associations to sanguine acceptance. The reviewer of the *Chicago Tribune* saw studying Oriental subjects as tantamount to encouraging their equal treatment with Christianity, arguing that 'professors of ... comparative philology naturally become expanders of the ancient religious ideas.'[67] Yet the majority of reviews were positive, including those in the more liberal Christian journals. The *National Baptist* suggested that Whitney's book should be read 'for its suggestive and liberalizing influence.' It was 'heartily' recommended 'to intelligent men generally ... and especially to pastors,' who needed to know more 'of the religion of that ancient people from whom we trace our own descent, and whose race qualities, moral and intellectual, [reflect] our own blood inheritance.'[68]

As Whitney came to be known as the American authority on philology, Oriental languages and Sanskrit, he received hundreds of requests for general and specific information.[69] The letters came from lay enquirers, ordinary individuals, scholars and famous names, such as R. W. Emerson, and H. S. Olcott, co-founder of the Theosophical Society with H. P. Blavatsky. These letters show how closely Americans identified Whitney with his areas of expertise and illustrate the extraordinary position that Whitney occupied. Whitney's transcendent identity meant that Sanskrit at Yale came to stand for much more than an academic course at a university: it became synonymous with a national source of an immensely important field of knowledge.

Conclusion

Said wrote that the relationship between the Orient and the Occident was essentially a relationship of power.[70] American Orientalism began after the Second World War when America fitted 'self-consciously into places excavated' by Britain and France, and in doing so acquired the same intellectual authority over the Orient that those nations had possessed.[71] Yet, as we have seen, Sanskrit became the source of a kind of intellectual power and cultural authority that American Orientalists used less to dominate the Oriental 'other' than to represent themselves, to authenticate an autonomous and distinctively American national, scholarly and intellectual modernity, and to challenge and refute their previous dependence on European traditions of knowledge and scholarship.

American Orientalism inherited many of the essentializing, racist and bigoted assumptions of European perspectives on the East. The public debates over Max Müller and Whitney in American newspapers display a deep discomfort with the implications of shared roots with Indians. Americans found it easier to abstract philological and philosophical knowledge and appropriate it while rejecting Indian methods of reading and interpretation. In this way they could treat Sanskrit in a form removed from its origins. Yet in doing so they were also consciously making an American field of knowledge. The reception of Sanskrit therefore allowed a dialogical interaction wherein Sanskrit could and did alter American intellectual and cultural consciousness. The more Americans could insist on their own interpretations, the more they could construct their own academic traditions, and prove their prowess in this most esoteric, intellectually advanced and internationally respected of fields, the more they could come into their own. American Orientalism became a mode of study, thought and cultural production that, as Said rightly pointed out, allowed power over the subject, but it also offered Americans a different kind of power, over their own, shifting, cultural identity.

This work is indebted to Said, and to Said's study of Orientalism. Yet, it has sought to offer another way of looking at Orientalism, in the context of nineteenth-century American Sanskrit scholarship, which ultimately clarifies the continuing relevance of *Orientalism* as a place to begin searching for alternatives. For, as Said once asked, in an essay arguing against the conversion of theory to 'cultural dogma,'[72] 'what is critical consciousness at bottom if not an unstoppable predilection for alternatives?'[73]

Notes

1. In the interests of brevity this work will refer to the 'United States of America' as 'America.'
2. Edward W. Said, *Orientalism* (New York: Vintage Books, 1979), 294–5.
3. Said, *Orientalism*, 1.
4. Said, *Orientalism* 1–2 (Said's emphasis).
5. Ibid.
6. Said, *Orientalism*, 4.
7. See, for example, Douglas Little's, *American Orientalism: The United States and the Middle East since 1945* (Chapel Hill, NC: University of North Carolina Press, 2002).
8. Raymond Schwab, *The Oriental Renaissance: Europe's Rediscovery of India and the East, 1680–1880*, trans. Gene Patterson-Black and Victor Reinking (New York: Columbia University Press, 1984).
9. Said, 'Raymond Schwab and the Romance of Ideas,' in *The World, the Text and the Critic*, 246–67. (Cambridge, MA: Harvard University Press, 1983), 250.
10. Said, 'Travelling Theory,' in *The World, the Text and the Critic* (Cambridge, Massachusetts: Harvard University Press, 1983), 226–7.
11. Said, 'Travelling Theory,' 226.
12. Ibid.
13. Ibid.
14. Said, *Orientalism*, 19.
15. Said, *Orientalism*, 22.
16. Ibid.
17. Dale Riepe's largely descriptive *The Philosophy of India and Its Impact on American Thought* (Springfield, IL: Charles C. Thomas, 1970) still represents the most extensive study of the history of Sanskrit in America, but Sanskrit is not the work's central concern. Critically engaged writing on American interactions with Indian ideas may be found in Partha Mitter's work on American Orientalism, and Susan Bean, *Yankee India: American Commercial and Cultural Encounters with India in the Age of Sail, 1784–1860* (Salem: Peabody Essex Museum, 2001). I am grateful to Professor Mitter for sharing his unpublished work with me.
18. C. D. Buck, 'Comparative Philology and the Classics,' *Transactions and Proceedings of the American Philological Association* 47 (1916), 65–83.
19. Said, *Orientalism*, 22.
20. Ibid, my emphasis.
21. George Steiner, 'The Mandarin of the Hour – Michel Foucault,' *New York Times*, 'Books,' 18 February 1971.
22. Ibid.

23. Michel Foucault, *The Order of Things: Archaeology of the Human Sciences* (London and New York: Routledge, 2007), 206.
24. Foucault, *The Order of Things*, 274.
25. Foucault, *The Order of Things*, 305.
26. Friedrich von Schlegel, *On the Language and Philosophy of the Indians* (1808), republished in *Aesthetic and Miscellaneous Works*, trans. E. J. Millington (London: Henry G. Bohn, 1849), 439, quoted ibid.
27. Von Schlegel, *On the Language*, 253.
28. Ibid.
29. Said, 'Raymond Schwab and the Romance of Ideas,' 263.
30. Maurice Bloomfield, 'Fifty Years of Comparative Philology in America,' *Proceedings of the American Philological Association* 50 (1919), 62.
31. Maurice Bloomfield, 'Notes of Recent Publications, Investigations and Studies,' *JHU Circular* 11, no. 99 (June 1892), JHU Archives.
32. Ibid.
33. C. W. Eliot, 'The New Education,' Part II of II, in *American Higher Education: A Documentary History*, eds. Richard Hofstadter and Wilson Smith, 632–47. (Chicago: University of Chicago Press, 1961), 637.
34. C. W. Eliot, 'The Aims of Higher Education,' in *Educational Reform: Essays and Addresses*, ed. Charles W. Eliot, 223–52 (New York: The Century Company, 1898), 225, [my emphases].
35. 1836 Flyer, Folder on Isaac Nordheimer, Acting Professor of German, Professor of German and of Oriental Languages, 1836–42, Faculty Material, NYU Archives.
36. Nordheimer was the only member of NYU's faculty at this time for whom we have evidence that he was familiar with Sanskrit. He was later appointed Professor of Oriental languages at New York University.
37. Isaac Nordheimer to unknown addressee/s, 1838. Isaac Nordheimer, Acting Professor of German, Professor of German and of Oriental Languages, 1836–42, Faculty Material, NYU Archives.
38. Ibid.
39. Ibid.
40. On the AOS's fiftieth anniversary a commentator declared that as the nation had 'long decided' that Whitney was 'the representative of American philology,' the previous half-century was the 'age of Whitney.' 'Fifty Years of American Oriental Studies,' n.d., newspaper clipping, Whitney Papers, Manuscripts and Archives Yale University (MAYU).
41. Yale University, 'About Yale, History,' http://www.yale.edu/about/history.html.
42. Ibid.
43. Benjamin R. Foster, 'Gibbs, Josiah Willard,' *American National Biography*, www.anb.org/articles/09/09-01085.html [accessed 29 May 2011].
44. 'Salisbury Letter,' 60.
45. Ibid.
46. Said, *Orientalism*, 294.
47. Ibid.
48. Ralph R. Rosenberg, 'The First American Doctor of Philosophy Degree: A Centennial Salute to Yale, 1861–1961,' *The Journal of Higher Education* 32, no. 7 (October 1961), 393.

49. Gilman to Salisbury, 30 September 1869, Salisbury Papers, MAYU.
50. Ibid., 5 [Gilman's emphasis].
51. Ibid., 7.
52. Ibid., 8.
53. *Yale Catalog, 1892–93*, MAYU.
54. William Dwight Whitney, *Sanskrit Grammar* (Cambridge, MA: Harvard University Press, 1879) and Charles Lanman, *A Sanskrit Reader: Text, Vocabulary and Notes* (Cambridge, MA: Harvard University Press, 1884).
55. Said, *Orientalism*, 3.
56. Stephen G. Alter, *William Dwight Whitney and the Science of Language* (Baltimore, MD and London: The Johns Hopkins University Press, 2005), 1.
57. Alter, *William Dwight*, 1–2.
58. Alter, *William Dwight*, xi.
59. Ibid.
60. Adam Nelson, 'Nationalism, Transnationalism, and the American Scholar in the Nineteenth-Century: Thoughts on the Career of William Dwight Whitney,' *The New England Quarterly* 78, no. 3, (September 2005), 374.
61. *Daily Chronicle*, 12 March 1864, newspaper clipping, Whitney Papers, MAYU.
62. Ibid.
63. 'Oriental and Linguistic Studies,' n.d., *The National Baptist*, newspaper clipping. Whitney Papers, MAYU.
64. Alter, *William Dwight*, xi.
65. Judith Ann Schiff, 'Advice for the Language-lorn,' March/April 2010, *Yale Alumni Publications Inc.* http://www.yalealumnimagazine.com/issues/2010_03/oldyale2425.html [accessed 25 May 2011].
66. Alter, *William Dwight*, 5.
67. *Chicago Tribune*, n.d., newspaper clipping, Whitney Papers, MAYU.
68. *National Baptist*, n.d., newspaper clipping, Whitney Papers, MAYU.
69. Schiff, 'Advice for the Language-lorn.'
70. Said, *Orientalism*, 5.
71. Said, *Orientalism*, 17.
72. Said, 'Travelling Theory,' 244.
73. Said, 'Travelling Theory,' 247.

6
Re-Arabizing the De-Arabized: The Mistaʿaravim Unit of the Palmach

Yonatan Mendel

It was a hot summer day in Palestine in August 1942. Shimʿon Somekh, a Baghdad-born Jew who had immigrated to the country a decade earlier, was teaching Arabic in Kibbutz Mishmar ha-ʿEmek. During one of the classes, the director of the educational institution stepped in and told him that someone was waiting for him outside. Somekh probably assumed that this had something to do with security. As a fluent Arabic speaker, the Haganah intelligence services contacted him frequently and used his knowledge of Arabic for security-oriented missions. But this time, the person waiting outside and the offer he made to Somekh were exceptional. This was Yigal Allon, one of the founders of the Palmach and its commander between 1945 and 1948.[1] Allon explained to Somekh that he represented 'a special Haganah unit which works in cooperation with the British army.' He asked Somekh to leave his teaching position and join the unit. 'The Jewish Yishuv needs you more than your students,' he explained to Somekh, and recruited him to the mistaʿaravim unit of the Palmach.[2]

This anecdote serves as an introduction to this article as it sheds light on three important phenomena. First, the significant use of the language skills of Arab-Jews in Zionist security organizations at the historical moment examined. Second, the link made between the Zionist intelligence forces and British efforts in the Middle East, which hints to the quasi-Orientalist connection between them. Third, and when taking into consideration that Somekh accepted Allon's offer and left his pedagogical duties, this anecdote demonstrates the superiority of 'Arabic-for-security' over 'Arabic-for-peace' within the Zionist population in Palestine, and suggests that it was around that moment in time that studying Arabic to integrate in the region, let alone using the language to maintain an Arab–Jewish identity, became practically impossible.

With regards to *Orientalism* and the debates surrounding it, this article strives to add some inside insights on the formation of the Oriental 'other' as reflected in the mistaʿaravim unit of the Palmach. As members of this unit had to learn 'how Arabs behave' and 'what Arabs eat' this piece solidifies our knowledge on the frozen, essentialist and never-changing image of the Orient as perceived by Orientalists. Moreover, this piece strengthens the notion that in the process of Orientalizing the other, there is an implied formation of the self. In the case examined here, this is demonstrated on two different levels. First, in the context of the grand Zionist–Palestinian conflict, Orientalizing the Palestinian-Arabs enabled the Zionist establishment to formulate a 'Jewish' image which was different from 'the Arab' one, and so served the political need for national 'homogeneousness,' even if imagined. Second, and with regards to the Arab-Jews, Orientalizing the Palestinian-Arabs and learn-ing how to *imitate* them enabled the members of the Mistaʿaravim unit to de-Arabize themselves, to sharpen the difference between themselves and 'the Arabs,' and so to 'prove' their Jewishness in Zionist political terms. The process of Orientalization, therefore, can be seen in this con-text as a 'rite of passage' in a struggle to be accepted into a powerful, hegemonic, political discourse, even if it meant denying one's cultural and historical self.

Ha-Shaḥar Unit: From the Syrian Platoon to the Israeli Defence Forces

The creation of the Palmach mistaʿaravim unit was an outcome of the growing cooperation between the Zionist movement and the British authorities in Palestine. This cooperation began before the Second World War[3] but intensified following its outbreak. Nazi Germany was a mutual enemy of the British Army and the Jewish people, a fact which brought some of the interests of the Haganah and the military forces of the British Mandate closer together. This anti-Nazi cooperation solidi-fied in June 1940 following the German occupation of France and the establishment of the Vichy government there. Britain's biggest concern was that Syria and Lebanon, which were under Vichy-French Mandate, would be used by the Axis powers as springboards for attacks on the Allied bases in the area, including in Palestine.[4] As a result, the Allied forces' headquarters contacted the Haganah and asked it to join the military effort against their mutual enemy.[5]

Cooperation on psychological warfare began immediately as two commanders in the Haganah, Yoseph Fein and Tuvia Arazi, established a network of agents in Syria. The network was operated by local Syrian-Jews and its main activity was the distribution of propaganda brochures against Nazi Germany.[6] Cooperation on military intelligence began with a course given by a British officer to groups of Haganah members in the Carmel Forest.[7]

In mid-1941, there was a crucial development as German bombers began landing in Aleppo on their way to Iraq to support Rashid al-Keelani's revolt against British domination. The British Army was in need of immediate intelligence to sabotage German progress in the Levant,[8] and at this point the idea of taking on Jewish individuals who immigrated to Palestine from Arab lands as intelligence agents was first proposed. Gamliel Cohen, one of the fathers of Israeli espionage, recalls:

> In 1941, the British proposed the leadership of the Zionist movement...to take advantage of the special potential hidden in the Mizrahi Jews[9] in Eretz-Yisrael, and to select from them intelligence agents...to be infiltrated and implanted in the Arab population in Syria and Lebanon...This revolutionary idea was adopted by Yitzhak Sadeh and Yigal Allon...and materialized under the British unit 'the Syrian Scam.'[10]

The 'Syrian Scam,' known by the Haganah as the 'Syrian Platoon' ('ha-Maḥlakah ha-Surit'), came into being immediately after the British proposal. It was comprised mostly of Syrian-born Jews and during May 1941 the first agents were planted in Damascus. Operating according to orders they received from the British headquarters they began collecting intelligence on specific targets, such as the oil refineries in Tripoli.[11] They also operated sabotage missions, including a series of explosions in Aleppo's military airport.[12]

In June 1941, the concept of Arabic-speaking Jewish agents was further institutionalized through a training course held in Tel Aviv. The course was headed by Major Nicholas Hammond, a Professor of Ancient Greece at the University of Cambridge, who during the war became the liaison officer between the British Special Operations Executive (SOE) and the Syrian Platoon. Under his command, a group of Arab-Jews were trained in a variety of subjects for 'Arab-related missions,' including Arab dress and dialects.[13]

Around the same period in time the Allied forces invaded Syria and Lebanon and reoccupied the area. Despite this new state of affairs, the British decided to continue operating the Syrian Platoon and in September 1941, 12 Arab–Jewish agents entered Syria and Lebanon, where they teamed up with their companions.[14] Their main tasks were to collect intelligence on pro-Nazi agents.[15]

A few months later, however, after Yigal Allon became the commander of the Syrian Platoon, the unit became increasingly disconnected from British interests and more oriented toward Zionist missions.[16] This process was expedited in 1943 as the German Army was defeated in North Africa, a development that decreased the British need for cooperation with the Haganah. This, combined with the intensification of the tension between British and Zionist forces in Palestine, as well as the Zionist–Palestinian political conflict in large, accelerated the termination of the Syrian Platoon and the launching of an independent unit of the Palmach.

In March 1943 the Syrian Platoon was officially dismissed, and its Arab–Jewish agents were ordered to end their activities and return to Palestine. Upon their return, they were asked by the Palmach to join a group of Jewish–Arab agents that had begun training in Al-Khureibah area in the Carmel Forest, forming 'the Arab Platoon' ('ha-Maḥlakah ha-'Aravit'). This unit was soon to be known as 'Ha-Shaḥar' ('The Dawn') and its main objective was to penetrate Arab cities and villages pretending to be Muslim or Christian Arabs and to take part in espionage activities. The scope of the activities of Ha-Shaḥar unit was broad, and it seems that the influence and significance of the unit were much greater than the actual number of its agents which from 1944 stabilized at 40–50 annually.[17]

The next section of this chapter analyses segments of the training programmes of the unit and investigates its deeper layers. However, before this, a more general overview of the unit's activity is needed. Within the wide spectrum of its missions, it is noteworthy that over the years 1943–47, members of Ha-Shaḥar took part in the formation of 'Tiḳei ha-Kfarim' ('The Village Files') of the Haganah, where more than 600 Palestinian villages and cities were mapped and information about them was gathered in preparation for possible future clash with the Palestinian-Arabs. The political information for the files was gathered by members of Ha-Shaḥar.[18] Furthermore, from 1945 onwards members of Ha-Shaḥar were planted in different industrial locations, considered by the Haganah as places from which anti-Zionist resistance might emerge. These locations included Haifa Port, the potassium factories near the Dead Sea and the British military camps that hired Jewish and Palestinian workers.[19] Members of Ha-Shaḥar were also planted in the big cities, including Jaffa, Ramla and Haifa, mostly as shopkeepers. They were sent to collect intelligence on British military bases and Palestinian figures and targets.[20] They were also sent to Palestinian celebrations and religious gatherings, including Friday prayers (mostly in Al-Aqsa Mosque in Jerusalem and Al-Jarīnī in Haifa) and the Nabi Musa and Nabi Rubin festivals.[21] Their activity consisted of more warlike missions as well. This included, for example, participation in the Haganah's 'Night of the Bridges' in 1946 when 11 bridges connecting Palestine to its neighbours were blown up;[22] surveillance on Arab leaders and British officers; assassinations (e.g., of a British police officer named Bruce,[23] and Palestinian fighters in ʿArab al-Sawārkah[24]); and more (see figure 6.1).

Ha-Shaḥar also operated outside the borders of Palestine. Representatives of this unit attended the coronation of King Abdallah in the Hashemite Kingdom of Transjordan in 1946,[25] opened businesses in Egypt, Syria and Lebanon (see figure 6.2), and visited Iraq.[26] These activities were further intensified following the 1947 Partition Plan and the overt clashes between Jews and Arabs in Palestine. Some members of the unit were then sent outside of Palestine to gather information about the preparations of the Arab armies, as well as to study the intentions of Palestinian refugees who fled from their houses. One of their missions was to convince these refugees that returning to Palestine was impossible.[27] Many of the members of this unit in fact used cover stories of being Palestinian refugees themselves.[28] During these activities, seven of its members were caught and killed in different places, including Gaza, Jordan and Jaffa.[29]

In August 1948, following the establishment of Israel, Ha-Shaḥar unit became part of the Israeli intelligence services of the IDF and was named Sherut Modiʿin 18 (Intelligence Services 18).[30] Ha-Shaḥar was dismissed in 1950 after all of its members returned from their missions abroad. At a meeting of Ha-Shahhar veterans held in the 1980s, its great significance was underlined by one of its members, Yaʿacov Nimrodi:

> Ha-Shaḥar was a central part of our intelligence services . . . The unit was the basis for many large operations that became known worldwide and for which nobody would ever take responsibility . . . From this unit emerged the Israeli Mossad, Shabak (General Security Service) and Military Intelligence . . . We were the starting point of Israeli espionage.[31]

Figure 6.1 Yaʿaquba Cohen, the Mistaʿaravim Unit (Palestine, 1948): Photo taken in Safed, just before the attack of the Haganah on the city. The Palmach Photo Gallery

Figure 6.2 Members of the Mistaʿaravim Unit (Lebanon, undated): Moshe ʿAdaki, Shaʾul Algavish and ʿAkiva Feinstein. The Palmach photo gallery

Ha-Shaḥar, Orientalism and the Demise of the Arab–Jewish Identity

Keeping Nimrodi's comment in mind, this article suggests that studying and analysing Ha-Shaḥar's main presuppositions can shed light on the deeper processes that took place during the crucial decade of 1940–50 in Palestine/Israel. As I argue, the emergence of Israeli 'presumptions' about the Arab people are processes which are connected to the activity and training of this unit. In security spheres like this one, some of the central 'Arab-related' aspects of the Zionist worldview were shaped and later transmitted to the newly created Israeli state, and have influenced the Israeli–Jewish collective memory, its relations with the Arab 'other' and its denial of the Arab 'self.'

An important departure point for this discussion is the Zionist essence of Ha-Shaḥar. As the unit was part of the Palmach it is probably superfluous to mention its Zionist characteristics. Nevertheless, a few interesting facts on the specific background of its members can shed light on the political process that resulted in the creation of the unit. Many members of Ha-Shaḥar began their Zionist political education in their home countries when they joined 'Ha-Ḥalutz' ('The Pioneer') youth movement, which was established with the core aim of encouraging young Jews to settle in Palestine.[32]

The movement operated from 1905 in North America and Europe but began its activities with Jewish Middle Eastern communities only in 1928.[33] Interestingly, this late decision to approach Arab-Jews was an outcome of Zionist *European* needs. It was connected to lands purchased in the Houran area (south-west Syria) by Edmond de Rothschild in order to settle them with Jews. However, as Chayim Weizmann, the head of the World Zionist Organization, could not convince the French authorities to allow Jews from Palestine, subjects of the British Mandate, to settle in French Mandate areas, the alternative Zionist method was to settle Syrian-Jews there, with the aim of making it a transition-base for Zionist immigration from Russia to Palestine.[34]

Thereafter, Ha-Ḥalutz members began organizing groups of young Damascene Jews and briefed them about the 'Houran Plan.' Some of these youngsters visited Palestine illegally and were familiarized with the Zionist cause,[35] but these efforts were heavily criticized by their parents and by the leadership of the Syrian Jewish community who objected the clandestine activity. On one occasion, they even informed the Syrian police about the Zionist activity and five members of Ha-Ḥalutz were arrested.[36]

The project of settling the Houran was eventually abandoned due to other problems, including serious administrative difficulties, but this scheme had spread the activity of Ha-Halutz from Europe and North America into the Middle East, and contributed significantly to the immigration of young Syrian Jews to Palestine.[37] Some of these youngsters decided to stay in Palestine, and during the 1930s–1940s they joined the Zionist military effort. Due to their flawless Arabic, many of them were recruited to intelligence-oriented missions, and some joined the Syrian Platoon of the Haganah and the Ha-Shahar unit of the Palmach.

Their operations required them to be sent back to their homelands, but this time with a fake identity. They thus completed a cycle in their short lives which symbolizes the crisis in the relations between Jews and Arabs in the region: they were born in Syria during the period of Arabic renaissance in which the Arab–Jewish identity emerged,[38] transformed by the Zionist education they received in Palestine, and finally returned to their birthplaces as secret agents.

Gamliel Cohen, who is considered to have been the first Zionist spy to operate in Arab lands, was one of these Syrian-Jews.[39] Yaʿacov Buqaʿi, who entered Jordan under the fake identity of a Palestinian refugee and was caught, executed and buried under the name Najib Ibrahim Hamouda, is another example of this Ha-Halutz–Ha-Shahar cycle.[40] David Shammash and Gideon Ben-David (both were born in Baghdad, joined Ha-Halutz as teenagers, immigrated to Palestine and ended their lives after being caught and killed in Jaffa as members of Ha-Shahar[41]) also represent a similar life story.

Another noteworthy fact that relates to the background of the Ha-Shahar members, and to the 'cycle' they made, is the tasks given to them upon immigrating to Palestine, which seem to gather around the positions of guarding, watching and patrolling. Interestingly, the Arab Platoon, from which Ha-Shahar unit emerged, was headed by Yizhak Hankin, one of the chief members of 'Agudat ha-Shomrim' ('The Zionist Watchmen Association').[42] Moreover, when Yeroham Cohen writes in his memoirs about becoming the head of Ha-Shahar unit, he mentions that he remembers the commander of the Palmach 'from the time I worked as a guard in 1937.'[43] Shaʾul Hayardi (Al-Wardy), who was born in Aden and immigrated to Palestine in 1931, also served a guard before he joined Ha-Shahar.[44]

This connection between members of Ha-Shahar and earlier 'guarding-related' positions held is probably not coincidental. It was in these spheres that many Arab-Jews could find work, and where they could both use their Arabic and 'physically' prove their loyalty

to the Zionist cause.[45] However, proving loyalty was not only important regarding the Zionist military efforts, but also the dominant Zionist
presumptions and discourse. A quote from Ya'aquba Cohen,[46] in which
he describes the desired new recruits of Ha-Shahar, demonstrates this:

> We are looking for [Jewish] people with good knowledge of Arabic
> and with an 'Arab mentality.' Most of our new recruits are from
> Mizrahi families, some were born here [Palestine] and some in
> the neighbouring countries...The difference between them is that
> those born in the neighbouring countries lacked valour and courage
> because they grew up in a Diasporic environment [lit. 'avira shel
> galut'] and some of these exilic customs [lit. 'galutiyut'] got stuck to
> them...for example, the lack of chutzpah.[47]

This quote serves as an indication of the way members of Ha-Shahar
adopted Zionist concepts, but of European origin, as a sign of their
belonging to the grand Zionist narrative. Ya'aquba suggests that the
Arab-Jews in their home countries were lacking 'courage' and 'chutzpah,' but those characteristics more than anything represented what
European Jewry perceived as its own 'deficiencies.' In other words,
the Arab-Jews who operated within the Zionist movement internalized European–Zionist assumptions such as the desire to create a
proud, healthy 'new Jew,' full of chutzpah.[48] Following the analysis of
Raz-Krakotzkin, it seems that 'the negation of exile' as a constructive
element of Zionist identity, is demonstrated in Ha-Shahar through the
use of Ashkenazi representations, but also through the physical return
of the Arab-Jews to their birthplaces, as spies.[49]

Another example of the way members of Ha-Shahar strove to
identify with the dominant European–Jewish experience can be seen in
Operation David (November 1948). During this mission, Eliyahu Riqa, a
Damascus-born Jew, was sent to blow up the Lebanese navy ship 'Igris'
which used to be Adolf Hitler's private yacht. Riqa, using the code name
Khalil Sidqi, recalls the moment he was first told about his mission:

> I received the photos of the target and looked at them carefully. 'Igris,'
> 'Hitler,' these words went straight into my head. 'I am going to blow
> up the personal boat of Hitler,' I said to myself. The name of the Nazi
> enemy rang in my ears like cymbals...A few moments before I made
> it to the yacht I pondered: what a wonderful opportunity has fallen
> into my lap...To me, it resembled our victory over Hitler...[50]

Riqa's memories of his feelings can help us to better understand the construction of the 'Mizrahi' identity in light of the European experience. Blowing up Hitler's yacht serves here two pillars of this formation. First, it allows the Arab-Jews to be 'part' of the Holocaust of European Jewry, in this case through the act of revenge, but in other cases, through acts of comparison.[51] Second, it confirms a powerful 'our' ('to me, it resembled *our* victory over Hitler') that puts the religio-national identification before one's homeland, culture or language.

Regarding Arabic language and culture, it is worth mentioning that members of Ha-Shaḥar were encouraged to deepen their knowledge in both, but only within the restrictions of the security 'license' granted to them.[52] It is therefore striking to uncover the way members of Ha-Shaḥar were encouraged to speak Arabic and consume Arabic culture as part of their anti-Arab missions.[53] As early as 1941, the training of the Syrian Platoon included 'sitting in coffee places in Jaffa, dressed like Arabs, playing backgammon and listening to Umm Kulthum, Farid al-Atrash and Muhammad Abd al-Wahab.'[54] Interestingly, these 'Arab culture' training sessions became routine in Ha-Shaḥar. For example, to buy clothes for their missions, members of the unit were sent to Arab flea markets in Haifa, Jaffa or Jenin, and part of their mission was always to drink coffee in one of the local shops.[55] Deni Agmon, who for two years served as the commander of the unit, mentions that this training was called 'practical tours' ('siyurim maʿasiyim'), which included 'eating and drinking in Arab restaurants, taking Arab buses, and playing games in Arab coffee places.'[56] Dror mentions the importance of the training that included taking part in social activities with Palestinian Arabs (see figure 6.3), such as parades and youth clubs, or 'playing table tennis in the Al-Najjādah club in Jaffa.'[57] These activities, according to Dror,

> were intensified after the 1947 Partition Plan...following which members of Ha-Shaḥar spread to different areas, including Jaffa, the Old City in Jerusalem, Nablus, Jenin, Ramla, Tiberia, Haifa and Gaza, where they were sent to visit markets, mosques, travel agencies and hotels, took buses and trains, read Arabic newspapers, preferably Al-Difāʿ, and participated in demonstrations and parties.[58]

This way of training, where 'being' Arab involved active and clandestine efforts, probably contributed to the differentiation made in Ha-Shaḥar between an 'Arab' and a 'Jew.' This was a unique reflection of similar and perhaps more comprehensive processes that took

Figure 6.3   Members of the Mista'aravim Unit (Palestine, 1948): Ya'acov Buqa'i (right) dressed in an Arab scout outfit, Moshe Sa'adi (centre) in Al-Najjādah uniform and Moshe Negbi dressed as an Arab notable. The Palmach Photo Gallery

place among the Mizrahi/Arab-Jewish community in Israel and Jewish-Israelis in general. This is demonstrated well in the Hebrew term used to describe the unit's activity, *hista'aravut*, and the unit's members, mista'aravim.[59] These phrases are a neologism made up of two Hebrew words, *histayut*, which means 'to disguise oneself,' and *hit'aravut*, which means 'to become Arab.'[60] The Palmach website adds to this by suggesting that the origin of the term is in the Arabic word *ista'raba* which is 'a situation in which people who are not Arab live and behave as Arabs.'[61] These explanations suggest that the mista'aravim were non-Arabs who disguised themselves to look, talk and behave *like* Arabs. This is an interesting description of a unit whose members were predominantly Arab-Jews whose first language was Arabic, and therefore can add to the literature about the denial of the Arab–Jewish identity within the Zionist movement and in the context of the conflict in Palestine/Israel.[62]

This partition between 'the Arab' and 'the Jew' can be also seen in the way the mista'aravim were viewed from outside the unit. Gideon Ben-David, for example, a Baghdadi-born Jew, immigrated illegally to Palestine in 1945 to later join Ha-Shahar. In Dror's book, this action is described as follows: 'Ben-David made his way in difficult conditions and while dressed up *as an Arab*.'[63] In 1947, after Ben-David was recruited to Ha-Shahar, he was caught during an intelligence mission in Jaffa together with David Shammash. They were tortured, but according to several sources did not admit they were mista'aravim. They were killed and buried in an unknown place under their code names, and their captors assumed they were Palestinian-Arabs who collaborated with the Zionist movement. A text written for the memory of Ben-David in his Kibbutz shows clearly the disconnection made between the Arab-Jews and the Arab people:

> Even after all the tortures you have gone through, your enemies killed you without knowing who you are and where you came from. You found your final rest in their impure cemetery, as they buried you like an Arab who betrayed his own people.[64]

Yet to be 'like an Arab' was actually the desire of the mista'aravim, a fact which is exemplified in their memoirs. When Yemen-born Sha'ul Havardi (Al-Wardy) wrote about his first Ha-Shahar mission in Jaffa, he remembers he stayed in a hotel on Butrus Street and that 'I grew a moustache and behaved *a-la-Franji* [in a posh way]...I simply imagined myself to be an Arab.'[65] Yeroham Cohen, who was also born to a Yemenite–Jewish family, used even stronger language when he described his Ha-Shahar experience in Syria in 1948. According to him:

> I identified with my role so much that when I came to visit in Israel I was afraid to speak Hebrew...Out of devotion, I became an Arab, in the full sense of the word...this identification, which was forced upon me, created a situation in which I just stopped hating Arabs.[66]

In his memoirs, Yitzhak Shushan (code name Abu-Sehayek) also made a clear distinction between 'the Arab' and 'the Jew.' Born in Aleppo in 1926, he remembers that his Jewish school decided to form a scout group. He recalls that 'when we walked in the streets nobody noticed our Jewishness...I think that I then realized that one can both be a Jew and look like an Arab.'[67]

One of the ways found to bridge the 'gap' between 'the Arab' and 'the Jew' by members of Ha-Shahar and Zionist historiography was the frequent use in inverted commas when using the word *Arabs*. When Ya'aqubah Cohen, for example, describes the mista'aravim who worked in the Dead Sea area he mentions that once 'a commander in the

Haganah saw on one of the Dead Sea boats an "Arab" who looked exactly like Naʿim Dahan from the mistaʿaravim.'[68] Similarly, when the IDF journal describes the trainings of the mistaʿaravim it uses the inverted commas strategy: 'Thanks to the courses given by Shimʿon Somekh, Ha-Shahar warriors became "Arabs" in all senses . . .'[69] The same punctuation is used in the Palmach official website. For example, with regards to the operation of blowing up a Palestinian–Arab-owned garage in Haifa, it is written that the two mistaʿaravim (Shushan and Cohen) drove away as fast as possible but by mistake hit a British military jeep. According to the Palmach website, 'The English drew their guns and began to search the "Arabs" but found no weapons.'[70]

The use of inverted commas, or the use of terminologies such as 'becoming an Arab' or 'looking like an Arab,' all serve a similar cause. They reassure the writer, as well as the reader, that the mistaʿaravim only *imitated* the Arabs. It so implies that the Arab-Jews were 'naturally' non-Arabs who actually had to go through a transformation of 'becoming' Arabs.

More importantly, this 'natural' differentiation between 'Jews' and 'Arabs' is connected to the Orientalist approach from which the Zionist movement drew its inspiration. This approach, which was also adopted by Arab-Jews who became part of the Zionist movement and ideology, is evident in the history and practice of Ha-Shahar. First, the idea to use Arab-Jews as mistaʿaravim was initially a British idea practised in Mandate Palestine, which points to the Orientalist spirit of the project.[71] Second, as the mistaʿaravim were part of the Palmach, it is important to bear in mind the general Orientalist approach of this organization. As highlighted by Almog, 'Arabism' was a status symbol in the Palmach, which included imitation of Oriental customs such as the drinking of black coffee, the setting of bonfires, the use of Arabic words and the adoption of Palestinian dabkeh dance steps.[72] Third, the actual name of the unit indicates its Orientalist roots. Ha-Shahar means 'The Dawn' in Hebrew, but this is an amendment of the original name of the unit, which was 'Ha-Shehorim' [lit. 'The Blacks']. This derogatory term, definitely in the Zionist context, was used by European–Ashkenazi Jews to insult Mizrahi Jews.[73] It is not known who originally chose this name for the mistaʿaravim unit, but it was changed as soon as the use of the term was criticized.[74]

The Orientalist characteristics of the unit, exemplified in the use of 'blacks' for Arab-Jews (in contrast to Ashkenazi 'whites'[75]), was also reflected in the discriminatory divisions inside the unit as many mistaʿaravim objected that all of the apprentices, warriors and agents of the unit were Mizrahi, and almost all of its commanders were Ashkenazi.[76] Yigal Allon (born under the name Yigal Peikowitz) , the Ashkenazi founder of Ha-Shaḥar, expressed this Orientalist 'black and white' spirit of the unit when saying that the mistaʿaravim needed to be 'black on the outside and white on the inside.'[77] By so stating and by using the black-and-white metaphor, Allon clarified the 'hierarchy' of Zionist Orientalism: at the top are those 'white both inside and out' (Ashkenazi), then come those 'black on the outside and white on the inside' (Arab-Jews) and at the bottom come those 'black on the outside and inside' (Muslim/Christian Arabs).

Orientalist elements can be also found in Ha-Shaḥar's training programme. For example, when Zionist political leaders from the Jewish Agency visited the unit, the mistaʿaravim hosted them in a Bedouin tent. This practice shows the patronizing, essentialist and also romantic lenses through which the mistaʿaravim unit looked at the Arab people and the way this 'knowledge' was circulated. This practice is especially striking when acknowledging that the vast majority of Palestinian-Arabs lived in houses, not in tents, and that most of them resided in urban spaces.

The Orientalist worldview was evident also when the mistaʿaravim greeted the guests in traditional Arabic greetings, and 'by putting one's hand on one's forehead and heart.'[78] They also sang Arabic songs, known to the mistaʿaravim as 'ho ho songs,' in loud voices.[79] Deni Agmon remembers that for these events the mistaʿaravim used to slaughter a sheep and cook it with rice and pine-nuts. According to him, this was because 'we wanted it to be easier for the mistaʿaravim to move naturally into the Arab area.'[80]

Gamliel Cohen remembers that emphasis was put on the external appearance of the mistaʿaravim, and that their training frequently included exaggerations such as an 'obligation to eat only with [their] hands.'[81] A document entitled 'Classes for Mistaʿaravim' from July 1943 confirms this training. It has information about ten specific classes that include the following: 'Peasant dress,' 'Putting on [Arab] dress,' 'Entering an [Arab] village looking for an acquaintance,' 'Being hosted in an Arab house,' 'Drinking coffee,' 'Eating,' 'Spending the time between the meal and sleeping time,' 'Sleeping,' 'Waking up' and 'Farewell.' The information provided is very detailed and includes instruction on the lighting of cigarettes, orders of greetings, politeness, correct terminologies and pronunciation, eating rice and meat with hands only, the importance of belching at the end of the meal, the importance of praising Allah frequently, instructions on how to ask for the toilet, noises that need to be made when waking up, and more.[82] These instructions perhaps attempted to give a social context to the places and societies in which the mistaʿaravim would operate,[83] but they seem to be influenced by a deeply Orientalist approach toward the Arab people. This approach categorizes all Arab people under a one-dimensional group and frozen in time.[84]

Moreover, emphasis on *Muslim* religious traditions was also used in an exaggerated way in Ha-Shahar. An interesting example of this attitude took place when some of the members of Ha-Shahar were approached by their neighbours in Syria, Lebanon and Palestine who wanted to match them up with women from their social circles. The mistaʿaravim asked their headquarters what they should do, and they were told to say that according to the shariʿa they must marry their cousins.[85]

Another interesting example of what seems to be the over-pious lenses through which the mistaʿaravim perceived the Arab world concerns the castration of a Palestinian-Arab from Bisan (Beit Sheʾan). The man, named Muhammad, was accused by the Haganah of the rape of two Jewish women. He was tried *in absentia* by the Haganah court and was sentenced to death. The leadership of the Ha-Shahar unit received the order to plan the operation and kill him. However, they asked the Haganah to 'allow' the mistaʿaravim to castrate him instead. They argued that this is what Muslim law demands in the spirit of 'a hand that stole should be cut off.' They received the Haganah's approval and after a few days a group of mistaʿaravim entered the person's house pretending to be Syrian warriors, asked him to come and help them with a weapon convoy and then took him to a distant place where he was castrated.[86]

This operation became a famed story in the Palmach generally, and in Ha-Shahar more specifically. Chaim Hefer, a famous Israeli poet, wrote at the time a song dedicated to the mistaʿaravim, which is called 'We Castrated You, Muhammad' ['Sirasnukha ya Muhammad']. This song became part of the repertoire of the mistaʿaravim, and according to the website of the Palmach 'they sang it dancing around the bonfire using oriental melody and trills.'[87]

This story hints at the Orientalist elements of *Ha-Shahar*, not only with regards to the 'Oriental celebrations' around the bonfire, but also with relation to the punishment itself. First, it hints to an Orientalist fascination with Arab sexuality. The almost uniform association made between 'the Orient and sex,' as observed by Said, was possibly also behind the decision to castrate the Palestinian man, as well as behind naming the song 'We Castrated You, Muhammad.'[88] Taking his sexual potency, and the name Muhammad may have even greater symbolism, possibly represented for the mista'aravim a metaphorical way to neutralize the power of the Arab 'other.'[89]

Second, it seems clear that the mista'aravim perceived Muslim religious law (shari'a) as unchanging. Obviously, just like Jewish religious law (Halakha) shari'a has undergone various interpretations since it was written. The choice of an un-interpreted text, however, indicates the Orientalist spirit of Ha-Shahar. 'The return to the beginning of Islam' while ignoring historical, political and economic changes stood at the heart of the decisions of the mista'aravim. Moreover, they neglected the fact that the literal implementation of the punishment 'a hand that stole should be cut off' was not customary in modern Palestine, and in the previous century was found mainly in Saudi Arabia, Afghanistan and Pakistan, far away (both physically and socially) from Palestine.[90] Viewing Islam as homogeneous, 'Islam is Islam' as Said commented,[91] seems to stand at the heart of the castration.

The way Arab–Jewish members of Ha-Shahar looked at the Arab communities in the Middle East as alien, almost less human, and definitely not as part of their culture, probably contributed to their ability to experience the Palestinian Nakba without identifying with the Arab trauma.[92] Strikingly, the mista'aravim not only used cover stories about being 'a Palestinian refugee who is waiting concernedly for his family'[93] or 'a Palestinian refugee whose brother was lost during the war,'[94] but were also implanted inside the convoys of Palestinian refugees and made their way with them to exile, all in order to create a more genuine cover story for the future and to provide updated intelligence to the Palmach. This was, for example, the case of Havakuk Cohen, whose mission was to join Palestinian refugees from Haifa.[95] Gamliel Cohen, using the code name Jamil, was also implanted in a group of Palestinian refugees who were dispossessed during the war.[96] Other members of Ha-Shahar were either 'put' in prison or in a detention center before being 'deported' to Syria, Jordan or Lebanon.[97]

Furthermore, the mista'aravim, who during the heated years of 1947–48 increased their operations in Palestine, reported to one another on new expressions used by Palestinian-Arabs and so improved their knowledge of colloquial Arabic. From November 1947 they mention one new phrase being used again and again in coffee shops, especially when the news spoke of Arab defeats in different locations. *Rāhat Falastīn* ('Palestine is gone') was the new phrase, and according to their memoirs it was an expression they began using frequently between themselves and during their operations.[98] Their apathetic attitude toward a very powerful and tragic phrase, especially for Arab people, contributes to our understanding of the depth of disconnection the mistaʿaravim felt toward the objects of their surveillance.

This does not mean that Palestinian suffering was left totally unnoticed. One of the mistaʿaravim, for example, was ordered to go to Haifa port and join one of the boats on which thousands of Palestinian refugees fled. When he reached the port he remembers 'the gloomy and terrifying sight... of thousands of people who were waiting on the quay which was empty of boats... shouts and weeping only increased the tumult.'[99] However, he left the place and continued to his next mission. Despite the shocking scenes, it was clear to him that it was not his Nakba.

Conclusion

Ha-Shaḥar unit is a case study that helps to shed light on processes and developments which took place within the Zionist movement in the 1930s and 1940s, such as new emphases on intelligence skills and organizations. Moreover, through the examination of the work of this unit, the Orientalist characteristics of the Zionist project in Palestine clearly emerge.

With regards to the members of Ha-Shaḥar, this article surveyed a historical process in which the Arab-Jews who immigrated to Palestine grew up as Arabic-speaking Jews, joined the Zionist movement where they underwent a process in which they shed their Arab cultural belonging and identity, and gained it again only in relation to Zionist security and political needs. 'Re-Arabizing the de-Arabized,' as this article is entitled, was a powerful journey that seems to symbolize the end of the Arab–Jewish identity. It demonstrates the rule, which is the de-Arabization of Jews, a process which was both a part and a result of the political conflict in Palestine, but it also shows the rigid boundaries drawn around the only exception to the rule that was permitted by the Zionist movement. In other words, it suggests that the only possible return of Jews to their Arab roots and culture permitted by Zionist ideology is through imitation and impersonation and only in the contexts of espionage, and military intelligence.

This article, therefore, has a tragic load in its cargo. It argues that those Arab-Jews who were most capable of understanding the Arab people not only did not serve as a 'bridge' between the Zionist-Europeans and the Arab people through the hyphen in their Arab–Jewish identity, but were exploited by and exclusively served the Zionist–Jewish movement's military wings and political needs. They were recruited not only to castrate a Palestinian rapist from Bisan or to explode a car bomb in Haifa, but to help formulate a society and a state which perceived the Arab as its opposite. Within these discursive boundaries which permeated into the State of Israel, Arab-Jews were allowed to call themselves Arabs, and were allowed to sit and play backgammon in Jaffa, read a Palestinian newspaper in Haifa and speak in Arabic with their Palestinian–Arab counterparts in Jerusalem, only if they carried a forged ID and only if using a fake name.

Acknowledgements

This article is based on a paper given in a University of Cambridge conference entitled *Jews of Arab Culture*, held in 2009. I would like to thank Prof. Yasir Suleiman who encouraged me to speak about this topic and who came up with its original title. I would also like to thank Ronit Chacham, Yael Azgad and Chloe Massey as well as the editors and reviewers of this book, who all read this article and gave me important and helpful comments.

Notes

1. The Haganah (meaning in Hebrew: 'The Defence') was the central and most powerful Zionist para-military organization operating in Palestine between 1920 and 1948, when it became the core of the Israeli Defence Forces (IDF). The Palmach (a Hebrew acronym that stands for 'The Strike Force') was established in 1941 as the elite fighting force of the Haganah.
2. The word 'Yishuv' (meaning in Hebrew: 'The Settlement') relates to the Jewish population of Palestine in the pre-state period. The quote is taken from: 'The Irgun Archive: Testimony of Shimʿon Somekh,' 154.26. See also: Gamliel Cohen [in Hebrew], *The First Mistaʿaravim* (Tel Aviv: Israeli Ministry of Defence, 2002), 37.
3. For example, in 1937 in the aftermath of the Arab Revolt, British Army officer Captain Orde Wingate established the Special Night Squads (SNS) in cooperation with the Haganah. See: Joel Beinin, *Workers and Peasants in the Modern Middle East* (Cambridge: Cambridge University Press, 2001), 96.
4. Robert Harkavy, *Strategic Basing and the Great Powers, 1200–2000* (London: Routledge, 2007), 79.
5. See, for example: Reuven Erlich [in Hebrew], *The Lebanon Triangle: The Policy of the Zionist Movement and the State of Israel towards Lebanon, 1918–1958* (Tel Aviv: Maʿarakhot, Israeli Ministry of Defence, 2000), 152; Yeroham Cohen [in Hebrew], *Palmach behind Enemy Lines in Syria* (Tel Aviv: Ha-Kibbutz ha-Meʾuhad, 1973), 11.

6. Anita Shapira, *Yigal Allon, Native Son: A Biography*, trans. Evelyn Abel (Philadelphia, PA: University of Pennsylvania Press, 2008), 111.
7. Yeroham Cohen [in Hebrew], *By Light and in Darkness* (Tel Aviv: ʿAmikam, 1969), 26.
8. Ashley Jackson, *The British Empire and the Second World War* (London: Hambledon Continuum, 2006), 154–5; Cohen, *By Light and in Darkness*, 26–8.
9. The term 'Arab-Jews' has been almost totally excluded from Israeli–Jewish discourse. Instead, other expressions, all 'Arab-free,' such as Mizraḥim ('Oriental') or Sephardim (descendants of Jews who lived in the Iberian Peninsula until the Spanish Inquisition) were adopted. For further reading see: Yehouda Shenhav, *The Arab Jews: A Postcolonial Reading of Nationalism, Religion, and Ethnicity* (Stanford, CA: Stanford University Press, 2006); Ella Shohat, 'Sephardim in Israel: Zionism from the Standpoint of Its Jewish Victims,' *Social Text*, no. 19/20 (Autumn 1988), 1–35.
10. Sadeh and Allon were both founders of the Palmach. Quoted in: Cohen, *The First Mista ʿaravim*, 11.
11. Yousef Qustika (code name Abu-Nuri) collected the intelligence on this target. The operation was never implemented as the boat of the warriors was lost and the faith of its people was never known (the boat carried 22 members of the *Haganah* and one British commander). See: Ian Black and Benny Morris, *Israel's Secret Wars: A History of Israel's Intelligence Services* (New York: Grove Press, 2003), 31; 'Preparations for the Departure of the 23 Yordei Hasira Boat' (Palmach Information Center): http://www.palmach.org.il/show_item.asp?levelId=42858&itemId=8607&itemType=0
12. Cohen, *By Light and in Darkness*, 28 and *Palmach behind Enemy Lines in Syria*, 40–1.
13. Cohen, *The First Mista ʿaravim*, 23 and *By Light and in Darkness*, 32.
14. Ibid.
15. Cohen, *Palmach behind Enemy Lines in Syria*, 67–70.
16. Allon's desired new orientation included the broadening of the unit's responsibilities to include assistance to the 'Mossad le-ʿAliyah Bet' (the Zionist institution in charge of the Jewish illegal immigration to Palestine) and establishing connections with Jews in Arab countries to provide them with information about the Zionist movement. See: Zvika Dror [in Hebrew], *The 'Arabists' of the Palmach* (Tel Aviv: Ha-Kibbutz ha-Meʾuhad, 1986), 23 and 43.
17. Information taken from: 'The Irgun Archive: Testimony of Shimʿon Somekh,' 154.26.
18. 'The Villages' Files' [in Hebrew] (Palmach Information Center): http://www.palmach.org.il/show_item.asp?levelId=38612&itemId=5528&itemType=0; Gil Eyal, *The Disenchantment of the Orient: Expertise in Arab Affairs and the Israeli State* (Stanford, CA: Stanford University Press, 2006), 85.
19. Dror, *The 'Arabists' of the Palmach*, 102–4; Yoav Gelber [in Hebrew], *The Intelligence in the Yishuv: 1918–1947* (Tel-Aviv: Defense Ministry, 1992), 604; for further reading about the British military camps and their policy of hiring Arab and Jewish workers, see: Zachary Lockman, *Comrades and Enemies: Arab and Jewish Workers in Palestine, 1906–1948* (Berkeley, CA and London: University of California Press, 1996), 292.
20. Cohen, *The First Mistaʿaravim*, 33.

21. 'Ha-Shaḥar Unit [in Hebrew]' (Palmach Information Center): http://www
.palmach.org.il/show_item.asp?levelId=38612&itemId=5533&itemType=0
22. Dror, *The 'Arabists' of the Palmach*, 122–3.
23. Ibid., 125–9.
24. Ibid., 134–5.
25. 'The Irgun Archive: Testimony of Shimʿon Somekh,' 154.26.
26. Dror, *The 'Arabists' of the Palmach*, 187–202. See also: 'Ha-Shaḥar
Unit' [in Hebrew] (Palmach Information Center): http://info.palmach.org.
il/show_item.asp?levelId=38612&itemId=5535&itemType=0.
27. See: Johnny Mansour [in Arabic], 'The Mistaʿaravim Unit: Beginning,
Crimes, Training and Tasks,' *Qaḍāyā Isrāʾīliyyā* 15 (2004), 14.
28. Dror, *The 'Arabists' of the Palmach*, 175, 192–3, 201, 220; ʿOdeda Yaʿari
[in Hebrew], *Contour Lines: The Story of Deni Agmon, the Commander of the
Mistaʿaravim Unit* (Tel Aviv: Beit ha-Palmach, 2006).
29. Dror, *The 'Arabists' of the Palmach*, 211–25.
30. Morris, *Israel's Secret Wars*, 43.
31. Dror, *The 'Arabists' of the Palmach*, 226 [my translation].
32. See, for example: David Mittelberg, *The Israel Connection and American Jews*
(Westport, CT: Greenwood, 1999), 6.
33. According to ʿAbbas, Ha-Ḥalutz movement (established in Syria in 1928) was
the first Zionist movement to operate in Arab lands. See: Avraham ʿAbbas [in
Hebrew], 'The History of Ha-Ḥalutz Movement in Syria and Lebanon,' *Shevet
ve-ʿAm* 3 (December 1958), 113–24.
34. This idea was put forward by Yehouda Almog. See: Ibid.
35. Zvi Ilan [in Hebrew] 'Ha-Ḥalutz in Syria and the Settlement in the Houran,'
Mi-Kan u-mi-Shaam: The Journal of the Damascus Jewry Organization in Israel
13 (April 2011), 16–17. See also: Shimʿon Kushnir [in Hebrew], *A Man in the
ʿAravah: The Story of Yehudah Almog* (Tel Aviv: ʿAm ʿOved, 1973), 21, 60–3.
36. 'Ha-Ḥalutz in Syria,' 16–17.
37. Ibid., 20–1.
38. Reuven Snir, ' "We Are Arabs before We Are Jews": The Emergence and
Demise of Arab-Jewish Culture in Modern Times,' *EJOS – Electronic Journal
of Oriental Studies* 8, no. 9 (2005), 1–47; Lital Levy, 'Historicizing the Concept
of Arab Jews in the Mashriq,' *Jewish Quarterly Review* 98, no. 4 (Fall 2008),
459–60.
39. Dror Mishani, 'Gamliel Cohen Died: One of Israel's Most Senior Intelligence
Agents,' [in Hebrew] *Arutz Sheva: Israel National News*, 17 July 2002: http://
www.inn.co.il/News/News.aspx/30272
40. Dror, *The 'Arabists' of the Palmach*, 222–4.
41. Ibid., 211–15.
42. Cohen, *The First Mistaʿaravim*, 30.
43. Cohen refers to his service in the *Notrim*, a Jewish police force set up by
the British during the 1936–1939 Arab Revolt. See: Cohen, *By Light and in
Darkness*, 47.
44. Dror, *The 'Arabists' of the Palmach*, 32.
45. Cf. Eyal, *The Disenchantment of the Orient*, 4, 23–4.
46. Yaʿaquba Cohen was born in Palestine to an Iranian–Jewish family. He
learned Arabic from a young age as he lived next to Sheikh Badr village in
Jerusalem.

47. Qtd. *The 'Arabists' of the Palmach*, 75.
48. For further reading about these characteristics in the Zionist discourse, see: Oz Almog, *The Sabra: The Creation of the New Jew* (Berkeley, CA and London: University of California Press, 2000), 78, 92, 114, 141.
49. Amnon Raz-Krakotzkin [in Hebrew], 'Exile within Sovereignty: A Critique of the "Negation of Exile" in Israeli Culture,' *Teʾoria u-Vikoret (Theory and Criticism)* 4 (Fall 1993), 23–55.
50. Roʿi Amos [in Hebrew], 'The Debt,' *Ba-Mahane: The weekly IDF Magazine* 46 (December 2010): http://dover.idf.il/IDF/News_Channels/bamahana/2010/46/14.htm [my translation].
51. See, for example, the way Zionist historiography and many Iraqi-Jews who live in Israel describe the 1941 'Farhud' (the two-day pogrom perpetrated in Baghdad) within the framework of the Holocaust of European Jewry. See: *The Arab Jews*, 140–1.
52. I use the term 'license' following Shenhav's analysis. See: ibid., 3.
53. Cf. ibid.
54. Cohen, *The First Mistaʿaravim*, 24.
55. Dror, *The 'Arabists' of the Palmach*, 63.
56. Yaʿari, *Contour Lines: The Story of Deni Agmon*.
57. Dror, *The 'Arabists' of the Palmach*, 81.
58. Ibid., 138.
59. The word *mistaʿaravim* (an active participle) refers in Hebrew to the people who are trained in *histaʿaravut* (gerund).
60. See: Ami Pedahzur, *The Israeli Secret Services and the Struggle against Terrorism* (New York: Columbia University Press, 2010), 19–20.
61. See: 'Histaʿaravut' [in Hebrew], (Palmach Information Center): http://info.palmach.org.il/show_item.asp?levelId=38612&itemId=5529&itemType=0.
62. See, for example: Reuven Snir, '"Ana min al-Yahud": The Demise of Arab-Jewish Culture in the Twentieth Century,' *Archiv Orientální* 74 (2006), 389.
63. Dror, *The 'Arabists' of the Palmach*, 213 (emphasis mine).
64. The eulogy in Kibbutz Beʾeri is quoted in: ibid., 214. It can be argued that from a pan-Arab viewpoint, Ben-David was indeed an Arab who betrayed his own people.
65. Qtd. *The 'Arabists' of the Palmach*, 33.
66. Ophir Ḥakham [in Hebrew], 'To Be Afraid 26 Hours a Day: The Palmach Mista ʿaravim Unit,' *Ḥamanit: The Israeli Military Intelligence Journal* (April 1991), 40 (my translation).
67. Qtd. *The ʿArabistsʾ of the Palmach*, 34.
68. Qtd. Ibid., 102–3. The Arab person on the Dead Sea boat was of course Naʿim Dahan.
69. 'Behind the Shadows' [in Hebrew], *Ba-Mahane: The IDF Weekly Magazine* 42 (2010): http://dover.idf.il/IDF/News_Channels/bamahana/2010/42/15.htm
70. 'The War of Independence: The Blowing-Up of the Garage in Haifa' (Palmach Information Center): http://www.palmach.org.il/show_item.asp?levelId=42858&itemId=8773&itemType=0
71. See the 'special potential hidden in the Mizrahi Jews' as quoted in footnote 10.
72. Almog, *The Sabra: The Creation of the New Jew*, 19.

73. Another derogatory term used by Ashkenazi-Zionists to describe Mizrahi Jews was 'schwartze chaies,' which means 'black animals' in Yiddish. See: Ella Shohat, 'Rupture and Return: Zionist Discourse and the Study of Arab Jews,' *Social Text* 75, no. 21 (Summer 2003), 50 and 'The Invention of the Mizrahim,' *Journal of Palestine Studies* 29, no. 1 (Autumn 1999), 5–20.

74. Rafi Sitton and Yitzhak Shushan [in Hebrew], *The People of Secrets* (Tel Aviv: Yediʿot Ahronot, 1990), 178.

75. See, for example: Dror Mishani [in Hebrew], *The Ethnic Unconscious* (Tel Aviv: ʿAm ʿOved, 2006), 29.

76. Dror, *The 'Arabists' of the Palmach*, 130–1.

77. Qtd. Ibid., 73–4.

78. Eyal, *The Disenchantment of the Orient*, 92.

79. Ibid.

80. Qtd. *Contour Lines*, *The 'Arabists' of the Palmach*, 62.

81. Cohen, *The First Mistaʿaravim*, 31.

82. Document entitled 'Classes for Mistaʿaravim,' dated 22 July 1943, found in: 'The Central Zionist Archives,' S25/22201.

83. For further reading on the successes and failures of training spies to be able to speak and behave according to social functions and situations, see: Florian Coulmas, 'Spies and Native Speakers,' in *A Festschrift for Native Speaker* (The Hague: Mouton, 1981), 355–67.

84. In a satiric piece written by Sayed Kashua in 2009, the writer mocked the Orientalist way in which Israeli mistaʿaravim units still perceive the Arab people. He argues that while all Arab-Palestinians in Israel drink macchiato, the only ones who still order black coffee with cardamom are the Jewish mistaʿaravim. See: Sayed Kashua, 'How to Be an Arab,' *Haaretz*, 16 October 2009.

85. Cohen, *Palmach behind Enemy Lines in Syria*, 143. Later on the problem was solved as *Ha-Shaḥar* began recruiting also women members from the Arab–Jewish community in Palestine. See: Dror, *The 'Arabists' of the Palmach*, 27.

86. Cohen, *Palmach behind Enemy Lines in Syria*, 106.

87. 'Ha-Shaḥar Unit: The Castration Operation' [in Hebrew] (Palmach Information Center): http://www.palmach.org.il/show_item.asp?levelId=38612&itemId=5899&itemType=0

88. See: Edward Said, *Orientalism* (New York: Vintage Books, 1978), 188–92.

89. This sexual/national neutralization can be demonstrated in the song, as one of its lines says: 'we will keep your balls [testicles] in formaldehyde/instead of bass you will sing soprano/because we castrated you, Muhammad.'

90. See, for example: Herbert J. Liebesny, 'Judicial Systems in the Near and Middle East: Evolutionary Development and Islamic Revival,' *Middle East Journal* 37, no. 2 (Spring 1983), 202–17; Fazlur Rahman, 'Islamic Modernism: Its Scope, Method and Alternatives,' *International Journal of Middle East Studies* 1, no. 4 (1970), 330.

91. Said, *Orientalism*, 107.

92. Approximately 700,000 Palestinian-Arabs were dispossessed during the years 1947–48. See: Avi Shlaim, *The Iron Wall: Israel and the Arab World* (New York: W. W. Norton, 2001), 31.

93. See for example: Shimʿon Ḥoresh (Haroush) '1924–2006: A Legend in His Lifetime,' 36.

94. Dror, *The 'Arabists' of the Palmach*, 180–1.
95. Ophir Ḥakham [in Hebrew], 'The Youngest of Them All: Ḥavakuk Cohen, the First Victim of the Palmach Mistaʿaravim Unit,' *Ḥamanit: The Israeli Military Intelligence Journal* (April 1991).
96. Yaʿari, *Contour Lines: The Story of Deni Agmon*.
97. Dror, *The 'Arabists' of the Palmach*, 201, 220.
98. Dror, *The 'Arabists' of the Palmach*, 81.
99. Qtd. *By Light and in Darkness*, 65.

7
Cannibalizing Iraq: Topos of a New Orientalism

Moneera Al-Ghadeer

In this chapter, I shall address the following questions: why has the foreign become associated with anxiety and devoid of the aesthetic fascination that marked its representation in nineteenth-century Orientalism? To what extent is the surge of an American Orientalist discourse intertwined with discursive violence against the Middle East? In what ways does this new Orientalist discourse on the Middle East reproduce the phantasm of cannibalism? In place of the nineteenth-century discourses that saw the Orient as a source of aesthetic value, the foreign has now become a source of anxiety that provokes cannibalistic manifestations. I will also explain that the figuration of cannibalism is mostly generated by the war on terror as projected onto Iraq and argue that the radical transformation of certain images of the ethnic other after 9/11 epitomizes a new Orientalist discourse that is devoid of cultural aesthetics. The central section of this chapter, 'Cannibalistic Spectacle,' introduces the notion of cannibalism as it relates to the emergence of a new Orientalist discourse instigated by American neo-imperial violence, with reference to the photographic images of the interrogation operation at Abu Ghraib prison. It also focuses on the disfiguration of the enemy and the ways in which torture tactics incorporate cultural, psychological and sexual appropriations, some of which are grounded in the earlier Orientalist framework. The final section of the chapter, 'Cultural Cannibalism,' reflects on the possibility of anti-cannibal ethics toward the other and a response to the new surge of Orientalism by drawing on Irigaray's and Derrida's arguments, specifically their investigation of the cultural and political modes of subjectivity that continually produce cannibalistic relations.

The new Orientalist discourse emerges in Western post-9/11 rhetoric. President Bush's first response to the attacks was replete with figurative descriptions of a conflict with an elusive enemy. He rendered this enemy in terms of a binary opposition between the civilized world and the barbaric while encouraging what Michelle Brown describes as 'retributive frames of punishment.' She writes:

> Retributive frames of punishment marked the contours of the war on terror from the beginning, as evidenced when President Bush assured the American public and the world in the hours after the events of September 11: 'Make no mistake: The United States will hunt down and punish those responsible for these cowardly acts,' those responsible being individuals, to employ the administration's binary rhetoric, who had 'burrowed' into the everyday life of Americans, the hidden 'cowards,' 'barbarians,' and 'evil-doers,' lurking in the 'shadows' and 'caves,' afraid to show their faces.[1]

From this perspective, the Arab or Muslim, seen without culture and outside civilization, epitomizes savagery. These phantasmal images structure the foreign as an other that 'burrows' its way into the body politic, thereby constructing a dialectic in which I constantly banish what threatens *me* by devouring it in order to sustain my life. Cannibalism, then, figures a continual devouring of the foreign once it has been transformed into a distant other on the political and cultural levels, projecting primitive characterizations onto what has been marked for annihilation and destruction.

Cannibalistic Spectacle

> It is the other implanted in me, the metabolized product of the other in me: forever an 'internal foreign body.'
> (Jean Laplanche, *Essays on Otherness*)

A grotesque anecdote from Iraq describes a soldier who 'kept a human finger in his wall locker during his entire tour of duty.' The severed parts of a human body were preserved not to be restored to life but to be relished as battlefield trophies or to satisfy a lingering cannibalistic desire. Apparently, this soldier is not alone in savouring the enemy's remains: another solider ate 'the charred flesh of an Iraqi civilian, the victim of an IED attack aimed at American forces.' Richard Sugg quotes these anecdotes narrated by Brad McCall, a former US soldier who deserted his unit and fled to Canada in 2007.[2] These fleeting moments illustrate the desire to devour the other. They evoke a cannibalistic scene in which the soldier relishes the enemy's flesh. Sugg explains that often 'the aggressors do not actually eat, but enact their dominance by cannibalistic gestures.'[3] Cannibalism generates empirical and symbolic associations ensnared in a realm of fascination. It signals a profound resistance to any argument about its manifestation in recent American media discourse. As Dan Beaver reports, 'Cannibalism evokes, as few other phenomena, a range of reflection from the most sublime metaphors of religious sacrifice to images of the most extreme murderous cruelty.'[4] Cannibalism converges with imperialism, reproducing as it does so imagined constructs of the colonized. Cannibalism often indicates a confrontation with the other in which the self, attached to its terrifying and grotesque craving, attempts to consume the other, sadistically assimilating the other to the same in order to overcome whatever the self perceives as alien and peripheral.

At first glance at the Abu Ghraib photographs, a number of historical references gush forth: Algerian prisoners tortured during the French conquest, shackled slaves and lynching.[5] Self-other relations are the fundamental dynamic inside Abu Ghraib that defines boundaries, righteously and schematically dividing the world into good and evil, civilized and primitive, while reactivating the repressed act of cannibalism. The photographs from Abu Ghraib cannot be isolated from the discourse of the war on terror, where one can easily recognize the paradigms that the soldiers enacted in these photos, unleashing the phantasm. In fact, the officers knew that President Bush and Secretary Rumsfeld had ruled that the Geneva Convention did not apply.[6] One of the characteristics in such images is the acting out of the fantasy in which the other is perceived as primitive, ultimately recasting a more savage and more transgressive Iraqi subject, unravelling further sensations of estrangement and alienation. We can see the prison's atrocity as a satire of imperialist power mocking its own consumption and cannibalistic desire.

Yet the Abu Ghraib photos also generate associations with rites, secret rituals, ceremonies of religious sacrifice, covert operations and fraternity or fight clubs. The latter association brings Žižek's observation to mind. He underlines a new fighting trend embedded in the war on terror, namely,

'toughman-fights,' in which only amateur men (and women also) engage in violent boxing matches, getting their faces bloody, testing their limits.... Although these fights stand under the sign of 'God bless America!' and are perceived by (most of) the participants

themselves as part of the 'war on terror,' one should not immediately
dismiss them as symptomatic of a redneck 'proto-Fascist' tendency:
they are part of a potentially redemptive disciplinary drive.[7]

As a reaction to the war on terror, 'toughman-fights' exemplify a
sadomasochistic tendency. 'Toughman-fights' are performed under the
motto 'God bless America,' they remain a small, communal ritual
aimed at restoring confidence and sanctuary. This violent ritual, then,
functions as the individual's talismanic protection against imminent
terror. On the other hand, we should not overlook the paradox in
this performance, what Žižek calls its 'redemptive disciplinary drive.'
I would suggest that the American soldier transgressively and defi-
antly performs a toughman-fight, but it is against the detainee at Abu
Ghraib. The detained terrorist, that manufactured monster, needs to
be brutally killed off and annihilated before he attacks the American
soldier, as expressed in the words of Graner, a soldier who participated in torturing the detainees: 'You know these guys can kill
people.'[8]

To be in prison is to be already under surveillance, but the camera
creates a doubling effect of being watched, observed and inspected.
Thus, not only is the detainee under the gaze of the guards and soldiers and the 'other soldiers [who] stopped by to view,' but there is
an anonymous and all-encompassing camera lens that violates and
cuts through the male body.[9] While the camera seems to represent an
authorized form of power, it also moves as a fictive force of an uniden-
tifiable gaze coming from elsewhere; it implicitly threatens to expose
the image of the tortured, humiliated detainee to the external world.
For the detainee, it is no longer a secret game when the soldiers are
mocking him and laughing inside a confined prison cell; he is haunted
by the fear of being publicly exposed. Hersh explains the gravity of
being exposed publicly: 'It was thought that some prisoners would do
anything, including spying on their associates – to avoid dissemination of the shameful photos to family and friends.'[10] The soldiers knew
very well that the camera amplified the apprehension of the detainees.
In the first place, these images were produced for the soldiers' own
consumption: they exchanged them and played them on their com-
puters, repeating the viewing of what they had already watched in the
prison cell. The detainees' gaze is absent from these photographs; either
because their faces are covered with sandbags or women's underwear or
because their gaze is averted by sheer dread or real disfiguration. The
photographer exposes a pornographic desire, which exposes the most

private and intimate body parts of an Iraqi male and completes this voyeuristic gaze. Theodore Nadelson notes that pornography is encouraged in war: 'The pornoerotic arouses, "gets men up"; that is, it makes them feel their ability at dominating and focuses them on aggression. American aviators were reportedly shown pornographic movies before they flew combat missions in the Gulf War.'[11]

In the Abu Ghraib photographs, the body is hollowed out by isolating its parts in the close-up shots; it doubles the pain of those spectators who may also experience shame and humiliation inflicted upon the national image with which they identify. We often hear these reactions toward the photographs juxtaposed with the moral greatness of 'our' civilization, but in the mainstream media little is expressed on behalf of the tortured detainee and his civilization. Scarry argues that war and torture follow a similar trajectory: 'In both war and torture, there is a destruction of civilization in its most elemental form.'[12] In this sense, detainees' testimonies will reveal how civilization is crushed within each prisoner's body and is turned into another war zone for the torturer. The torturer's power reduces the detainee's body into partial injured objects, constantly reminding the detainee of the soldier's power and control over him. The detainee is traumatized by the soldier's excessive appetite for defacement. These photographs show ghostly corpses or stripped bodies hung for display, scarred, exposed and piled up as bare flesh to reconstruct a scene perversely populated by disquieting and sexualized bodies, which eventually fulfils the fantasy that the other is archaic, ungovernable and wild. The incorporation of masculinity and nudity serves as both symbolic castration and manifestation of victorious rites. When looking at the Abu Ghraib photographs, a throng of menacing images floods the scene especially when one attempts to reflect on the implication of crowding naked, Iraqi men into the frame while soldiers inflict physical and verbal brutality upon them. The prison, according to these visual renderings, turns into a zone that incarcerates threatening masculinity, prompting a simulacrum of the threatening male figures, the 9/11 suicide hijackers, Bin Laden, Saddam Hussein, his sons, al-Zarqawi, al-Zawahiri and, more recently, Hassan Nasrallah. (Of course, the mainstream US media do not differentiate between these figures politically or ideologically.) One should bear in mind that creating and reproducing these icons of monstrosity does not banish them entirely, and there will be other monstrous figures, motivating a new justification to hunt them down. Baudrillard complicates the idea of the demonized or evil other:

It all comes from the fact that the Other, like Evil, is unimaginable. It all comes from the impossibility of conceiving of the Other – friend or enemy – in its radical otherness, in its irreconcilable foreignness. A refusal rooted in the total identification with oneself around moral values and technical power. That is America that takes itself for America and which, bereft of otherness, eyes itself with the wildest compassion.[13]

Accordingly, the American political discourse installs provocative inscriptions like those that Bush used after 9/11 in a desperate attempt to identify and put a face on this elusive enemy who will always be 'unimaginable' and 'inconceivable.'[14] If the relation between self and other is fashioned by identification and mimetic affinity, it will only prompt gazing into a narcissistic reflection in which the self cannot perceive the other's alterity. In this sense, America cannot accept resistance or 'opposition,' following Baudrillard's thesis.[15] The desire to eliminate this opposition, as noted earlier, pervades the configuration of masculinity that is always essentialized and consequently associated with Arab and Muslim men, who, in turn, trigger war rhetoric. This anxiety promotes tracking and profiling of certain racially marked men.[16]

In all of the photographs, we can trace libidinal and sadistic excess. While the camera takes snapshots, it comes to resemble a horror movie, which is the privileged site of cannibalism in American popular culture. In his insightful analysis of *The Silence of the Lambs*, Cary Wolfe cites Stephen King, who addresses transgression and sociality in horror fiction. King explains:

> Horror appeals to us because it...is an invitation to indulge in deviant, antisocial behavior by proxy – to commit gratuitous acts of violence, indulge our puerile dreams of power, to give in to our most craven fear. Perhaps more than anything else, the horror story says it's okay to join the mob, to become the total tribal being, *to destroy the outsider.*[17]

If we, momentarily and provisionally, perceive of Abu Ghraib files and photographs as influenced and informed by horror films and read them along with King's statement, we will realize they are an enactment of prohibited acts and the indulgence of an unconscious craving. But of course, we will retreat after recognizing that what occurred at Abu Ghraib is the act of horror itself without the fictional proxy.

What occurred was the spontaneous engagement in menacing excesses designed 'to destroy the outsider.' Documented in these photographs are many acts of physical and sexual ruthlessness committed against Iraqi detainees; these acts range from attaching electric wires to different parts of the body, including male genitals; punching; beating with hard objects; slapping; kicking; pouring cold water; 'isolating detainees "in the hole" for thirty days with possible thirty days extension'; and using dogs to attack them.[18] Once again, are these acts performed to satisfy a craving of some unconscious fear, if we follow King's remark? What if there is a haunting of a cannibalistic desire that has been awakened after indulging in the fantasy and its transgressive way? In addition to the physical brutality, a long narrative of sexual abuse and sadistic acts unfolds in these photographs, turning the detainees into submissive savages during a cannibalistic rite, a ritual in which there is an inability to tolerate the staged unruly Iraqis. These cannibalistic trends trigger antagonistic behaviour toward the other. What binds these soldiers in committing these violations? Along with Stephen King's remark, Žižek reminds us of another communal bond by highlighting that 'what "holds together" a community most deeply is not so much identification with the Law that regulates the community's "normal" everyday circuit, but rather *identification with a specific form of transgression of the Law.*'[19]

These images depict Iraqi men in sadomasochistic and pornographic settings where rape and sodomy prevailed. Many detainees describe that they were coerced into being naked with their heads in sandbags, or into wearing women's underwear, which was sometimes used to cover up their faces in preparation for interrogation. One detainee writes in his statement that 'they stripped me from my clothes ... and I spent 6 days in that situation.'[20] Shalal, also known as 'The Man Behind the Hood,' says in a graphic testimony that he 'was kept in the cell without clothes for two weeks,' then was given a blanket, which he draped over his body, and was 'placed ... on top of a carton box containing can [sic.] food,' electrocuted and photographed.[21] His well-known photograph emphasizes the temporality of torture and the disavowal of his vulnerability. Some detainees were forced to masturbate in front of other detainees, the soldiers and the camera. Others were thrown into sexual positions with other naked male prisoners or were threatened with rape; a soldier was 'sodomizing a detainee with a chemical light' and a 'broom stick.'[22] One detainee explains that the soldiers forced him to rape a 15-year-old, then went further to crush him morally and psychologically by inscribing 'I'm a rapist' on his leg and taking pictures of him naked. Most of the detainees' statements indicate that they were exposed to these sexual violations during the holy month of Ramadan. In addition to the centrality of the materiality of body for the torturer, the detainee's moral values were stripped of their context, appropriated, displaced and emptied out, rendering them an indispensable site for torture. Behavioral Science Consultation Teams (BSCTs or 'biscuits' – we need to keep the acronym in mind) use 'a psycho-cultural approach to exploiting the prisoner's religion.'[23] For instance, they shave the 'detainee's beard or hair (to *neutralize* Muslims in the interrogation setting).'[24] The appropriation of the prisoner's culture, sacred rituals, identity and everything that marks his difference becomes a weapon that is turned against him, presupposing his surrender to the dominant soldier. Following the previous testimonies, we can trace how presumed cultural taboos that were once produced and conceived in an earlier Orientalist discourse are replayed upon the detainees' flesh in communal humiliation and abuse to spark a powerful return of new Orientalism.

The body of the detainee becomes a target, engendering prohibited acts indicative of perversion and sexual pathology:

> They stripped me of all my clothes, even my underwear. They gave me women's underwear, that was rose color with flowers in it and they put the bag on my face. One of them whispered in my ear, 'today I am going to fuck you,' and he said this in Arabic. Whoever was with me experienced the same thing. That's what the American soldiers did, and they had a translator with them.... And he called me 'faggot' because I was wearing the woman's underwear, and my answer was 'no.'[25]

> I saw Grainer punching one of the prisoners right in his face very hard when he refused to take off his underwear and I heard them begging for help. And also the American soldiers told to do like homosexuals (fucking).[26]

These statements demonstrate that the soldiers involved in torture insist on utilizing modes of sexuality and homosexuality to assault and humiliate the detainees. They intensify the prisoners' wounds by giving them malicious names like 'Faggot,' 'The Claw,' 'The Ice Man,' 'Gus,' 'Shitboy' and 'Taxi Driver.' Shalal states, 'the soldiers marked my forehead with the words "Big Fish" in red. All the detainees in this camp are considered "Big Fish." '[27] By replacing the proper name with a mocking or assaultive 'label,' it indicates a cynical mutilation and disfiguration of the detainee's identity. These offensive nicknames are, in fact, similar to aliases; some of the torturers also work under pseudonyms and aliases.[28] This name-calling disfigures the proper name, and the detainee's identity is mutilated in order to mock him and reduce him to a thing by obliterating his subjectivity. This is ultimately an attempt to banish him from memory and likewise erase the tracks of the criminal act. For these indications, special attention must be given to more than 100 'ghost detainees' whose records are missing or not available because the CIA did not list their names.[29] One could consider a disfigured America created, to a certain extent, by the war on terror that has been camouflaging political agency and ethical responsibility. Secret and undercover operations, use of aliases, embedded journalists, security alerts, military tribunals, black sites (100 secret detention centres, some of which were built in Morocco, Romania, Guantánamo Bay [referred to as Strawberry Fields] and Thailand [called Cat's Eye]),[30] surveillance under the Patriot Act, and finally the turning away from acknowledging violence in Abu Ghraib prompted a deformation of America, an America that has abandoned civil and human rights. This deformation contributed to the denial of violence and held sway over the question of justice in the public sphere.

The verbal violence practiced at Abu Ghraib brings in the discussion of assaultive speech and its wounding effects. Charles R. Lawrence III points out the relationship between furious speech and physical injury by explaining 'the immediacy of the injurious impact of racial insults.' He compares 'the experience of being called' a racist or hateful name to 'receiving a slap in the face. The injury is instantaneous.'[31] In *Excitable Speech*, Judith Butler aligns her reading with Lawrence's.[32] She emphasizes, 'Certain words or certain forms of address not only operate as threats to one's physical well-being, but there is a strong sense in which the body is alternately sustained and threatened through modes of address.'[33] In view of the fact that the detainees were forced into performing homosexual acts, it is impossible not to recall the American military's former prohibition on homosexuality. Butler observes, 'The term "homosexual" was disallowed as part of a self-ascription or self-definition on the part of military personnel. The term itself was not banished, but only its utterance within the context of self-definition.'[34] Moreover, the language of the military policy, according to Butler, 'is explicitly constructed as contagious and offensive conduct.'[35] Following Butler's analysis, I will ask: while we are aware of the American military's regulation on homosexual self-definition, how can we read the enactment of prohibited fantasies within an imperative structure that demands and deploys homosexual utterances and images? Where do these homophobic portrayals of Iraqi men come from? Can they be attributed to 'the magical power' of the taboo and the unconscious desire to violate it? The installation of the taboo, its conscious and unconscious workings against what has been prohibited, and the emergence of a desire to violate can be traced in the images from Abu Ghraib. The crew behind these photographs is driven to stage prohibited acts of torture, rape and sodomy while deploying hateful speech and dehumanizing the detainees. While the taboo condemns these acts, it paradoxically instigates a powerful desire to transgress because 'the magical power that is attributed to taboo is based on the capacity for arousing temptations' according to Freud.[36] The 'magical power' of the taboo is associated with some sort of infectious, transmittable disease in Freud's language that spreads out to other prohibited sites. Once the desire to defy what has been prohibited travels to the unconscious, it produces a set of intricate violations that imply that the taboo has lost its primary aim, leading to the Abu Ghraib images.

Intertwined within the sexual images is a returning Orientalist presupposition about Arabs and sexuality. But what motivates the imagination to come up with these systematic methods of sexual torture? Hersh refers to the reliance of the American military on Patai's well-known text, *The Arab Mind* (1973):

> The book includes a twenty-five-page chapter on Arabs and sex, depicting sex as a taboo vested with shame and repression...The Patai book, an academic told me, was 'the bible of the neocons on Arab behavior.' In their discussions, he said, two themes emerged – 'one, that Arabs only understand force and, two, that the biggest weakness of Arabs is shame and humiliation.'[37]

Clearly, the Orientalist enclosure reproduces fundamental generalizations and caricatures about what constitutes an Arab mind, as if there is such an object to begin with that can be encapsulated along with the forces of its phobias and fantasies. The preoccupation with the Arab mind is profoundly anchored in an earlier Orientalist discourse. One example of these biases about the Arab mind will take us back to Said's discussion of a lecture delivered by H. A. R. Gibb in 1945. Gibb contends:

> *The Arab Mind*, whether in relation to the outer world or in relation to the process of thought, cannot throw off its intense feelings for the separateness and the individuality of the concrete events. This is,

I believe, one of the main factors lying behind that 'lack of a sense of law'... the characteristic difference in the *Oriental*.[38]

Gibb disavows the Arab's rationality and asserts that his 'mind' does not understand legality, thus indicating that he is a savage who lives in constant anarchy. Said rightly interrogates Gibb's statement: 'What is the meaning of "difference" when the preposition "from" has dropped from sight altogether?'[39] In the case of Patai, the obsession with the Arab mind and sexuality is really nothing new since it pervades Orientalist discourse, a point Said explores thoroughly in *Orientalism*. Said characterizes Patai's book by highlighting its reductive and compressed scope:

> Much of his paraphernalia is anthropological – he describes the Middle East as a 'culture area' – but the result is to eradicate the plurality of differences among the Arabs (whoever they may be in fact) in the interest of one difference, that one setting Arabs off from everyone else. As subject matter for study and analysis, they can be made to permit, legitimate, and valorize general nonsense.[40]

The Abu Ghraib photographic images bear the marks of European colonialism while cannibalizing the rhetoric of Orientalism, engendering a spectacle saturated with depictions of this Arab mind and its deviant attitude toward sexuality. In an unprecedented way, these sexual presuppositions and caricatures are manufactured in military schools. Patai's book becomes an enabling mode to imagine, presume and then believe the myth of how the so-called Arab mind thinks of gender and sexuality. Thus, these reductive Orientalist guidelines present a difficult task for experts and advisers rushing from the departments of area studies, political science and social sciences to share their insights about the Middle East and provide analysis of the ethnic other. This rush to provide knowledge is nothing new: Said observed this phenomenon in the American political apparatus almost four decades ago. He asserts: 'Thus the militarily-national-security possibilities of an alliance, say, between a specialist in national character analysis and an expert in Islamic institutions were soon recognized, for expediency's sake if for nothing else.'[41] Furthermore, BSCTs prepared the psychological torture plan or the interrogation strategies.[42] Once Patai's clichés and biases are re-encoded, twisted and mystified of course, they create this surge of new Orientalist imagery. The Abu Ghraib files illustrate the military application of these new Orientalist clichés and formulas, but what we see is an eruption of the pathology of violence. The Iraqi bodies are coerced to disclose what violates the normative, that is, madness, homosexuality, animality and criminality. But how can we begin to understand the convergence of these categories and their symbolic functioning as a fertile zone for torture? Butler aptly cautions us against a geopolitical discourse that tries to conflate and equalize these different constructs and their symbolic configuration. She writes:

> It seems crucial to resist the model of power that would set up racism and homophobia and misogyny as parallel or analogical relations. The assertion of their abstract or structural equivalence not only misses the specific histories of their construction and elaboration, but also delays the important work of thinking through the ways in which these vectors of power require and deploy each other for the purpose of their own articulation.[43]

The discourse on Abu Ghraib deploys and generates what resides on the empire's peripheries – Arab, homosexual, animal and many more – in order to produce sheer reflections in a mirror so that these characterizations multiply resistance while, in fact, they all amplify the discourse of power, as Butler indicates.

Cultural Cannibalism[44]

> I kill it and remember it…I interiorize it totally and it is no longer other.
>
> (Derrida, *The Ear of the Other*)

Thus far, my argument about the cannibalization of Iraq concerns the emergence of a new Orientalism promoted by colonial violence and media representation of a disfigured and devoured 'enemy.' What motivates figuring this 'enemy' in such gothic and graphic imagery, that is to say, as the archaic depiction of the Orientalized other? Is it the acting out of a suppressed mourning, a mode of melancholia? Is it possible to call for an anti-cannibal ethics during the atrocities of war? We have seen how the self is threatened with destruction, its sovereignty destabilized and its democratic image affected by violence from elsewhere. The prisoner abuse at Abu Ghraib discloses a topos of a new American Orientalism. After the exposure of these atrocities and others, an obsessive desire arises to discard and suppress violence. In *Oath Betrayed*, Steven H. Miles highlights this suppression:

Torture by American soldiers must be a different kind of torture: 'torture lite.' It must be an isolated event, the work of a 'few bad apples' or a local command breaking down.[45]

These relentless efforts to mask the consequences of aggression and thrust violence aside produce a discursive structure in which the act of cruelty is persistently and rhetorically conjured away as 'torture lite,' a 'few bad apples,' 'a glitch,'[46] 'the poor training of a handful of troops' and 'the hillbilly defense,' among other examples.[47] These tropes avert and preclude the reading of violence and torture to deflect criticism of the transgressive acts. Such deflection is mostly at the level of the tropological language that is deployed by the speakers to deny and turn away from accountability when cruelty is committed by the colonizer against a liminal other. These semantic and rhetorical configurations proclaim that there is no other violence but the violence committed by the culturally and racially circumscribed other. The failure of the new Orientalist discourse to entirely repress the other and the inability to respond to torture and bear its moral consequences cannot be dismissed or neutralized since such a denial generates a rejection of, and return to, mourning, which is continually resisted, masked and disavowed insofar as it hinges on melancholic underpinnings. The symbolic internalization and incorporation of the other during a melancholic trajectory of loss is often derailed by unconscious resentment and/or resistance. Theorists have noted that the process of cannibalism always fails in the melancholic incorporation of the other as a lost but indigestible object. In *Mémoires: For Paul de Man*, Jacques Derrida faces the impossibility of mourning and describes how the ego that refuses to mourn the friend's death turns instead to assimilate his remnants, unconsciously internalizing him and incorporating him into the self to protect and memorialize him. The other dies but lives in the recesses of the self. Derrida postulates that 'if death comes to the other, and comes to us through the other, then the friend no longer exists except *in* us, *between* us . . . . He lives only in us.'[48] Whether this devouring is induced by an unconscious turn or is part of an impossible mourning, the self cannot entirely digest the other's remnants, resulting in a failed cannibalism. Derrida acknowledges the inevitability of this cannibalistic move that attempts to interiorize and integrate the other but does not annihilate or obliterate him: 'We cannot cannibalize the other.'[49] This impossibility is imperative in installing an ethics of alterity.

Symbolic cannibalism threatens to perpetually reduce the other into the self-same relation in cultural politics. The mode of camouflaging violence and repeatedly turning away from addressing the scenes of horrific aggression and destruction in Iraq paradoxically entails a turn to figurative cannibalism. The displaced cruelty involves a drifting to another cannibalism that is cultural, an apt metaphor formulated by Luce Irigaray's conceptualization of self-other mediated relations.[50] Irigaray's notion of the unethical devouring of the other allows us to reconsider how the other – which characteristically has emerged through the rhetoric of war on terror barely consumed and never digested – construes homecoming as a spectral desire and fantasy. The violently cannibalized other is materialized into fetishistic cultural manifestations. Precisely because cannibalizing and interiorizing of the other is oftentimes unspoken, unsymbolized and suppressed, the other subsequently re-emerges to haunt us in a rather inverted way, in a space of cultural cannibalism, motivating a desire to devour the other's cultural attributes, music, artistic objects, exotic souvenirs, cuisine, language and so forth. In this way, denying violent acts primarily and ironically relies on the inevitability of cannibalism, a redevouring of the other after his injury or death. Deutscher insightfully traces this politics of nonappropriation: 'Cultural cannibalism,' to use Luce Irigaray's metaphor, is the unethical reduction of the other to the status of 'me' or 'mine,' rather than s/he to whom I make the address, s/he who addresses me, in the 'entre deux.'[51] Irigaray asserts: 'To you it constitutes an overture, to the other who is not and never will be mine.'[52] Irigaray calls into question cultural and political modes of subjectivity that continually inaugurate appropriation and cultural cannibalism. She cautions us about conventional relations with the other and calls for re-establishing new political and cultural programmes, beginning with a philosophical revision of 'the syntax of communication' demonstrated in her book's title: *I Love to You*.[53] A restructured object relation necessitates that the other should not occupy the direct or indirect object spatial and grammatical position in which the 'I' projects its intentional reflexivity and revolves around the objectified 'you.' This restructured communication does not hinge on power relations but emerges from conscious reciprocity and integrity.

What can be done to avoid the unethical relationship with the other in a political environment of cultural cannibalism, and how can we begin such a transformative approach to the politics of mediation? What ethical strategy would inaugurate nonappropriative self–other relations outside American neo-imperialist structures? Irigaray calls for anti-cannibalistic relationality through cultural, economic, legal and linguistic reform. This reform would engender a restructuring of the symbolic representation of difference and improve mediation between subjects. The relationship with the other must refrain from solipsistic and self-reflexive terrains marred by cultural cannibalism. An indefatigable critical reform of the cultural appropriation of the other is one way of installing an ethics of alterity.

Notes

1. Michelle Brown, ' "Setting the Conditions" for Abu Ghraib: The Prison Nation Abroad,' *American Quarterly* 57, no. 3 (2005), 981.
2. See Richard Sugg, 'Eating Your Enemy: Richard Sugg Searches History to Explain the Phenomenon of Aggressive Cannibalism, Following Recent Allegations from Iraq,' *History Today* 58, no. 7 (2008), 20.
3. Ibid.
4. See Dan Beaver, 'Flesh or Fantasy: Cannibalism and the Meanings of Violence,' *Ethnohistory* 49, no. 3 (2002), 671, 672.
5. Consider Susan Sontag, 'Regarding the Torture of Others: Notes on What Has Been Done – and Why – to Prisoners, by Americans,' *New York Times Sunday Magazine*, 23 May 2004, 26–7.
6. Steven H. Miles, *Oath Betrayed* (New York: Random House, 2006), 68.
7. Slavoj Žižek, *Organs Without Bodies* (London: Routledge, 2004), 174.
8. Graner made this statement 'in an April 2005 statement to the Army Criminal Investigation Command.' See Michael Scherer and Mark Benjamin, 'Other Government Agencies,' *The Abu Ghraib Files*, http://www.salon.com/news/abu_ghraib/2006/03/14/chapter_5/index.html
9. Cited in the psychological assessment in Karen J. Greenberg and Joshua L. Dratel, eds., *The Torture Papers: The Road to Abu Ghraib* (Cambridge: Cambridge University Press, 2005), 449.
10. Seymour Hersh, *Chain of Command: The Road from 9/11 to Abu Ghraib* (New York: HarperCollins, 2004), 44.
11. See Theodore Nadelson, *Trained to Kill: Soldiers at War* (Baltimore, MD: Johns Hopkins University Press, 2005), 133. Nadelson quotes H. Kurtz, 'Correspondents Chafe over Curb on News,' *Washington Post*, 26 January 1991.
12. See Elaine Scarry, *The Body in Pain* (Oxford: Oxford University Press, 1985), 61.
13. Jean Baudrillard, *The Spirit of Terrorism* (New York: Verso, 2002), 62.
14. See Brown, 'Setting the Conditions.'
15. Baudrillard, *Spirit of Terrorism*, 63.
16. This differs from the conventional European colonial discourse, which was preoccupied with the female body as a topos to be conquered and upon which the colonizer declares the Oriental's defeat. For example, Alloula presumes that the colonizer appropriates the female body to defeat the Algerian man. See Malek Alloula, *The Colonial Harem*, trans. Myrna Godzich and Wlad Godzich (Minneapolis, MN: University of Minnesota Press, 1986), 122.
17. Cary Wolfe, *Animal Rites* (Chicago: University of Chicago Press, 2003), 98; italics mine.

18. Miles, *Oath Betrayed*, 55. Also, all of the mentioned violations are documented in detainees' testimonies and in the investigation statements. See Greenberg and Dratel, *Torture Papers*, 416.
19. Slavoj Žižek, *The Metastases of Enjoyment: Six Essays on Women and Causality* (London: Verso, 1994), 55; italics in the original.
20. Greenberg and Dratel, *Torture Papers*, 505.
21. Professor Ali Shalal's testimony, 'The Man Behind the Hood,' presented to the War Crimes Commission on 19 February 2007, in Kuala Lumpur, Malaysia, presents a detailed account of the violations committed in the Abu Ghraib prison. See the full transcript of Shalal's testimony at Ali Shalal, 'Torture at Abu Ghraib: "The Man Behind the Hood,"' *Global Research*, 27 April 2009, http://www.globalresearch.ca/index.php?context=va&aid=13379
22. Ibid.
23. Miles, *Oath Betrayed*, 57.
24. Miles, *Oath Betrayed*, 56; italics mine.
25. Greenberg and Dratel, *Torture Papers*, 503.
26. Ibid.
27. See Shalal, 'Torture at Abu Ghraib.'
28. In fact, those who committed torture disguised their identity and used aliases. 'Who was in charge of Abu Ghraib – whether military police or military intelligence – was no longer the only question that mattered. Hardcore special operatives, some of them with aliases, were working in the prison.' See Seymour M. Hersh, 'The Coming Wars: What the Pentagon Can Now Do in Secret,' *The New Yorker*, 24 and 31 January 2005, http://www.newyorker.com/archive/2005/01/24/050124fa_fact
29. See 'Iraqi "Ghost Detainees" Could Number 100,' *Guardian Unlimited*, 10 September 2004, http://www.guardian.co.uk/international/story/0,,1301712,00.html
30. Recently the *New York Times* disclosed more information about secret prisons, torture and its 'architects.' See David Johnston and Mark Mazzetti, 'Interrogation Inc.: A Window into C.I.A.'s Embrace of Secret Jails,' *New York Times*, 13 August 2009, http://www.nytimes.com/2009/08/13/world/13foggo.html?ref=us. Also consider Scott Shane, 'Interrogation Inc.: 2 U.S. Architects of Harsh Tactics in 9/11's Wake,' *New York Times*, 12 August 2009, http://www.nytimes.com/2009/08/12/us/12psychs.html?_r=1&em
31. Kimberlè Williams Crenshaw, Richard Delgado, Charles R. Lawrence III and Mari J. Matsuda, *Words That Wound: Critical Race Theory, Assaultive Speech, and the First Amendment* (Boulder, CO: Westview Press, 1993), 67.
32. Judith Butler, *Excitable Speech: A Politics of the Performative* (London: Routledge, 1997), 4.
33. Butler, *Excitable Speech*, 5.
34. Butler, *Excitable Speech*, 104.
35. Butler, *Excitable Speech*, 107.
36. Sigmund Freud, *Totem and Taboo*, trans. James Strachey (New York: Norton, 1950), 35.
37. Hersh, 'The Coming Wars.'
38. H. A. R. Gibb, *Modern Trends in Islam* (Chicago: University of Chicago Press, 1947), 7; italics mine. A longer version of the quotation is cited by Said. See Said, *Orientalism*, 105–6.

39. Said, *Orientalism*, 106.
40. Said, *Orientalism*, 309.
41. Said, *Orientalism*, 107.
42. Miles, *Oath Betrayed*, 53.
43. Judith Butler, *Bodies That Matter* (London: Routledge, 1993), 18.
44. I am evoking Luce Irigaray's notion of cultural cannibalism, to which I will return later in this section. See Luce Irigaray, *I Love To You: Sketch for a Felicity Within History*, trans. Alison Martin (New York: Routledge, 1996).
45. Miles, *Oath Betrayed*, 23.
46. For example, 'Rumsfeld's explanation to the White House, the official added, was reassuring: "We've got a glitch in the program. We'll prosecute it". The cover story was that some kids got out of control.' See Hersh, 'The Coming Wars.'
47. Carol Mason 'examines the way U.S. media and government officials deflect criticism by deploying a hillbilly defense against accusations of American terror and military extremism.' See Carol Mason, 'The Hillbilly Defense: Culturally Mediating U.S. Terror at Home and Abroad,' *NWSA Journal* 17, no. 3 (2005), 39.
48. Jacques Derrida, *Mémoires: For Paul de Man*, trans. Cecile Lindsay, Jonathan Culler, Eduardo Cadava and Peggy Kamuf, ed. Avital Ronell and Eduardo Cadava (New York: Columbia University Press, 1989), 28.
49. See Penelope Deutscher, 'Mourning the Other, Cultural Cannibalism, and the Politics of Friendship (Jacques Derrida and Luce Irigaray),' *Differences: A Journal of Feminist Cultural Studies* 10, no. 3 (1998), 163.
50. See Irigaray, *I Love To You*. For Maggie Kilgour, imperialism is cultural cannibalism. See Maggie Kilgour, 'The Function of Cannibalism, at the Present Time,' in *Cannibalism and the Colonial World*, ed. Francis Barker, Peter Hulme, and Margaret Iversen (Cambridge: Cambridge University Press, 1998), 240–1.
51. Deutscher raises a valuable question: 'Does mourning involve a necessary cannibalism of the other since s/he is reduced to object of my memory?' Evidently, a process of incorporation takes place in mourning, a movement similar to cannibalism, but in order for the self to preserve the alterity of the other, this cannibalistic movement is impossible. See Deutscher, 'Mourning the Other,' 161.
52. See Irigaray, *I Love To You*, 117.
53. Irigaray, *I Love To You*, 113.

8
Confessions of a Dangerous (Arab) Mind

Andrea Teti

Introduction

A third of a century after the publication of Edward Said's *Orientalism* and after Michel Foucault's death, it is difficult to think of two intellectuals who have been more influential not just within their respective fields, but whose influence has travelled beyond the confines of their disciplines. The intellectual and personal relationship between Edward Said and Michel Foucault – particularly the former's assessment of the latter – has been the subject of a considerable amount of controversy, generated not least by Said himself. Said's very public disenchantment with Foucault's theoretical project and its political implications – in particular, Foucault's supposed unwillingness to translate 'insurrectionary scholarship' into political activism – has been the subject of much debate, not least because it resonates with much (mostly positivist) criticism of post-structuralism generally, and because it came from such a prominent figure, noted for both his contribution to post-positivist theory and for his activism on the Palestinian question. One would not be alone in finding this reading of Foucault's analysis and of his political practice questionable,[1] but the aim of this contribution will not be to offer yet another attempt to 'rule' over the dispute by arriving at a 'correct' interpretation of these two intellectuals' thought, not least because it attempts to take seriously warnings by both scholars concerning the political implications of ruling on 'truth.' Said and Foucault shared a concern for those moments in which power presented itself as natural and commonsensical, and in the idea of subjectivity – particularly the subjectivity of the Author(ity) – as a key moment through which the particular presents itself as universal, the subjective as objective. From this point of view, the very debate over what Foucault or Said 'really meant' and whether the invectives of the latter or the veiled comments of the former are 'justified' (that is speak the 'truth') about each other ends up falling into the trap of the Author(ity), the tricks of which both Said and Foucault sought to demystify.

Thus, after an initial review of the terrain of the debate between positions ascribed to Said and Foucault, this contribution will concentrate on points of convergence which might emerge from their respective texts. In doing so, the analysis offered will attempt to refrain from invoking one or the other (text) as authority, and disregard the question of whether these texts' authors would have agreed with either the interpretations offered or the uses to which texts and interpretations are put. Rather, this chapter will first draw parallels between Said's analysis of Orientalism as a discourse and, respectively, Foucault's analysis of confession as a discourse, the 'regime of truth,' and the political implications of such perspectives with particular attention to the relation between power, subjectivity and resistance. Broadly, the argument offered will be that reading Orientalism as a 'veridic discourse' and therefore as a 'regime of truth' makes it possible to highlight the operation of Orientalism as a confessional mechanism, which in turn affords a broad view of the contemporary politics of truth in which Orientalism plays such an important part. This raises the question of the relation between subjectivity, power and resistance within Orientalist discursive contexts – what Foucault might have called the strategic function(s) of this kind of 'veridic discourse' – where a confessional perspective affords purchase both on the formation of subjectivities and the possibilities of resistance, both of which Said's own analysis is often said to lack.[2] In sketching a Foucaultian development of the analysis of Orientalism, this article hopes to contribute not only a theory of resistance compatible with Said's analysis, but also to help understand the processes through which it 'manages and even produces' the Orient.

Birth of a Cottage Industry

Said famously acknowledges Foucault's influence on *Orientalism*[3] in the form of a tribute to the idea of 'discourse' in *The Archaeology of Knowledge* and in *Discipline and Punish* as well as Foucault's development of other concepts essential to his own analysis such as archaeology, genealogy and the archive. One of the reasons for Said's increasing distance from Foucault was, in Said's own estimation, connected to political differences on Palestine.[4] From his participation in a spring 1979 seminar held at Foucault's house – but organized by Sartre and de Beauvoir – on the Arab world, Said perceives Foucault as 'strongly pro-Israel.'[5] However, the account of the seminar remains patchy, and elsewhere Said himself is tentative about claiming Foucault was indeed pro-Israeli.[6] Thus, rather than providing evidence to support conclusions on Foucault's position, Said's recollection is valuable as an account of what led him to perceive political distance from Foucault – and this is valuable insofar as it helps explain the analytical distance Said tries to put between himself and Foucault.

There is a second dimension of Said's political distance from Foucault, namely what Said takes to be the passive, uncritical and apolitical stance adopted by most of those who follow French theorists such as Foucault and Derrida down the post-structuralist path. Focusing on deconstruction and understanding the machinery of power alone, had – in Said's estimation – led to a kind of moral nihilism and political passivity neutralizing the political potential of the role of the intellectual in critiquing power. Said famously accused these theorists of turning literary theory into a mostly academic exercise retreating 'into a labyrinth of "textuality," dragging along with it the most recent apostles of European revolutionary textuality – Derrida and Foucault – whose trans-Atlantic canonization and domestication they themselves seemed to be encouraging.'[7] Said also attacks Foucault for supposedly taking 'a curiously passive and sterile view not so much of the uses of power, but of how and why power is gained, used, and held onto'[8] to the point that he became 'uninterested in any direct political involvement of any sort.'[9] The sad result, Said claims, is that the question of a theory of power 'has captivated not only Foucault himself but many of his readers,' and its principal effect has been to is to 'justify political quietism with sophisticated intellectualism.'[10] Moreover, Said suggests that by 'ignoring the imperial context of his own theories, Foucault seems actually to represent an irresistible colonizing movement that paradoxically fortifies the prestige of both the lonely individual scholar and the system that contains him.'[11]

Finally, Said claims there are purely analytical differences between him and Foucault, arguing that while Foucault remains a structuralist at heart, his own work is informed by a humanism which allows for the possibility of (successful) resistance against power.[12] For Said's Foucault, 'everything is an aspect of the process of the carceral society,'[13] a 'conception [which] has drawn a circle around itself, constituting a unique territory in which Foucault has imprisoned himself and others with him'[14] with the end result that, rather than a champion of resistance to power, Foucault became 'the scribe of domination.'[15] By contrast, Said claims that – thanks also to the influence of E. P. Thompson's *The Making of the English Working Class* – he himself moved beyond the idea that society could be reduced to 'just the smooth working out of a massive system of domination,' emphasizing that he 'separated from Foucault at that point.'[16]

The 'accusation' that Foucault was obsessed with power and that his work denies the possibility of resistance was one Said was partly responsible for popularizing. Aside from fact that some have pointed out the lack of a theory of resistance in Said's own work,[17] there is plenty of evidence that Foucault never intended his work to be interpreted this way and, more importantly, that it need not be interpreted this way, as the following section will show. In response to a question about his alleged nihilism and determinism, however, Foucault said he was 'astounded to learn that people could have seen the affirmation of an inescapable determinism in my historical studies,' claiming that his work aimed to emphasize precisely the opposite, the contingency and immanence of social structures.[18]

For this reason, when Said claims he is not arguing 'that Orientalism unilaterally determines what can be said about the Orient, but that it is the whole network of interests inevitably brought to bear on (and therefore always involved in) any occasion when that peculiar entity "the Orient" is in question'[19] one might hear more than an echo of Foucault's argument that 'power relations are mobile relations, that is, they may become modified, they are not given once and for all'[20] and, beyond this, that 'in relations of power, there is necessarily a possibility of resistance, because if there were no possibility of resistance – of a violent resistance, of flight, of ruse, of strategies that invert the situation – , there would be no power relations at all.'[21]

Said's representation of the analytical distance between him and Foucault is problematic on two levels: first, as a claim about this supposed difference itself, and secondly in terms of the tensions it raises in Said's own position. The first claim can be disputed not only on the kind of grounds outlined above – based on claims explicitly made by Foucault for and in his own work – but also on the basis of the elements of convergence which will be described below. The issue of Said's internal (in)consistency is one which he was aware of and defended, arguing that it was entirely intended.[22] For present purposes, the most important aspect of this inconsistency both analytically and politically is that Said at times relies on the idea that discourses are 'artificial,' violating the truth of a reality beyond discourse, and at other times berating those, like Foucault, who follow through the implications of this position on the constructedness of representations and therefore of identities to the logical conclusion that there is no ontologically fixed fundamental truth about the social. This is in spite of Said's suggestion of precisely such an ontological mutability in his claim that such artificial representations 'manage – and even *produce* – the Orient.'[23] It is not just, as Kennedy puts it, that Said alternates 'between the idea that true representation is theoretically possible and the opposite position that all representation is necessarily misrepresentation,'[24] but that there seems to be an unresolved but analytically and politically crucial tension over the relationship between representation and ontology at the heart of Said's work on Orientalism. It is precisely in relation to this tension that a different reading of Foucault could have been useful.

Orientalism as a 'Regime of Truth'

It is unfortunate that Said did not draw on Foucault's work on the 'regime of truth' and on the specific mechanism of confession. For all Said's criticism of Foucault, there are striking parallels between Said's texts on Orientalism and Foucault's on the relation between knowledge, truth and power. It is regrettable that certain misunderstandings and a (perceived) political differences on the question of Palestine prevented Said from greater engagement with what Foucault was writing at very time his own analysis of Orientalism was taking shape.

Two passages of an interview given by Foucault on the relationship between truth and power provide an excellent introduction to the paradigm he offers to think about their interrelation, and display a considerable resemblance to Said's own work definition of Orientalism. The first passage points out the status of truth and the political implications of such claims. Here, for a discourse, the claim to tell the truth about its object is the lynchpin of a whole network of relations of power:

> [B]y truth I do not mean 'the ensemble of truths which are to be discovered and accepted,' but rather 'the ensemble of rules according to which the true and the false are separated and specific effects of power are attached to the true' [...] it's a matter not of a battle 'on behalf' of truth, but of a battle around the status of truth and the economic and political role it plays. [...] 'Truth' is to be understood as a system of ordered procedures for the production, regulation, distribution, circulation, and operation of statements. 'Truth' is linked in a circular relation with the systems of power which produce and

sustain it, and to effects of power which induces and extends it. A 'regime' of truth.[25]

Nearly simultaneously, Said variously defines Orientalism as:

- the corporate institution for dealing with the Orient [...] by making statements about it, authorizing views on it [...] teaching it, settling it, ruling over it;[26]
- a style of thought based upon an ontological and epistemological distinction made between 'the Orient' and (most of the time) 'the Occident'[27];
- a way of coming to terms with the Orient that is based on the Orient's special place in European Western experience,[28] [which is]
- particularly valuable as a sign of European-Atlantic power over the Orient [because it is] a *veridic discourse* about the Orient.[29]

Orientalism's power as a discourse lies in its ability to claim that it is not *a* truth, but *the* truth about the Orient. This claim to veridiction is essential in Said's argument that Orientalism is 'a Western style for dominating, restructuring, and having authority over the Orient.'[30]

Reading these statements side by side, it does not seem a stretch to argue that these perspectives are fundamentally compatible, both in their analysis of the politics of truth-telling, and in its entanglements with power, and therefore in its political implications. In both cases discourses on truth are 'veridic' because they supply 'rules according to which the true and the false are separated.' In both cases, this veridiction is produced by identifiable mechanisms (Said's 'corporate institution' or Foucault's 'systems of power') and produces 'effects of power' (political, economic and so on) by 'authorizing views' but also 'inducing and extending' this power, enabling it to teach, settle, and rule, and essentially establish the conditions for its own (re)production. Moreover, in both cases these discourses of truth have political functions/effects precisely because they present themselves as *the* truth about a particular subject. The contexts in which these veridic discourses emerge, the forms they take and the effects they have – not least in their own reproduction – suggest that both are 'linked in a circular relation' with power. Indeed, if one followed each recurrence of 'truth' in Foucault's definition with the phrase 'about the Orient,' one might easily imagine the statement having been written about Orientalism.

A second resemblance between these texts can be found in relation to the underpinnings of truth-telling/-claiming discourses, specifically in the political economy of truth-production. Said calls Orientalism a 'corporate institution' which promotes a 'style of thought.' This resonates closely with Foucault's approach to truth as the result of a particular political economy. While it is the case, as Bové points out, that Said did not acknowledge Foucault's work on the regime of truth,[31] there is ample space for convergence on the (re)productive nature of the relationship between power, knowledge and truth. Foucault's analysis presents the discursive realm of a regime of truth as inextricable from a political economy:

> In societies like ours, the 'political economy' of truth is characterized by five important traits. 'Truth' is centred on the form of scientific discourse and the institutions which produce it; it is subject to constant economic and political incitement (the demand for truth, as much for economic production as for political power); it is the object, under diverse forms, of immense diffusion and consumption (circulating through apparatuses of education and information whose extent is relatively broad in the social body, notwithstanding certain strict limitations); it is produced and transmitted under the control, dominant if not exclusive, of a few great political and economic apparatuses (university, army, writing, media); lastly, it is the issue of a whole political debate and social confrontation ('ideological' struggles).[32]

Said's famous definition of Orientalism as the 'the *corporate institution* for dealing with the Orient [...] by making statements about it, authorizing views on it [...] teaching it, settling it, ruling over it,'[33] 'dominating, restructuring, and having authority over [it]'[34] and his claim that such a discourse has the effect/power to 'manage – and *even produce* – the Orient politically, sociologically, militarily, ideologically, scientifically, and imaginatively'[35] provide more than just a hint at a truth-producing framework underpinning this 'style of thought' that is much like Foucault's claims about the political economy of (the (re)production of) truth. Said's text certainly appears compatible with the view of Orientalist discourse as 'linked in a circular relation with the systems of power which produce and sustain it, and to effects of power which induces and extends it.'[36] Indeed, replacing 'truth' with 'Orientalism' in Foucault's passage above yields a surprisingly familiar image of Orientalism, and would pre-figure later analyses of neo-Orientalism.[37]

Confessions of a Dangerous (Arab) Mind

Foucaultian regimes of truth and Saidian veridic discourses therefore seem to have more than a little in common. This begs the question of what *kind* of regime of truth Orientalism might be. Here another tool developed by Foucault – confession – may shed some light.

Foucault's analysis of confessional discourse[38] identifies a mechanism in which a certain number of steps are discernible: first, a canon of normality is established (the state of sinlessness) as the goal to which all individuals ought to aspire (emancipatory project); second, a force is identified which leads all individuals to deviate from that norm (sinfulness); third, a framework is put in place to redeem sinners and achieve emancipation (confession). In this mechanism, two subject positions are clearly identifiable – the confessor and the sinner – as well as a number of 'effects of power,' ranging from the hierarchical relation of authority between sinner and confessor to the way 'knowledge' is produced and the consequences of accepting or resisting this framework.

Confession works first and foremost by establishing a canon of 'normality' – and therefore of deviance and pathology – through what Foucault calls a 'specification of individuals': the Sinner is marked by sinfulness (deviance), while the Confessor is gatekeeper to the state of grace (the norm). In the confession manuals Foucault analyses, sin is presented as an ever-present force driving individuals to fall from grace (that is, to deviate from the norm, especially through sexuality). On the one hand, therefore, individuals are provided with a goal to which to aspire and it is enjoined upon them to redeem themselves. On the other hand, they are defined as having an intrinsic force within them that inevitably leads to a fall from grace.

Orientalist discourse operates in much the same way. Through its depiction of the West's Other, Orientalism presents a particular narrative of Western Selfhood as well as of the Arab-Islamic Other. These two subject positions display properties strikingly similar to those of Sinner and Confessor in confessional discourse: the cultural essentialism which marks out Arab-Islamic alterity as fundamentally and dangerously deviant closely mirrors the construction of sin and deviant pathology in Foucault's text. Specifically, the Arab-Islamic Other is presented as not accidentally, but inherently deviant (by its nature authoritarian, irrational, religious, stagnant and so on) while the Western Self is presented as the objective to which to aspire (egalitarian, rational, secular, advanced and so on).[39] The texts Foucault examines present the causality of deviance as diffuse, latent, polymorphous and inextinguishable. When Said shows how Orientalist discourse attributes precisely these characteristics to the Oriental Other – for example tropes around trustworthiness and rationality – it is difficult not to hear Foucault describing the pathology buried deep in the Sinner's nature as 'obscure,' 'elusive by nature (*il est de sa nature d'échapper*); its energy and its mechanisms escaped observation (*se dérobent*)'[40] such that 'its causal power was partly clandestine.'[41]

There are several 'effects of power' that flow from the articulation of the Occident–Orient relation in this 'confessional' way. Here, it is important to emphasize the similarity in the way truth is defined and produced in these discourses, namely through what Foucault calls the 'method of interpretation.' The way what counts as 'truth' – about subjectivities, about their (respective) goals and relations – is produced is crucial for reasons readily apparent from both Said's and Foucault's texts. Primarily, these discourses are explicitly given the remit of 'telling the truth' about their respective domains, not least because this truth is vital to the greater objective of emancipation (that is of normalizing deviance). Since alterity is defined as inherently deviant from the outset, however, the game is rigged. Emancipation is framed in connection with cognate discourses about Civilization, Progress, Modernization, Democratization and so on. But this convergence between emancipatory and essentialist dimensions creates a truth which, so long as the underpinnings of that discursive framework remain unchallenged, entraps the Other, condemning it to never fully achieving the emancipatory task it is set. After all, if the 'Arab Mind' is by its nature incapable of enlightened rational thought or if 'Islam is incompatible with democracy,' then no matter how far an individual or a society might 'progress,' they are inevitably doomed to fail. Whether the Other 'accepts' the terms of this rigged 'game' – and therefore admits an 'original sin' which by definition it can never transcend and accepts the Western/Normal Self's authority – or whether it rejects it altogether, thereby opening itself to the 'legitimate' application of discipline, these discourses inevitably discipline the Other.

This (re)presentation of the Oriental Other's nature as inherently deviant – a dissimulated, dangerous and inescapable causality – has several important implications. Specifically, the latent nature of Orientalist Islam's causality elicits the need for *constant, endless* and *ubiquitous* surveillance.[42] As with the sinfulness of sexuality in confession, the 'passional impulses' built into the very nature of the Oriental Other might manifest themselves at any time and in any place: society and its political agents must be constantly monitored for even the slightest hint that such dangers might manifest. As a source of not simply contingent but of pathological deviation, Arab-Islamic alterity thus becomes a 'police' matter, 'not something one simply judged, [but] a thing one administered, [...] regulated for the good of all.'[43] The risk posed by Islam's latent causality thus transforms the specification of the (Western) Norm into a 'grid' – provided by Orientalism's classical motifs described above – identifying possible kinds of deviation and the sites at which these might manifest. As a result, the supposedly neutral and objective taxonomy of a machinery of observation transubstantiates into lines of penetration established all around the Arab-Islamic Other's body politic, into a taxonomy of surveillance. While the avowed aim of this surveillance is to prevent and neutralize deviation and more generally to bring about the 'reformation' of the deviant Other, this can never, of course, be achieved given the nature of alterity as pathological by assumption. This combination of an avowedly emancipatory/reformatory aim and a latent, polymorphous and deviant causality transforms Orientalism into a *carceral space*, the fundamental function of which is to govern the Other by framing its purpose as emancipation – *re*formation – on this confessional discourse's own terms, and by disciplining its (inevitable) failures.

One function of confessional discourse's 'carceral' property is the application of discipline, and as Said's analysis claims, one of Orientalism's central functions is precisely to authorize views which make it possible to settle and rule over the Orient. In confessional discourse, the qualitative discrimination between normal and pathological and between Self and Other is central to the legitimization of disciplinary interventions upon the Other. As Foucault argues: 'there where one finds a society of normalization, there where one finds a power which is [...] in the first instance [...] a bio-power [...] racism is indispensable as a condition in order to be able to put someone to death.'[44] Here, 'racism' can be read in a straightforward literal sense, but also metaphorically, as pathology: confessional discourses legitimize the application of discipline against the Other by recourse to its essential – and essentially threatening – alterity, clearly mirroring the way Said sees Orientalist discourse as operating. Just like it is the ontological character of sexuality in itself which presents a permanent and existential threat to the purity – and therefore the eternal life – of the soul, the Oriental Other in general and the Arab-Islamic Other in particular are representations not simply of contingent difference with Western Selfhood – although this it is this dimension which has increasingly been emphasized, not least since Said's critique – but of ontological irreconcilability. Both sex and Otherness need first to be framed as expressions of the pathological, and only then can disciplinary inter-ventions against them be justified: once they come to be understood as pathological, they also become the target for 'corrective' or at least pro-tective practices. Paraphrasing Said: once it becomes possible to make statements about and authorize views on this Other based on its special place in the Western Self's imagination, it also becomes possible to rule over it.[45]

Moreover, this play of alterity and discipline is intimately involved in the (re)production of identities at an ontological level. It is important to note that the confessional structure of this discourse not only inserts bodies (politic) into a dynamic which authorizes the exercise of discipline by upon the Orient, but tends to (re)produce (Oriental) failures (in civilizing, modernizing, democratizing and so on). Just as for Orientalism in Said, the continued existence of such a radical – and radically dangerous – Other has a precise function. While on a superficial reading, disciplinary intervention is aimed at eliminating the threat to the body (politic) which comes from such pathology, on another more fundamental level its existence, alterity and danger are inextricable from the process by which the 'normal' Self can establish its own identity. From this vantage point, conversely, it also becomes clear that Orientalism's imperialist impulse is not simply subservient to a gratuitous desire to colonize, but, as Said noted elsewhere, is woven closely into the processes whereby Western cultures formulate their own identities. These are precisely the implications of Said's emphasis on 'the Orient's special place in European Western experience.'[46]

Perhaps even more significantly, in the way that it produces 'truth,' Orientalism like Confession disenfranchises the (deviant) Other from shaping the truth of its own condition. The Other is placed in a position in which it is unable to authorize a different account of itself – for example, reconciling democracy and Islam, or different visions of modernity – without falling foul of the discourse's canons of 'normality' and therefore laying itself open to 'corrective' disciplinary intervention. Indeed, the role of the Oriental Other, as of the Sinner, is to confess its deviations to the Occidental Self, whose task it is to then adjudicate on the Other's nature. As Foucault observes:

[t]ruth did not reside solely in the [confessing] subject [...] It was constituted in two stages: present but incomplete, blind to itself, in the one who spoke; it could only reach completion in the one who assimilated and recorded it [...]. [T]he revelation of confession had to be coupled with the decipherment of what it said.[47]

This decipherment could only be carried out by a subject in the Confessor's position: for Orientalism, the position of ('Western') emancipation.

It is important to note that in this process not only is truth being produced by a particular subject position, but that there are two truths which are being produced symbiotically. The Other must

> speak the truth (but since it is the secret and is oblivious to its own nature, we reserve for ourselves the function of telling the truth of its truth, revealed and deciphered at last) and we demand that it tell us [...] that truth about ourselves which we [the 'emancipated' Self] think we already possess in our immediate consciousness.[48]

It is in this sense that Orientalism, like Confession, is a 'style for dominating, restructuring, and having authority over' *both* the Self and the Other, a discourse which must 'manage – and even produce'[49] them both simultaneously, a 'corporate institution' which produces a whole range of inextricably linked subjectivities 'by making statements about them, authorizing views on them, settling them, and ruling over them.'[50]

Subjectivity, Power and Resistance

Thinking about Orientalism as a confessional discourse also affords purchase on the role, possibilities and obstacles to resistance against Orientalism itself, helping to formulate that conceptualization of resistance Said is accused of lacking.

If the analogy between the operation of Orientalism and Foucault's analysis of confession is correct, it can be extended to the role of the latter as a 'machinery of incitement,' an analytical grid whose effect is not limited to simply describing nor even disciplining its object's 'deviance,' but extends to actually generating it. From this point of view, Orientalism's confessional configuration in itself generates the subject position of power, but it also produces its counterpart in the form of subjectivities which occupy the position of resistance, if in no other form than deviation from the canonical goals set by Orientalist discourse.

In Foucault's analysis, confession was the lynchpin of the particular configuration of power relations because it was inextricable from the production of certain subjectivities. As outlined above, these subjectivities are clustered around two positions, that of the Normal Self (the Occident), and that of the Deviant Other (the Orient). Two categories of subjectivities can be discerned with respect to the latter: one which attempts to achieve the emancipatory task it is set within the framework, the other which resists this role.

Today, liberal interventionism perhaps best exemplifies the attempt by the Normal Self to produce a subjectivity for the Other in its own image. These interventions take on a range of forms, for example seeking to reform target populations by 'providing a positive example, through the promotion of market democracy via trade, aid, cultural and political exchange – or the withdrawal of these [...] – right up to coercive intervention and statebuilding.'[51] Despite protestations to the contrary, these were the characteristics of Western governments' democracy-promotion programmes – those very programmes whose failure was so starkly highlighted by the 'Arab Spring.'[52]

But most revealingly, from the standpoint of the normal Self in a confessional framework, policy failures, from 'minimalist' interventions by cultural example or financial enticement, all the way to 'maximalist' state-building or 'liberal intervention,' 'must be put down [...] to shortcomings in other areas,' exempting either the Western Self or the framework itself from any responsibility.[53] Instead of a critical re-examination, the paradoxical result is to produce an imperative to *'change the target culture right up to the reconstruction of every individual in society.'*[54] This is precisely the aim of a whole range of discourses cognate to Orientalism, from Civilization to Modernization, and from Development and Democratization to 'good governance.' Indeed, one could argue that it is precisely the attempt to 'change the target culture right up to the reconstruction of every individual' which lies at the heart of attempts to promote democracy in the Middle East or to 'integrate' European Muslims (for example, the debate over *hijab* or 'European Islam').

But a confessional discursive configuration also produces a second kind of subjectivity which resists the application of the framework itself. In relation to sexuality, a key source of pathological deviance for the literature he examines, Foucault argues that 'the dissemination and reinforcement of heterogeneous sexualities [is] linked together with the help of the central element of confession that compels individuals to articulate their sexual peculiarity.'[55] This is not simply a 'weak hypothesis' that diverse sexualities are pre-existing and that a disciplinary grid is imposed upon them, redefining them as 'deviant' behaviours to be disciplined in order to 'normalize' them, but rather a 'strong hypothesis' that these sexualities are produced not least by and through the observational framework itself. In other words, in this process of observation, Othering and disciplining, the supposedly transparent framework within which the Other is conceived of shifts from being an external and neutral taxonomical grid to becoming an instrument of scrutiny and therefore of production. But because alterity as defined in this discourse is fundamentally pathological, frameworks of observation also come to act as *devices of saturation*, seeking out alterity in the most minute details of an individual's or a society's practices in what becomes a kind of self-fulfilling prophecy. In so doing, the taxonomical structure of such nominally neutral frameworks comes to operate as *lines of penetration*, lines along which failure to fulfil expectations legitimizes disciplining the deviant Other. However, insofar as they are channels for the administration of discipline, these lines of penetration also become sites of resistance, and in so doing help engender the very dangerous alterity they avowedly seek to neutralize.

Analogously, for Orientalism, the 'grid of observation' built around the motifs of Western Selfhood and transposed into the categories and analytical taxonomies of Orientalism and its cognate frameworks – Civilization, Modernization, Democratization and so on – becomes a grid through which the Western Self can police its Oriental Other to detect any potentially dangerous 'deviance.' This grid legitimizes disciplinary interventions in order to 'inoculate' both Oriental and Western bodies politic against pathological deviance, but also simultaneously continuously (re)generating that deviance. This standpoint offers the possibility of a coherent reading not just of Orientalism *per se*, but also of the interplay between 'Western' and 'Eastern' discourses, both between 'West' and 'Middle East,' and in the complexities of political debates in postcolonial Arab states – in relation, for example, to nationalism, (neo- and cultural) imperialism, religion, democracy, Islam and ultimately modernity. In this sense, a Foucaultian development of the analysis of Orientalism furnishes not only a theory of resistance, but also helps understand the processes through which it 'manages and even produces' the Orient, not least 'imaginatively.' If Orientalism as a discourse displays confessional properties, and if it can be shown to operate as a machinery of incitement, resistance is far from impossible: it is inevitable. An Orientalist discursive formation produces the very alterity which Normal Selfhood finds threatening and aims to eliminate, and in legitimizing disciplinary interventions against this alterity, it both attempts to eliminate that alterity and facilitates its reproduction.

What a confessional perspective also affords is the sophistication to differentiate between difference *kinds* of resistance. Foucault has been accused – not least by Said himself – of underplaying resistance, even as a possibility. He certainly appeared conservative about the possibilities of resistance in another famous exchange, the 1971 debate with Noam Chomsky.[56] Yet while Foucault's writing is certainly concerned with the way power operated to shape subjectivity – 'processes of subjectivation' which make individuals into subjects 'in both senses of the word' – he also analysed 'heterotopias,'[57] spaces in which other identities and social organizations are possible, and where there is no single hegemonic power. These are spaces of resistance, or more precisely spaces in which alternatives to hegemonic power configurations can be thought, and from which challenges might be brought. Indeed, Foucault berates political and legal theory precisely because for all its critiques of monarchy and absolutism, it has not yet 'cut off the king's head.'[58] They have not been radical enough: they still conceive politics in terms of sovereign power, and in doing so are deemed to reproduce their flaws by another name.

Foucault's texts therefore pose the problem of 'genuine' resistance and alternatives to power, offering a lens through which to interrogate resistance but without foreclosing its possibility. A confessional perspective suggests caution about the intrinsic merits of any resistance, but also allows one to ask whether a particular form resistance has the potential to effect (structural) change by subverting the power configuration within which it occurs, or whether it ends up reproducing that configuration in a different guise. This is a point on which many political opponents would agree, from notable currents of Islamist thought for which Western cultural imperialism includes ideas such as secularism and nationalism, to conservative theorists of 'polyarchic' democracy.[59]

Finally, it should be noted that Foucault's analysis of confession includes a point made in the margins but which is of fundamental importance, not least in the case of Orientalism, namely the observation that occupying the position of the Confessor or the Sinner, the normal or the deviant, is inextricable from pleasure(s): the pleasure of exercising power, or of rebelling. Here the use of psychoanalytic theoretical perspectives suggests itself to reflect on both the pleasures and desires of power/resistance, and on resistance as rupture of the confessional organization of power. The latter also suggests a second sense in which resistance can be thought, that is not just as opposition to the Confessional hierarchy – after all, resistance in those terms can serve, through the legitimate invocation of discipline, to reinforce the confessional organization of power – but of undoing that form of power in its entirety. In this sense, the confessional economy of power provides a 'structural' criterion through which to measure the success of any change.

Conclusions

The distance Said placed between his work and Foucault's is well known, but the potential for convergence contained in their respective work is too great to ignore. In particular, this contribution has offered a perspective on Said's *Orientalism* from the standpoint of the mechanism of Foucault's analysis of confession. Ultimately, both can be read as an organization of subjectivities around two opposed subject positions – one, the Normal Self, the second an inherently Deviant Other – such that the discourses which give rise to this organization superficially provide a pathway for the Other to eliminate its deviance while making that emancipatory trajectory ultimately impossible.

There are many issues which in this context could only be hinted at – such as the role of desire and pleasure in the formation and play of confessional and Orientalist subjectivities – while others could not be broached at all, from the idea of the dispositive to governmentality, to the proper topography of a 'confessional Orientalism.' This analysis also comes with important caveats. First, it does not and cannot claim that the politics of Orientalist discourse(s) – particularly its 'social scientific turn' or its post-9/11 securitization – are *exhausted* by their confessional dimensions, nor inevitably bound to these. On the contrary, they are embedded far broader politics of spectacles, simulations and (il)liberalisms. Moreover, the confessional logic sketched above does not apply equally to all discourses articulating relations between the 'West' and all its Others, a difference which itself begs attention. Nor, finally, does this analysis tackle the crucial question of the nexus formed by the study of 'political transitions' – modernization, development, democratization and so on – and the political economies underpinning these truth-telling machineries. However, reading Orientalism as a confessional discourse affords purchase on a series of issues in Said's approach, including a theory of resistance, the interplay between power and resistance, and criteria through which to assess the nature of change.

The 'confessional' organization of such discourses and subjectivities also raises questions, such as the reason for this kind of configuration to exist at all. In relation to governmental power, Foucault retrieves one of the original meanings of economy, *oikonomia*, organization fit for a particular purpose. Given its resilience in the face of a third of a century of post-Orientalist scholarship, one might well ask what the particular purpose of Orientalist discourse is. One answer is provided by Said himself in terms of the political functionality of Orientalism in legitimizing, in both its classical and social scientific guises, a whole series of exercises of power. A fragment from Foucault's Preface to *History of Madness*, read from a confessional standpoint, provides perhaps a more radical suggestion:

> In the universality of Western Reason [*ratio*], there is a split [*partage*] which is the Orient: the Orient thought of as origin, dreamt of as the vertiginous point from which are born nostalgias and promises of a return, the Orient offered to the West's colonizing reason yet indefinitely inaccessible, because it remains [*demeure*] forever the limit: night of the beginning in which the West formed itself but in which it drew a dividing line [*ligne de partage*], the Orient is everything for it that it is not, notwithstanding which it still must seek its own original [*primitive*] truth in it.[60]

My thanks go to Ziad Elmarsafy, Anna Bernard and Andrea Mura for comments on earlier drafts. This chapter is based on an article published in *Foucault Studies*.

Notes

1. For example, Paul A. Bové, 'Intellectuals at War: Michel Foucault and the Analytics of Power,' *SubStance* 11, no. 4 (1982–3), 36–55.
2. For example, Robert Young, *White Mythologies: Writing History and the West* (London and New York: Routledge, 1990); Aijaz Ahmed, *In Theory: Classes, Nations, Literatures* (London: Verso, 1992); William Ashcroft and Pal Ahluwalia, *Edward Said*, 2nd edn (London: Routledge, 2009), 65–7.
3. Edward W. Said, *Orientalism* (London: Penguin, 2003), 3.
4. It is, however, clear that the tensions between Said's work and Foucault's – particularly the implications of the latter's for the former's run far deeper than such a disagreement, however important. For a sustained analysis of the politics of Said's and Foucault's respective positions, see Bové, 'Intellectuals at War.'
5. Said reported becoming disenchanted with the couple because they 'knew nothing about the Arab world and were both fantastically pro-Israel' in *Interviews with Edward Said*, eds., Amritjit Singh and B. G. Johnson (Jackson: Mississippi University Press, 2004), 75, and then recounts the famously pro-Palestinian Gilles Deleuze telling him of a disagreement between him and

Foucault on the question of Palestine (what about we do not know), infer-
ring Foucault was pro-Israeli and had wanted to avoid the topic with Said for
this reason. As Racevkis points out, however, Foucault's views on the Israel
were far from one-sided. In a 1982 interview, he condemned the massacre of
Palestinians in the camps of Sabra and Shatila which the IDF were responsible for allowing it to happen, expressing distrust in both Menachem Begin
and Yasser Arafat. Michel Foucault, *Dits et écrits*, vol. I–II (Paris: Gallimard,
2001), 1168.
6. See Said, *Diary*, for his account of the meeting and a response to criticisms.
7. Said, *The World, the Text, and the Critic* (Cambridge: Harvard University Press,
1983), 3. Offering a diagnosis of the ills of contemporary literary criticism,
Said finds that 'our critical ethos is formed by a pernicious analytic of blind
demarcation by which, for example, imagination is separated from thought,
culture from power, history from form, texts from everything that is *hors
texte*, and so forth' (*The World, the Text*, 169). 'What puzzles me is not only
how someone as remarkably brilliant as Foucault could have arrived at so
impoverished and masochistically informed a vision of sound and silence,
but also how so many readers in Europe and the United States have routinely
accepted it as anything more than an intensely private, deeply eccentric,
and insular version of history.' Said, *Reflections on Exile and Other Literary and
Cultural Essays* (London: Granta, 2000), 523.
8. Said, *The World, the Text*, 221.
9. Said, *Power, Politics and Culture* (New York: Vintage Books, 2001), 77.
10. Said, *The World, the Text*, 245. It ought to be pointed out that Foucault always
resisted formulating a theory of power, but rather focused on providing tools
for an analytic of power, arguing that 'theories' of power were inextricably involved in the (re)production of particular forms of political order in
the first place. For example, Michel Foucault, *History of Sexuality, Vol. 1: The
Will to Knowledge* (London: Penguin, 1998), 82–3; Said, *Interviews with Edward
Said*, eds. A. Singh and B. G. Johnson (Jackson: Mississippi University Press,
2004), 63.
11. Said, *Culture and Imperialism* (London: Vintage, 1993), 278.
12. '[U]nlike Michel Foucault [...] I do believe in the determining imprint
of individual writers upon the otherwise anonymous collective body
of text constituting a discursive formation like Orientalism' (Said,
Orientalism, 23).
13. Said, *The World, the Text*, 65.
14. Said, *The World, the Text*, 245.
15. Said, *The World, the Text*, 138.
16. *Interviews with Edward Said*, 101.
17. Citing *White Mythologies* and *In Theory*, Ashcroft argues that 'for all his
dissenting analysis of Western discourse, Said has no theory of resistance'
(Ashcroft and Ahluwalia, *Edward Said*, 65).
18. Foucault, *Dits et écrits*, 693.
19. Said, *Orientalism*, 3.
20. Foucault, *Dits et écrits*, 720.
21. Ibid. For an overview of the debate concerning Said's misappropriation of
Foucault, see Ashcroft and Ahluwalia, *Edward Said*; Young, *White Mythologies*;
James Clifford, *The Predicament of Culture: Twentieth Century Ethnography*,

Literature, and Art (Cambridge, MA: Harvard University Press, 1988) and Ahmad, *In Theory.*

22. Said claims he 'designed [Orientalism's theoretical inconsistency] that way' (Said, *Criticism*, 137) to challenge 'the sovereignty of the systematic method' (*Orientalism*, 673) and to develop a notion of non-coercive knowledge 'which was deliberately anti-Foucault' (Said, 'Edward Said,' in *Criticism in Society*, ed. Imre Salusinszky, 123–48 (New York and London: Methuen, 1987), 137). This again suggests a problematic understanding of Foucault's approach to ontology, truth, and to the relation between theory and power.

23. Said, *Orientalism*, 3. Emphasis added.

24. Valerie Kennedy, *Edward Said: A Critical Introduction* (Oxford: Polity, 2000), 29.

25. Foucault as cited in *The Foucault Reader* ed. Paul Rabinow (London: Penguin, 1991), 74.

26. Said, *Orientalism*, 2.

27. Ibid.

28. Said, *Orientalism*, 1.

29. Said, *Orientalism*, 6; emphasis added.

30. Said, *Orientalism*, 3.

31. Bové, 'Intellectuals at War.'

32. Foucault, *Reader*, 73.

33. Said, *Orientalism*, 2; emphasis added.

34. Said, *Orientalism*, 3.

35. Said, *Orientalism*, 3; emphasis added. Elsewhere in *Orientalism*, Said writes ' "the Orient" is itself a constituted entity, and the notion that there are geographical spaces with indigenous, radically "different" inhabitants who can be defined on the basis of some religion, culture or racial essence proper to that geographical space is equally a highly debatable idea' (322).

36. In *Beginnings*, emphasising both his proximity to and distance from Foucault' regime of truth,' Said writes that Orientalism is 'a new habit of thought, *a set of rules for knowledge to dominate truth*, to make truth as an issue secondary to the successful ordering and wielding of huge masses of actual present knowledge' (*Beginnings: Intention and Method* (New York: Columbia University Press, 1985), 291; emphasis added). Here, the analysis implies an underpinning 'objective' truth: this presents a significant difference with Foucault's text, but also with passages cited earlier in which Said seems to indicate the 'Orient' being actively (ontologically) produced by the veridic discourses of these corporate institutions.

37. For an early, brilliant but much-neglected analysis of neo-Orientalism – a social scientific 'reincarnation' of earlier generations of Orientalism rooted in the humanities – albeit not formulated in explicitly Foucaultian terms, see Yahya Sadowski, 'The New Orientalism and the Democracy Debate,' in *Political Islam: Essays from Middle East Report*, eds. Joel Beinin and Joe Stork (London: I. B. Tauris, 1997), 33–50.

38. Foucault, *Will to Knowledge*, 17–21, 59–73.

39. There are of course various versions of this argument, from those focusing on Arab culture (for example Raphael Patai) to the role of Islam (for example Elie Kedourie), both in 'humanist' terms, such as the ones Said analyses in *Orientalism*, or in more 'sublimated' social scientific terms such as those

detected in Sadowski's groundbreaking analysis of early democratization theory.

40. The reflexive form renders the crucial property that sin deceives the sinning Other as much as the Confessor. This also reinforces the Confessor's right to deliberate on the truth of the Sinner's acts and avowals.

41. Foucault, *Will to Knowledge*, 66; emphasis added. The original French renders the crucial property that sin deceives the sinning Other as much as the Confessor, which reinforces the Confessor's right to deliberate on the truth of the Sinner's acts and avowals.

42. This is precisely one of the functions to which data-gathering exercises such as those routinely performed in assessments of 'civil society' can be turned.

43. Foucault, *Will to Knowledge*, 24.

44. Foucault, *Il faut défendre la société – Cours au Collège de France, 1975–1976* (Le Foucault Electronique v. 2001/Folio Editions, 1977), 228. '[l]à où vous avez une société de normalisation, là où vous avez un pouvoir qui est [...] en première instance, en première ligne, un bio-pouvoir [...] le racisme est indispensable comme condition pour pouvoir mettre quelqu'un à mort'.

45. Said, *Orientalism*, 1–2.

46. Said, *Orientalism*, 1.

47. Foucault, *Will to Knowledge*, 66–7.

48. Foucault, *Will to Knowledge*, 69; emphasis added.

49. Said, *Orientalism*, 3.

50. Said, *Orientalism*, 2.

51. Beate Jahn, 'The Tragedy of Liberal Diplomacy: Democratization, Intervention, Statebuilding (Part I),' *Journal of Intervention and Statebuilding* 1, no. 1 (2007), 92.

52. The recent events of the 'Arab Spring' provide a reminder of how quickly and effectively such mechanisms operate. The uprisings defied and surprised scholarship and policymaking, exploding Orientalist myths and challenging the West's own hegemonic narratives about the superiority of liberal democracy. And yet attempts to 'orientalize' the uprisings soon emerged, for example by crediting Gene Sharp, American theorist of non-violent change whose work was used by Freedom House, with providing the intellectual spark which made the uprisings possible. See Rabab El-Mahdi, 'Orientalising the Arab Uprisings,' *Jadaliyya*, 11 April 2011, http://www.jadaliyya.com/pages/index/1214/orientalising-the-egyptian-uprising [accessed 30 January 2012].

53. Jahn, 'The Tragedy of Liberal Diplomacy,' 93.

54. Ibid.; emphasis added.

55. Foucault, *The Will to Knowledge*, 61.

56. The debate is reproduced in John Rajchman, *The Chomsky-Foucault Debate* (New York: The New Press, 2006), and available online at http://www.youtube.com/watch?v= kawGakdNoT0

57. Foucault's lecture *Of Other Spaces* was given in Tunisia in 1967, but was not authorized for publication until the spring of 1984: http://foucault.info/documents/heteroTopia/foucault.heteroTopia.en.html. The original French version is available here, with additional commentary by Foucault: http://foucault.info/documents/heteroTopia/foucault.heteroTopia.fr.html

58. Foucault, 'Interview with Alessandro Fontana and Pasquale Pasquino,' in *The Foucault Reader*, ed. Paul Rabinow (London: Penguin, 1991), 63.
59. Embodying a Western liberal tradition sceptical of democracy, Robert Dahl, for example, argues that active participation by lower-class citizenry is likely to have negative effects on democracy. See Dahl, *Polyarchy* (New Haven, CT: Yale University Press, 1971), 89. Despite considerable differences between them, Gaetano Mosca, Vilfredo Pareto, Max Weber, Alois Schumpeter and Samuel Huntington all variously incarnate this liberal scepticism of mass democratic participation.
60. Foucault, *Dits et écrits* 1, 189–90.

9
The 'War on Terror' and the Backlash against *Orientalism*

Robert Spencer

> A person skilled in the 'art' of questioning is a person who
> can prevent questions from being suppressed by the dominant
> opinion
>
> (Hans-Georg Gadamer, *Truth and Method*, p. 361)

The last few years have witnessed a vigorous backlash against
Orientalism. Edward Said's most influential work has been accused
of sweeping denunciations of Western scholarship about the Orient
as well as knee-jerk anti-Americanism and even covert support for
terrorism and radical Islam. His critical stance on Western colonialism
and especially Zionism meant that Said was no stranger to abuse
and misrepresentation, from Edward Alexander's coinage of the epithet 'Professor of Terror'[1] to Justus Weiner's baseless claim that he
had invented his status as a Palestinian and a refugee. Said's argument in *Orientalism* is, of course, that the purportedly disinterested
study of the Orient frequently perpetuates age-old prejudices about the
East that make it easier to denigrate the region and justify its domination. However over-determined its reception was by specifically academic and institutional trends, *Orientalism*'s confrontational tone and
its appearance in the late 1970s along with its author's forthright advocacy of the Palestinians' national aspirations meant the book was soon
caught up in the passionate ideological disagreements surrounding the
Iranian Revolution, the hostage crisis, Israel's accelerating expansion-
ism after the 1967 war and the election of the first Likud government in
1977, and the general audibility of the Arab and Islamic worlds. In short,
this was a book pitched into the tented field of political controversy.

I wish to analyse and censure what I am characterizing as the
'backlash' against *Orientalism*. I want to show how Ibn Warraq's

Defending the West, Martin Kramer's *Ivory Towers on Sand* and Robert Irwin's *For Lust of Knowing* take *Orientalism* to task for what they see as an excessively critical account of both Western scholarship about the Middle East and Western powers' involvement in the region. As I see it their aim is not to join the extremely fertile and necessary discussion underway in Middle East and postcolonial studies about how to generate knowledge (as opposed to ignorance) about the Middle East, a discussion that did not begin with *Orientalism* and certainly did not finish with it; they wish rather to close that discussion down. Theirs is a manifestly anti-intellectual project aimed at stifling debate and discrediting an articulate opponent of mainstream preconceptions about Islam and the Arabs. It is also an anti-political project, concerned not with stimulating wider discussion about the consequences and intentions of Western power in the Middle East but with preventing those discussions from taking place. Far from engaging with Said's arguments, as scholars in Middle East and postcolonial studies have done, sometimes sympathetically and sometimes unfavourably but almost always *critically*, Warraq, Kramer and Irwin have chosen either to slander Said and those influenced by his work or to distract from the substance of Said's arguments with quibbles about the errors of fact and interpretation contained in *Orientalism*.

What they have not done, or perhaps, given the strength of their faith in the possibility of pure and disinterested scholarship, have not been capable of doing, is take on board Said's contention that scholarship about the Middle East does not take place away from the contexts, perspectives and interests in which all humanly produced knowledge is shaped. They have not been in a position, therefore, to encourage the kind of intellectual and political self-questioning that Said espoused over 30 years ago and that has become even more necessary in the wake of the terrorist attacks of 2001 and the ill-starred 'war on terror,' not to mention what Perry Anderson calls 'the concatenation' of the Arab Spring.[2] My first point, which once the layers of misrepresentation are peeled away is also Said's, is that this kind of introspection is an intrinsic part of humanistic investigations into the literatures, cultures and societies of the Middle East. These are hermeneutic undertakings and it is in their nature to give rise not to dogma but to debates between interpretations. My second point is that a useful political or, to use a Saidian term, worldly function is performed by scholars in the humanities when they foster such debates, not when they kowtow to received wisdom about the Middle East's backwardness and passivity.

Said had little enough time for his critics' complacent faith in what V. S. Naipaul once called 'our [that is the West's] universal civilization.'[3]

Yet he also rejected James Clifford's suggestion that he should steer clear of 'the totalizing habits of Western humanism.'[4] Said resolved instead 'to be critical of humanism in the name of humanism.'[5] He contested the violent and hypocritical humanism espoused by European and North American powers, which Noam Chomsky has dubbed 'the new military humanism.'[6] Said defended an alternative definition of humanism: humanism in the intellectual sense of 'what the humanities do' (foster knowledge and self-knowledge) and humanism in the sense of human rights (a principled commitment to the value and equality of *all* human life and a permanent end to the habit of confusing one specific culture with humanity as a whole). These two aspects of humanism are linked in *Humanism and Democratic Criticism*. For it is the capacity for introspection (what the philologist Leo Spitzer calls 'the power bestowed on the human mind of investigating the human mind'[7]) that leads, ideally, to a concertedly critical attitude toward 'Western' political elites' complacent faith that their beliefs and actions embody and promulgate humanity's highest ideals.

By 'Western' here I certainly do not mean to write in the manner of those intellectuals and political leaders usually referred to as 'neo-conservatives' (a term that surely prompts the objection that there was not much that was particularly 'neo-' about Cheney and co's unselfconscious belief in the 'free market' and American military power). Nor am I anxious to ape the rhetoric of the 'anti-Western' zealots of radical Islam who, ironically, share the 'neocon' belief that the world consists of two vast and entirely dissimilar camps ('the West' and its adversaries) destined to fight it out for pre-eminence. Given the cogency of Neil Lazarus's warning that 'the West' is a deceptive term that conceals the actual political and economic (as opposed to geographic) origins of colonial power and ideologies,[8] perhaps we would be better advised to drop such undiscriminating terms as 'West' and 'East' in deference to Said's insight in *Orientalism* that the ideology the book sets out to describe and denounce is 'ultimately a political vision of reality' that promotes an insuperable difference between West and East.[9] The task that Said set himself was to achieve alternative perspectives on this relationship in order to bring into view alternative visions. A comprehensive perusal of *Orientalism* and, even more so, of Said's other works, reveals that his argument is emphatically not, as his detractors would have us believe, that the histories and traditions of 'the West' are irredeemably malevolent or that 'the West's' 'enemies' should be applauded. To the contrary, for Said it is possible for scholars to produce understanding and even visions of human community and to do so, moreover, via a fidelity to the ideal of humanism, an intellectual and political tradition on which no culture or region can claim a monopoly.

To appreciate the lasting relevance of *Orientalism* one need only recall the republication in 2002 of *The Arab Mind* by Raphael Patai, a cultural anthropologist who taught at Columbia and Princeton. Patai's egregious book, rightly dismissed as 'general nonsense'[10] in *Orientalism*, is a work of the most capaciously sweeping generalizations about the Arab world which nevertheless served, according to the investigative journalist Seymour Hersh, as the 'bible of the neocons on Arab behaviour.'[11] Disturbingly, in the light of the revelations from Abu Ghraib prison in Iraq, Patai holds forth on Arabs' alleged susceptibility to sexual humiliation. This compilation of racist clichés has even been used, we learn from the effusive preamble by one Norvell De Atkine (a retired US Army colonel and former head of Middle East studies at Fort Bragg), as a textbook at the JFK Special Warfare School and as an authority on such matters as 'the modal personality traits that make them [that is the Arabs] susceptible to engaging in terrorist actions.'[12]

Orientalism places scholars on their guard against this sort of confusion between scholarly know-how and political power. Yet it is hardly without its flaws. Indeed *Orientalism*, as Lazarus has argued, is in many ways untypical of Said's work as a whole.[13] Neil Larsen identifies two Orientalisms vying within the text: the humanist and the Foucauldian, the one seeking out knowledge and valuing truth, the other writing off truth as a fiction produced in the service of power.[14] It is the former that brings down the curtain, as it were, and is the approach that Said favoured in his subsequent writings. What is too rarely noticed is that in its final section *Orientalism* does countenance scholarship that provides its readers with knowledge about other cultures and societies. Said concludes *Orientalism* by drawing readers' attention to scholars like the anthropologist Clifford Geertz, the Marxist historian and sociologist Maxime Rodinson, and the ethnographer and pied-noir Jacques Berque. Though they were thoroughly versed in the disciplines of Orientalism and could be characterized as being in various ways 'outsiders' to the regions that they studied, these thinkers were nevertheless 'capable of freeing themselves from [Orientalism's] old ideological straitjacket.'[15] Given the right degree of methodological self-questioning, of distrust of prevailing doctrines about the region being studied, and of painstaking responsiveness to that region's detail and diversity, independent minds like theirs can cut through misapprehension and give rise to understanding.

I would not have undertaken a book of this sort if I did not also believe that there is scholarship that is not as corrupt, or at least as blind to human reality, as the kind I have been mainly depicting [...] The trouble sets in when the guild tradition of Orientalism takes over the scholar who is not vigilant, whose individual consciousness as a scholar is not on guard against *idées reçues* all too easily handed down in the profession [...] For if Orientalism has historically been too smug, too insulated, too positivistically confident in its ways and its premises, then one way of opening oneself to what one studies in or about the Orient is reflexively to submit one's method to critical scrutiny [...] [Berque and Rodinson demonstrate] a direct sensitivity to the material before them, and then a continual self-examination of their methodology and practice, a constant attempt to keep their work responsive to the material and not to a doctrinal preconception.[16]

The task enjoined here and in Said's later work is to identify as well as actively contest the prevalence of Orientalist representations. Not least in the final chapter of *Orientalism* itself, as well as more fully in *Covering Islam* and *The Question of Palestine* (which as Abdirahman Hussein notes 'were meant to clarify and refine the original thesis'[17]), Said both raises the possibility of non-coercive knowledge and demonstrates that possibility by trying to represent faithfully to his readers the experiences and aspirations of his compatriots: 'I have tried here,' he writes toward the end of the latter book, 'to present the Palestinians as *representable* – in terms of our collective experience, our collective sense of things, our collective aspirations, above all, as a real and present (because historical) reality.'[18] The rigour and insistence of Said's critique of Orientalist forms of knowledge is matched therefore only by the alacrity with which, after *Orientalism*, he proceeded to outline alternatives.

Said's point therefore, in *Orientalism* and even more explicitly in its sequels, is that the diverse peoples and societies which we have been taught to see, reductively, as 'the East' are not doomed to remain closed books to 'Western' minds. Indeed, the implication is that such categories as 'East' and 'West' are inadmissible, something made much more explicit in Said's later critique of Samuel Huntington's crude 'clash of civilizations' thesis. One's membership of a culture or society and the ways in which one then approaches other cultures and societies is influenced by any number of standpoints, affiliations and identities, such as class, gender, religion, sexuality and so on. Taken together these things fatally undermine any idea that the world is divided into homogeneous and unchanging camps and force us instead to conceptualize the world as multifarious, internally divided, dynamic and even, ultimately, reconcilable.[19] It is fair to say therefore, as Lazarus and Timothy Brennan have done, that Said's work did not share the mainly anti-humanist premises and principles that characterize much of the work that *Orientalism* inspired.[20] Interestingly, Said did not trace his own method to Foucault and Jacques Derrida, philosophers whose ideas dominated the field of postcolonial studies in its formative years. To the contrary, he incurred a debt to the methods and principles of humanist intellectual practice as elaborated by American literary critics like R. P. Blackmur, Richard Poirier and Lionel Trilling and especially by the half-forgotten tradition of German comparative philology. The careful elucidation of texts by great philologists like Leo Spitzer and especially Erich Auerbach provided Said with a model for attentive, penetrating and, once he had adapted and extended their ideas, both intellectually and *politically* self-conscious scholarship. Scholarship can and ought to give rise to knowledge and self-knowledge. Moreover, it should be humanistic in the second and even more important sense of being inspired by as well as devoted to engendering visions of the world to set against the divisive ideologies of racial and national exclusivism from which the German philologists had fled in the 1930s.

Said was attracted by the philological method, particularly as it is set out in Auerbach's little manifesto 'Philologie der *Weltliteratur*,' which Said co-translated in the late 1960s, and as it is deployed in Auerbach's magnum opus *Mimesis*. There is a continuous oscillation in *Mimesis* between the large theme or idea on the one hand and the individual detail on the other. Despite its quixotic aim to provide a history of the representation of reality in Western literature, this remarkable book nevertheless deduces its extensive conclusions from the most scrupulous and even microscopic immersion in the techniques and nuances of particular plays, poems and novels. The philologist, as Auerbach explains, should follow the intrinsic momentum of his own work, radiating outwards from an exegesis of a representative passage of prose or verse to an explication of the whole of the text in question, its contexts, connections and consequences and of the historical developments of which it forms a part.[21] Only on the basis of the knowledge he accrues from a close attention to texts is the scholar qualified to speak authoritatively of the wider situations in which those texts were composed and in which they circulate. Philology is a method that rewards close textual scrutiny without sacrificing general insight.

It is well known that Auerbach credited the existence of *Mimesis* to the unavailability of a well-stocked European library during his wartime exile in Istanbul and to his consequent reliance not on the disconcertingly vast amount of critical literature on, for example, the New Testament and Dante's *Divine Comedy* but on the details and complexities of the texts themselves.[22] What gives the book its enduring authority is not its compendiousness but its erudition, as well as its ability to draw general conclusions from convincing analyses of specific examples: all accomplished in spite and even because of the scholar's physical distance or exile from the milieu with which he is concerned. Distance, in short, need not debilitate the careful scholar. Awareness of that distance makes one conscious of the gaps in one's knowledge and of the biases and misunderstandings that inevitably lie between one and the phenomena that one studies. Such a scholar is thus careful not to operate with the unearned authority of the sage who throws out pronouncements without real knowledge of or sympathy with the subject of his enquiries. Moreover, distance ought to lead to an enhanced awareness of one's own personal and scholarly deficiencies and to an enforced preoccupation with particulars. 'In any event,' as Auerbach remarks in his study of Latin rhetoric, 'such a method compels us to look within ourselves and to set forth our consciousness of ourselves here and now, in all its wealth and limitations.'[23]

Similarly, Said's point in *Orientalism* is that all knowledge is admixed with presuppositions, theories and even personal biases. Our analyses are therefore most illuminating when we are conscious of these obstacles to the production of dependable knowledge, willing to reflect on them and resolved to prevent them from dominating or dictating one's work. Such sharp-eyed engagement with the shape and detail of other cultures leads, potentially, to a new scepticism about the broad-brushed dogmas that usually write those cultures off as nugatory and inferior. Far from being motivated by a fanatical anti-Westernism, therefore, Said's work was guided by an abiding (as well as critical and creative) fidelity to a distinctively European intellectual tradition. It was humanism that allowed Said to develop a form of scholarship that sought to produce and disseminate knowledge about, for example, the Middle East, Islam and the lives of the Palestinians, albeit knowledge reliant on a scrupulous attention to detail as well as a strict intellectual self-consciousness. In short, humanism, which is not a distinctively 'Western' idea but which Said learnt about chiefly from European thinkers like the philologists, was Said's guiding principle.[24] Humanism is the art of self-criticism. Just as the distinctive human faculty is, as we have seen, 'the power bestowed on the human mind of investigating the human mind,' so for Auerbach the business of criticism is 'a process of formulation and interpretation whose subject matter is our own self.'[25] Humanism necessitates self-analysis, not for its own sake but for that of the broadened horizons it opens up, the knowledge it makes possible and the broad sympathies it helps to instil. It is, Said explains, radically democratic and insubordinate as well as possessed of an inclusive 'catholicity of vision.'[26]

What, therefore, are we to make of those critiques of Said's work that accuse him of hostility to 'the West' and dogmatic attacks on European scholarship? I think we should conclude that far from being fair assessments they are in fact tendentious polemics. Take, for example, Martin Kramer's *Ivory Towers on Sand: The Failure of Middle Eastern Studies in America*. Kramer is a former director of the Moshe Dayan Center for Middle Eastern and African Studies at the University of Tel Aviv, named after the Israeli general and defence minister during the 1967 war. His critique of the development of Middle East studies in the US since the publication of *Orientalism* is published by the Washington Institute for Near East Policy (WINEP). WINEP describes itself as 'an education foundation [for] supporting scholarly research and informed debate on U.S. interests in the Near East.'[27] But here those interests are not debated so much as slavishly endorsed. The contradiction between subservience to so-called US interests and the values of education, scholarship and debate does not seem to have occasioned much reflection on the part of Kramer, the Institute's Wexler-Fromer Fellow, or on that of its distinguished patrons listed at the back of the book. On the board of advisors can be found an impressive list of foreign policy bigwigs including Paul Wolfowitz; the late Jeane Kirkpatrick (Reagan's ambassador to the UN and anti-communist hawk); ex-US ambassador to Israel Samuel W. Lewis; the military strategist Edward Luttwak; the plutocrat Mort Zuckerman; veteran of the Iran-Contra affair Robert McFarlane; Republican Party hanger-on Richard Perle; and a veritable throng of ex-Secretaries of State including Warren Christopher, Lawrence Eagleburger, Alexander Haig, George Schultz and, inevitably, Henry Kissinger. *Ivory Towers on Sand* is not a measured work of scholarship or even a work of scholarship at all but a tract produced on behalf of a partisan political organization. It is a trashy screed devoted to the task of flinging mud.

Kramer's thesis is that in the last 30 years American centres for the study of the Middle East have been overrun by Said's disciples.[28] Middle Eastern studies has been 'crippled' by the 'revolution' 'unleashed' by

Orientalism.[29] He alleges that Said's work helped introduce academia to a more or less overt sympathy for political Islam.[30] Academic study of the Middle East since the uprising triggered by *Orientalism* has also been politically biased.

> Orientalism made it acceptable, even expected, for scholars to spell out their own political commitments as a preface to anything they wrote or did. More than that, it also enshrined an acceptable hierarchy of political commitments, with Palestine at the top, followed by the Arab nation and the Islamic world. They were the long-suffering victims of Western racism, American imperialism, and Israeli Zionism – the three legs of the orientalist stool.[31]

Said's critique of mainstream scholarship has led, according to Kramer, to the erection of barriers to keep out any scholar who is not from the Middle East or who does not conform to the socialist and anti-Israel creeds of 'the new orthodoxy'[32]; to a clannishness and conformism that have reduced Middle East Studies to 'a politburo of the likeminded'[33]; to the intimidation of scholars with differing views; to 'antigovernment zealotry'[34]; and to unabashed cheerleading for Palestinian and Islamic causes. Kramer judges the field to be almost wholly irrelevant on account of what he argues is Middle East studies' poor record in predicting events in the region.[35] Kramer does not want scholars but clairvoyants who can foretell events and then forewarn the government. His book is based on the frankly anti-intellectual assumption that a major scholarly field ought to exist solely for the purpose of serving the state. Who can deny that scholarship has public responsibilities? But what Kramer fails to recognize is that the public is not the same thing as the government.

He ends with a threat, a spot of flag waving and a cheery forecast that younger scholars will soon produce more useful studies of Islam and the Middle East. They can do this, apparently, by making their work relevant to the public, which for Kramer means the state.

> Middle Eastern studies must regain their relevance, or risk becoming 'Exhibit A' in any future case against public support for area studies. They can best achieve this by discovering and articulating that which is uniquely American in the American approach to the Middle East. The idea that the United States plays an essentially beneficent role in the world is at the very core of this approach.[36]

Accordingly, Kramer recommends increased federal scrutiny of Middle East studies centres in the US in order to make sure they are spreading the word about the state's beneficence. One is reminded of Bertolt Brecht's quip about the 1953 uprising in the GDR: since the people had forfeited the confidence of the regime then perhaps the regime should dissolve the people and elect another.[37] Maybe because American intellectuals no longer tell their government what it wants to hear, an exasperated government would be well advised to disband them and find some that do. Hence the increasing popularity of scholarship located not in universities but in the think tanks that seem to proliferate in Washington like bacteria on a Petri dish, including WINEP, the Heritage Foundation, the Council on Foreign Relations, the American Israel Public Affairs Committee (AIPAC) and the Nixon Center for Peace and Freedom (an Orwellian title if ever there was one), not to mention innumerable other organizations that exist not to analyse, still less to question, American foreign policy but to cheer it on and jockey for government funds.[38]

Kramer's depiction of Middle East scholars as docile acolytes of Said is wide of the mark. As Zachary Lockman, Professor of Middle Eastern and Islamic Studies at New York University, has pointed out, *Orientalism* was not the first work to call into question some of the methodologies and presuppositions of mainstream scholarship about the Middle East.[39] Nor has it been immune to some very cogent criticisms and qualifications from within the disciplines of Middle East and postcolonial studies, as we shall see. Thanks in part to Said's intervention, which has been analysed and discussed but never unquestioningly endorsed, those disciplines have been the site of a very vigorous debate about the relationship between scholarship and power. Kramer's only contribution to this debate has been to assert that the role of the scholar, the intellectual and the student is to be at the beck and call of what he calls 'the centers of American decisionmaking.'[40] His book is a farrago of affronts and accusations, of faulty reasoning and boorish complaints about the temerity of newfangled scholars to question the altruism and objectivity of the US government.

Ibn Warraq's aim in *Defending the West* is equally one-sided: to portray 'Western civilization,'[41] without pausing even once to consider the contentiousness of that category, as the home of rationalism, universalism and self-criticism. In truth, however, there is little evidence of any of these qualities in his repetitive tirade. Not a word of criticism of 'the West' will be heard here. Not even the institution of slavery occasions a moment of contrition or self-doubt.[42] Here the virtues of 'the West' are

monotonously extolled and 'Islamic civilization' correspondingly belit-
tled for its comparative mediocrity and weakness.[43] Ibn Warraq bemoans
'the totally pernicious influence of Edward Said's *Orientalism*' which, he
asserts, 'taught an entire generation of Arabs the art of self-pity,' 'encouraged the Islamic fundamentalist generation of the 1980s, bludgeoned
into silence any criticism of Islam, and stopped dead the research of
eminent Islamologists who felt their findings might offend Muslim sensibilities and who dared not risk being labeled "Orientalist".'[44] As he
sees it, Said's purpose was to 'trawl through Western literature for filth
to besmirch Western civilization,'[45] 'all the while spewing forth hatred
of the country that took him in.'[46] Said's work has spawned acolytes
who possess a 'Manichaean worldview'[47] according to which 'Western'
scholarship along with the West's presence in the world are invariably
nefarious and harmful. *Orientalism* provided, Warraq alleges, a 'formula'
for 'those unable to think for themselves' by encouraging an unthinking
cultural relativism.[48] Said is even accused of 'destroying' the disciplines
of history and literary criticism.[49] No evidence is given of course, and
no scholars are named. These shrill and essentially baseless accusations
are accompanied by nasty insinuations about, for example, Said's experiences at prep school![50] They culminate in Ibn Warraq's wild claim that
'[t]he most pernicious legacy of Said's *Orientalism* is its implicit support for religious fundamentalism,'[51] 'whose impact on world affairs,'
he concludes the first part of the book by reminding us, 'needs no
underlining.'[52]

Said was a one-man fifth column! *Orientalism* unfastened the gates
and in streamed a legion of young Saidians who dedicated themselves to denouncing the US and thereby weakening its defences.
By calling into question the altruism and benevolence of American
power and by subjecting a scholarly discipline to critical evaluation Said
had single-handedly sapped the West's strength and self-confidence.
'[I]mpressionable youth,' Ibn Warraq frets, are now 'unwilling to defend
the West against the greatest threat that it has faced since the Nazis.'
Said's work was 'a master fraud that bound American academics and
Middle East tyrants in unstated bonds of anti-American complicity.'[53]
'Unstated' is the key word here: 'unstated' anti-Americanism, 'unstated'
sympathy for terrorism and tyranny, and 'unstated' religious fundamentalism. 'Unstated,' however, because as we shall see Said never stated
these things and indeed, at every opportunity took care to state the
opposite.

Diatribes like Warraq's and Kramer's suffer far more grievously from
the faults of which they accuse *Orientalism*: the copious use of sweeping

and utterly unsubstantiated generalizations, the cursory and selective use of evidence, an intemperate and polemical tone, not to mention a bullying contempt for alternative points of view. The reason for these prickly indictments of *Orientalism* is to be found, I believe, in their shared hostility to theory: by which I mean their aversion to the sort of critical reflection on methods and precepts that most scholars engage in routinely but which the likes of Kramer and Warraq, who are not scholars in any sense but men who make a living by flattering the powerful, see as unnecessary impediments to the process by which sensible minds gain access to reality. In the words of the historian Maya Jasanoff:

> Said wanted to break down what he saw as a false 'distinction between pure and political knowledge.' Does that mean that facts do not exist, or that evidence does not matter? Certainly not. But it does mean that scholars ought to be aware of the circumstances governing the kind of knowledge that they produce and circulate.[54]

No such awareness holds back Kramer or Warraq. They are wedded to a frankly naïve faith that scholarship can be entirely disinterested and that truth can be accessed with ease by minds unencumbered by anything as whimsical and pusillanimous as theory or self-knowledge.

In *For the Lust of Knowing*, Irwin at least does us the favour of identifying some of the flaws in *Orientalism*. He censures Said's neglect of the laudably non-tendentious contributions made to the field of Orientalism by Marxist scholars (Rodinson aside),[55] Said's factual mistakes[56] and the occasional selectiveness of his evidence,[57] his sometimes fallible knowledge of Middle Eastern history,[58] his inattention to the prestige enjoyed by German Orientalism at a time when Germany had no colonies,[59] his travestying of Karl Marx's writings on India[60] and his relative inattention to the question of how to improve the study of the Middle East instead of simply criticizing its deficiencies.[61] Yet there is no reason why these objections should prompt us to dismiss *Orientalism* altogether. We should instead take the view that Said's larger point about the importance of becoming conscious of one's own political and intellectual preconceptions before dealing with entities as complex, politically fraught and humanly significant as whole cultures, societies and religions ought to be retained as well as clarified, refined and developed.

This lesson has not been lost on postcolonial scholars, despite their awareness of *Orientalism*'s flaws. Dennis Porter, James Clifford,

Neil Lazarus and Robert Young have all, albeit from very different intellectual perspectives, noted the methodological contradictions in *Orientalism*.[62] Bart Moore-Gilbert regrets that *Orientalism* neglected to stress the weak points and limitations of the discourse of Orientalism and therefore failed also to emphasize the possibility of resistance both at the sharp end of colonialism's operations and within imperial culture itself.[63] John Mackenzie notes the varied manifestations of popular Orientalism,[64] Leila Gandhi the ways in which metropolitan subcultures in late nineteenth-century Britain actually opposed colonial expansion,[65] Joseph Massad the complex relationship between Orientalism and sexuality,[66] and Crystal Bartolovich and others both the consistent opposition of Marxists to colonial expansion and the possibility that Said's predominantly textual analyses might usefully be combined with a materialist sensitivity to social and economic structures.[67] Reina Lewis, Billie Melman, Nupur Chaudhuri and Margaret Strobel have all reminded us that women take part in Orientalism not just as aesthetic or discursive metaphors for certain facets of inferiority (which is what Said argues in *Orientalism*[68]) but also as participants in colonial expansion and as artists and writers who question and even subvert Orientalist and imperialist discourses.[69]

While a little quarrelsome at times and very fond of bad puns and mixed metaphors, Daniel Varisco has provided a constructive, not to say remarkably comprehensive, survey of the many responses to *Orientalism*. Though he values Said's larger points about the need for acuity and self-consciousness when studying the Middle East and Islam and though he agrees with Said about the dangers of complicity between scholarship and power, Varisco contends that *Orientalism* was basically an exercise in clearing the space necessary for better work to be produced on these subjects, both in Said's later writings and in those of other scholars: 'better' in the sense of being more intellectually and politically self-conscious and therefore more willing to get outside or at least to scrutinize and evaluate prevailing doctrines about the Middle East and Islam. Such undertakings are more necessary than ever, Varisco considers, given the US' and European powers' ever greater and more confrontational involvement 'with buyable governments and bombable people in the Middle East.'[70] Varisco argues, and I agree with him, though I wouldn't use these terms, that the goal of serious scholarship about the Middle East is to 'improve understanding of self and other, not to whine endlessly or wallow self-righteously in continual opposition.' 'It is time,' as he puts it, more agreeably, 'to read beyond *Orientalism*.'[71]

Orientalism is valuable because, as Varisco indicates, it 'stimulated a necessary debate in English-speaking academe that has hardly abated'[72] about how to produce knowledge as opposed to ignorance about other societies and cultures. That debate predated *Orientalism*,[73] was then galvanized by it, and has outlasted and in some ways superseded it. But Kramer and Ibn Warraq are not interested in debate except insofar as they can reduce it to an undignified slanging match. They wish to shout down their opponents or else place hands over their mouths. Both men decline to engage with the substance of the argument put forward in *Orientalism* and instead bandy about scurrilous accusations. Irwin tries to discredit the whole by cavilling about parts, to show, for example, that Said must have been wrong about Orientalism because his translations of Goethe and Flaubert contained flaws. As Maya Jasanoff has pointed out, 'Irwin's factual corrections, however salutary, do not so much knock down the theoretical claims of *Orientalism* as chip away at single bricks. They also do nothing to discount the fertility of *Orientalism* for other academics.'[74] The really pernicious aspect of the slurs and misrepresentations put forward by Said's critics is that they would close down vital discussions about the interpretive frameworks as well as the social, institutional and political contexts in which knowledge about the Middle East, like all humanly acquired knowledge, is produced. Only the most naïve minds could scorn this dialogue because they assume, mistakenly of course, that facts speak for themselves and can presented without any scrutiny of one's own predilections and prejudgements.

Said's opponents also close their eyes to his principled opposition to terrorism, tyranny and fundamentalism. They persist in claiming, absurdly, that when it came to violence and dictatorship in the Arab world Said 'praised those things with faint damns.'[75] In fact his damns were quite loud and insistent. It will not do to allege that after September 2001 Said 'put the terrorists' case for them, just as he had put the case for Saddam Hussein.'[76] On the contrary, Saddam along with the zealots who brought down the Twin Towers were denounced by Said in the strongest possible terms: 'No cause, no god, no abstract idea can justify the mass slaughter of innocents',[77] he told the readers of the Arab newspapers *Al-Ahram* and *Al-Hayat* in the days after the attacks. In addition, the mediocrity and cupidity of Arab leaders were repeatedly laid bare by Said (he numbered Arafat and his lackeys among these venal regimes[78]), as were, in passages Irwin must have skipped, the 'morally repugnant and politically disastrous'[79] suicide bombings and 'the bizarre failures of logic, moral reasoning, and appreciation of human life that lead [in the Arab world] either to leaps of religious enthusiasm of the worst kind or to a servile worship of power.'[80]

It is necessary to recall Said's opposition to these things because the effort to understand the Middle East is not a matter of merely academic concern. It involves intellectual, moral and ultimately political choices. Approaching the region with a sense of its detail and complexity, seeing it as a product of history rather than as a manifestation of some unchanging essence, and undertaking the kind of critical self-reflection on orthodox preconceptions to which the likes of Kramer and Warraq are evidently allergic, are vital processes if engagement with places like the Middle East is to be based on self-knowledge and human solidarity rather than bumptious self-congratulation and a fawning deference to those in power. This is a point that must be restated insistently. Debate should be encouraged not kept in check if we are to engage with the Middle East in more perspicacious and nuanced as well as more enlightened and both morally and politically effective ways. This objective is obviously not possible if we rely for information on partisan news organizations, mainstream politicians and the inexpert punditry of retired generals, hacks, think tank habitués and other 'insiders.' Rajiv Chandrasekaran allows us to glimpse the consequences of this fraudulent wisdom when he reports seeing Coalition Provisional Authority staff in Baghdad's 'green zone' thumbing through the *Complete Idiot's Guide to Understanding Iraq* and a 1970s tourist guide to Baghdad.[81] One need only read Chandrasekaran's hair-raising tale of religiose and parochial bureaucrats praying in the viceroy's office each morning before going to work rearranging a country about which they knew virtually nothing to be convinced of how crucial it is that painstaking and conscientious study of the Middle East should cut through the fog thrown up by soundbites and fixed ideas.

'There are such things as pure scholars,' writes Irwin.[82] That this is not the case is what Said's book sets out to prove. The errors and exaggerations that Irwin discovers in *Orientalism* distract us from but do not affect this larger insight: that knowledge is affected by context and in particular by the overbearing contexts of institutional, economic, political and even military power. I am claiming that the fantasy of scholarly disinterest and the consequent aversion to self-scrutiny paves the way to intellectual complacency. If left unchallenged it compounds the kind of unselfconscious faith in the purity of one's own motives and the flawlessness of one's own culture that resulted in the unmitigated catastrophe of the war in Iraq and the wider 'war on terror.'

Equality, dialogue and self-knowledge were Said's watchwords, maxims taken from the ideal of humanism that he followed and that he believed to have been born from Europe's better self. Therefore, let us do Said the justice of giving his work the kind of scrupulous attention with which he urged us to approach the peoples and societies of the Middle East. Said's work is, I believe, a radical affirmation of humanist scholarship and values.[83] Yet it repudiates the claims made by the US and its auxiliaries to be the custodians of those traditions. Said's humanism should be set against the counterfeit humanism of his detractors, for whom freedom, democracy and human rights are benefactions to be dispensed by powerful states. *Orientalism* points up the political surroundings in which scholarship is conducted; it would be a surprise therefore if it were not itself an intensely and passionately, albeit openly, political intervention. It is indeed a book tied, as Said puts it, 'to the tumultuous dynamics of contemporary history',[84] one that is concerned not just with assessing an important scholarly field but with questioning prejudices and encouraging understanding about a strategically important and resource-rich as well as distinctive, complex and powerfully human part of the world. What has been misplaced in the nationalist and religious passions unleashed since 2001, as Said complained, is 'a sense of the density and interdependence of human life, which can neither be reduced to a formula nor be brushed aside as irrelevant.'[85] *Orientalism* should be read today as a potent corrective to the prejudices as well as to the ideological complacency that made possible the abominations perpetrated at Abu Ghraib as well as the depredations visited on Iraq, and that permit the violence meted out unremittingly to the Palestinians. For Said the term 'Orientalism' names a durable system of misrepresentations that can be combated by scholarship that is so methodologically self-conscious and so meticulously attentive to the details and complexities of the region being studied that it succeeds in producing and propagating knowledge, in broadening horizons, as well as giving rise to understanding and human sympathy. The backlash against Said's work has the aim of discrediting the radical pedagogical and, ultimately, political potential of these ideas. It would discourage the practice of questioning and self-questioning, which after all is what scholarship is all about.

Acknowledgements

Versions of this paper were first presented at two symposia: '*Orientalism, Thirty Years Later*', hosted by the Department of English at the University of York on 1st November 2008, and '*Orientalism and its Critics*' at the

American University of Beirut on 1st June 2009. I would like to express my gratitude to the organizers and participants at these events for the stimulating discussions that took place on both occasions.

Notes

1. Edward Alexander, 'Professor of Terror,' *Commentary* 88, no. 2 (1989), 49–50.
2. Perry Anderson, 'On the Concatenation in the Arab World,' *New Left Review* 68 (2011), 5–15.
3. V. S. Naipaul, 'Our Universal Civilization,' *Manhattan Institute*, http://www .manhattan-institute.org/html/wl1990.htm [accessed 11 January 2012].
4. James Clifford, *The Predicament of Culture: Twentieth-Century Ethnography, Literature, and Art* (Cambridge: Harvard University Press, 1988), 271. Said engages with Clifford's arguments very generously in *Humanism and Democratic Criticism* (New York: Columbia University Press, 2004), 8–9.
5. Said, *Humanism and Democratic Criticism*, 10.
6. Noam Chomsky, *The New Military Humanism: Lessons from Kosovo* (London: Pluto, 1999).
7. Leo Spitzer, *Linguistics and Literary History: Essays in Stylistics* (Princeton, NJ: Princeton University Press, 1948), 24.
8. Neil Lazarus, 'The Fetish of "the West" in Postcolonial Theory,' in *Marxism, Modernity and Postcolonial Studies*, eds. Crystal Bartolovich and Neil Lazarus (Cambridge: Cambridge University Press, 2002), 43–64.
9. Edward W. Said, *Orientalism* (Harmondsworth: Penguin, 1985 [1978]), 4.
10. Said, *Orientalism*, 309.
11. Seymour M. Hersh, *Chain of Command* (Harmondsworth: Penguin, 2005), 39.
12. Norvell B. De Atkine, Foreword to *The Arab Mind*, by Raphael Patai (New York: Hatherleigh Press, 2002), x.
13. Neil Lazarus, *Nationalism and Cultural Practice in the Postcolonial World* (Cambridge: Cambridge University Press, 1999), 11. I too have argued that *Orientalism*'s inattention to resistance makes it a somewhat anomalous work in Said's oeuvre, *Cosmopolitan Criticism and Postcolonial Literature* (London: Palgrave, 2011), 166–76.
14. Neil Larsen, *Determinations: Essays on Theory, Narrative and Nation in the Americas* (London: Verso, 2001), 27.
15. Said, *Orientalism*, 326.
16. Said, *Orientalism*, 326–7.
17. Abdirahman A. Hussein, *Edward Said: Criticism and Society* (London: Verso, 2002), 230.
18. Edward W. Said, *The Question of Palestine* (New York: Vintage, 1992 [1979]), 231–2.
19. Edward W. Said, 'The Clash of Definitions,' in *Reflections on Exile and Other Literary and Cultural Essays*, ed. Said (London: Granta, 2000), 569–90.
20. Neil Lazarus, 'Representations of the Intellectual in *Representations of the Intellectual*,' *Research in African Literatures* 36, no. 3 (2005), 116; Timothy Brennan, *Wars of Position: The Cultural Politics of Left and Right* (New York: Columbia University Press, 2006), 93–125.

21. Erich Auerbach, 'Philology and *Weltliteratur*,' trans. Maire and Edward Said, *The Centennial Review* 13 (1969), 12–16.

22. Erich Auerbach, *Mimesis: The Representation of Reality in Western Literature*, trans. Willard R. Trask (Princeton, NJ: Princeton University Press, 1968 [1953]), 557. See Edward W. Said, *The World, the Text, and the Critic* (Cambridge: Harvard University Press, 1983), 5–9.

23. Erich Auerbach, *Literary Language and its Public in Late Latin Antiquity and the Middle Ages*, trans. Ralph Manheim (London: Routledge, 1965), 21.

24. That humanism is not an exclusively 'Western' idea is the argument put forward by George Makdisi. It is well known that humanism's Renaissance origins are in the teaching of rhetoric, erudition, polymathy and multilingualism. Less widely appreciated is that humanism took shape at least two centuries before the Italian Renaissance in the Islamic colleges, universities and madrasahs of Baghdad, Sicily and Andalucía. Evidence of this tradition's formative impact on European scholarship can be seen in Latin and vernacular translations of Arabic texts, institutional similarities and academic traditions of assessment and qualification, as well as in the importance placed in both traditions on eloquence, deliberation and self-teaching. For Makdisi the heritage of humanism is 'the work of both, the civilization of classical Arabic Islam and that of the Christian Latin West' (*The Rise of Humanism in Classical Islam and the Christian West* (Edinburgh University Press, 1990), 350). As Said puts it, 'too much is known about other traditions to believe that even humanism itself is exclusively a Western practice' (Said, *Humanism and Democratic Criticism*, 53–4).

25. Auerbach, *Mimesis*, 549.

26. Said, *Humanism and Democratic Criticism*, 27.

27. Martin Kramer, *Ivory Towers on Sand: The Failure of Middle Eastern Studies in America* (Washington, DC: The Washington Institute for Near East Policy, 2002), 138.

28. Kramer, *Ivory Towers on Sand*, 31.

29. Kramer, *Ivory Towers on Sand*, 22.

30. Kramer, *Ivory Towers on Sand*, 55.

31. Kramer, *Ivory Towers on Sand*, 37.

32. Kramer, *Ivory Towers on Sand*, 121.

33. Kramer, *Ivory Towers on Sand*, 92.

34. Kramer, *Ivory Towers on Sand*, 84.

35. Kramer, *Ivory Towers on Sand*, 2.

36. Kramer, *Ivory Towers on Sand*, 129.

37. Bertolt Brecht, *Poems: 1913–1956*, eds. John Willett and Ralph Manheim (London: Methuen, 1976), 440.

38. See Zachary Lockman's discussion of the marginalization in the US of university-based scholars and the increasing prominence of interested think tanks and ill-informed pundits, *Contending Visions of the Middle East: The History and Politics of Orientalism* (Cambridge: Cambridge University Press, 2004), 241–51.

39. Zachary Lockman, 'Behind the Battles over US Middle East Studies,' http://www.merip.org/mero/interventions/lockman_interv.html [accessed 10 July 2010] Said's antecedents include the Egyptian Marxist Anouar Abdel Malek's

'Orientalism in Crisis,' *Diogenes* 44 (1963), 104–12; Samir Amin's, *Arab Nation* (London: Zed, 1978); and Hichem Djait's, *L'Europe et l'Islam* (Paris: Seuil, 1978).

40. Kramer, *Ivory Towers on Sand*, 80.
41. Ibn Warraq, *Defending the West: A Critique of Edward Said's 'Orientalism'* (New York: Prometheus, 2007), 11.
42. Warraq, *Defending the West*, 247.
43. Warraq, *Defending the West*, 246.
44. Warraq, *Defending the West*, 18.
45. Warraq, *Defending the West*, 27.
46. Warraq, *Defending the West*, 29.
47. Warraq, *Defending the West*, 13.
48. Warraq, *Defending the West*, 245.
49. Warraq, *Defending the West*, 267.
50. Warraq, *Defending the West*, 43.
51. Warraq, *Defending the West*, 53.
52. Warraq, *Defending the West*, 54.
53. Warraq, *Defending the West*, 247.
54. Maya Jasanoff, 'Before and After Said,' *London Review of Books*, http://www .lrb.co.uk/v28/n11/jasa01_.html [accessed 8 July 2010].
55. Robert Irwin, *For Lust of Knowing: The Orientalists and Their Enemies* (London: Allen Lane, 2006), 254.
56. Irwin, *For Lust of Knowing*, 282.
57. Irwin, *For Lust of Knowing*, 298.
58. Irwin, *For Lust of Knowing*, 283.
59. Irwin, *For Lust of Knowing*, 127, 130–1.
60. Irwin, *For Lust of Knowing*, 295.
61. Irwin, *For Lust of Knowing*, 300.
62. Clifford, *The Predicament of Culture*, 264; Denis Porter, '*Orientalism* and Its Problems,' in *Colonial Discourse and Postcolonial Theory*, ed. Laura Chrisman and Patrick Williams (London: Harvester, 1993), 151; Lazarus, "Representations of the Intellectual in *Representations of the Intellectual*", 115–16; and Robert Young, *White Mythologies: Writing History and the West* (London: Routledge, 1990), 129–32.
63. Bart Moore-Gilbert, *Postcolonial Theory: Contexts, Practices, Politics* (London: Verso, 1997), 49–53.
64. John M. Mackenzie, *Orientalism: History, Theory and the Arts* (Manchester: Manchester University Press, 1995).
65. Leila Gandhi, *Affective Communities: Anticolonial Thought, Fin de Siècle Radicalism and the Politics of Friendship* (Durham, NC: Duke University Press, 2006).
66. Joseph A. Massad, *Desiring Arabs* (Chicago: The University of Chicago Press, 2007).
67. Crystal Bartolovich, 'Introduction: Marxism, Modernity, and Postcolonial Studies,' in *Marxism, Modernity and Postcolonial Studies*, 1–16.
68. Mackenzie, *Orientalism*, 207.
69. Reina Lewis, *Gendering Orientalism: Race, Femininity and Representation* (London: Routledge, 1996); Billie Melman, *Women's Orients: English Women and the Middle East, 1718–1918: Sexuality, Religion and Work* (London:

Palgrave Macmillan, 1992); and Nupur Chaudhuri and Margaret Strobel, *Western Women and Imperialism: Complicity and Resistance* (Bloomington, IN: Indiana University Press, 1992).

70. Daniel Martin Varisco, *Reading Orientalism: Said and the Unsaid* (Seattle, WA: University of Washington Press, 2008), 294.
71. Varisco, *Reading Orientalism*, 304.
72. Varisco, *Reading Orientalism*, 36.
73. Lockman, *Contending Visions*, 148–81.
74. Jasanoff, 'Before and After Said.'
75. Irwin, *For Lust of Knowing*, 308.
76. Irwin, *For Lust of Knowing*, 308.
77. Edward W. Said, *From Oslo to Iraq and the Roadmap* (London: Bloomsbury, 2004), 110.
78. Edward W. Said, *The End of the Peace Process: Oslo and After* (London: Granta, 2002).
79. Said, *From Oslo to Iraq*, 238.
80. Said, *From Oslo to Iraq*, 378.
81. Rajiv Chandrasekaran, *Imperial Life in the Emerald City: Inside Iraq's Green Zone* (New York: Vintage, 2007), 167.
82. Irwin, *For Lust of Knowing*, 302.
83. Other discussions of the importance of humanism in Said's thought include Emily Apter, 'Saidian Humanism,' *boundary 2* 31, no. 2 (2004), 35–53; Paul Bové, 'Continuing the Conversation,' *Critical Inquiry* 31, no. 2 (2005), 399–405; Saree Makdisi, 'Said, Palestine and the Humanism of Liberation,' *Critical Inquiry* 31, no. 2 (2005), 443–61; W. J. T. Mitchell, 'Secular Divination: Edward Said's Humanism,' *Critical Inquiry* 31, no. 2 (2005), 462–71; and Robert Spencer, 'Edward Said and the War in Iraq,' *New Formations* 59 (2006), 52–62.
84. Edward W. Said, 'Preface' to *Orientalism* (London: Penguin, 2003), xii.
85. Said, 'Preface' to *Orientalism*, xx.

10
'The Defeat of Narrative by Vision': Said and the Image

Nicholas Tromans

There often seems to have been something of the *fin-de-siècle* symbolist in Edward Said. It is there in the hint of dandyism of course, but I'm thinking of his way of morphing one register of experience into another – music into politics into media analysis into literature – in brilliant successions of quicksilver translations. But the characterization stalls once we consider that Said had almost nothing to say about the visual arts (or architecture), and indeed confessed that he felt inclined to 'panic' when invited to speak on the subject, as he was by the visual studies theorist W. J. T. Mitchell in 1998.[1] Mitchell tried gamely to draw Said out on the topic, managing to elicit some intriguing early memories of museum visiting in Cairo and some preferences among the masters of European painting. But an effort to turn the conversation to more general thinking about the visual by raising the seeable/sayable division in Foucault led the remainder of the conversation into much more familiar Saidian territory.[2]

In his essay 'Secular Divination: Edward Said's Humanism,' published in the 2005 number of *Critical Enquiry* devoted to 'Continuing the Conversation' with Said, Mitchell looked back on the 1998 interview and sought to interpret Said's apparent aversion to the visual.[3] In a couple of long and dense paragraphs toward the end of this piece, Mitchell tentatively suggests a parallel with one of Said's luminaries, the Enlightenment pioneer of a secular philosophy of history, Giambattista Vico. Vico distinguished between the true, revealed religion of the Bible, based on the unmediated perception of divinity and the prohibition of idolatry, and the alternative gentile traditions rooted in divination, that is, the reading of 'sensible signs.'[4] Mitchell points to the paradox that Vico's own New Science is rooted in this 'science of auspicial divinity,'[5] for secular criticism assumes as its role the analysis of systems of humanly generated meanings masquerading as idols and totems:

> Divination might be seen, paradoxically, as a distinctly *secular* hermeneutics in contrast to the sacred hermeneutic tradition grounded in the Bible. Divination is associated with the interpretation of human and natural objects – auguries based in the material body and its states, prophecies based in the formal alignments of stars or the behavior of animals, or diagnoses based in the analysis of dreams and (most notably) in graven images and works of art.[6]

Mitchell concludes by suggesting that Said shares with Vico a tragic sense of humanity being unable ever to entirely extract itself from these systems of visual signs. Myths, legends and illusions may be shattered, but what remains will always be another set of representations, never a purely clear view. To pause before an image, then, is to acknowledge the limits of critical work. This might suggest failure, or, in Mitchell's reading, it confesses language's 'bafflement' – Said's preferred term for aporetic wisdom.

In Said's own writing, there are good examples of images being interpreted in precisely this way, as the point of exhaustion of argument. In *Orientalism*, a book devoted to representations but which almost entirely overlooks images, one of Said's *bêtes noires* is the early Victorian Egyptologist Edward William Lane. Said describes the introductory pages to Lane's sprawling *Manners and Customs of the Modern Egyptians* (1836) in terms of a narrative unable to support itself, with the appearance of images being the indication that the inevitable implosion has taken place. Lane is seeking to explain the Egyptian character as a function of the local climate, a strategy which soon leads him to contradict himself:

> and soon [we] are bogged down in descriptions, complete with charts and line drawings, of Cairene architecture, decoration, fountains, and locks. When a narrative strain re-emerges, it is clearly only as a formality.[7]

These diagrams represent, then, the collapse of Lane's argument, and reveal for Said a larger aspect of Orientalism, namely the conflict between narrative and vision. The latter implies, for him, a static, panoptical composition which cannot accommodate intricate narrative. Personal stories are erased through the image's ultimately territorial requirements – the process which Said, later in *Orientalism*, terms 'The defeat of narrative by vision.'[8] In this paper I am going to pursue some of the implications, for Said and for his legacy, of this notion of the image as boundary. For the younger Said, the visual register appears to deny authentic narrative: it seems in some way to occupy and shut down the spaces required by language. But for the later Said, a few examples of visual communication came to be valued precisely on account of their ability to speak in ways which went beyond what words might say. I will also consider some of the implications of Said's attitudes toward images for the academic study of visual culture.

Said repeatedly invited the interpretation of his thinking through his biography, and his 1999 memoir *Out of Place* certainly encourages the idea that a suspicion of the image developed early on in his life. The account of Said's childhood describes his father's excessive passion for capturing all family gatherings and outings on camera, determined to fix an image of a stable and successful existence. Borrowing the terms of Foucault's account of disciplinary surveillance, Said writes of his longing to escape 'my father's unforgiving optical grid':

> I remember that as I grew older – certainly by age eleven or twelve – I felt that the ritual of doing the same thing over and over in front of my father's camera was becoming more and more disconcerting. This awareness coincided with my wish somehow to be disembodied. One of my recurrent fantasies … was to be a book, whose fate I took to be happily free of unwelcome changes, distortions of its shape, criticism of its looks.[9]

Thus the passionate identification with literature was born from a phobia of images. In keeping with this almost mythic account, it was apparently the panoptical patriarch himself who offered a solution to the young Said's growing anxiety over being looked at:

> To be looked at directly, and to return the gaze, was most difficult for me. When I was about ten I mentioned this to my father. 'Don't look at their eyes; look at their nose,' he said, thereby communicating to me a secret technique I have used for decades. When I began to teach as a graduate student in the late fifties I found it imperative to take off my glasses in order to turn the class into a blur that I couldn't see. And to this day I find it unbearably difficult to look at myself on television, or even to read about myself.[10]

Again, for the study of literature to proceed, the gaze has to be dissolved or otherwise gotten out of the way. Of course these autobiographical passages prompt the sceptic to ask just how much pain it can have caused Said to appear on camera given his visual conspicuousness from the 1980s onwards. (As I write these words, images of a handsome middle-aged Said gaze in all directions from the covers of books lying on my study floor.) A former student of Said's, Aram Veeser, notes in his recently published memoir that 'Edward Said was often photographed. He had a knack for organizing the image.'[11] 'Organizing' is a rather interesting choice of word, suggesting a certain arm's-length distance in Said's dealing with images even when he consented to work with or through them.

Sticking with Said's biography and his own use of it to explicate his lines of thought, his 1970 essay on 'The Arab Portrayed,' an account of media representations of the 1967 Arab–Israeli War, has an important role as the germ of *Orientalism* and as marking the point at which Said became politicized in the Palestinian cause.[12] Here he complains of the ways in which contrasting images of the two sides in the conflict were evoked in America, the Israelis as individuals with personal narratives, with histories and so with tragic status, the Arabs on the other hand as an undifferentiated mass, darkly threatening the scene from somewhere offstage. As Said was to object on many occasions over the following years, the Palestinians had become invisible, disembodied.[13] Which is to say, they had achieved precisely the state Said tells us he himself had longed for as a boy when confronted with his father's lens. We might say that it was Said's commitment to the 'invisible' Palestinians which was the dynamic in his eventual acceptance that images and representations could not be avoided – that if we do not provide them for ourselves then someone else will do it for us.

Said's *Orientalism* was a thoroughgoing assault upon images of Arabs in the sense of stereotypes – descriptions which were replicated and rein-forced until they appeared natural and fixed, deterring any deviation from the representation they offered. The book cast these stereotypes as active, allied to – if not agents of – European imperialism. But the idea of the image as a tool of control was itself a hardy stereotype, breed-ing many replicas of itself in academic writing, and providing an all too easily available opinion to offer in regard to any visual representa-tion of 'the Orient.'[14] The gaze in general was equally easy to figure as something inherently malign, a coercive structure keeping the subordi-nate in their place. Martin Jay has surveyed this theme as it appears in modern philosophy, most notably in Foucault and Lacan, in his 1993 book *Downcast Eyes: The Denigration of Vision in Twentieth-Century French Thought*, in which Said makes a brief appearance. Jay references Said's characterization, which we have already mentioned, of the Orientalists' vision as a panorama, that wrap-around representation of territory so popular in the nineteenth century (and, intriguingly, adopted by some Arab rulers in the twentieth[15]) which suppressed the significance of any micro-narrative aspiring to take place within the bounds of its epic parameters.[16] In principle the same might of course be said of any kind of composition, but political implications immediately emerge when a composition explicitly purports to capture the likeness of territory. Mitchell has interpreted the colonial landscape – as painted by European artist-travellers – as a prelude to conquest, as a fictitious series of spaces from which to begin the very real pronouncements of possession.[17] In his 1998 interview with Said, Mitchell hints at these issues, leading Said to return to one of his regular themes, the relationship between territory and the possibility of narrative: space as a prerequisite of story.[18] The reader cannot help but feel a little frustration that Said will not talk specifically about images at this point in the conversation. He seems to veer away from the topic of visual representations of the territories of Israel/Palestine and from the relationships between narratives and images (one definition of which is signs *in space*) just when such subjects seem so relevant to his concerns. Although Said himself stopped shy of the image in this case (or rather he again stopped shy *at* the image), some of the politically committed geographical writings on modern conflicts in the Middle East, fusing analysis of visual technologies and of political ideologies, have been among the most creative to be produced under his influence.[19] And while Said left others to pursue this more precise critique of visual practices, on other occasions he explored the possible roles images might have in interrupting narratives in a productive way.

During the 1980s Said developed the critique of representation offered in *Orientalism* by addressing the ways in which Orientalist stereotypes were available also to those being ostensibly represented to reclaim, reform and reply to.[20] In 1985 he commented in an interview that 'Representations are a form of human economy...I don't think there is any getting away from them – they are as basic as language,' suggesting that the response to Orientalist discourse could never be simply to reject its imagery, but had also to provide other, better representations.[21] At this time Said was completing his only major project with a central visual component, *After the Last Sky: Palestinian Lives*, a book of photographs by the Swiss photojournalist Jean Mohr which Said selected and used as the inspiration for a melancholy text reflecting on everyday Palestinian experience and his own distance from it.[22] The collaboration had come about through Said's admiration of an earlier alliance of Mohr's, with the writer John Berger. In their book, *Another Way of Telling* (first published in French in 1981), Berger used Mohr's photographs of the remains of peasant life in Europe to attempt a novel mode of narrative where pictures which seemed to declare an almost brutal realism were recast as illustrations to texts which hovered somewhere between fictionalized biography and reportage.[23] Said reviewed the English version of *Another Way of Telling* in *The Nation*, praising Berger's effort to wrest personal narrative history – albeit in fictive mode – from authorized institutional narratives, and he fell especially for one particular photograph of the lined face of an impossibly hard-working old man.[24] But Said ends his review asking Berger how his emphasis upon memory and upon subjective alternatives to dominant ideologies might impact political activism: what were the future implications for this new way of remembering?

Whether Said himself succeeded in making good this political gap in his own collaboration with Mohr is far from clear.[25] He set about the project, to borrow Veeser's phrase, by organizing the images. Browsing Mohr's Geneva archive of several thousand shots of Palestinians taken at various times since 1948, Said improvised four loose themes under whose rubric he selected prints: *States/Interiors/Emergence/Past and Future*. The method, he recalled, was self-consciously musical, with little attention paid to the specific facts of the images' date, location or immediate context. The intention was to follow Berger in disrupting the predictable narratives carried across from fiction into journalism, and to represent instead 'Fragments, memories, disjointed scenes, intimate particulars' which could not be corralled into a unifying story leading somewhere conclusive.[26] So, at least went the aspiration, the image's capacity to baffle conventional narratives would now be turned to political advantage. But for someone so very far removed from the people and places described in the book (Said had not been in Palestine for nearly 40 years), this was a precarious strategy, for surely he risked appearing to subsume Mohr's sprawling archive of Palestinian experience into his own personal narrative of exile. In fact, with extraordinary irony, when the strategy did come up against its limits, it was precisely because of the intimacy of one of the photographs with Said's own family history. In the text of *After the Last Sky*, Said relates how, when showing the photographs he had chosen to his sister, she had pointed out to him something he had managed to overlook – that a portrait of an old lady wearing heavy spectacles, a hairnet and a warm smile was not just a charismatic old body but was in fact Mrs Farraj, a distant relation whom Said now remembered meeting in the 1940s. Abruptly and disorientingly a new semantic register is opened, more personalized than that signalled in the individualized yet anonymous other photos; and where can that leave those other images in comparison, except as, in some degree, types after all? As Said confessed, 'Something has been lost,' leaving a sense that 'the representation is all we have.'[27] Perhaps this is the best example in Said's work of an image marking the end of the road for a process of analysis.

Said, with characteristic candour, did not omit the portrait of Mrs Farraj from *After the Last Sky*, but did remove it from its intended sequence (*Interiors*), placing it aside in a kind of coda to that section. Thus it interfered only minimally in the central method of the book which involved getting the pictures within each section to speak together rather than individually, avoiding the static understanding of the image in which a single space is mapped through a unique composition, the completeness of which appears to preclude further development. It was in large part this same attraction of the image-sequence which appealed to Said in Joe Sacco's classic graphic novel *Palestine*, first published in the 1990s, to which Said provided a celebratory preface in 2001. Sacco spent several weeks in Gaza and the West Bank over the winter of 1991–92, and his 'comic' is a memoir of his efforts to understand the people he encountered there. The imagery is an unsparingly ugly species of caricature, emphasizing, for example, grotesquely exaggerated mouths, which has its roots in the political satire of the Weimar Republic and which seems to aim to reinforce the author's honest account of his own preconceptions, fears and failures. With a few exceptions, the pictures evoke a claustrophobic subjectivity, where the disorientation of overcrowded social spaces echoes the bewilderment of Sacco's political understanding. On one page he describes himself discovering a copy of Said's *Orientalism* in the Gaza flat of an American English teacher. With typical self-deprecating irony, Sacco wishes he could remain at the comfortable apartment reading Said rather than keep his appointment at the Jibaliya Refugee Camp.[28] In his 2001 preface, Said returned the compliment, writing that 'Sacco's art has the power to detain us, to keep us from impatiently wandering off in order to follow a catch-phrase or a lamentably predictable narrative of triumph and fulfillment' and: 'certainly his images are more graphic than anything you can either read or see on television.'[29] By graphic Said must mean specific: Sacco's method of dealing with 'Palestine' only through the personal histories of the individuals he meets provides the antidote to the media's treatment of Arabs en masse that Said had been complaining about since the 1967 War.

After the hesitations to speak about the image which we have noted in Said, especially in his 1998 interview with Mitchell, there is almost a sense of relief that in the last few years of his life he found some images of Palestine to celebrate, even enjoy, and it is intriguing that these should have been the work of a creative artist, albeit one in a *Sachlichkeit* tradition, rather than that of, say, a photographer in the mould of Mohr. Said wrote at least one other introductory text for an artwork referring to Palestine – his essay 'The Art of Displacement: Mona Hatoum's Logic of Irreconcilables' which appeared in the catalogue for the artist's 2000 Tate exhibition *The Entire World as a Foreign Land*. The show comprised pieces describing an everyday domestic world in which it had become impossible to carry on living, a tragi-comic environment in which the objects appeared as 'mundane instruments of a defiant memory' creating a space marked by 'changes in everyday materials and objects that permit no return or real repatriation' but which are nevertheless 'unwilling to let go of the past that they carry along with them like some silent catastrophe.'[30] At this stage in his life, Said was often invited to contribute some comment or imprimatur to works with a Palestinian theme of many kinds. But while the texts he wrote on Sacco and Hatoum are just two of several such supportive statements, they are also sincere appreciations and lead us to wonder what, had he lived, Said might ultimately have been induced to write about that special category of the image, the fine arts.

In the 1998 interview, Mitchell manages to get Said, again with hesitation it seems, to think back to some of the museum experiences which had moved him over the years. Said recalls no encounter with Western art during his youth in Cairo, 'So the painterly and the picturesque were, to me, very obscure. There were no keys to them.'[31] Mitchell does however succeed in prompting Said to recall some of the alternative visual spectacles on offer in 1940s Cairo, specifically the recently established popular museums which included a waxworks display and the huge Agricultural Museum at Giza. At the latter, the young Said was powerfully struck by the grotesque specimens of veterinary pathology – exhibits which still have a kind of abject allure today. In an article on Egyptian museums published a few years ago, the journalist Fayza Hassan asked:

How horrific could a museum dedicated to agriculture really be? To find out, head upstairs to the mounted animal heads, hacked-up birds and stuffed croc gallery. Next door, the communicable diseases exhibit features giant models of mange, pickled diseased livers, a blown-up camel's stomach, crucified guinea pigs and a hair ball the size of a grapefruit recovered from a horse's intestine.[32]

Meanwhile, at the waxworks museum (now indefinitely closed for renovation), the exhibits were said to melt in the summer. Hassan delights in recording how 'Cleopatra's nose droops to her chin and sweaty severed limbs litter the floor. One unnamed princess wanders aimlessly in search of her missing head.' From these formative experiences Said seems to have developed something of a taste for the sensationally morbid.[33] The Western artworks which Said names to Mitchell as having remained with him tend to be images of human decay, deformation or decomposition. He mentions the contorted bodies of El Greco, Rodin and Francis Bacon, and especially admires the horrific imagery and expressive painterliness of Goya, specifically *Saturn Devouring his Children*: 'There's a kind of gentleness in the middle of all the violence that impresses me a great deal.'[34] In a similar vein is another of Said's favourites, Ivan Albright's *The Picture of Dorian Gray*. Painted for the 1945 film based on Wilde's story, this gothic-burlesque piece represents the horrific decay which the portrait of Dorian underwent to allow its original to retain his beauty. In light of these preferences we can see more easily how the ragged features of the old man in Berger and Mohr's *Another Way of Telling* and the vulnerable lumpiness of Sacco's Palestinians would have appealed to Said.

Said also names to Mitchell as favourite artists Cézanne and Picasso, both again painters associated with the decomposition of the human body, particularly the latter's *Demoiselles d'Avignon*, one of the great treasures of New York's Museum of Modern Art. But beyond this, the way that Cubism combines different viewpoints superimposed upon one another, fracturing the ostensible subject into related but disjointed facets, allowed it entry into Said's repertoire of metaphors for the Palestinian experience, one epithet for which, offered in *The Question of Palestine*, is 'cubistic.'[35] Later, another preferred visual metaphor – applied approvingly to various subjects – became traditional Islamic geometric decoration. When describing the process of selecting the photographs for *After the Last Sky* according to loose structural themes rather than specific subject matter, Said suggested he was working as if with 'the nonrepresentational art of the Islamic world.'[36] As we have already noted, the process was equally supposed to be musical, and as Said developed a fondness for the model of contrapuntal interpretation in his later work, this equation between the abstract pattern-making to be found in both music and Islamic decoration came to seem significant. Indeed, it is clear that the attraction of Islamic decoration was a function of the model of counterpoint favoured by the later Said. Earlier he had not been so appreciative of Islamic design, even allowing himself to write, in *Covering Islam* (1981), that 'it is perhaps true that Islam has produced no very powerful visual aesthetic tradition,' a jarring moment in the midst of a painstakingly ruthless exposure of the laziness of others' writings on Islam.[37]

These references to Said's limited comments on Western art lead us to the question of his influence upon and legacy for art history, a discipline which today finds its boundaries threatened by the more dynamic neighbouring, or enveloping, field of visual studies. The basics of this story can be told simply. In the 1980s, art historians looked at European paintings of the Orient and found there self-serving Western stereotyped representations comparable to the writings which Said had analysed in *Orientalism*. From the 1990s a more contrapuntal reading has become standard, in line with Said's own development – that is, the participation of 'Orientals' in their own representation by others, and dialogues between 'Orientals' and 'Occidentals,' were emphasized. But without Said's unrelenting focus on the urgent political crises in the Arab world, the political aspect of the critique of Orientalist visual culture risks evaporating into elaborate patterns of influence.

The nineteenth-century French Salon painter Jean-Léon Gérôme seemed from the start the most obvious place to begin transferring Said's approaches in *Orientalism* from literature to art. Gérôme worked in a highly polished classical style which allowed him to describe architectural and still-life details with a reality effect that seemed to carry across to the human content of his Egyptian and Turkish subjects, in which women bathed naked and men appeared pious or ferocious in picturesque costumes. Linda Nochlin used Gérôme, along with his Orientalist predecessor Delacroix, as the main theme in her 1983 essay 'The Imaginary Orient' which detailed the ways in which these artists edited the reality they experienced for political and imperial ends, how their apparent Orientalist expertise often turned out to be a fraud, and how poorly they compared with the progressive art of a figure such as Manet whose flattened spaces and self-consciously cropped compositions confessed the inherent artificiality of the Western representational tradition.[38] Nochlin's essay appeared at the highpoint of the intellectual war of independence of art history, as the discipline sought to assert its status within the academy by vociferously picking fights with museum curators, its parent professionals. Nochlin's essay began as an exhibition review, and ended with a call to art historians to abandon the neutral documentary methodologies of the archive in favour of techniques imported from more critical fields such as film studies. The article has enjoyed an after-life, in proportion to its scope, scarcely less prolonged than Said's *Orientalism* itself, being described by the art historian Frederick Bohrer in 2005 as 'still matchless' and by one of Said's longest-winded critics, Ibn Warraq, in 2007, as 'offensive,' 'tendentious,' 'calumniating' and even as 'degrading the Orient.'[39] The essay's long-maintained position at the centre of the debates around Orientalism and the visual arts – it is now nearly 30 years old – seems hard to account for until we reflect that neither Nochlin nor anyone else ever extended the ambitions of that article to the length of a full book. The project of transferring Said's original critique of Orientalism to the visual arts seemed somehow unnecessary because everyone could imagine, more or less, how it would read from Nochlin's paper which itself persisted in the literature as a kind of telling fragment (to borrow one of Nochlin's own favoured metaphors of modernity) of that larger possibility.[40]

Said had in fact himself considered Gérôme's brand of Orientalism in *Covering Islam*, where he marvels at the capacity of the American media to remake the world according to its own needs. In that book he laments how easily a painting by Gérôme, which he represents as kitsch but harmless in its original guise, so easily became a crudely conceived cover for *Time* magazine in April 1979, the month of the founding of the Islamic Republic of Iran:

> [T]he cover was adorned with a Gérôme painting of a bearded muezzin standing in a minaret, calmly summoning the faithful to prayer; it was as florid and overstated a nineteenth-century period piece of Orientalist art as one could imagine. Anachronistically, however, this quiet scene was emblazoned with a caption that had nothing to do with it: 'The Militant Revival.' There could be no better way of symbolizing the difference between Europe and America on the subject of Islam. A placid and decorative painting done almost routinely in Europe as an aspect of the general culture had been transformed by three words into a general American obsession.[41]

Here Said reads the meaning of the image(s) almost entirely in terms of location. The shift from Europe, where the painting formed part of an extended family of repetitive iconography, to America, where, standing alone, the picture is compelled to illustrate the headline, is decisive. While our first reaction to re-reading this passage may be nostalgia for a time when such coverage might be seen only as an American problem, we can also see that Said appears to be attributing to Gérôme a far less settled meaning than that insisted upon by Nochlin, to whom his art was inherently bad and reactionary. Said thus in effect anticipates the kinds of site-specific analyses of Orientalist *imagery* that have become the norm in recent years in contrast to the former castigation of certain European Orientalist *painters* for not being nearer the front of the queue for the future according to Modernism's chronology of things.

The tide turned in the 1990s at conferences, and in the resulting essay collections, where dialogue and counterpoint became the standard models.[42] A simple but highly effective piece by Emily Weeks on a portrait by David Wilkie of the Egyptian Pasha, Mehemet Ali, painted in Alexandria in 1841, helped crystallize the new approach.[43] The Pasha, observed Weeks, had dictated carefully to the British artist how he wished to be portrayed, and Wilkie had duly followed his instructions. The image was thus jointly authored by sitter and portraitist and, despite Wilkie's thoroughgoing immersion in Orientalist stereotypes, could not be seen as Orientalist in the simple old sense. The same period saw a new focus upon Western art's engagement with the Ottoman Empire, especially at Istanbul, a place to which the original theory of Orientalism did not travel well, given the complex recycling of images among artists there from many different backgrounds, and the existence of what has been labelled Ottoman Orientalism, the phenomenon of metropolitan Turks constructing peripheral identities for their imperial subjects.[44] Osman Hamdi Bey, the Turkish archaeologist, museum official and painter of traditional Ottoman costume and architecture, personifies this alternative mode of Orientalism and in consequence has become one of the most widely discussed figures of the late nineteenth century among art historians.

The counterpoint model of cultural interaction and the history of art in Istanbul were made for one another, but by this point in our sketch of recent art–historical writing, Said has vanished from the picture. To take a recent, and fairly typical example of mainstream academic work in this area, none of the essays in *The Poetics and Politics of Place: Ottoman Istanbul and British Orientalism* (2011) feel the need even to pay homage to Said, except now as an historical phenomenon in the archives of the literature.[45] There are indeed few grand reputations deferred to in such work, the trend of which is toward micro-history, with a strong scepticism regarding generalization. The editors' introduction to *The Poetics and Politics of Place* warns of the dangers of polarities and insists on semantic multiplicity and above all on complexity. I do not want to argue that they are wrong, or indeed that there is any deficiency in such work. What I am going to claim is that there seems to be a certain disingenuousness within Western art history today when it deals with Middle Eastern subject matter, or at least that art–historical *institutions* are guilty of this.

In 2008–09 I attended several academic conferences which tied in, explicitly or just conveniently, with the thirtieth anniversary of Said's *Orientalism* (one of them being of course the multidisciplinary event on which the present book is based). The two principal art-related events in London in this period were the Courtauld Institute's *Framing the Other: 30 Years After Orientalism* (26 April 2008) and the Tate's *Contemporary Art in the Middle East* (22–23 January 2009). Both were excellent. But I was struck by the apparent need to bring in as keynote speakers people unconnected with the art world, not, or not just, to provide larger context, but quite clearly to supply the politics. At the Courtauld, Robert Fisk did his usual heady mixture of autobiography and horror stories, while at the Tate the special guests were the geographer Derek Gregory and the Palestinian poet and former PLO representative Mourid Barghouti – both figures associated in different ways with Said whose posthumous presence was thus in effect vicariously effected. The only regret one might reasonably have felt at being offered the chance to hear such significant speakers was that the balance between the aesthetic and political, which Mitchell praises Said for maintaining in his texts, seemed possible for art history only by balancing itself against other modes of writing. The point about disingenuousness, then, is that art history wants its complexity and its politics, but it does not seem to believe itself able to embrace both simultaneously.

The study of images in the aftermath of Said really need have no such diffidence. There is plenty of scope for this academic field to recover something of the dynamic political relevance that the conferences I have mentioned seemed to feel they lacked. For example, clearly the best way to translate Said's original formula of Orientalism into the visual register, rather than asking whether this or that painting was flattering or otherwise to its subject matter, is to examine how the West has historically denied the visual competence of the Oriental. That is, traditions of iconophobia and aniconism within certain Islamic societies were exaggerated into an accusation that Islam was inherently retarded in vision, incapable of proper perspective upon the world.[46] I have argued elsewhere that in the case of the Victorian painter of Palestine, William Holman Hunt, these assumptions of optical superiority directly informed his evolving Zionist politics.[47] More recently, the American neo-realist painter John Currin has spoken of how he sees his erotic imagery in part as retaliation for 9/11, and pornography generally as (another) last stand of Western visual culture mounted against the supposed alternative of Islamic iconoclasm.[48] Nor do we have to think very hard to find other examples in Western culture of Islam being held to blame for placing impediments on a 'natural' desire to look.[49] A related set of questions could be set out around what we might term 'the permission to represent,' that is, the investigation of the relationship between power and the possession of technologies for generating representations. Consider how important it has appeared for those Westerners wishing to influence the Middle East to induct their allies in the techniques of the observer. One could, for example, assemble an interesting iconographic album of European Arabists demonstrating to their friends how to use the view-finder of a camera or weapon. In a popular book about T. E. Lawrence 'of Arabia,' I find a 1918 photograph of an RAF pilot demonstrating to a Bedu man the sight of the machine gun mounted on his biplane. The image is captioned 'The Arabs were fascinated and heartened by the military technology that Britain supplied.'[50] Given the current flourishing British arms trade in the Middle East, how contemporary that sounds.

Edward Said never really became comfortable writing about images, despite some of the enthusiasms of his later years which I have described. His first model of Orientalism seemed to shy away from any visual representation as necessarily involving some kind of territorial assertion which risked compromising the independent voice of the critic. Later, Said showed a greater sympathy toward the image's habitation of space, toward its embodiment, seeing in this a potential to express certain human predicaments, among them the sense of displacement which he felt Hatoum's sculpture succeeded in describing. For those of us writing on images in the wake of Said, the challenge is to recognize, with him, the tendency of pictures to confound autonomous, independent narratives. To confront the inherently spatial, localized nature of images should lead us to an understanding of the personal and political *relationships* which they always establish.

Notes

1. W. J. T. Mitchell, 'The Panic of the Visual: A Conversation with Edward W. Said' (1998), in *Edward Said and the Work of the Critic: Speaking Truth to Power*, ed. Paul A. Bové (Durham, NC: Duke University Press, 2000), 31–50.
2. See Mitchell, 'The Panic of the Visual,' 42, where Deleuze's account of the distinction between *le visible et l'énonçable* in Foucault is cited: cf. Gilles Deleuze, *Foucault* (Paris: Éditions de Minuit, 1986), 55–75. For a suggestion that while Foucault moved from the seeable to the sayable, Said followed the reverse trajectory, see Joseph Massad, 'Affiliating with Edward Said,' in *Edward Said: A Legacy of Emancipation and Representation*, eds. Adel Iskandar and Hakem Rustom (Berkeley, CA and London: University of California Press, 2010), 35ff.
3. W. J. T. Mitchell, 'Secular Divination: Edward Said's Humanism,' *Critical Inquiry* 31, no. 2 (2005), 462–71.
4. Giambattista Vico, *The New Science* (1730), trans. Thomas Goddard Bergin and Max Harold Fisch (Ithaca, NY: Cornell University Press, 1948), 7.
5. Vico, *New Science*, 309.
6. Mitchell, 'Secular Divination,' 495–7. Mitchell might have reinforced his argument by mentioning Vico's use of Vaccaro's elaborate allegorical frontispiece to his book as a pictorial basis upon which to begin to expound his New Science.
7. Edward W. Said, *Orientalism* (1978) (London: Penguin, 1985), 162.
8. Said, *Orientalism*, 239.
9. Edward W. Said, *Out of Place: A Memoir* (London: Granta, 1999), 76.
10. Said, *Out of Place*, 55.
11. H. Aram Veeser, *Edward Said: The Charisma of Criticism* (New York: Routledge, 2010), 1. Veeser, who describes himself as a 'sceptical admirer' of his subject, has taken his interest in the performative side of Said so far as to have developed a touring performance work in which he re-enacts Said's demolitions of his interlocutors in public debates.
12. Edward W. Said, 'The Arab Portrayed,' in *The Arab-Israeli Confrontation of June 1967: An Arab Perspective*, ed. Ibrahim Abu-Lughod (Evanston, IL: Northwestern University Press, 1970), 1–9.
13. See, for example, David Barsamian and Edward W. Said, *Culture and Resistance: Conversations with Edward W. Said* (London: Pluto, 2003), 20.
14. For a more sophisticated attempt to use the concepts of image and picture in an analysis of colonialism in the Arab world, see Timothy Mitchell, *Colonising Egypt* (Berkeley, CA and London: University of California Press, 1991).
15. Ralph Hyde, *Panoramania! The Art and Entertainment of the 'All-Embracing' View* (London: Barbican Art Gallery, 1988), 272, 275.
16. Martin Jay, *Downcast Eyes: The Denigration of Vision in Twentieth-Century French Thought* (Berkeley, CA and London: University of California Press, 1993), 295.
17. W. J. T. Mitchell, 'The Imperial Landscape' (1984), reprinted in *Landscape and Power*, ed. W. J. T. Mitchell (Chicago: University of Chicago Press, 2002), 5–34.

18. Mitchell, 'Panic of the Visual,' 43–4. See further Derek Gregory, 'Edward Said's Imaginative Geographies,' in *Thinking Space*, eds. Mike Crang and Nigel Thrift (London: Routledge, 2000), 302–48; and William V. Spanos, *The Legacy of Edward W. Said* (Urbana, IL: University of Illinois Press, 2009), 26–69.
19. I am thinking especially of Derek Gregory, *The Colonial Present: Afghanistan, Palestine, Iraq* (Oxford: Blackwell, 2004).
20. See Edward W. Said, 'Orientalism Reconsidered', in *Reflections on Exile and Other Essays* (Cambridge, MA: Harvard University Press, 2000), 198–215.
21. From a 1985 interview with Jonathan Crary and Phil Mariani in Edward W. Said, *Power, Politics and Culture: Interviews with Edward W. Said*, ed. Gauri Viswanathan (London: Bloomsbury, 2004), 41–2.
22. Edward W. Said (photographs by Jean Mohr), *After the Last Sky: Palestinian Lives* (1986) (New York: Columbia University Press, 1999). The title of the book was borrowed from a line in Mahmoud Darwish's poem 'The Earth is Closing on Us.'
23. Berger's collaboration with Mohr went back to their 1967 classic *A Fortunate Man* about an English country doctor. See John Roberts, *The Art of Interruption: Realism, Photography and the Everyday* (Manchester: Manchester University Press, 1998), 128–43.
24. Edward W. Said, 'Bursts of Meaning' reprinted in *Reflections on Exile*, 148–52. For the photograph which so struck Said, see John Berger and Jean Mohr, *Another Way of Telling* (Cambridge: Granta, 1989), 293. *Another Way of Telling* was one of the tiny number of books about images to warrant an honourable mention anywhere in the text or notes to Said's *Culture and Imperialism*: Edward W. Said, *Culture and Imperialism* (London: Chatto & Windus, 1993), 405. Also mentioned are T. J. Clark on Manet and Paris, and Malek Alloula on popular postcards of harem scenes (133–4, 222).
25. On *After the Last Sky*, see John Hawley, 'Edward Said, John Berger, Jean Mohr: In Search of an Other Optic,' in *Paradoxical Citizenship: A Tribute to Edward Said*, ed. Silvia Nagy-Zekmi (Lanham, MD: Lexington, 2006), 203–10 and Mustapha Marrouchi, *Edward Said at the Limits* (New York: State University of New York Press, 2004), 107–25.
26. Said, *After the Last Sky*, xi.
27. Said, *After the Last Sky*, 84.
28. Joe Sacco, *Palestine* (Seattle: Fantagraphics Books, 2001), 177.
29. Edward W. Said, 'Homage to Joe Sacco,' in Sacco, *Palestine*, v, iii. Said also suggests that comic images generally 'in their relentless foregrounding ... seemed to say what couldn't otherwise be said ... defying the ordinary processes of thought' (ii).
30. Edward W. Said, 'The Art of Displacement: Mona Hatoum's Logic of Irreconcilables,' in *The Entire World as a Foreign Land*, ed. Mona Hatoum (London: Tate Gallery, 2000), 17.
31. Mitchell, 'Panic of the Visual,' 39.
32. Fayza Hassan, 'Museums Across Egypt,' *Egypt Today*, April 2006.
33. Conceivably, the youthful Said's taste was informed by the Surrealism which flourished in Cairo at this period: see Samir Gharieb, *Surrealism in Egypt and Plastic Arts* (Cairo: Prism, 1986). Thanks to Peter Gran for this suggestion.
34. Mitchell, 'Panic of the Visual,' 33.
35. Edward W. Said, *The Question of Palestine* (London: Routledge & Kegan Paul, 1979), 122.

36. Mitchell, 'Panic of the Visual,' 36; see also 45.
37. Edward W. Said, *Covering Islam: How the Media and the Experts Determine How We See the Rest of the World*, 1981 (London: Vintage, 1997), 66.
38. Linda Nochlin, 'The Imaginary Orient' (1983), in Nochlin, *The Politics of Vision: Essays on Nineteenth-Century Art and Society* (New York: Harper & Row, 1989), 33–59.
39. Frederick N. Bohrer, 'The Sweet Waters of Asia,' in *Edges of Empire: Orientalism and Visual Culture*, eds. Jocelyn Hackforth-Jones and Mary Roberts (Oxford: Blackwell, 2005), 136 n.2; Ibn Warraq (pseud.), *Defending the West: A Critique of Edward Said's Orientalism* (Amherst, NY: Prometheus, 2007), 342. Ibn Warraq (341–2) makes much of Nochlin's false claim that the Arabic inscription on the tiled wall in Gérôme's *The Snake Charmer* is illegible, a mistake in which Said is implicated as Nochlin had consulted him on the question (Nochlin, 'Imaginary Orient,' 57–8 n.7). Said had himself chosen the *Snake Charmer* as the cover illustration for the paperback edition of *Orientalism* in 1979: Daniel Martin Varisco, *Reading Orientalism: Said and the Unsaid* (Seattle, WA: University of Washington Press, 2007), 25–6. He later singled Nochlin's article out for praise in 'Orientalism Reconsidered' (213).
40. Linda Nochlin, *The Body in Pieces: The Fragment as a Metaphor of Modernity* (London: Thames & Hudson, 1994).
41. *Covering Islam*, 16–17.
42. No sooner had the counterpoint model for cultural interaction become conventional than Said himself began to express doubts about its suggestion of a dominant theme which needs to be responded to, and even talked of substituting the less hierarchical model of *heterophony* (Veeser, *Edward Said*, 124, 129).
43. Emily Weeks, 'About Face: Sir David Wilkie's Portrait of Mehemet Ali, Pasha of Egypt,' in *Orientalism Transposed*, eds. Julie Codell and Dianne Sachko Macleod (Aldershot: Ashgate, 1998), 46–62.
44. See Ussama Makdisi, 'Ottoman Orientalism,' *American Historical Review* 107, no. 3 (2002), 768–96.
45. Zeynep Inankur, Reina Lewis and Mary Roberts, eds., *The Poetics and Politics of Place: Ottoman Istanbul and British Orientalism* (Istanbul: Kıraç Foundation, 2011), 99.
46. Finbarr Barry Flood's forthcoming book, *Islam and Image: Aniconism, Iconoclasm, and the Economy of Representation*, promises to be a significant survey of this theme.
47. Nicholas Tromans, 'Palestine: Picture of Prophecy,' in *William Holman Hunt*, eds. Carol Jacobi and Katherine Lochnan (Toronto, ON: Art Gallery of Ontario, 2008), 135–60.
48. David Usborne, 'John Currin: The Filth and the Fury,' *The Independent*, 16 March 2008.
49. See Joan Wallach Scott, *The Politics of the Veil* (Princeton, NJ: Princeton University Press, 2007).
50. James Barr, *Setting the Desert on Fire: T.E. Lawrence and Britain's Secret War in Arabia, 1916–18* (London: Bloomsbury, 2006), photograph between 172–3; cf. Frank Gardner, *Blood and Sand* (London: Bantam, 2006), photograph between 260–1 for a comparable image of Omani Bedu women with a BBC film camera.

11
How Much Is Enough Said? Some Gendered Responses to *Orientalism*

Joanna de Groot

In the 35 years since the publication of Edward Said's text *Orientalism* there has, of course, been debate and polemic around the agenda established by that text.[1] Other sections in this volume explore a number of these avenues, but the focus of this piece will be on one of the most paradoxical aspects of *Orientalism*'s legacy: its engagement, or lack of it, with questions and categories of gender and sexuality.[2] This paradox is rooted in the ways in which *Orientalism* both opened up and constrained gendered analyses of the modes of knowledge, representation and power used in 'western' depictions of 'the East.' Statements in the original text linked the cultural and ideological production of 'the East' by Europeans to concepts of 'Oriental' effeminacy and of European sexual opportunity in, and fantasy about, people and societies in the Middle East and North Africa.[3] Yet the propositions about such links did not establish any systematic analysis of the gendered and sexualized character of modern 'Orientalisms.' While this may have been understandable in the 1970s when the impact of feminist thought in the wider academy was limited, it sits oddly with the dissident method, tone and content of Said's text. Indeed, Said marginalized and dismissed the emergent discipline of women's studies as vulnerable to the influence of 'pressure group complicity.' His construct of 'Orientalism' made conventional androcentric assumptions about scholarship and cultural production, and worked with *un*gendered notions of 'men.'[4] This contrasts ironically with the confidence with which Said considered that he could speak from his position as a Palestinian, which critics might also have characterized as compromised by 'pressure group complicity.' A dozen years later Said could describe feminism as 'a site where things happen,' and note the disruptive power of Joan Scott's recent article on gender as a category of analysis. However, disregarding the extensive influence of that text, he added that to argue that 'out of it one can derive a particular position strikes me as quite false and quite wrong,' and chose one work on British women in Nigeria to stand for the rich new debate on gender and imperialism.[5] Subsequent debates over *Orientalism* have given less attention to gender and sexuality than to other intellectual and political issues.[6] Yet the references to 'Orientalist' themes of sex and sensuality, to the use of exotic/erotic female images, and to gendered and sexualized depictions of dominance and subordination, provide fertile suggestions about the significance of gender and sexuality as categories of analysis on the terrain it outlines.

Not surprisingly, the challenge posed by these suggestions and limitations has been taken up in studies of the mutually constitutive relationships of Western femininities, masculinities and sexualities, and Western constructions and depictions of 'the East.'[7] While expanding the discussion of the gendered character of various imperial relationships, this scholarship converged with critiques of ethnocentrism in Euro-American feminist thought and practice, and of its contradictory complicities with colonial and imperial power.[8] If critical work on *Orientalism* has not always given adequate attention to gender issues, this body of scholarship is testimony to the contradictory but productive legacy of Said's work.

Leaving aside the varying conceptual frameworks chosen by the contributors to this body of scholarship, two aspects of the debate have particular interest for me. First, arguments often focus on particular texts, times and places, raising questions about the relationship of such specificity to larger propositions on representation, empire and Orientalism. Studies of exchanges between European and Ottoman women, of the engagement of Bengali *bhadralok* with British ideas of gender and nation, or of 'imperial' aspects of French and British culture, have opened up complexities and contradictions in any simple notion either of a binary opposition between 'Orient' and 'Occident,' or of 'Orientalism' as a 'corporate institution.'[9] At the same time they deepen understanding of some of the deep structures of thought and feeling which shaped the ideas and practices of Europeans who were involved with 'the East.' While some texts deploy detailed scholarship in order to challenge, if not dismiss, the validity of such persistent structures, others have established the importance of attention to particular locations and times in the past, while continuing to find the broader framework relevant.[10] I would argue that although close readings of specific situations and phenomena are a familiar form of empiricist resistance to conceptual and theoretical approaches to literature, history and art, they can also be used to strengthen, test and enrich our grasp of concept and theory.

Second, scholarship influenced by *Orientalism* raises questions about the relationships between cultural products and the material and political worlds within which cultural production takes place. Art, literature, music and architecture can usefully be understood as *forms of social action*, that is creative endeavours undertaken by human agents in specific historical circumstances, while also existing as objects/texts whose genre, structure, imagery and meanings merit analysis in their own right. This is not just a matter of connecting cultural production to the structures of patronage, art markets or professional formation upon which they relied very directly; it also directs attention to chronologically and culturally specific bodies of ideas, beliefs, assumptions and values which shape any particular society and its cultural practices. As Behdad argues, it is possible to use a notion of 'Orientalism' derived from Said's text, treating it neither as a 'neutral' term in intellectual, literary or art history, nor as a 'one size fits all' label for an ideological discourse of power. Rather, it can be used to study the networks of material, political and aesthetic connections underpinning cultural production. This can also enable scholars to investigate and interpret combined and uneven relationships between 'discrete objects, specific individuals, and concrete practices.'[11] Rather than working with ideas of opposition or distinction between materialist analysis, aesthetic appreciation, and political critique, recent work on 'imperial' or 'exotic' aspects of European literature, like histories of European archaeology, tourism or medicine in the Middle East, has considered just such complexities.

To pursue these two themes further I shall explore two specific sites of cultural production and debate where the analytical tools of gender and Orientalism can be tested. Separated in space and time, they allow the use of comparative methods to consider the value of the 'Saidian' paradigm and gender analysis, the complexities of each case and the intersections of cultural and material phenomena. First, I examine the career and work of the Ottoman painter and cultural grandee Osman Hamdi Bey (1842–1910). I focus on the relatively unexplored gendered aspects of his painting, and on notions of cultural hybridity as alternatives to binary oppositions of 'East'/'West' or 'self'/'other' which rather misconceive late Ottoman culture. This will support a reassessment of Orientalizing readings of the *'harem'* trope in visual depictions of 'Eastern' female and domestic subjects. Secondly, I shall consider recent debate and scholarship around what commentators frequently term 'veiling' as it has been reconfigured in Middle Eastern, South Asian and North African societies and diasporas over the last three decades. I consider the recent history of female dress codes and practices in those settings as a case study in the politics of culture/culture of politics, reading it through the lenses of gender analysis, genealogical narrative, and Orientalist and counter-Orientalist discourse.

In my discussion of Osman Hamdi Bey, I consider his role as a 'modern'/modernizing male of the Ottoman elite, embedded in established patterns of power and patronage, influenced by 'western' notions of order and progress, and performing specific versions of masculinity and domesticity. I revisit his paintings of 'Oriental' scenes shaped by the iconic work of the French Orientalist artist Jean-Léon Gérôme, while pursuing their own distinctive agenda. My analysis challenges the binary formulations and gender blindness of *Orientalism*, while showing that its concerns with the role of power and knowledge in relations between Europeans and people in the Middle East are enriched, not devalued, by it. It suggests that those relations are best understood in terms of fluidity, discomfort and hybridity, and deploys the idea of 'speaking back'[12] to Orientalism to explore them further.

For some commentators, Osman Hamdi Bey's work as 'founder' of the Istanbul Archaeology Museum and the Istanbul Academy of Fine Arts make him a significant contributor to Turkish advances to 'modern' cultural forms and achievements. His paintings and cosmopolitan responses to work and travel in the Ottoman lands have been analysed as exemplars of 'Ottoman Orientalism.'[13] His collecting and organizing of Hellenistic and Hittite antiquities for museums enacted modern Ottoman views of the pre-Ottoman past of those lands at a time when dissident nationalisms and external pressures challenged its dominance. It responded creatively as well as defensively to Ottoman incorporation into European dominated circuits of great power politics and global economic activity, in which they participated on unequal terms. The Ottoman government had its own agendas of reasserting central control over subject territories, and of adapting and appropriating European administrative and military practices for its purposes.[14] Albeit cautious and conservative, the regime's interest in reform led it to encourage the education of military and civilian officials, or young men destined to become such officials in 'modern,' 'western' practices. In Istanbul, Salonika, Paris or Berlin, such men encountered ideas and experiences which stimulated interest in reform, influencing Young Ottoman and Young Turk groups seeking to radicalize or shape official *tanzimat* (reform) policies from the 1860s.[15]

Although involving the imitation and importation of 'western' practices, ideas and institutions, these changes also shaped mutually constitutive relationships between Ottomans and Europeans. Europeans' sense of their own modernity and superiority was shaped by what they saw as their role as agents of Ottoman 'improvement,' ranging from technology transfer and financial investment to models of educational and political reform and secular knowledge. However, male members of the Ottoman elite and upwardly mobile educated urban middle strata came to define themselves through active negotiations, responses or resistances to such external influences. As officials, soldiers and intellectuals they had their own agency in reform activities, and contributed to cultural and material transformations especially in urban areas. Their work involved creative syntheses of indigenous and imported influences, as when a Young Ottoman patriot used the traditional form of a praise poem to express his commitment to liberty and reform, or when secular government schools referred both to Islam and to the 1876 constitution.[16] It also established masculine and masculinist tropes of 'modern' Ottoman authority.

The roles played by Osman Hamdi Bey exemplify such developments. The son of a ethnic Greek adopted into an elite Ottoman family, Hamdi Bey spent nine years of his youth in Paris where he undertook legal studies and then artistic training with the prominent academic and Orientalizing artists Gérôme and Boulanger. This early experience combined the established formation patterns of the Ottoman governing class with new trends. The recruitment of members of subordinate or minority groups within the empire into central government, and the role of family and patronage in the advancement of officials dated back to the sixteenth century. In the nineteenth century, government policy and family aspiration looked to new forms of education and training for the governing elite, either in Europe or along European lines. Emerging from this hybrid elite formation, Hamdi Bey's Parisian experiences were a basis for his entry into the state apparatus, backed by his administrator father's influence. He began his career with the reformer Midhat Pasha in Baghdad, pioneering modernizing Ottoman governance as a metropolitan official in a provincial outpost. Rather than pursuing political change, as Midhat did, he took up administrative posts in Istanbul, and via his father's patronage was tasked with presenting Ottoman culture at the 1873 Vienna International Exposition.[17] He put his knowledge of Western languages and technologies at the service of the ruling regime, turning toward cultural management, and beginning to produce paintings, as he would do for the rest of his life.

His administrative and archaeological work in the provinces of the Ottoman Empire, like his paintings of carpet merchants, Muslim shrines and genre scenes can be seen as expressions of '*Ottoman* Orientalism,' an imperial style for restructuring, and dominating the subject peoples of that empire.[18] The restructuring of the Ottoman regime in the nineteenth century refigured its relations with those peoples. It included violent repression of 'dissident' groups, revived central controls on provincial government, modernizing initiatives and the redesigning of the ethno-religious *millets* (communities) into which Ottoman subjects were administratively organized. This entailed the movement of officials and experts from Istanbul to the provinces to govern, build roads and telegraph lines, set up schools and hospitals or rebuild urban centres. While introducing or reinforcing European influences, such men were also Ottoman imperial agents dealing with local elites and varied communities. Their 'civilizing mission' was rooted in traditions of Ottoman dynastic power, the new culture of elite Ottomanism, and the modernizing agendas of the state. Eldem's readings of Hamdi Bey's letters to his father from Baghdad in the late 1860s and his accounts of life and archaeological work in south-eastern Anatolia and Kurdistan in the 1880s reveal a hybrid blend of Western cultural codes and Ottoman imperial culture.[19]

Quoting a general indictment of 'backwardness' in Ottoman society from an 1870 letter of Hamdi Bey, Eldem includes the following without comment:

What do you see in families? Nothing but corruption, depravity, fights, divorces. They are infested by slavery and lose their morality to odalisques. The wife does not submit to her husband's will, and the husband fails to respect his wife. He goes his way as she goes hers. They have never held hands. They have never formed a family. The children are abandoned. The mother has never thought of them. Entrusted to a slave who thinks that s/he is moveable property, these poor children are left to vegetate while the mother goes to the Sweet Waters to dirty and roll in the mud a name she carries but hates. And all this happens just because a ridiculous convention in our degenerate customs requires that a man should close his eyes before taking a wife. A convention which requires that a marriage should not result from the free will of a man and a woman but rather from an agreement between their parents.[20]

What is striking about this 'modern' critique is its choice of the sexual and the familial as markers of 'backwardness.' The use of household slaves as sexual or parental substitutes, failure to perform 'proper' marital or mothering roles, female sexual promiscuity and arranged marriages, are condemned as undermining progress and decency. Hamdi Bey aligns with those who depicted new possibilities for women and marriage in novels, pursued education for women, or satirized dress reform, creating gendered discourses of nation, empire and society. These characterized the growing role and confidence of the *afrangi* (Westernized) members of the modernizing elites and urban commercial, professional and entrepreneurial classes.[21] Like them he placed gender roles, norms and relations at the centre of Ottoman responses to European influence, and of the Orientalizing reformist discourse of its elite. Depictions of reformed femininity, and, as I argue, of masculinity also, are woven into his agenda as an artist and as a man. Figures of the modest domestic woman and family, and the responsible Ottoman official and family man run through his artistic work and self-presentation.

Hamdi Bey pursues such issues through explicit ripostes to the dominant European images of odalisques, dancers and naked women in Oriental baths exemplified in the paintings of Gérôme. He paints 'Turkish' interiors where men wearing 'historic' costumes beside Ottoman tiled fireplaces are offered coffee by modestly dressed wives rather than being serviced by a group of exotically semi-clad odalisques.[22] Bourgeois domesticity interacts with Eastern glamour, Ottoman discourses of the past and a display of technical skill (his legacy from Gérôme) countering male European *harem* fantasy with specifically Ottoman male views of modern marriage. The glamorous but fully covering 'Turkish' dresses with contemporary head covering worn by the women in his interior scenes, of women socializing, arranging flowers or at their toilette with female servants, renegotiated 'exotic' European stereotypes.[23] Hamdi Bey depicts women whose restrained body language challenges European Orientalist convention, deploying historicized settings with 'modern' French touches to furniture and décor. Blends of Ottoman tradition and modernity were configured through gender and class dynamics in his street scenes. Women wearing up-to-date versions of the *feraje* (long outer coat), *yashmak* (head and face cover), and parasols gather and converse, while men of the 'traditional' urban classes (street vendors, beggars, religious specialists) in 'ethnic' dress are placed near the edges or in the background.[24] Elite women enact modest modernity in public, just as in other paintings they enact literacy and piety, reading Qur'ans or visiting shrines in his favourite close-fitting but modest yellow outfits. These dress styles, so different from the Western clothing worn by women and girls in his own family, enact the complex politics of dress, gender and modernity in nineteenth-century Istanbul.

One dramatic approach to these themes is a painting called *The Mihrab* in which a woman, allegedly based on his wife, sits on an inlaid Qur'an reading-stand in a mosque niche (*mihrab*) indicating the direction of Mecca with religious books scattered on the floor around her.[25] The fifteenth-century style of the *mihrab* tile mosaic, the stand, and the metal incense burner and candlestick frame the single central figure in signifiers of Islam and its artistic practices and traditions. They suggest the Hamidian regime's use of history and religious legitimation and a new relationship to Islamically inspired objects, now become exhibits in the Imperial Museum of which Hamdi Bey was director. Shaw sets *The Mihrab* within Ottoman cultural practices as narratives of Ottoman civilization, the rule of Adbul Hamid, and new Ottoman nationalism.[26] However, the gender dynamics of this painting with its unusual presentation of a central female figure merit equal attention. The dissonance between the woman in Hamdi Bey's signature form-fitting yellow dress sat upright staring ahead and the setting in which she is posed offers a number of unstable meanings. Is this dramatic dominant figure disrupting 'traditional' piety, learning and Ottoman relationships to their past, with its secular female presence in a domain historically dominated by male authority? Is it redirecting and re-energizing religious practice by refiguring old Turco-Persian tropes linking human and spiritual love, such as referring to the beloved as the *qibla* (the direction of Mecca), in a contemporary form? What does it mean to gender and sexualize the past and present in this way?

Clearly a Saidian approach has supported this discussion of art, knowledge and power in their late Ottoman setting as it has equally benefitted from gender theory and categories. If the Saidian binary of subordination and domination only partially captures the complexities of that setting, any effective gender analysis needs to engage with men and masculinity as well as women and femininity. Analysis of Hamdi Bey should turn to that hitherto rather neglected aspect and consider the formation of his own hetero-masculine persona and his artistic depictions of masculinity. As noted, Hamdi Bey and his father were products of the modernizing efforts of nineteenth-century Ottoman rulers and male elites. Usually discussed in terms of state reconstruction or of new patterns of culture, social life and political thought, these initiatives can also be understood as refiguring masculinities. As yet there is little research on associations between modernity, male hetero-normativity and colonialism in the late Ottoman context comparable to Massad's and Najmabadi's work on the Arab lands and Iran,[27] but poten-tial areas of changing masculinity can be suggested. This might include gender analysis of reforms in male dress, with the *stambouline* frock coat, and later European male suits and the fez, replacing the 'traditional' robes and head wear of Ottoman bureaucrats, and European military uniforms appearing among Ottoman soldiers. Such changes signified not only state policy, but also shifting performances and meanings of manliness. Scholars could likewise consider the gender aspects of educational reform, linking masculinities, the modernizing of profes-sional formation and identity, and the reconstitution of male roles in Ottoman families.

These themes surface in Hamdi Bey's self-presentation in photographs and paintings. Like other elite men he used photographic technology, and a European genre of family portrait photos, to present himself as a 'modern' father with his daughters, all in European dress, and as the patriarch among his family outside their modern house.[28] Such depictions parallel photographic portraits of him as a professional *afrangi* cultural administrator at his desk, as a confident public man, hands in the pockets of his European suit, or as a modernized Ottoman establishment figure in fez and suit. The slightly dandyish orchid in the buttonhole of the middle-aged Hamdi Bey recalls earlier images of him as a dashing if respectable *boulevardier* in his youth. Depictions in informal dress among objects in the museum and on excavation sites with ancient finds, or with fellow experts and workers in local dress, establish him within his all-male profession, and thus within the classed and ethicized structures of late Ottoman masculinity. A patriarch with two successive French wives, he is shown engaging with modern knowl-edge, art objects and provincial subordinates. His cultural authority was recognized by collaborations and honorary doctorates from Western universities (recorded in photographs) and by his place in the Ottoman official hierarchy.

Despite his *afrangi* formation, Hamdi Bey did not restrict himself to cultural emulation in his self-presentation. In the 1870s he had presented himself as an exotic Ottoman of the past whose costume and weapons evoked that historical form of masculinity, and his features appear on ethnically dressed figures in his own 'Orientalist' genre paint-ings, 'speaking back' to Gérôme's genre scenes of Oriental men. He used himself as model in works like *The Tortoise Trainer* (1906) and perhaps

The Arms Seller (1908). One revealing visualization of his complex relationship to Gérôme's practice is a photograph of him working in his
studio on the Orientalizing work *The Arms Seller*, whose figures are based
on himself and his son, wearing his European three-piece suit and soft
Turkish shoes. His modern male artistic presence, echoing French portrayals of 'the artist in his studio,' is posed not with a live nude female
model (as often with that genre) but with his painting of exotic Oriental
male figures. The ambiguous doubling of Hamdi Bey's presence in the
photo presents linked and opposed forms of 'traditional' and 'modern'
Ottoman masculinity, and stages the intersections between patriarchal
family relations, public life and male careers in late Ottoman society.[29]

Another version of Ottoman masculinity is seen in a series of Hamdi
Bey's works using his own facial features on figures dressed as a *hoja*
(holy man) engaged in pious Muslim activities. Wearing a 'traditional'
robe and white head cloth tied on with a scarf, this figure appears in
the background of a street scene, as a solo figure reading a holy book,
at a tomb, or mosque door, and in groups of men reading and discussing religious topics in mosque settings.[30] He positions this image
within scenes of traditional male homosociality and piety, rather distant from the world of modern archaeology and cultural administration
which framed his career. This may show Hamdi Bey's engagement with
the politics of the Hamidian regime, which buttressed its authoritarian
and modernizing government with claims to the caliphate and general
support for Islam. It also echoes Orientalist depictions of Muslim men
engaged in religious rituals by artists like Gérôme,[31] 'speaking back' to
them through the subversive addition of his own presence within such
scenes. This associates modern Ottoman men with religion less as a
timeless tradition than as a relevant contemporary practice linking cultural authenticity, faith and patriotic Ottomanism. It produces a hybrid
relationship to Islam, here signified through a European trope often
deployed to disempower it, and an equally hybrid relationship to the
French Orientalist art tradition in which Hamdi Bey had trained, show-
casing its techniques and assumptions, but claiming pictorial space for
different purposes.

Osman Hamdi Bey's career, his image, and his artistic output thus
exist in a real but unstable relationship to the paradigms set out in
Orientalism. It would be hard to understand them without acknowledging the roles of power/knowledge relations, intertextuality, and Western
styles for dominating, managing and structuring 'the Orient.' These
were manifest in European assertions of their capacity to investigate the
ancient past of the Ottoman land through modern scholarship, and to

shape its future with rational scientific authority, as well as their material and political power. As a cultural manager Hamdi Bey attached himself to these viewpoints, as he did to the practice of depicting an exotic ethnic 'Orient' in visual art. Yet adaptations of, and resistances to European Orientalism were as much part of his life and practice as were Orientalist elements in his museology and painting. When he took the carpet seller subject favoured by Orientalist painters, and placed ethnic-exotic carpet merchants beside an unimpressive European in a colonialist helmet perched alongside wife, child and local guide, he reframed the trope from a 'local' viewpoint.[32] It matches the ironic and hybrid messages sent by his photo portrait as a modern Orientalizing artist contrasted with his painting of himself in archaic Ottoman dress looking at a female model (in that ubiquitous yellow dress) set in an equally archaic Ottoman interior.[33] A Saidian approach does only partial justice to these gendered complexities and cultural dilemmas.

Hybridity and gender are equally important conceptual tools for the analysis of current contests and debate over the dress codes of women in the Middle East or among Middle Eastern and South Asian diasporas. As I have argued elsewhere, those contests have a complex genealogy combining gendered European Orientalist imaginings, with equally gendered Middle Eastern nationalist, reformist and anti-colonial agendas, and postcolonial religious revivalisms and cultural nationalisms of recent decades.[34] The last quarter century has seen regular attention in Western media to the presentation and politics of 'veiling' – the dress codes of head and/or body covering associated with women in societies in the Middle East and North Africa or with women identified as Muslim.[35] Press coverage of women wearing *chadors* during the upheavals in Iran in 1979 and of the new theocratic regime's concerns with female 'veiling' included the American Kate Millet's supposedly 'feminist' intervention in the conflict over that issue. The climate created by the Iranian Revolution in the 1980s generated greater Western attention to 'Islamist' trends and movements in Algeria, Turkey and Egypt, including much writing on headscarves and 'veils.' In the 1990s hostile discussion of the Taliban regime in Afghanistan foregrounded their treatment of Afghan women, including enforced wearing of the *burqa* (an indigenous all-over women's head and body cover). It is notable that this issue had *not* preoccupied Western coverage of Afghan movements, including the Taliban, during their Western-backed war with the Russians in the 1980s. The *'burqa* trope' shaped western coverage of the US/UK military intervention in Afghanistan, whose attack on the 'pro-terrorist,' 'fundamentalist' Taliban was partly legitimated as supporting the 'rescue' of Afghan women. This produced numerous references to the *burqa*, including remarks by a well-known progressive lawyer and wife to the UK prime minister.[36]

Nor has media attention to female dress codes been solely a matter of representing far-away people of whom Western audiences know little. The French 'headscarf affair' of 1989, with its controversy over whether girls could wear the head covering considered appropriate by some Muslims when they went to school, linked the 'veiling' issue[37] to questions about cultural pluralism in French society and the secularity of the French state. This debate reappeared in sharper form in 2004 when the French government brought in legislation to restrict the use of blatantly religious items of clothing in state schools, which in fact focused on girls' wearing of head-coverings in conformity with Islamic dress codes. As with debates around arranged marriage, clitoridectomy or 'honour killings' in particular communities in Europe, views on the control of women's bodies combined with anxiety over immigration and cultural diversity, and with racial prejudice and stereotyping, as well as with woman-centred agendas. Again, while some of Said's questioning of Western styles for dominating the East may be relevant, the dynamics of gender, and of contemporary racial, postcolonial and transnational politics can be shown to be equally relevant.

Attention to 'veiling' has featured in Iran, Egypt and Turkey as much as in the Western media over recent decades. From public, scholarly and official engagement with 'good'/'bad' *hijab* in Iran under the Islamic Republic[38] to legal, political and administrative contests over female head-covering in Turkey[39] and in Egypt,[40] controversy has engaged women and men, politicians and religious specialists, civil society and state authorities. A complex set of diverse, if overlapping, interests and beliefs has informed contests over the morality, practicality and symbolic significance of women's use/non-use of particular forms of head, body or face covering. In the twenty-first century, concern with codes of female self-covering is a significant component of cultural and political discourses in 'Middle Eastern' and 'Islamic' societies and communities, as well as marking European and North American depictions of those societies or communities. Veiling and unveiling are subjects of social and governmental and social sanctions (including physical punishment), of ideological differences, and of conflicts of practice or interest between groups and individuals. Testimony from Turkish teachers, North African migrants to Holland, Egyptian and Iranian activists, and Moroccan women indicates a complex range of choices, possibilities and constraints around 'veiling' which form part of their daily lives.[41] These women locate their choices and difficulties within the context of loyalties to faith and community, of dress codes as matters of choice and empowerment, and of cultural authenticity, repression and autonomy. Debates by religious specialists, intellectuals and political organizations show how belief, theory and legitimation in relation to 'veiling' are contested and hence political issues. Official, communal and legal regulation of 'veiling' demonstrates the role of power and the presence of power relations, pitting authority against choice, and conformity against diversity. The adoption or removal of 'veils'[42] have been acts of political assertion and resistance expressing opposition to 'foreign' intrusion and state regulation, claims to classed, gendered or patriotic rights and identities, aspirations for change, or loyalty to religion and cultural tradition.

Since the use/non-use of dress codes for women has become heavily politicized since the later nineteenth century, the histories or genealogies of such politics are central to any analysis of this phenomenon. There is a narrative of the politics and practices of veiling in Middle Eastern societies, created by historians of state-building, social reform, popular culture, fashion, and religious or political debate and movements in Iran, Algeria, Turkey or Egypt.[43] There is a parallel narrative of Western depictions and judgements of veiling in art, scholarship, literature and the media, which has been the domain of much of the scholarship stimulated by *Orientalism*. There is also the question of the impact of the latter upon the former, and one fruitful line of enquiry into the cultural politics of veiling as a signifier is to examine its history with a Saidian focus on culture and imperialism, combined with attention to gender politics, and to Middle Eastern 'speaking back' to European Orientalism. A historical approach allows us to follow the emergence, intertwining and persistence of many-sided, unstable and contested views and practices around veiling within the complex relations of dominance and subordination based on gender, colonial power and class formations. It also enables us to consider the interactions of culture, politics and social structures and practices. What follows is a brief exposition of the genealogy of current discourses around veiling, showing how it has been shaped by the conjunctures of imperial Orientalism, Middle Eastern anti-colonialism, and postcolonial resistance. This will be the basis for some reflections on the conceptual challenges posed by such a genealogy.

Our starting point is the 'moment' of Western Orientalism in its powerful nineteenth-century form. Within the spectrum of gendered and sexualized constructions of 'the Orient' associated with European involvement in the Ottoman lands, Iran and North Africa, images of veils and veiling had a prominent place. In addition to providing verbal or visual markers of the erotic, alluring, available 'Other' to be desired, denigrated or dominated, if not all three, it served as a signifier of Western relationships to 'the East,' and was internalized within *Western* sexual vocabularies. The metaphor of unveiling was used for the acquisition and appropriation of knowledge of 'distant' people and places (domestic slums as well as 'foreign' cultures) by privileged Europeans. It was associated with the modernization or religious conversion of 'native' peoples. It shaped the politics of control and improvement associated with colonial power. Images of veiling and unveiling in western narratives of heterosexual desire, seduction and romance placed the trope of 'Oriental' sexuality *within* the Western imaginary, as an internal 'other' making desire safe as exotic fantasy. They also played a role in the practices of colonial power. From the provision of veils for girls attending schools in French colonial Algeria in the 1850s to efforts to encourage their removal a century later, intervention over veiling was a part of a colonial presence which was invested both in sustaining ethicized boundaries between rulers and subjects and in a *mission civilisatrice* which sought to 'modernize' indigenous groups. British missionaries in India, American equivalents in the Ottoman lands and colonial administrators in Egypt engaged with similar concerns.[44] The veil was thus a politically charged object or issue entwined with gender and colonial power relations. As a term serving these multiple purposes it ignored the variegated forms and codes of body and head covering among different groups of women, let alone men, in the Middle East. A practice which had formerly expressed the local cultures and power relations of veil users and their communities was now also shaped by global relations between those communities and European power.

The role of veils/veiling as Western signifiers of the 'Orientalness' of an 'Orient' characterized by the oppression of women, by sexualization and by subjugation to repressive Muslim precepts or backward customs, generated varied responses within the Middle East. A second conjunctural 'moment' saw the use of the veiling/unveiling issue as symbol and signifier of 'national' self-assertion, of cultural 'authenticity' and of social progress. Male reformers and nationalists in Iran, Egypt and the Ottoman lands discussed veiling alongside female education and the reform of marriage in their projects for progress, modernization and emancipation from European dominance, in which the 'woman question' played a powerful role. The unveiling and public exposure of 'our' women became a theme to mobilize male opposition to foreign or anti-Muslim influences whether Iranian religious leaders in the 1870s and modernizing intellectuals in the 1890s, Indian nationalists like Tilak at the turn of the twentieth century, or Algerian *'ulama'* in the 1930s.[45] It was seen as a desirable element in schemes to improve women's lives like reforms in polygamy and access to formal education, and satirized as part of the 'backwardness' from which reformers and nationalists sought to distance their societies. Beyond this, the question of female veiling also played a part in nationalist and reformist debates over the position of women in 'the nation' as equal or subordinate partners, as citizens and as patriots.[46] Women writers and activists in those areas assessed the primacy of the 'veiling issue' against other concerns about their inclusion and empowerment as persons and citizens and entered into sophisticated negotiations with Western influences and conventions.[47] By the early twentieth century, veiling had acquired a dense range of political and cultural meanings shaped by all these discourses, while in material terms established practice, social change and fashion were also key determinants of actual behaviour.

Twentieth-century nationalists, state-builders and modernizers in the Middle East were thus heirs to an already complex set of perceptions, and aspirations which persisted and shifted in the eras of late colonialism, decolonization and postcolonial crises. Just as discourses of religion and cultural authenticity, including established female dress codes, fed into anti-colonial nationalism, so too did the discourses of secularist modernization and state-building, including reform *for* (rather than *by*) women. Veiled/unveiled women as signifiers of national honour and culture, of national progress and modernity were staples of male political rhetoric and flagship government policies in Iran, Egypt and republican Turkey, and figured in male reworking of hetero-normative domestic and sexual norms. Politically and culturally active women also engaged in varied ways with discourses of veiling/unveiling in relation to motherhood, patriotism, education and autonomy. They lived with difficult choices between the gender politics which might lead them to emphasize women's needs and interests, and the politics of anti-colonial nationalism and statism, each cross-cut by their urban/rural, class and religious affiliations.[48]

As femininities, and indeed masculinities, were being refashioned, at least for some classes, it was the *polyvalence* of veiling as a cultural practice and as symbol which characterized those processes, even if Western observers still deployed images of veiling as exotic/traditional and unveiling as 'modern.' While different participants in these debates (male, female, pious, secularizing, radical, gradualist) took varied positions on these questions, they all contributed to the embedding of questions of veiling as broader issues in the shaping of independent progressive nations in the Middle East and North Africa. Commentators have noted that they were often addressed less as matters where women should determine and follow their own views and preferences than as symbolic issues of state and national identity.[49] It is notable that advocates of unveiling like Kasravi and Kermani in Iran, Qasim Amin in Egypt or Gokalp and Ataturk in Turkey argued that it would produce social and national progress while asserting male superiority and reformed female domesticity as foundations of the modernized state and society. As Reza Shah, the authoritarian modernizing ruler of Iran, reportedly put it in 1936, 'It is easier for me to die than to take my wife unveiled among strangers, but I have no choice. The country's progress requires that women must be set free and I must be the person to do this.'[50]

In the era of decolonization, Cold War and the making of a postcolonial world order which included Muslim migration to Western Europe, contests among various stakeholders over veiling were reconfigured. However, this was in part shaped by the still powerful legacies of cultural nationalism, communal politics, state-led modernization and religious/secular debate established over preceding decades, including discourses of veiling/unveiling.[51] Some of the promises of the new nations established in the Middle East after 1945 were embodied in the veiled/unveiled figures who signalled progress and tradition, 'authentic' and modern identities. The unravelling of these promises helped to constitute a third conjunctural 'moment' in which new layers of meaning were added to the existing politics and discourse of veiling. Hopes for prosperity and autonomy in postcolonial Middle Eastern states were frustrated by the difficulties of material development within unequal relationships to the global economy, and by the growing reliance of ruling regimes on repression and the cultivation of privileged groups of clients and supporters. Self-determination and empowerment were put in question by the entanglements of Middle Eastern states in the great power politics of the Cold War and its aftermath, and the persistently unresolved Palestinian/Israeli question. Urban and cross-border migrations, like the spread of formal education and new employment patterns, unmade and made communities with new structures, pressures and opportunities. Such changes and frustrations stimulated renewal in religiously inflected movements for national and social self-assertion against the neo-colonial power of American influence and the failures of ruling regimes. The discrimination and racism experienced by

Middle Eastern and South Asian migrants to Europe, and its combined and uneven relationship with processes of assimilation, separation and anti-racist politics, opened up spaces for the development of political and re-figured Muslim activity and ideas.[52]

Within this context the politics of veiling was prominent. As with the ideas of the new Muslim movements more generally, the adoption and promulgation of 'modest,' pious, *hijabi* dress was less a return to 'traditional' practices than a re-configuration of veiling to meet the convergent concerns of religion and contemporary circumstances. New forms and variants of head and body covering have been developed by women in Turkey, Egypt and Europe, just as the state regulation of veiling in the Islamic republic in Iran has been modified and adapted in gestures of resistance and autonomy. This has inspired new creative and entrepreneurial initiatives in the sphere of fashion which link women's choices in this area of their lives to the world of twenty-first-century consumption and self-expression through dress.[53] Many women who adopted new styles of Islamic dress did so in defiance of family or peer opinion, and in conjunction with a determination to pursue education and professional employment, and to be socially and publicly active. Their politics of negotiation and self-assertion coexisted uneasily with other discourses of control over women and of gender inequity, also deployed by some advocates of veiling.[54] Whether veiling affirmed female obedience and manly resistance to defeat, repression, and to Western or local elite corruption, or whether it was a modern, personal and portable signifier of decent gender separation, allowing women to be both religiously committed and publicly active, was and is a contested question. Such contests paralleled differences over female autonomy among Muslims a century earlier, and echoed difficult discussions about the form and content of 'modern' religious precept and practice in 'new Muslim' movements, and about the possibilities, if any, of Muslim feminism. While Algerian-born Marnia Lazreg argues passionately that present-day 'reveiling' is neither an unconstrained choice for women who adopt it, nor in their interests, authors like el-Guindi and Göle argue for more complex readings.[55]

This brief narrative has challenged the widespread reading of the 'veiling issue' through the binaries of religion/secularism, repression/emancipation, modernity/tradition, Muslim/Western and reactionary/liberal. At no time has the politics of veiling been a matter of monolithic positions or binary oppositions. Authoritarians have enforced both veiling and unveiling while advocates of 'progress' or 'freedom' have both supported and condemned them. Just as the gendered debate on veiling has been inflected by class and generational difference as well as religious and secular ideas, so religious/secular confrontations over veiling have been entwined with nationalist, reforming and conservative agendas alongside those of class and gender. Veiling issues have both shaped and been shaped by the politics of women's advancement, of nation making, of religious revival, of anti-colonialism, of hetero-normative masculinity, of elite social engineering, of visions of a better society and of populist resistance. They have never been within the sole control of those most directly concerned – women who choose to veil or not to veil – although women have certainly been active on the political terrains where the issues have been addressed. If the many layers or strands of meaning which the practice of veiling now carries mean that there is no straightforward narrative to present, it is equally the case that its contemporary significances are best grasped by historicized and gendered analysis.

Such an approach also challenges the revived Orientalizing depictions of veiled and 'oppressed brown women' exotic, vulnerable, needing to be 'rescued from brown men' (in Spivak's phrase) now frequent in the media. It draws insights from the practices of anthropological and ethnographic discussions of women and dress codes.[56] This has a certain irony, granted the historic role of anthropology and ethnography in the shaping of colonial and Orientalist discourses of exotic others, primitive cultures and traditional customs. However, this critical and gender-aware anthropology not only accesses subaltern voices and views with respect but also offers analyses of the intersections of meaning and material life, of subordination and agency, and of attachments to and adaptations of established viewpoints practice. In presenting women and their communities as agents if not controllers of their own lives, such work opens up alternatives to Islamophobic or Orientalizing judgements.

However, that type of specificity runs the risk of endorsing a cultural relativism which denies the realities of dominance and subordination within Middle Eastern societies in the name of rejection of cultural imperialism. As Berktay argues for feminist analysis, in seeking to avoid judgemental labelling of particular views or practices, commentators can end up colluding with those who control, repress or exploit others in their own society, and with practices which are contentious within that society.[57] One way to move on from this dilemma might be to use notions of intersectionality to unpack the tensions and convergences between the different power regimes – gender, postcolonial, class, governmental, generational – within which people function and the modes of acceptance or resistance which they produce.[58] This could support commitment to what Eisenstein has called 'polyversality' as a form of relativism to be balanced with recognition of cross-cultural themes and common concerns.[59] It is significant that these conceptual innovations have emerged within the gender and feminist debate on ethnocentrism, pluralism and universal, although in a way they also bring discussion back to Said's later reflections on humanism and the postcolonial condition. Perhaps this is a fitting note on which to conclude a gendered interrogation of *Orientalism*.

Notes

1. For example, James Clifford, *The Predicament of Culture: Twentieth-Century Ethnography, Literature and Art* (Cambridge, MA and London: Harvard University Press, 1988), 255–76; Bryan Turner, 'Outline of a Theory of Orientalism,' in *Orientalism*, ed. Edward W. Said (London: Routledge 2000), vol. 1, 1–31; Zachary Lockman, *Contending Visions of the Middle East* (Cambridge: Cambridge University Press, 2004), 182–267; Lila Abu-Lughod, 'Orientalism and the Middle East in Middle Eastern Studies,' *Feminist Studies* 27, no. 1 (2001), 101–13; Daniel Martin Varisco, *Islam Obscured: The Rhetoric of Anthropological Representation* (New York: Palgrave Macmillan, 2005). Much useful scholarship on Said is collected in Patrick Williams (ed.) *Edward Said*, 4 vols. (London: Sage, 2000).

2. See, for example, Lisa Lowe, *Critical Terrains: French and British Orientalisms* (Ithaca, NY and London: Cornell University Press, 1994); Deniz Kandiyoti, 'Contemporary Feminist Scholarship and Middle East Studies', in *Gendering the Middle East*, ed. Deniz Kandiyoti (London: I. B. Tauris, 1996), 1–28; Joanna de Groot, ' "Sex" and "Race": The Construction of Image and Language in the Nineteenth Century,' in *Sexuality and Subordination: Interdisciplinary Studies of Gender in the Nineteenth Century*, eds. Susan Mendus and Jane Rendall (London and New York: Routledge, 1989), 89–128.

3. Edward W. Said, *Orientalism* (London: Penguin, 2003), 6, 8, 62–3, 72, 103, 118, 146–7, 149, 166–7, 182–4, 186–8, 190, 206–8, 211–12, 244, 286–7, 311–12.

4. Said, *Orientalism*, 96, 97, 104.

5. 'Interview with Edward Said,' in *Edward Said: A Critical Reader*, ed. Michael Sprinker, 221–64. (Oxford and Cambridge, MA: Blackwell 1992), 248–9; the piece of work in question is Joan Scott, 'Gender: A Useful Category of Analysis,' *American Historical Review* 91, no. 5 (1986), 1056–61.

6. The recent volume edited by Ghosh includes only one piece dealing with those themes, and Varisco's recent extensive study does not really engage with them either. Ranjan Ghosh, ed., *Edward Said and the Literary, Social, and Political World* (London: Routledge, 2009); Daniel Varisco, *Reading Orientalism: Said and the Unsaid* (Seattle, WA: University of Washington Press, 2007).

7. On 'Orientalist' art works and intercultural contacts in the Ottoman Empire, see Reina Lewis, *Gendering Orientalism: Race, Feminism and Representation*

(London and New York: Routledge, 1996) and *Rethinking Orientalism: Women, Travel and the Ottoman Harem* (London: I. B. Tauris, 2004); Joan del Plato, *Multiple Wives, Multiple Pleasures: Representing the Harem, 1800–1875* (Madison and Teaneck, NJ: Farleigh Dickinson Press, 2002); Mary Roberts, *Intimate Outsiders: The Harem in Ottoman and Orientalist Art and Travel Literature* (Durham, NC: Duke University Press, 2007). On Orientalizing texts, see Ruth Bernard Yeazell, *Harems of the Mind: Passages of Western Art and Literature* (New Haven, CT: Yale University Press, 2000) and Antoinette Burton, *Empire in Question: Reading, Writing and Teaching British Imperialism* (Durham, NC: Duke University Press, 2011). Recent works on sexuality and empire include Richard Phillips, *Sex, Politics, and Empire: A Postcolonial Geography* (Manchester: Manchester University Press, 2006); and Joseph A. Massad, *Desiring Arabs* (Chicago: University of Chicago Press, 2007).

8. See, for example, Chandra Talpade Mohanty, *Feminism without Borders* (Durham, NC: Duke University Press, 2003); Zillah R. Eisenstein, *Against Empire: Feminisms, Racism and the West* (London: Zed Press, 2004); Ann Laura Stoler, *Carnal Knowledge and Imperial Power: Race and the Intimate in Colonial Rule* (Berkeley, CA and London: University of California Press, 2002); Mirinalini Sinha, *Colonial Masculinity: The 'Manly Englishman' and the 'Effeminate Bengali' in the Late Nineteenth Century* (Manchester: Manchester University Press, 1995).

9. For example, Lewis, *Rethinking Orientalism*; Sinha, *Colonial Masculinity*.

10. Examples of the former are John M. Mackenzie, *Orientalism: History, Theory and the Arts* (Manchester: Manchester University Press, 1995) and Robert Irwin, *For Lust of Knowing: The Orientalists and Their Enemies* (London: Allen Lane, 2006). Examples of the latter include Michael J. Franklin, 'Introduction' to *Representing India: Indian Culture and Imperial Control in Eighteen-Century British Orientalist Discourse* (London: Routledge, 2000); Joanna de Groot ' "Brothers of the Iranian Race": Manhood, Nationhood and Modernity in Iran 1870–1914,' in *Masculinities in Politics and War: Gendering Modern History*, eds. Stefan Dudink, Karen Hagemann and John Tosh (Manchester: Manchester University Press, 2004), 137–56; Nebahat Avcioglu, *'Turquerie' and the Politics of Representation* (Farnham: Ashgate, 2011); Zeynep İnankur, Reina Lewis and Mary Roberts, eds., *The Poetics and Politics of Place: Ottoman Istanbul and British Orientalism* (Seattle, WA: University of Washington Press, 2011).

11. Ali Behdad, 'Orientalism Matters,' *Modern Fiction Studies* 56, no. 4 (2010), 7711, which develops its general argument with reference to photography in and about the Middle East.

12. This concept has been productively used by Zeynep Celik in 'Speaking Back to Orientalist Discourse,' in *Orientalism's Interlocutors: Painting, Architecture, Photography*, eds. Jill Beaulieu and Mary Roberts (Durham, NC and London: Duke University Press, 2002), 19–42, which deals in part with Osman Hamdi Bey.

13. Wendy Shaw, *Possessors and Possessed: Museums, Archaeology and the Visualization of History in the Late Ottoman Empire* (Berkeley, CA and London: University of California Press, 2003); Ussama Makdisi, 'Ottoman Orientalism,' *American Historical Review* 107, no. 3 (2002), 768–96.

14. For a general context see M. Şükrü Hanioğlu, *A Brief History of the Late Ottoman Empire* (Princeton, NJ and Oxford: Princeton University Press, 2008); Suraiya N. Faroqhi, *The Later Ottoman Empire* (Cambridge: Cambridge University Press, 2006); Halil İnalcık and Donald Quataert, *Economic and Social History of the Ottoman Empire 1300–1914* (Cambridge: Cambridge University Press, 1997).

15. See Selim Deringil, *The Well Protected Domains: Ideology and the Legitimating of Power in the Ottoman Empire 1876–1908* (London: I. B. Tauris, 1997); Fatma Müge Göçek, *Rise of the Bourgeoisie, Demise of Empire: Ottoman Westernisation and Social Change* (New York and Oxford: Oxford University Press, 1996).

16. See Şerif Mardin, *The Genesis of Young Ottoman Thought* (Syracuse, NY: Syracuse University Press, 2000); Nazan Cicek, *The Young Ottomans: Turkish Critics of the Eastern Question in the Late Nineteenth Century* (London: Tauris Academic Studies, 2010).

17. The details of Hamdi Bey's early career are summarized in Shaw, *Possessors and Possessed*, 97–9.

18. Makdisi, 'Ottoman Orientalism'; Edhem Eldem, 'An Ottoman Traveller to the Orient: Osman Hamdi Bey,' in *The Poetics and Politics of Place: Ottoman Istanbul and British Orientalism*, ed. Zeynep İnankur, Reina Lewis and Mary Roberts (Istanbul and Seattle, WA: University Washington Press, 2011), 63–82 and *Un Ottoman en Orient: Osman Hamdi Bey en Irak* (Paris: Actes Sud, 2010).

19. Eldem, 'An Ottoman Traveller,' 184–90.

20. Osman Hamdi Bey in Baghdad to Edhem Bey in Istanbul April 1870, quoted in *Un Ottoman en Orient*, 99.

21. See Deniz Kandiyoti, 'Woman as Metaphor: The Turkish Novel from the Tanzimat to the Republic,' in *Urban Crises and Social Movements in the Middle East: Proceedings of the CNRS-ESRC Symposium Paris, May 23–27th, 1986*, eds. Kenneth Brown *et al.* (Paris: L'Harmattan, 1989), 140–52; Zehra F. Arat, ed., *Deconstructing Images of 'The Turkish Woman'* (New York and Basingstoke: Palgrave, 2000); Gocek, *Rise of the Bourgeoisie*.

22. Two paintings of this type are called *Girl Bringing Coffee* dating to 1881.

23. Examples include *Harem* (1880), *Girl Putting Flowers in a Vase* (1881), *Girl Combing Another Girl's Hair* (1881, 1882), *Girl Musicians* (1880, 1882), *Girl with a Vase* (1880).

24. For example, *At the Mosque Door* (1891), *Women Strolling* (1887), *Women with Ferace* (1904).

25. *The Mihrab* (1901), private collection, in Shaw, *Possessors and Possessed*, 181; colour reproduction accessed at http://flickr.com [accessed 12 January 2012].

26. Shaw, *Possessors and Possessed*, 172–82.

27. Afsaneh Najmabadi, *Women with Mustaches and Men without Beards* (Berkeley, CA and London: University of California Press, 2005); Massad, *Desiring Arabs*.

28. See the photographs at http://okulweb.meb.gov.tr/48/11/731023/html/ohb.html, http://tr.wikipedia.org/wiki/Osman_Hamdi_Bey and at http://www.sanalmuze.org/image/osh02.htm [accessed 15 January 2012].

29. See photos at http://osmanhamdibey.tumblr.com/ and http://www.define gizemi.com/forum/arastiralim-tartisalim/karakus-tumulu-ve-nemrut-tumulu su-t16738.html [accessed 15 January 2012], and Wendy Shaw, *Ottoman*

Painting: Reflections of Western Art From the Ottoman Empire to the Turkish Republic (London and New York: I. B. Tauris, 2011), 81–3.

30. Examples would be *Hodjas at a Mosque* (1891, another version 1907), at http://www.tarihnotlari.com/osman-hamdi-bey; *Dervish at a Prince's Tomb* (1908), at http://www.forumgercek.com/showthread.php?t=69714; *Outside the Rustem Pasha Mosque* (1905) at http://www.tarihnotlari.com/osman-hamdi-bey [accessed 16 January 2012].

31. Between *Prayer in the House of an Arnaut Chief* (1857) and the last years of his career (1895–1903), Gérôme painted more than 20 prayer scenes set in mosques and (like Hamdi Bey) at the tombs of sultans; he also painted several muezzins and a *mufti* reading. See the full catalogue of his paintings in Gerald Ackermann, *The Life and Work of Jean-Léon Gérôme* (Paris: ACR, 1986), 206–7, 216–17, 218–19, 228, 242–3, 244–5, 274–5, 292–3, 294–5.

32. Hamdi Bey, *Carpet Merchants* (probably 1880s) at http://www.turkotek.com [accessed 12 January 2012].

33. Hamdi Bey, *Artist in His Studio*, reproduced in *Ottoman Painting*, 85 from Cezar, *Osman Hamdi.*

34. Joanna de Groot, 'What Goes Around Comes Around: "Veiling," Women's Bodies, and Orientalisms Past and Present' (paper presented at the *International Congress of Historical Sciences*, Sydney, 2005).

35. For comment see Lila Abu-Lughod, 'Do Muslim Women Really Need Saving? Anthropological Reflections on Cultural Relativism and Its Others,' *American Anthropologist* 104, no. 3 (2002), 783–90.

36. This involves *selecting out* this phenomenon from among the many variants of dress code relating to concealing/revealing body parts which might include conventions of covering among men like the Touareg, concerns over 'topless' female bathing attire in Europe, or nun's veils. This selectivity gives to the material discussed below a particular resonance. More generally it is important to be very clear that *all* forms and codes of bodily presentation in *any* period or society can be understood as material and cultural signifiers with political and symbolic power.

37. The terms *hidjab/hijab* (Arabic term for head-covering), *voile* (veil), *tchador/chador* (the Persian language term for the head-to-foot covering worn by Iranian women) and *foulard* (scarf) all appeared in French media coverage. See Diana R. Blank, 'A Veil of Controversy: The Construction of a "Tchador Affair" in the French Press,' *Interventions* 1, no. 4 (1999), 536–54; see also Joan Scott, *The Politics of the Veil* (Princeton, NJ: Princeton University Press, 2007).

38. See Haleh Afshar, *Islam and Feminisms: An Iranian Case Study* (Basingstoke: Macmillan, 1998); Faegheh Shirazi, *The Veil Unveiled: The Hijab in Modern Culture* (Gainesville, FL: University Press of Florida, 2001), 92–108.

39. See Elizabeth Ozdalga, *The Veiling Issue: Official Secularism and Popular Islam in Modern Turkey* (Richmond, Surrey: Curzon, 1998), 40–8.

40. See Fadwa El Guindi, *Veil: Modesty, Privacy, and Resistance* (Oxford and New York: Berg, 1999); Arlene Elowe MacLeod, *Accommodating Protest: Working Women, the New Veiling and Change in Cairo* (New York: Columbia University Press, 1991).

41. See Ozdalga, *The Veiling Issue*, 51–85; Azza Karam, 'Veiling, Unveiling and Meanings of the Veil: Challenging Static Symbols,' *Thamyris* 3, no. 2 (1996), 219–36; Annelies Moors, ' "Islamic Fashion" in Europe: Religious Conviction, Aesthetic Style, and Creative Consumption,' *Encounters* 1, no. 1 (2009), 182–9.

42. Thus far I have self-consciously placed the words 'veil,' 'veiling' and 'unveiling' in scare quotes to indicate that they are symbolic and ideological rather than descriptive terms, as well as being an unhelpful and mystifying, single concept supposedly naming a whole diverse range of garments and dress codes. In order not to clutter the text or irritate readers I now desist from this, urging them to keep in mind the problematic nature of these terms.

43. See Camron Amin, *The Making of the Modern Iranian Woman: Gender, State Policy, and Popular Culture, 1865–1946* (Gainesville, FL: University Press of Florida, 2002); Beth Baron, *Egypt as a Woman: Nationalism, Gender and Politics* (Berkeley, CA and London: University of California Press, 2005); Yesim Arat, 'Nation Building and Feminism in Early Republican Turkey', in *Turkey's Engagement with Modernity: Conflict and Change in the Twentieth Century*, eds. Celia Kerslake, Kerem Öktem and Philip Robins (Basingstoke: Palgrave Macmillan, 2010), 38–54; Marnia Lazreg, *The Eloquence of Silence: Algerian Women in Question* (New York and London: Routledge, 1994).

44. See, for example, K. Pelin Basci, 'Shadows in the Missionary Garden of Roses: Turkish Women in American Missionary Texts,' in *Deconstructing Images of 'the Turkish Woman,'* ed. Zehra Arat (New York and Basingstoke: Palgrave, 2000), 101–25.

45. See Najmabadi, *Women with Mustaches*, 132–55; Amin, *Making of the Modern Iranian Woman*, 25–37; Lisa Pollard, *Nurturing the Nation: The Family Politics of Modernizing, Colonizing, and Liberating Egypt* (Berkeley, CA and London: University of California Press, 2005), 100–31; Baron, *Egypt as a Woman*.

46. See, for example, Muhammad Karim Khan Kermani, 'Nasiriyya' (c.1870), in his *Collected Persian essays*, ed. Kerman, 1967–9, 395–6, quoted in Mangol Bayat, *Mysticism and Dissent: Socio-Religious Thought in Qajar Iran* (Syracuse, NY: Syracuse University Press, 1982), 85.

47. See Margot Badran, *Feminists, Islam and Nation: Gender and the Making of Modern Egypt* (Princeton, NJ: Princeton University Press, 1991); Beth Baron, *The Women's Awakening in Egypt* (New Haven, CT and London: Yale University Press, 1994); Parvin Paidar, *Women in the Political Process in Twentieth Century Iran* (Cambridge: Cambridge University Press, 1995), 30–77; Aynur Demirdirek, 'In Search of the Ottoman Women's Movement,' in *Deconstructing the Image of the 'Turkish Woman,'* ed. Zehra Arat (New York and Basingstoke: Palgrave, 2000), 65–82.

48. Joanna de Groot, 'Coexisting and Conflicting Identities: Women and Nationalisms in Twentieth Century Iran,' in *Nation, Empire, Colony: Historicizing Gender and Race*, eds. Ruth Roach Pierson and Nupur Chaudhur (Bloomington, IN: Indiana University Press, 1998), 139–65.

49. See, among others, de Groot, 'What Goes Around' and 'Coexisting and Conflicting Identities.'

50. Interview with Muhammad Baheri (8 August 1982) for the Iranian Oral History Project, quoted in Afsaneh Najmabadi, 'Hazards of Modernity and

Morality: Women, State, and Ideology in Contemporary Iran,' in *Women, Islam, and the State*, ed. Deniz Kandiyoti, 48–76. (Basingstoke: Macmillan, 1991), 73.

51. See Wilson Chacko Jacob, *Working Out Egypt: Effendi Masculinity and Subject Formation in Colonial Modernity* (Durham, NC and London: Duke University Press, 2011).

52. See Saba Mahmood, *The Politics of Piety: The Islamic Revival and the Feminist Subject* (Princeton, NJ: Princeton University Press, 2005).

53. See Emma Tarlo, *Visibly Muslim: Fashion, Politics, Faith* (Oxford and New York: Berg Publishers, 2010).

54. See, for example, the views expressed by Sakineh, a rural migrant to Tehran who participated in the 1979 revolution, in *Le discours populaire de la revolution Iranienne*, eds. Paul Vieille and Farhad Khosrokhavar (Paris: Contemporaneite, 1990), vol. 2, 345–64.

55. Marnia Lazreg, *Questioning the Veil: Open Letters to Muslim Women* (Princeton, NJ and Oxford: Princeton University Press, 2008); El Guindi, *Veil*; Nilüfer Göle, *The Forbidden Modern: Civilisation and Veiling* (Ann Arbor, MI: University of Michigan Press, 1996).

56. Mahmood, *Politics of Piety*, and Tarlo, *Visibly Muslim*.

57. Fatmagül Berktay, 'Looking from the "Other" Side: Is Cultural Relativism a Way Out?' in *Women's Studies in the 1990s: Doing Things Differently*, eds. Joanna de Groot and Mary Maynard (Basingstoke and New York: Macmillan and St. Martin's Press, 1993), 110–31.

58. Developed by feminist thinkers on law and sociology, 'intersectionality' is a term used for conceptualizing and investigating the multi-faceted relations of power and difference which are simultaneously shaped by gender, ethnic, class, sexual, colonial, age or other distinctions and connections. Early formulations include Kim Crenshaw, 'Demarginalising the Intersection of Race and Sex: A Black Feminist Critique of Antidiscrimination Doctrine, Feminist Theory and Antiracist Policy,' in *Feminist Legal Theory*, ed. D. Kelly Weisberg (Philadelphia, PA: Temple University Press, 1993), 383–95 and 'Mapping the Margins: Intersectionality, Identity Politics and Violence against Women of Colour,' *Stanford Law Review* 43 (1991), 363–77. Later contributions include Leslie McCall, 'The Complexity of Intersectionality,' *Signs* 30, no. 3 (2005), 1771–800; and Jennifer Nash, 'Rethinking Intersectionality,' *Feminist Review* 89, no. 1 (2008), 1–15.

59. Eisenstein, *Against Empire*.

12
Said's Impact: Lessons for Literary Critics

Nicholas Harrison

> [T]here is a mind of society, and it is this mind that we address, tutor, doctor, inform, evaluate, criticize, reform. Our role is highly mediated and subtle, insidious even, but as a class of people our impact on the on-going life of society in its day-to-day and even long-term affairs is very diffuse, hence minimal.
>
> (Edward Said on literary critics/
> teachers of literature, 1976)

Very few literary critics can expect their work to have the sort of impact achieved by Edward Said. He positioned *Orientalism*, his best-known book, against 'an implicit consensus [...] building up for the past decade in which the study of literature is considered to be profoundly, even constitutively nonpolitical,' and lamented the fact that literary critics tended to apply their techniques only to strictly literary objects.[1] If that consensus was real, *Orientalism*, published in 1978, helped shatter it. Said's angry critique of Western attitudes toward the East has been widely and enduringly influential, and not only because his topic had evident political gravity. The book also set an example methodologically. Others could take inspiration from Said's willingness to break through disciplinary boundaries, and could adapt Said's concept of 'Orientalism' to launch a critique of, say, 'Africanism,' drawing in diverse situations and materials. A significant amount of the activity inspired by *Orientalism* has accordingly taken place outside the literary-critical realm, and a fair proportion of it outside universities. And that dimension of the book's legacy is tied to its own fundamental impetus to link academic and literary materials with, and in some important sense give priority to, a wider world of politics and conflict.

To put the last point in slightly different terms, the book's impact relied in part on its own emphasis on 'impact.' For anyone connected with UK universities, this term has become highly charged, as it has recently and controversially entered the official criteria by which UK funding bodies assess academic research, and refers primarily to impact outside the academic world. This shift in the official expectations around research is taking place alongside drastic changes to the funding of teaching, with the sudden trebling in English universities of the fees paid by 'home' and EU students, and the withdrawal of government funding for the teaching of many university subjects (but not all; although the justifications for this policy are couched primarily in the rhetoric/ideology of 'the market,' the market is not being trusted to deliver enough doctors, say).[2] Many people consider the new policies anti-intellectual and, especially in the case of the new fee régime, anti-egalitarian, and even more people consider them reckless: one of the remarkable things about the policies is that many of their effects, including their financial effects, were and are somewhat unpredictable even in the short term, notably to those who devised the policies. In the case of 'impact,' however, the predictable and deliberate effect has been the intensification of pressure on academics to consider ways in which they may exert an influence beyond the university.[3]

This chapter will use the work of Edward Said to think through some of the ways in which the work of the academic literary critic/teacher may be justified in such a context, and may or may not be aligned with the idea of 'impact.' That idea of impact has met with widespread opposition, often from researchers who seemingly have little reason to fear it in terms of immediate professional self-interest, since they work in disciplines that habitually feed directly into patented technology, new drugs or changes in government policy. It is also widely assumed, however, that the notion of impact and some of the other changes to university culture will foster, and have fed on, a climate that is especially hostile to non-vocational disciplines such as literary studies and music. On one level, then, the 'impact agenda' could be said to crystallize widespread doubts about the worth of research and scholarship in the humanities. On another level, it could be said simply to formalize what is already a legitimate and arguably intrinsic ambition for academic work across varied fields, that is, the ambition to change the way people think or to have some other sort of effect on the culture at large.

As far as the 'impact agenda' is concerned, Said's whole career may appear exemplary: first, in the sense that *Orientalism* and some of his other publications had effects far beyond the literary-critical realm that was his homeland as teacher and researcher; and secondly, in that his academic work propelled him into positions of political engagement and influence beyond the university. I will argue, however, that the example he set literary critics is often unclear, and sometimes flawed. I should clarify that although my chapter will centre on literature/literary criticism, and although some of the views cited toward the end of the chapter suggest grounds for privileging literature over some other possible objects of study, I believe that my central arguments could be extended into other cultural/academic spheres, such as film and film criticism. I will begin by considering Said's advocacy of the role of the public intellectual, since Said's fulfilment of that role is perhaps the most conspicuous way in which he himself had an impact beyond the academy. It is indisputable that his political commitments were linked to and consistent with the politicizing thrust of his work as a critic; my analysis, however, will cast doubt on the idea that such links help validate the critical work itself, especially insofar as the critical work is about literature. In the second section of the chapter I will argue that when the Said of *Orientalism* hesitates over how to incorporate literature, and certain literary-critical reflexes, into his argument, he reveals the incommensurability between, on the one hand, a lingering commitment to certain literary texts and forms and to literary-critical methodologies, and on the other hand, a drive to prioritize over all other considerations, including possible distinctions between literary and non-literary texts, the putative political impact of 'Orientalist' texts in general. From there I will move to arguments for a certain separation of the aesthetic and the academic from the political, drawing also on Said's writings about music. Finally, I will focus on issues of 'impact' in education, particularly literary-critical education. If, today, there is any sort of consensus among academic critics about 'the study of literature,' it is certainly not that it is 'profoundly, even constitutively nonpolitical.' On that point, the lessons of *Orientalism* have been learned. What may be more evident today than it was in 1978, however, is that doubts about the special status attributed to literature in the study of literature can come from varied sources, and may be fed by basic indifference or outright hostility to the sort of academic sphere in which Said's own work took root.

Academics and Intellectuals

In *Representations of the Intellectual* Said paints the intellectual as a lonely, somewhat anti-social, heroic figure. He characterizes the intellectual 'as exile and marginal, as amateur, and as the author of a language that tries to speak the truth to power.'[4] If this is a model for literary critics, it is not one that many of us seem naturally to fit. This is not the place to rehearse in general terms the pedigree of Said's vision of the intellectual, which others have explored, found inspiring, and criticized.[5] Nor is my intention to disparage that vision of the intellectual. Instead, starting from certain equivocations in Said's account of the relation of the intellectual to universities and to teaching, I want to ask what literary critics worried about 'impact' should learn from this dimension of Said's work.

There is a frequent assumption in Said's writing, and sometimes an argument, that academic professionals, especially in the humanities, are particularly well positioned to become intellectuals. Admittedly there is some variance in his use of the term 'intellectual,' but it is clear that he favours the politicized sense captured in the phrase 'speaking the truth to power.' At one point he states: 'intellectuals are individuals with a vocation for the art of representing, whether that is talking, writing, teaching, appearing on television.'[6] Later the category broadens when he speaks somewhat negatively of 'the increased number of twentieth-century men and women who belong to a general group called intellectuals or the intelligentsia – the managers, professors, journalists, computer or government experts, lobbyists, pundits, syndicated columnists, consultants who are paid for their opinions.'[7] Readers may share Said's misgivings about the ways 'expertise' may be fetishized or may be less expert than it seems (and no-one, surely, is in favour of pseudo-expertise), but some important distinctions disappear in this list: few people would be inclined to call 'computer experts' or 'managers' as such 'intellectuals.' And just after this, Said remarks: 'To accuse all intellectuals of being sellouts just because they earn their living working in a university or for a newspaper is a coarse and finally meaningless charge.'[8] The main point Said is making here is that one should not succumb to cynicism, but his phrasing carries the assumption that for the most part intellectuals do indeed work for universities or newspapers, or both, and legitimately so.

At another moment Said cites Russell Jacoby's argument about the regrettable disappearance from today's world of the non-academic intellectual. He initially describes Jacoby's argument as 'unimpeachable.' Glossing Jacoby, Said remarks: 'today's intellectual is most likely to be a closeted literature professor, with a secure income, and no interest in dealing with the world outside the classroom.' Such a person is not an intellectual at all in Said's primary, positive sense, of course; but this slippage in Said's terminology is another indication that he assumes all academics are prospective intellectuals, and it is clear he shares some of Jacoby's distrust of professors who appear uninterested in 'the world outside the classroom,' or who 'write an esoteric and barbaric prose that is meant mainly for academic advancement and not for social change.'[9] These paraphrases of Jacoby raise various questions. Is there really such a thing as a teacher who has 'no interest in dealing with the world outside the classroom'? What does 'dealing' mean? And what falls 'inside' the classroom, for instance when you are studying a novel about the Carthaginian wars, or about contemporary immigration, or even a campus novel? Is all 'esoteric' prose also 'barbaric'? And how well is the range of possible ambitions for academic prose captured in the alternative between 'academic advancement' and 'social change'?

Among other things, Said's remarks about intellectuals convey a certain ambivalence about being an academic and about teaching. (Teaching, I should note in passing, is another activity that academic prose may seek to inform; I shall return to this later.) Said disagrees with Jacoby on some points, and sticks up for US universities, but his use of a kind of *style indirect libre* often blurs the boundaries between their points of view, which in itself may be revelatory of Said's mixed feelings. Moreover, at moments in *Representations of the Intellectual* Said seems to *oppose* the single-minded energy of the intellectual to the stasis and conformism of the teacher. He comments that 'unlike teachers and priests, who seem more or less to remain in place, doing the same kind of work year in and year out, organic intellectuals are always on the move, on the make,' and describes the early career of Joyce's Stephen Dedalus as 'a seesaw between the blandishments of institutions like the church, the profession of teaching, Irish nationalism, and his slowly emerging and stubborn selfhood as an intellectual.'[10] One could also see an implicit distrust of academics in Said's praise of the 'amateur' intellectual and his suspicion of 'expertise,' a suspicion that was already evident in *Orientalism*.

Perhaps the most striking statement made by Said about the political bubble in which academic literary criticism may appear to exist (or may have appeared to exist around the time *Orientalism* was published) is the 1982 essay 'Opponents, Audiences, Constituencies and Community,' from which I quoted at the beginning of this chapter. 'Opponents, Audiences...' leads off with an anecdote about Said's conversation with an academic publisher at the annual conference of the MLA (the Modern Language Association, of which Said would later be president). Said asked about the sales and circulation of books of literary criticism, and the publisher replied that his press reckoned to sell about 3000 copies of each book. (Said considered this derisory, of course, whereas the day I achieve those figures, I'll be tempted to buy a yacht.) The circulation of these texts is a matter, Said surmises, of 'three thousand advanced critics reading each other to everyone else's unconcern,'[11] the sort of thing one can imagine certain politicians and university managers wanting, but not quite daring, to say. It is at this moment Said describes 'an implicit consensus [that] has been building up for the past decade in which the study of literature is considered to be profoundly, even constitutively nonpolitical.' He goes on to voice suspicion of specialism, commenting:

> To an alarming degree, the present continuation of the humanities depends, I think, on the sustained self-purification of humanists for whom the ethic of specialization has become equivalent to minimizing the content of their work and increasing the composite wall of guild consciousness, social authority, and exclusionary discipline around themselves.[12]

Said calls for 'interference,' 'breaking out of the disciplinary ghettos in which as intellectuals we have been confined.' More than that, he attacks two famously political literary critics, Fredric Jameson and Terry Eagleton, for accepting a state of 'cloistral seclusion from the inhospitable world of real politics.' The 'crucial next phase,' he says, is 'connecting these more politically vigilant forms of interpretation to an ongoing political and social praxis.'[13]

I have already suggested that this line of argument seems a natural one in the wake of *Orientalism*, and that the intellectual links between *Orientalism* and Said's political advocacy are clear thematically and also methodologically, in the sense that the book gave priority to questions of political or ideological impact. What is less clear is whether all other critic-teachers could and should follow Said's advice, and his example, when it comes to activity outside teaching and criticism. How far, then, should extra-academic commitments such as Said's be accepted as a necessary corollary of certain sorts of academic work? And how far does or should the possibility, desirability or even the actuality of such engagements serve to legitimate academic activities as such?

We may accept that the sort of position occupied by Said as a public intellectual was and remains a desirable one, but the first problem to consider is how many critic-teachers could take on such a role. More than do at the moment, no doubt, but in universities around the world there are very large numbers of critics. The MLA currently has more than

30,000 members spread across more than 100 countries. These 30,000 people must be only a small proportion of the world's total collection of academics who are prospective public intellectuals, given that membership is unusual in many countries, and that the MLA by no means covers all disciplines. As a grouping of prospective intellectuals the MLA has the great advantages of being US-based and communicating primarily in English, and so being central to many global political and academic networks. Still, not many of these 30,000 can realistically hope to achieve the eminence, or to effect the prominent political interventions, of a Chomsky, or a Said.

It may be, of course, that Said had a relatively broad conception of valid forms of extra-academic 'political and social praxis.' I would assume he approved of the extra-curricular activities of Gayatri Chakravorty Spivak, one of his eminent colleagues at Columbia, who is similarly known and admired for combining with her academic work some practical and political activities, for example, in raising literacy levels in India and Bangladesh. This less public form of extra-academic engagement is of a sort where opportunities for involvement are effectively limitless; and as in Said's case, Spivak's involvement in this activity seems consistent with her publications. The consistency between the academic and extra-academic work of Said or Spivak does not show that the link between the two spheres is necessary, however. As we have already seen, Said for one certainly did not wish to treat academic qualifications, positions and publications as prerequisites for public intellectuals or activists. Moreover, the eminent academic work that may help establish a political platform can be at a considerable distance, as in Chomsky's case, from the political terrain on which the academic intervenes. In the end the disconnection between Chomsky's academic work in linguistics and his political work has no bearing, in principle or in practice, on the legitimacy or effect of his political interventions. And the opposite must be true too: Chomsky's work as a professor, like Said's or Spivak's, is neither validated nor invalidated by his political activities, and would not in itself be any less or more legitimate if he spent more or less of his time engaged in those political activities.[14] In the end, there is something perverse and self-defeating about trying to justify academic work by showing that its practitioners can or must engage in extra-academic activity. In other words, we are no closer to a coherent justification of the academic work with which Said, and we, began; and that justification, which must somehow lie in the work itself, is what the 30,000 MLA members, and the rest of us, need.

Orientalism and the Impact of Literature

This returns us to *Orientalism*, the sort of book that Said was professionally committed to producing.[15] I have suggested already that if *Orientalism* was influential far beyond Said's home discipline of comparative literature, it was partly because the book had an anti-canonical thrust, and because its focus went far beyond literature. These characteristics can be seen when Said lumps literary writers in with propagandists, economists, administrators and the other objects of his criticism. Early in the introduction, he states:

> a very large mass of writers, among whom are poets, novelists, philosophers, political theorists, economists, and imperial administrators, have accepted the basic distinction between East and West as the starting point for elaborate theories, epics, novels, social descriptions, and political accounts concerning the Orient, its people, customs, 'mind,' destiny, and so on.[16]

On some level that is crucial to *Orientalism*, then, novels and poems are not to be distinguished from theories or political accounts; and as I indicated at the start of this chapter, what Said sought to emphasize here was their 'impact,' or their supposed impact. 'How did philology, lexicography, history, biology, political and economic theory, novel-writing, and lyric poetry *come to the service* of Orientalism's broadly imperialist view of the world?' he asks.[17] With such lists Said evoked then flattened distinctions of language, register, intention and so on, in order to argue that the varied writings by these diverse figures all fed into 'Orientalist discourse' and the politics associated with it. Frequently in *Orientalism* it seems, then, that Said has knocked great literary figures from their pedestals. For example, when stressing the prevalence and the coercive weight of the 'textual attitude' to the East, Said states: 'Orientalism imposed limits upon thought about the Orient. Even the most imaginative writers of an age, men like Flaubert, Nerval, or Scott, were constrained in what they could either experience of or say about the Orient.'[18] He talks later of an 'operation, by which whenever you discussed the Orient a formidable mechanism of omnicompetent definitions would present itself as the only one having suitable validity for your discussion.'[19] Nerval and Flaubert 'preferred Lane's descriptions to what their eyes and minds showed them immediately,' according to Said; and within their work one can find many of the familiar topoi of Orientalism.[20]

Despite all this, the literary writers whom Said most admired, including Flaubert and Nerval, seem to keep slipping off the hook. When Said remarks, for instance, 'Not only does a learned Orient inhibit the pilgrim's musings and private fantasies; its very antecedence places barriers between the contemporary traveler and his writing,' the argument seems at first to be the one we have just seen about 'omni-competent' Orientalist definitions recirculating unchallenged in literary texts among others. On this occasion, however, Said continues: '*unless*, as was the case with Nerval and Flaubert in their use of Lane, Orientalist work is severed from the library and *caught in the aesthetic project*' (my italics).[21]

In attempting to flesh out the idea of the 'aesthetic project' and to justify the exceptional status he wished to attribute to writers such as Flaubert and Nerval, Said offers a taxonomy of three curiously *ad hominem* 'intentional categories,' ascribing complicatedly, self-consciously different projects to writers in each notional group.[22] He then states:

> The paramount importance of Nerval and Flaubert to a study such as this [. . .] is that they produced work that is connected to and depends upon the kind of Orientalism we have so far discussed, *yet remains independent from it.* [. . .] *What mattered to them* was the structure of their work as an *independent, aesthetic, and personal fact* [. . .].

> On the one hand, therefore, the scope of their Oriental work exceeds the limitations imposed by orthodox Orientalism. On the other hand, the subject of their work is more than Oriental or Orientalistic (even though they do their own Orientalizing of the Orient); it *quite consciously* plays with the limitations and the challenges presented to them by the Orient and by knowledge about it.[23]

> (My italics throughout)

This is less than clear, and less than convincing. There are some peculiar turns of phrase (what does it mean to talk of 'the structure of their work as [. . . a] personal fact'?), and the focus on intention and self-consciousness is anomalous given that, as I have already emphasized, one of *Orientalism*'s founding gestures is to give a certain priority to texts' political influence. This implies that Said's primary concern should be reception, that is, the way Flaubert's and Nerval's writings flowed into Orientalist mentalities. From that perspective the notion of intention would help only if Said showed why 'what mattered to them' may have mattered to their readers (which I would assume it often did), or should matter to us. To put it another way, we need some account of how the aesthetic 'independence' these writers reportedly sought became the kind of independence Said attributed, at least at moments, to their writing.

One might expect the question of aesthetic independence to come into focus in Said's more detailed discussions of Flaubert's and Nerval's writing, but in *Orientalism* he pays little attention to their principal literary texts, drawing instead on their letters and notebooks. This muddies the waters, as the letters and notebooks do not typify the work for which primarily the writers are valued and granted special status. Indeed, letters and notebooks do not necessarily form part of their 'aesthetic project' in the crucial sense. Nor does Said say much about the history of reception of the works under scrutiny. Both issues, however – the literary nature of certain key texts, and the extent and nature of the writers' audiences – appear vital to Said's concerns. Historically, partly because of conventions of genre (including 'literature' as a genre), readers have brought different expectations to different texts, and different levels and forms of authority have attached to those texts. And some texts, not only because of their particular themes and style but by virtue of their form or genre, may have offered experiences and even insights not available elsewhere, and so may have played a distinctive role in shaping certain realms of experience or climates of opinion. For such reasons (which I am stating rather baldly here), aesthetic conventions and the modes of reception associated with them are important, or should be important, to a project such as *Orientalism*.

Rather than resolving the tensions that run through Said's treatment of the literary in *Orientalism*, however, such arguments, if pushed a little further, tend to heighten them. I have just suggested that even if your main concern about a group of literary texts is their putative influence, there is a methodological need to give due weight to the complicated, slowly shifting reading conventions specific to 'literature' and to different genres, such as 'theories, epics, novels, social descriptions, and political accounts,' since those conventions must have shaped the varied reactions elicited by those diverse texts. But the conventions are a complicated matter: where the literary is concerned, they may involve subtle and potentially disconcerting manipulations of frame and form, possible irony, and so on; they may involve the reader in complex experiences whereby linguistic reference is at once activated and suspended, or deflected, and whereby, in the case of fiction, the reader's 'belief' is premised on a kind of unbelief; and they allow considerable space for different readers to react in different ways, for example, in terms of what they find moving, or what they feel the text is 'trying to say.' Moreover, the variability of literary conventions lies also in the varying weight given to those conventions, from one reader or community of readers to another, and from one historical moment to another. The conventions are changeable, they are not universal, and in some respects they are fragile.

There is much more to be said about all this, but I hope it is already apparent that any serious attempt to take account of the conventions of and around literary texts will tend to blur rather than to sharpen one's understanding of the texts' 'impact.' Two incommensurable methodologies are in play, one literary-critical, the other socio-political. They refuse to coalesce into a single vision of the socio-political work that is done by literature, or should be done by literary criticism. The two approaches may be juxtaposed and may 'speak' to each other, in ways I have just discussed: so if and when socio-political methodology hits the problem that the socio-political impact of literary texts is impossible to measure, literary-critical methodologies may elucidate why. But the light cast by literary-critical methodology does not *disprove* the argument, or the hunch – whose political force tends to compel attention in a way that methodological niceties may not – that in practice, on balance, texts such as those discussed by Said, including those by Flaubert and Nerval, merged into the wider currents of Orientalism and other forms of prejudice. Accordingly, critics who feel that their primary concern is or should be with socio-political impact are likely to be worried that dedicating themselves to literature or literary criticism is a waste of time, or worse; and critics who do concentrate on literature will struggle to justify that decision on a certain political level. I noted just now that some texts, and genres, may offer insights and experiences not available elsewhere; and I would stand by my subsequent remark, that such texts may thus have played a particular role socio-politically, for example, in influencing opinion. But the first point – that some texts and genres may offer insights and experiences not available elsewhere – could also stand on its own: one may not know or care much about the history of those texts' circulation, and in any case, one may not have any real sense of the nature or degree of their historical influence. At this point, one is close to some notion of distinctive literary value; and one must be closer to Said's reasons for hesitating to treat Flaubert and Nerval as mere grist to the mill of Orientalism, or of *Orientalism*.

'The Aesthetic Project': Literature, Music and Criticism

One of the points I want to draw from this analysis of the place of literature in *Orientalism* is that academic literary critics are committed, not always consciously or willingly or even coherently, but by the nature of their work, to the idea that 'the aesthetic project' has an adequate degree of independence, and of merit, to make it a justifiable pursuit in the face of other possible and actual demands on their energies, including pressing political injustices. In the realm of literary criticism, however, both this commitment to the notion of aesthetic value and what I have presented as the incommensurability of different methodologies may be less than manifest when many critics are 'critical' about the objects of their attention in active and far-reaching ways, on political grounds and often for good reason. In that context, the foundational reliance of literary criticism on some notion of literary value may be clarified, I believe, through analogies and points of contact between literary criticism and another of Said's areas of activity, music criticism. Said's critical excursions into the world of music are among the things that made him seem suspiciously 'high cultural' to some observers. All the same, even anti-canonical and political critics would in general be reluctant, I imagine, to dismiss music criticism as a waste of time. And most might also accept, I assume, that music criticism or theory would struggle to find value if music itself did not already have value. Yes, music and music criticism alike have political aspects, and economic aspects; but it is implausible that the fundamental value or 'impact' of music can be expressed in such terms.

As a non-specialist I cannot hope to explore these issues around music in detail, and will limit myself to some brief remarks closely attached to Said's writing – starting with his account of a formative experience of music, and of music criticism, in his memoir *Out of Place*. Said recalls being enraptured as a teenager in Cairo by an orchestral performance of Schubert, Mozart and Beethoven conducted by Wilhelm Furtwängler, who had been tried after the Second World War for having collaborated with the Nazis. Partly to reflect his ignorance at the time, Said says relatively little about that history and the enduring controversy around Furtwängler (who was acquitted); but he does recall his dismissive reaction to 'a cousin's amateurish speculation that the Fifth's motto was "Fate's knocking at the door."' 'What I discerned in the piece, thanks to Furtwängler,' he goes on, 'was something I believed instinctively to be without any such concept. "Music is music," I remember responding, partly out of impatience, partly out of my inability to articulate what it was about the music that moved me so specifically and wordlessly.'[24]

The idea that music's effects can be at once specific and 'wordless' seems suggestive, and hard to dispute. In this area, too, though, Said appears to have been pulled in different directions. At this moment in his memoir he insists, explicitly and implicitly, on a certain distance separating musical experience from speech and from political context, but elsewhere one can see his urge to assimilate music more closely to verbal language and even to politics. This urge marks his discussions of Glenn Gould, among others. It is with Gould in mind (and in order to leave no doubt about the high value to be attached to pianism) that Said, when advocating the role of the intellectual, remarks: 'being an intellectual is not at all inconsistent with being an academic or a pianist for that matter.'[25] He bolsters that claim in writing about Gould's performances of Bach: according to Said,

> the drama of Gould's virtuosic achievement is that his performances were conveyed not only with an unmistakably rhetorical style but as an argument for a particular type of statement, which most musical performers do not, perhaps cannot, attempt. This is, I believe, nothing less than an argument about continuity, rational intelligence, and aesthetic beauty in an age of specialized, antihuman atomization.[26]

These are exhilarating ideas, and they are powerfully expressed, but there is a level at which Said appears to be struggling here to reconcile his admiration for Gould with his primary, narrower definition of the intellectual as 'the author of a language that tries to speak the truth to power.' It seems quite right that Gould could aptly be described as an intellectual, and that he changed musicians' and audiences' understanding of Bach and of performance. Yet it is not clear that he can aptly be described as the 'author' of a 'language'; and neither in Said's account nor in reality did his defining achievement lie in 'speaking the truth to power.' This suggests that a wider definition of legitimate intellectual work is needed, and one that is less to do with power. Relatedly, even though Said's rhetoric is compelling when he describes musical performance as 'argument,' that description is surely partial at best. One might compare Said's comment in *Musical Elaborations*, 'the narrative of liberation [...] still holds great power for me. But if that narrative does not have room for all the small narratives of liberation such as those I feel when reading a novel or listening to a work of music, then

I want no part of it.'[27] He is keen to link both novels and music to 'narratives of liberation,' but a certain hesitancy seems to be built into this sentence: one does not usually speak of 'feeling' a narrative, and the words 'I feel' may be taken as an acknowledgement that when it comes to music, and perhaps even novels, the 'small narratives of liberation' he finds or feels or projects may be quite subjective. Yet their 'small-ness,' or even imaginariness, is not, for him, a reason to abandon music in favour of realms whose political aspects are more fundamental and more distinct.

In relation to the principal concerns of my chapter – that is, with literature and literary criticism rather than music – one could retort that the relation of novels to 'narratives of liberation' may be closer than that of music; but according to my earlier arguments, literary criticism also undercuts its own legitimacy if it allows novels to be reduced to political narratives, or socio-historical documentation, and if it concedes that political narratives must always be its final reference point. Com-parison of literary criticism with music criticism would tend, then, to encourage literary critics to recognize the dependence of literary criti-cism on the distinctive value of literature; to accept a certain distance from politics as constitutive of their field; to be modest in their expec-tations, rhetorical or real, about the specifiable or measurable impact that the great majority of literature and literary criticism can hope to achieve; and to develop or maintain somewhat distinctive vocabular-ies and modes of attention, in order to do justice to their objects of attention and to the experiences they produce.

It could also be objected that many of the arguments I have just touched on concerning the validity and specificity of the 'aesthetic project' work better for music or literature than for criticism.[28] If, as Said suggests, Glenn Gould makes an argument for 'aesthetic beauty,' the 'argument' lies primarily in the aesthetic beauty that listeners find in Bach's music and Gould's playing; and while comparable arguments around beauty may be made for literary texts, I don't expect a large number of people to feel that way about my chapter. But as I empha-sized earlier, the modes of attention that maintain literature within the 'aesthetic project' and valorize it involve elaborate, sometimes frail conventions. Critics help promulgate those conventions both through their curatorial choices, and through their explicit and implicit advo-cacy of modes of reading that stand in a creative, dialectical relationship to the hermeneutic and affective richness of their objects. And at this point, we are talking not only about criticism, but also about teaching.

Edward Said and Literary Education

When asked, in an interview of 1997, which role he found most comfortable, that of writer, activist or teacher, Said replied, 'that of a teacher,' and went on: 'I've never used my classes to talk about political activism of the kind that I've done. I've stuck pretty carefully to the notion that the classroom is sacrosanct to a certain degree.'[29] In an essay of 1996 he wrote:

> the role of the member of the academy, the teacher, the scholar, the professor, is principally to [sic] his or her own field. That is to say, I think that there's no getting away from the fact that, speaking now as a teacher, my principal constituency is made up of my students; and therefore, there is no substitute, no amount of good work on the outside, no amount of involvement, that is a substitute for commitment not only to one's students, but also to the rigors of the discipline in which one finds oneself.[30]

In another interview, published in 1994, he stated:

> I don't advocate, and I'm very much against, the teaching of literature as a form of politics. I think there's a distinction between pamphlets and novels. I don't think the classroom should become a place to advocate political ideas. I've never taught political ideas in a classroom. I believe that what I'm there to teach is the interpretation and reading of literary texts.[31]

All these remarks are likely to be surprising to anyone who knows Said only by reputation; and, for reasons I hope already to have illuminated, they will be surprising to many who are familiar with Said's writing. To recap: this is partly because a central premise and implication of his most influential book, *Orientalism*, is that in crucial respects the 'distinction between pamphlets and novels' – a distinction reasserted in that last quotation – may be spurious, or a diversion from the vital issue of texts' impact on the world. (As we have seen, however, Said himself does not fully accept that premise, even within *Orientalism*.) Partly it is because Said was an eloquent advocate of the idea that it is desirable and even necessary for the critic/intellectual to break out of disciplinary and academic 'ghettos,' and to do 'good work on the outside,' becoming involved in 'an ongoing political and social praxis.'

There is another reason Said's expressions of commitment to teaching may be surprising. He paid relatively little attention to education in his major works, and when he did discuss education, it was often in pejorative terms – something we glimpsed earlier in his tendency to praise the intellectual at the expense of the teacher. His personal background was no doubt a factor here: in *Out of Place*, his portrait of his own education is often painfully antipathetic. Few of his experiences at colonial/colonial-era schools or even at university inspired him; more typical is his bitter memory of the 'cruel, impersonal, and authoritarian Englishmen' among his 'variously comic and/or maimed teachers.'[32] This autobiographical material certainly has wider resonances, but what is more important for my present purposes is that a certain suspicion of education also runs through much of Said's critical work, and through that of his successors. In *Culture and Imperialism* Said cites admiringly the research of his former student Gauri Viswanathan, whose book *Masks of Conquest: Literary Study and British Rule in India* argues that English as a discipline came into its own in the colonial age, and was tied to 'the imperial mission of educating and civilizing colonial subjects.'[33] When an education journal ran a special issue on Said in 2006, its editors, Fazal Rizvi and Bob Lingard, wrote:

> education was a central site for the exercise of colonial power, both in the metropolitan centre where it was through education that the legitimizing discourses of the colonial adventures were justified, and in the colonial societies, where education provided the structuring mechanisms of asymmetrical relations of power. [...] It was in and through educational institutions that students came to first accept as natural and inevitable the links between colonial power and knowledge.[34]

And according to the Said of *Orientalism*, this process continues today. In 'Orientalism Now,' he wrote:

> there is no Arab educational institution capable of challenging places like Oxford, Harvard, or UCLA in the study of the Arab world, much less in any non-Oriental subject matter. The predictable result of all this is that Oriental students (and Oriental professors) still want to come and sit at the feet of American Orientalists, and later to repeat to their local audiences the clichés I have been characterizing as Orientalist dogmas. Such a system of reproduction makes it inevitable that the Oriental scholar will use his American training to

feel superior to his own people because he is able to 'manage' the Orientalist system; in his relations with his superiors, the European or American Orientalists, he will remain only a 'native informant.'[35]

In this regressive 'system of reproduction,' in other words, universities, at least with regard to the 'Arab world,' inculcate clichés and racialized hierarchy: knowledge is no more than pseudo-knowledge; teachers are characterized by self-interest and feelings of superiority; and passive students soak it all up.

I cannot enter into the detail of these arguments, which I do not want to dismiss too quickly and which in some instances (including Viswanathan's book) centre specifically on colonial-era education and consider carefully the different functions education has served in different contexts. Nevertheless, at a general level I think these are strikingly negative pictures of education's aims and effects. Given that there is also an assumption here that colonial mentalities persist into the present, in academia and elsewhere, there is clearly a risk that the momentum of such arguments carries these critics to a point where their own involvement in education appears untenable. Said's writings seem at moments to be nearing that point, or at least, as we have seen, to be marked by odd tensions and silences as the possibility of radical self-contradiction and self-negation looms into view. Yet as we saw at the start of this section, Said also spoke passionately about his commitment to teaching, to the teaching of literature in particular, and to the idea that the classroom should in some sense be insulated from politics. In the remainder of this chapter, I want to look further at those pedagogical commitments, launching off from the interview from which I drew my epigraph.

Discussing the work of the critic-teacher in 1976, Said remarked:

[A] literary professional whose main base of operation is the university must realize that he exists in a condition of institutionalized marginality, so far as the system of political power is concerned. Of course we cannot deny that as teachers of literature, as disseminators of high culture, as transmitters of civilization (pick your favourite function) we do introduce and keep alive irrefutable things in the life of society. As Lionel Trilling once said, there is a mind of society, and it is this mind that we address, tutor, doctor, inform, evaluate, criticize, reform. Our role is highly mediated and subtle, insidious even, but as a class of people our impact on the on-going life of society in its day-to-day and even long-term affairs is very diffuse, hence minimal. Unlike social scientists, we cannot play – and there is no machinery for us to employ if we wanted to play – the role of consultants to business, industry, or government. No member of our profession has achieved political prominence. To some extent we are technicians doing a very specialized job; to a certain degree also we are keepers of, kept by, and tutors to the middle and upper classes, although a great deal of what we are interested in as students of literature is necessarily subversive of middle class values. The point is that institutionally, university literary critics/scholars are de-fused, and held nicely in check.[36]

Here again we see the tensions that run through many of Said's accounts of the work of the 'literary professional' in the university. He valorizes the critic-teacher's curatorial role; he views that role as a politically conservative one in some respects; and in other respects, he associates literature with subversion, and shows confidence in literature's distinctive powers. One reason he has mixed feelings about teaching literature is that universities, perhaps especially the humanities, usually cater to a privileged stratum of society;[37] another is his perception that the direct impact of teachers of literature on society ('impact' is his word, on this occasion) is 'very diffuse, hence minimal.' His strongest claims for teaching – 'we do introduce and keep alive irrefutable things in the life of society [. . .] there is a mind of society, and it is this mind that we address, tutor, doctor, inform, evaluate, criticize, reform' – are offered, oddly, as a kind of concession ('Of course we cannot deny . . .'), and are quickly undermined. It is hard to see exactly what is meant by the word 'insidious,' especially coupled with 'but,' but it can't be good; and the abstraction of 'the mind of society' allows Said's emphasis to shift away from education and toward the extra-academic world. That leads to the claim that the impact of critics/teachers of literature is minimal, our contact with industry or business regrettably slight and indirect. The last sentence, like the first, implies that the lack of demand for literature specialists to serve as consultants to government and industry is an unfortunate side-effect of 'institutional' arrangements. Such ideas take on a different colouring in light of those drastic changes to institutional arrangements in the UK that I discussed in my introduction, which imply that literary critics' lack of direct influence on industry or policy is in some sense stigmatized by the government's funding agencies.

This brings us to the first of the points on which I want to insist in conclusion. Some literary critics may find their way to 'impact' of the approved sort, and some may succeed in reaching positions of political influence. I have been trying to show, however, that there is no real basis on which such individuals can serve as generalizable examples for critics and teachers of literature, unless as part of an argument for dismantling their disciplines. But this is not to say that the work of most critics and teachers has no impact. One of the fundamental functions of academic criticism (as I noted earlier in passing, and as is surely readily apparent) is to shape critics' own teaching, and prospectively that of fellow academics. Criticism has this effect not only through its content, but also through its commitment to scholarship, accuracy, logic, evidence and, as I suggested earlier, a degree of expertise. Moreover, teaching and research share a commitment to some notion of originality, which is valorized in students as well as in primary texts and in criticism itself. Among other things, the commitment to originality makes teaching renew itself and remain 'on the move' (to echo a phrase used by Said in describing intellectuals). Neither scholarship nor originality, it should be noted, is any guarantee of 'impact' in the realm of publishing, or outside the academy; indeed, it is not difficult to think of respects in which those qualities may be an impediment to impact in the official sense. Yet if original works of criticism flow into teaching, and if teaching is thought of not abstractly in terms of a societal 'mind' but in terms of the students whom we 'address, tutor, doctor, inform, evaluate, criticize, reform,' the potential influence or impact exerted by teacher-critics sounds quite significant; and our institutions and disciplines – and even the 'system of political power,' if it supports those institutions and disciplines – no longer seem to be de-fusing us. All of this suggests, in other words, that teaching should be thought of as a fundamental form of 'social and political praxis' through which critics reach a significant audience and disseminate their ideas, and the primary arena in which 'impact' is systematically achieved in the humanities. Not to acknowledge this role for teaching, and its link to criticism, is a significant blindspot in many of Said's arguments about the work of the critic-intellectual, and also, more pressingly for current UK academics, in the official definition of academic 'impact,' which, as I implied earlier, seems to channel a perverse prejudice against pedagogical and intellectual impact 'within' universities.[38]

The other side of my argument, however, and my other principal conclusion, is that the notion of impact is inadequate to the kind of influence that literature teachers may hope to achieve, or should try to achieve, in their daily work. I suggested earlier that elements of a critique of 'impact' could be glimpsed between the lines of *Orientalism*, as Said struggled with his sense that literary works by Nerval and Flaubert may not simply have fuelled Orientalism, and that their writing may have value whether or not on balance, in its context, it did fuel Orientalism – something one has no way of establishing for sure. Even in *Orientalism* it is clear that Said felt he had a duty, as critic and teacher, to do justice to their writing on something like its own terms. And perhaps, when we observe Said wavering over literature in *Orientalism*, one relatively simple way to explain his contradictory impulses is in terms of the distinction between, on the one hand, texts that he, as a specialist in comparative literature, taught or might teach, texts on which the views of Said and his students were likely to be slowly formed, mixed and mutable, and on the other hand, those texts that he was passing through swiftly on the way to a political point. Yet in general within *Orientalism*, I suggested, and within much of the work influenced by it, that dimension of critical/pedagogical practice lost out to the drive to develop a more direct sort of political argument. Indeed, the influence of *Orientalism* seems to have been won in part through its downplaying of the specificity of literature, and of literary criticism.

As we have already seen, however (when, for instance, Said declared that his main task was teaching 'the interpretation and reading of literary texts'), he sometimes went much further in valorizing the aesthetic, and in tying it to his practice as a teacher. Something of this alternative emphasis was even incorporated into the 25th-anniversary edition of *Orientalism* that appeared in 2003, for which Said provided a new preface. He wrote:

> this book and, for that matter, my intellectual work generally have really been enabled by my life as a university academic. For all its often noted defects and problems, the American university – and mine, Columbia, in particular – is still one of the few remaining places in the United States where reflection and study can take place in an almost-utopian fashion. I have never taught *anything* about the Middle East, being by training and practice a teacher of the mainly European and American humanities, a specialist in modern comparative literature. The university and my pedagogic work with two generations of first-class students and excellent colleagues has made possible the kind of deliberately meditated and analyzed study that this book contains, which for all its urgent worldly references is still a book about culture, ideas, history, and power, rather than Middle Eastern politics *tout court.* That was my notion from the beginning, and it is very evident and a good deal clearer to me today.[39]

In several respects these comments on the 'American university' form quite a contrast to those I quoted from 'Orientalism Now' (which continued to form part of *Orientalism* in 2003, of course). When the Said of 2003 says the nature of his work is 'a good deal clearer to me today,' he acknowledges his change of perspective. Perhaps the most obvious change concerns his relation to the university institution; and although Said's special affection for his own university is understandable, I do not think the contrast he wished to draw was between an almost-utopian Columbia and the dystopias of UCLA, Harvard and Oxford. His more profound tribute was to the sort of academic and intellectual freedom he found, and wanted to see sustained, in many universities around the world, including freedom from governments' immediate political agendas. One might compare Said's comments on his involvement in 1977–82 in a project to establish a humanities curriculum for a Palestinian open university, about which he explained: 'The general consensus was that education for us [Palestinians] had to be a form of national self-affirmation, which I found antithetical to my interests.'[40] In their desire to harness education to immediate political ends, Said's Palestinian sponsors were far from unusual, of course, and Said addressed the relation between nationalism and education, notably literary and historical education, in more general terms in the Introduction to *Culture and Imperialism*, where he wrote:

> Defensive, reactive, and even paranoid nationalism is, alas, frequently woven into the very fabric of education, where children as well as older students are taught to venerate and celebrate the uniqueness of *their* tradition (usually and invidiously at the expense of others). It is to such uncritical and unthinking forms of education and thought that this book is addressed – as a corrective, as a patient alternative, as a frankly exploratory possibility.[41]

The other, more subtle – but related – shift of emphasis in the 2003 Preface concerns Said's attitude toward his disciplinary affiliation, and the teaching that was part of it. Naturally, he still hoped to have an impact on the way people thought; but he appeared more willing to accept that his influence would likely be primarily in the academic and cultural area, and that his ideas would feed into – and had emerged from – a kind of dialogue both with other specialists, and with his students. When he wrote that he was 'by training and practice a teacher of the mainly European and American humanities, a specialist in modern comparative literature,' and that 'for all its urgent worldly references

[*Orientalism*] is still a book about culture, ideas, history and power, rather than Middle Eastern politics *tout court*,' his point, clearly, was not that he was incompetent to talk about Middle Eastern politics because untrained in political theory. Nor, clearly, was he asserting that literary texts are divorced from politics, or denying that teaching in comparative literature may be politicizing in various senses. Rather, he was insisting that he was engaged in an exercise that was primarily cultural and academic, and that its value was associated inextricably with a certain distance from politics, a distance helping to create the exploratory space in which literary texts, his critical work and his students met.

In future I hope to go further with this argument about the intimate entanglement of particular conceptions of teaching, criticism and literature, and their relation to academic freedom and independent thought. To end the present chapter, however, I want to draw attention to some last reflections on this topic by Said, notably in a couple of his less well-known texts. In 'Identity, Authority and Freedom: The Potentate and the Traveler,' he writes:

> Our model for academic freedom should [...] be the migrant or traveler: for if, in the real world outside the academy, we must needs be ourselves and only ourselves, inside the academy we should be able to discover and travel among other selves, other identities, other varieties of the human adventure.

The teacher should not be a 'potentate' trying to 'reign and hold sway'; rather, like the traveller, she or he should seek not power but 'motion,' and should display and encourage 'a willingness to go into different worlds, use different idioms, and understand a variety of disguises, masks and rhetorics.'[42] To me this argument against any crude notion of pedagogical influence also sounds like an argument in favour of the teaching of literature.

That theme is taken up more explicitly in 'The Book, Critical Performance, and the Future of Education,' a text that offers some striking images of Said's love of reading ('I recall with embarrassing vividness that the great fantasy of my early and delinquent school days was the fond dream that I myself might shuffle off my mortal coil and become a book [...], being read and handed around by friends and perhaps even left behind in a train compartment'[43]). Here Said argues that 'the activation rather than the stuffing of the mind is [...] the main business of education,' that it comes from 'a sustained encounter with the actualities of reading and interpretation,' and that the study of literature can play a privileged role.[44] He quotes extensively from Richard Poirier, the last of his quotations ending:

> 'None [other than literature] can teach us so much about what words do to us and how, in turn, we might try to do something to them which will perhaps modify the order of things on which they depend for their meaning. To Literature is left the distinction that it invites the reader to a dialectical relationship to words that is allowable nowhere else.'[45]

To this, Said adds:

> And of course it is in the teaching of literature, a unique situation purposely removed both from the bustle of everyday life as well as the direct political impingements of society, that such a relationship described by Poirier can occur. Dialectical because in tension not only with the inquiring mind of the student and teacher but with socio-political values imposed by a party, a political agenda, or a worldly authority.[46]

I would note finally that closely comparable arguments (again drawing on Poirier) can be found in Said's late work *Humanism and Democratic Criticism*, which should, I believe, be read as an essay on teaching as much as on criticism. In it Said states categorically: 'I do not believe that, like the social sciences, the humanities must address or somehow solve the problems of the contemporary world,' adding later: '[I]n the main, I would agree with Adorno that there is a fundamental irreconcilability between the aesthetic and the non-aesthetic that we must sustain as a necessary condition of our work as humanists.'[47]

Such descriptions of literature and the aesthetic will sound reactionary to many critics today, notably in the whole area of postcolonial studies influenced by *Orientalism*, just as some of Said's rhetoric about teaching will sound old-fashioned. *Orientalism* both drew on and fuelled a wider crisis of critical confidence in the value of high culture, in itself and in education; along with a good proportion of critical and theoretical writing at least since the Second World War, it gave expression (if very ambivalently, as we have seen) to the fear that the West's greatest works of literature and of art were complicit in its most murderous ideologies, and that any defence of the partial or utter 'independence' of those works, recirculated in schools, universities and the world at large, made their treacherous ideological subcurrents less visible and so more pernicious. When, in *Humanism and Democratic Criticism*, Said speaks of 'the enlightening and, yes, emancipatory possibilities of close reading,' the political spark may still be there, but to some it will seem disappointingly faint.[48] Be that as it may, the constitutive and necessary distance of humanities education from certain socio-political demands now feels like a paradoxically unavoidable topic for those who, like Said, remain committed, by their praxis if not by all their pronouncements, to the value of literature as something to study and to teach.

Notes

1. Edward W. Said, 'Opponents, Audiences, Constituencies and Community' (1982), in *Reflections on Exile, and Other Literary and Cultural Essays*, 118–47. (Cambridge: Harvard University Press, 2000), 132.
2. I have used 'UK universities' then 'English universities' to reflect the fact that the REF affects all UK universities, whereas there are significant differences between arrangements for fees and maintenance grants in different parts of the UK. The detail of these differences is not important here; indeed, in addressing the UK situation through Said, I am assuming that certain basic issues are international in scope.
3. For those unfamiliar with the specific policies and debates mentioned in this paragraph and the next, a decent starting point is Stefan Collini's article 'Impact on Humanities', *Times Literary Supplement*, 13 November 2009, 18–19, and the responses to it in subsequent issues of the *TLS* up to 4 December 2009. See also note 38.
4. Edward W. Said, *Representations of the Intellectual* (New York: Vintage, 1996), xvi.
5. See, for example, Saree Makdisi, 'Edward Said and the Style of the Public Intellectual,' in *Edward Said: The Legacy of a Public Intellectual*, eds. Ned Curthoys and Debjani Ganguly (Melbourne: Melbourne University Press, 2007), 21–35.
6. Said, *Representations*, 12–13.
7. Said, *Representations*, 68.
8. Said, *Representations*, 69.
9. Said, *Representations*, 70–1, discussing Russell Jacoby, *The Last Intellectuals: American Culture in the Age of Academe* (New York: Basic Books, 1987).
10. Said, *Representations*, 4, 16. Said does indicate that Dedalus's pursuit of personal independence is self-defeatingly extreme; but on one level this reinforces my point, in that negative connotations are attached almost casually, and in passing, to the teaching profession.
11. Said, 'Opponents, Audiences,' 127.
12. Said, 'Opponents, Audiences,' 132, 139. The phrase 'the present continuation of the humanities depends' is intriguingly ambiguous.
13. Said, 'Opponents, Audiences,' 147.
14. Of course, if someone like Said calls for 'an ongoing political and social praxis,' understood to mean activity outside the academy, he will risk being

called a hypocrite if he spends none of his own time in that way. Yet even if that charge of hypocrisy were to stick, it would not, in itself, invalidate his arguments.

15. For an exploration of the relationship between notions of profession, professorship and literature, see Jacques Derrida, *L'Université sans condition* (Paris: Galilée, 2001), a book that began life as lectures on the future of the university and the 'humanities.'
16. Said, *Orientalism* ([1978] New York: Vintage Books, 2003), 2–3.
17. *Orientalism*, 15. My italics.
18. *Orientalism*, 43.
19. *Orientalism*, 156.
20. *Orientalism*, 177.
21. *Orientalism*, 168. The phrase 'severed from the library,' which carries anti-academic overtones, is a strange one to apply to these writers, as will be clear to anyone who has struggled with the web of allusions in Nerval's *Chimères* (1854) or has read Flaubert's major Orientalist work, *Salammbô* (1862), a lurid novel set in Carthage in the third century BC.
22. *Orientalism*, 157–8.
23. *Orientalism*, 181.
24. Said, *Out of Place* (London: Granta Books, [1999] 2000), 102.
25. Said, *Representations*, 72–3.
26. 'The Virtuoso as Intellectual,' Chapter 6 of *On Late Style: Music and Literature against the Grain* (New York: Pantheon Books, 2006), 132. That essay bemoans the fact that most intellectuals lack knowledge of music; comparably, Rokus de Groot concludes his interesting essay 'Edward Said and Polyphony' by saying 'for music to serve as a model for humanistic emancipation, music education is essential.' In *Edward Said: A Legacy of Emancipation and Representation*, eds. Adel Iskandar and Hakem Rustom (Berkeley, CA and London: University of California Press, 2010), 204–26. See too the ending of Said's essay 'The Book, Critical Performance, and the Future of Education,' *Pretexts: Literary and Cultural Studies* 10, no. 1 (July 2001), 9–19.
27. Said, *Musical Elaborations* (London: Chatto & Windus, 1991), 98; quoted by Lindsay Waters, 'In Responses Begins Responsibility: Music and Emotion,' in *Edward Said and the Work of the Critic: Speaking Truth to Power*, ed. Paul A. Bové (Durham and London: Duke, 2000), 97–113.
28. Michael Bérubé makes this sort of point in 'The Utility of the Arts and Humanities,' in *Rhetorical Occasions: Essays on Humans and the Humanities* (Chapel Hill, NC: University of North Carolina Press, 2006), 71–89.
29. Said, 'I've Always Learnt during the Class,' interview with Damayanti Datta (*The Telegraph*, Calcutta, 1997), reprinted in *Power, Politics and Culture: Interviews with Edward W. Said*, ed. Gauri Viswanathan (London: Bloomsbury, 2004), 280-3: 280–1.
30. Said, 'On Defiance and Taking Positions' (1996), in *Reflections on Exile*, 500–6, 500–1.
31. Said, *The Pen and the Sword: Conversations with David Barsamian* (Edinburgh: AK Press, 1994), 77–8. Said makes a similar point in *Representations*, 88.
32. Said, *Out of Place*, 183. For the sake of any Englishmen reading this chapter, I should clarify that 'cruel,' 'impersonal' and 'authoritarian' are all meant negatively.

33. Gauri Viswanathan, *Masks of Conquest* (New York: Columbia, 1989), 2. See Said, *Culture and Imperialism* (first published 1993; London: Vintage, 1994), 42, 101, 109.

34. Fazal Rizvi and Bob Lingard, 'Introduction,' *Discourse: Studies in the Cultural Politics of Education* 27, no. 3 (September 2006), 293–308, 294.

35. *Orientalism*, 323–4.

36. Said, interview in *Diacritics* 6, no. 3 (Fall 1976), 30–47, 47.

37. I do not have space to discuss universities' role in the socio-cultural reproduction of the middle classes, but that is another issue that presents itself with increased force under the new financial arrangements for universities in the UK and elsewhere. One of the problems disguised by the abstract phrase 'the mind of society' (as Said suggests by switching his attention to issues of class) is the constitution of the student body.

38. I believe my point stands despite some shifts in the terrain since the debates mentioned in note 3. See http://www.ref.ac.uk/pubs/, especially paragraphs 140–3 of *Assessment Framework and Guidance on Submissions* of July 2011, and the *Panel criteria and working methods* of January 2012. In the latter document, among the 'Indicative range of impacts' for disciplines including English, Languages and Music is: 'Informing and influencing the form or the content of the education of any age group in any part of the world where they extend significantly beyond the submitting HEI [Higher Education Institution]' (89). This holds open a certain space for academic/educational 'impact'; but the influence of one's research on one's own courses, or on courses within one's own university, is still excluded (if it were not, 'impact' could scarcely be made a separate criterion). In any case, the dominant current assumption within universities about the 'impact agenda' is that it must involve reaching outside universities.

39. *Orientalism*, xvi–xvii.

40. 'I've always learnt during the class,' 282.

41. *Culture and Imperialism*, xxvi. Similar points are made on 20 and 331.

42. Said, 'Identity, Authority and Freedom' (1991), republished in *Reflections on Exile*, 386–404, 403–4.

43. Said, 'The Book,' 10.

44. Said, 'The Book,' 14. Having agreed to discuss 'the future of education,' Said felt impelled in this essay to comment, 'I should first dispel any thought here that I am an expert on education: I am not although I have been a teacher for almost 40 years' – a remark that would support the argument that academic critics often show a peculiar reticence about their role as teachers. The essay also offers an encomium to books as objects, in my view making too much of the contrast between books and electronic media.

45. Poirier, *The Renewal of Literature: Emersonian Reflections* (London and Boston: Faber, 1987), 133 4.

46. Said, 'The Book,' 15.

47. Said, *Humanism and Democratic Criticism* (New York: Columbia, 2004), 53, 62–3. In the last quotation Said is presumably using the notion of academic 'work' as I have tried to use it throughout this chapter, to encompass teaching as well as criticism.

48. Said, *Humanism and Democratic Criticism*, 67.

Bibliography

Edward Said

Said, Edward W. *Music at the Limits: Three Decades of Essays and Articles on Music*. London: Bloomsbury, 2008.

——. *On Late Style: Music and Literature against the Grain*. London: Bloomsbury, 2006.

——. 'Literary Theory at the Crossroads of Public Life.' In *Power, Politics and Culture: Interviews with Edward W. Said*, edited by Gauri Viswanathan, 69–93. London: Bloomsbury, 2005.

——. 'My Right of Return.' In *Power, Politics and Culture: Interviews with Edward W. Said*, edited by Gauri Viswanathan, 443–58. London: Bloomsbury, 2005.

——. *From Oslo to Iraq and the Roadmap*. London: Bloomsbury, 2004.

——. *Humanism and Democratic Criticism*. Basingstoke: Palgrave Macmillan, 2004.

——. *Interviews with Edward Said*. Edited by Amritjit Singh and B. G. Johnson. Jackson, MS: Mississippi University Press, 2004.

——. *Power, Politics and Culture: Interviews*. London: Bloomsbury, 2004.

——. *Orientalism*. London: Penguin, 2003.

——. 'Preface' to *Orientalism*, xi–xxiii. London: Penguin, 2003.

——. *The End of the Peace Process: Oslo and After*. London: Granta, 2002.

——. 'Homage to Joe Sacco.' In *Palestine*, edited by Joe Sacco, i–v. Seattle, WA: Fantagraphics Books, 2001.

——. 'Bursts of Meaning.' 1982. In *Reflections on Exile and Other Literary and Cultural Essays*, edited by Edward W. Said, 148–52. London: Granta, 2000.

——. 'Diary.' *London Review of Books* 22, no. 11 (1 June 2000): 42–3.

——. 'Orientalism Reconsidered.' *Cultural Critique* 1 (Autumn 1985): 89–107 and in Said, *Reflections on Exile and Other Essays*, 198–215. Cambridge, MA: Harvard University Press, 2000.

——. *Out of Place*. London: Vintage, 2000.

——. *Reflections on Exile and Other Literary and Cultural Essays*. London: Granta, 2000.

——. 'The Art of Displacement: Mona Hatoum's Logic of Irreconcilables.' In *The Entire World as a Foreign Land*, edited by Mona Hatoum, 7–17. London: Tate Gallery, 2000.

——. *After the Last Sky: Palestinian Lives*, photographs by Jean Mohr. New York: Columbia University Press, 1999.

——. *Beginnings: Intention and Method*. 1975. London: Granta, 1997.

——. *Covering Islam: How the Media and the Experts Determine How We See the Rest of the World*. 1981. London: Vintage, 1997.

——. *Representations of the Intellectual: The 1993 Reith Lectures*. New York: Vintage, 1996.

———. *Peace and Its Discontents: Essays on Palestine in the Middle East Peace Process.* New York: Vintage, 1995.

———. *The Politics of Dispossession: The Struggle for Palestinian Self-determination, 1969–1994.* New York: Vintage, 1994.

———. *The Pen and the Sword: Conversations with David Barsamian.* Edinburgh: AK Press, 1994.

———. *Culture and Imperialism.* London: Vintage, 1993.

———. *The Question of Palestine.* 1979. New York: Vintage, 1992.

———. *Musical Elaborations.* London: Chatto & Windus, 1991.

———. 'Edward Said.' In *Criticism in Society*, edited by Imre Salusinszky, 123–48. New York and London: Methuen, 1987.

———. *The World, the Text, and the Critic.* Cambridge, MA: Harvard University Press, 1983.

———. 'Raymond Schwab and the Romance of Ideas.' In *The World, the Text and the Critic*, 246–67. Cambridge, MA: Harvard University Press, 1983.

———. 'Interview.' *Diacritics* 6, no. 3 (1976): 30–47.

———. 'Michel Foucault as an Intellectual Imagination.' *boundary 2* 1, no. 1 (1972): 1–36.

———. 'The Arab Portrayed.' In *The Arab–Israeli Confrontation of June 1967: An Arab Perspective*, edited by Ibrahim Abu-Lughod, 1–9. Evanston, IL: Northwestern University Press, 1970.

———. *Joseph Conrad and the Fiction of Autobiography.* Cambridge, MA: Harvard University Press, 1966.

Orientalism

Abdel Malek, Anouar. 'Orientalism in Crisis.' *Diogenes* 44 (1963): 104–12.

Abu-Lughod, Lila. '*Orientalism* and the Middle East in Middle Eastern Studies.' *Feminist Review* 27, no. 1 (2001): 101–13.

Al-ʿAzm, Sadik Jalal. 'Orientalism and Orientalism in Reverse.' In *Forbidden Agendas: Intolerance and Defiance in the Middle East*, edited by Jon Rothschild, 349–76. London: Saqi, 1984.

———. 'Orientalism and Orientalism in Reverse.' *Khamsin* 8 (1981): 5–26.

———. 'Orientalism, Occidentalism, and Islam: Keynote Address to "Orientalism and Fundamentalism in Islamic and Judaic Critique: A Conference Honoring Sadik al-Azm."' *Comparative Studies of South Asia, Africa and the Middle East* 30, no. 1 (2010): 6–13.

Ashcroft, William and Pal Ahluwalia. *Edward Said.* 2nd edn. London: Routledge, 2009.

Barbour, Richmond. *Before Orientalism: London's Theatre of the East, 1576–1626.* Cambridge: Cambridge University Press, 2003.

Barsamian, David and Edward W. Said. *Culture and Resistance: Conversations with Edward W. Said.* London: Pluto, 2003.

Bar-Yosef, Eitan. *The Holy Land in English Culture 1799–1917: Palestine and the Question of Orientalism.* Oxford and New York: Clarendon Press and Oxford University Press, 2005.

Bayoumi, Moustafa and Andrew Rubin. 'An Interview with Edward W. Said.' In *The Edward Said Reader*, edited by Moustafa Bayoumi and Andrew Rubin, 419–44. New York: Vintage, 2000.

Beaulieu, Jill and Mary Roberts, eds. *Orientalism's Interlocutors: Painting, Architecture, Photography*. Durham, NC and London: Duke University Press, 2002.

Behdad, Ali. 'Orientalism Matters.' *Modern Fiction Studies* 56, no. 4 (2010): 709–28.

Boehmer, Elleke. 'East Is East and South Is South: Post-Colonialism as Neo-Orientalism.' In *Edward Said*, edited by Patrick Williams, 116–27. Thousand Oaks, CA: Sage, 2001.

Bohrer, Frederick N. 'The Sweet Waters of Asia.' In *Edges of Empire: Orientalism and Visual Culture*, edited by Jocelyn Hackforth-Jones and Mary Roberts, 121–38. Oxford: Blackwell, 2005.

Bové, Paul A. *Edward Said and the Work of the Critic: Speaking Truth to Power*. Durham, NC and London: Duke University Press, 2000.

Brennan, Timothy. 'The Critic and the Public: Edward Said and World Literature.' In *Edward Said: A Legacy of Emancipation and Representation*, edited by Iskandar and Rustom, 102–20. Berkeley, CA and London: University of California Press, 2010.

———. 'The Illusion of a Future: "Orientalism" as Traveling Theory.' *Critical Inquiry* 26, no. 3 (2000): 558–83.

Cochran, Peter. 'Edward Said's Failure with (Inter Alia) Byron.' In *Byron and Orientalism*, edited by Peter Cochran, 183–96. Newcastle: Cambridge Scholars Press, 2006.

Curthoys, Ned and Debjani Ganguly. *Edward Said: The Legacy of a Public Intellectual*. Melbourne, VIC: Melbourne University Press, 2007.

Dirks, Nicholas. 'Edward Said and Anthropology.' In *Edward Said: A Legacy of Emancipation and Representation*, edited by Iskandar and Rustom, 86–101. Berkeley, CA and London: University of California Press, 2010.

Ghosh, Ranjan, ed. *Edward Said and the Literary, Social, and Political World*. London: Routledge, 2009.

Gran, Peter. 'Review of *Orientalism*, by Edward Said.' *Journal of the American Oriental Society* 100, no. 3 (1980): 328–31.

Gregory, Derek. 'Edward Said's Imaginative Geographies.' In *Thinking Space*, edited by Mike Crang and Nigel Thrift, 302–48. London: Routledge, 2000.

Harrison, Nicholas. ' "A Roomy Place Full of Possibility": Said's *Orientalism* and the Literary.' In *Edward Said and the Literary, Political and Social World*, edited by Ranjan Ghosh, 3–18. New York and London: Routledge, 2009.

Hawley, John. 'Edward Said, John Berger, Jean Mohr: In Search of an Other Optic.' In *Paradoxical Citizenship: A Tribute to Edward Said*, edited by Silvia Nagy-Zekmi, 203–10. Lanham, MD: Lexington, 2006.

Huggan, Graham. '(Not) Reading Orientalism.' *Research in African Literatures* 36, no. 3 (2005): 124–36.

Hussein, Abdirahman A. *Edward Said: Criticism and Society*. London: Verso, 2002.

Ibn Warraq (pseud.). *Defending the West: A Critique of Edward Said's Orientalism*. Amherst, NY: Prometheus, 2007.

Inankur, Zeynep, Reina Lewis and Mary Roberts, eds. *The Poetics and Politics of Place: Ottoman Istanbul and British Orientalism*. Istanbul: Kıraç Foundation, 2011.

Irwin, Robert. *Dangerous Knowledge: Orientalism and Its Discontents*. Woodstock, NY: Overlook Press, 2006.

———. 'Edward Said's Shadowy Legacy.' *The Times*. http://entertainment.timesonline.co.uk/tol/arts_and_entertainment/the_tls/article3885948.ece [accessed 6 July 2010].

Iskandar, Adel and Hakem Rustom, eds. *Edward Said: A Legacy of Emancipation and Representation*. Berkeley, CA and London: University of California Press, 2010.

Jasanoff, Maya. 'Before and After Said.' *London Review of Books*. http://www.lrb .co.uk/v28/n11/jasa01_.html [accessed 8 July 2010].

Kennedy, Valerie. *Edward Said: A Critical Introduction*. Oxford: Polity, 2000.

Lewis, Reina. *Gendering Orientalism: Race, Femininity and Representation*. London: Routledge, 1996.

———. *Rethinking Orientalism: Women, Travel and the Ottoman Harem*. London: I. B. Tauris, 2004.

Little, Douglas. *American Orientalism: The United States and the Middle East since 1945*. Chapel Hill, NC: University of North Carolina Press, 2002.

Lockman, Zachary. *Contending Visions of the Middle East: The History and Politics of Orientalism*. Cambridge: Cambridge University Press, 2004.

Lowe, Lisa. *Critical Terrains: French and British Orientalisms*. Ithaca, NY and London: Cornell University Press, 1991.

Macfie, Alexander Lyon, ed. *Orientalism: A Reader*. New York: New York University Press, 2000.

Mackenzie, John M. *Orientalism: History, Theory and the Arts*. Manchester: Manchester University Press, 1995.

Makdisi, Saree. 'Said, Palestine and the Humanism of Liberation.' *Critical Inquiry* 31, no. 2 (2005): 443–61.

Makdisi, Ussama. 'Ottoman Orientalism.' *American Historical Review* 107, no. 3 (2002): 768–96.

Marrouchi, Mustapha. *Edward Said at the Limits*. New York: State University of New York Press, 2004.

Massad, Joseph A. 'Affiliating with Edward Said.' In *Edward Said: A Legacy of Emancipation and Representation*, edited by Iskandar and Rustom, 23–49. Berkeley, CA and London: University of California Press, 2010.

Mitchell, W. J. T. 'The Panic of the Visual: A Conversation with Edward W. Said.' 1998. In *Edward Said and the Work of the Critic*, edited by Paul Bové, 31–50. Durham, NC and London: Duke University Press, 2000.

———. 'Secular Divination: Edward Said's Humanism.' *Critical Inquiry* 31, no. 2 (2005): 462–71.

Morton, Stephen. 'Terrorism, Orientalism, and Imperialism.' *Wasafiri* 22, no. 2 (2007): 36–42.

Porter, Denis. '*Orientalism* and Its Problems.' In *Colonial Discourse and Postcolonial Theory*, edited by Laura Chrisman and Patrick Williams, 150–61. London: Harvester, 1993.

Prakash, Gyan. 'Orientalism Now.' *History and Theory* 34, no. 3 (1995): 199–212.

Racevskis, Karlis. 'Edward Said and Michel Foucault: Affinities and Dissonances.' *Research in African Literatures* 36, no. 3 (2005): 83–97.

Rice, James P. 'In the Wake of Orientalism.' *Comparative Literature Studies* 37, no. 2 (2000): 223–38.

Sadowski, Yahya. 'The New Orientalism and the Democracy Debate.' In *Political Islam: Essays from Middle East Report*, edited by Joel Beinin and Joe Stork, 33–50. London: I. B. Tauris, 1997.

Spanos, William V. *The Legacy of Edward W. Said*. Urbana, IL: University of Illinois Press, 2009.

Spencer, Robert. 'Edward Said and the War in Iraq.' *New Formations* 59 (2006): 52–62.

Turner, Bryan. 'Outline of a Theory of Orientalism.' In *Orientalism*, edited by Edward Said, 1–31. London: Routledge, 2000.

Varisco, Daniel Martin. *Reading Orientalism: Said and the Unsaid*. Seattle, WA: University of Washington Press, 2007.

Veeser, H. Aram. *Edward Said: The Charisma of Criticism*. New York: Routledge, 2010.

Viswanathan, Gauri. *Power, Politics and Culture: Interviews with Edward W. Said*. London: Bloomsbury, 2004.

Williams, Patrick, ed. *Edward Said*. 4 vols. London: Sage, 2000.

General bibliography

Abbas, Avraham. 'The History of Ha-Halutz Movement in Syria and Lebanon' [in Hebrew]. *Shevet ye-ʿAm* 3 (1958): 113–24.

Abou-El-Haj, R. A. 'Historiography in Western Asia and North African Studies since Saʿid's *Orientalism*.' In *History after the Three Worlds*, edited by Arif Dirlik, Vinay Bahl and Peter Gran. Lanham, MD: Rowman & Littlefield, 2000.

Abu-Lughod, Lila. 'Do Muslim Women Really Need Saving? Anthropological Reflections on Cultural Relativism and its Others.' *American Anthropologist* 104, no. 3 (2002): 783–90.

Ackermann, Gerald. *The Life and Work of Jean-Léon Gérôme*. Paris: ACR, 1986.

Afshar, Haleh. *Islam and Feminisms: An Iranian Case Study*. Basingstoke: Macmillan, 1998.

Ahmed, Aijaz. *In Theory: Classes, Nations, Literatures*. London: Verso, 1992.

Al-ʿAzm, Sadik Jalal. *Dhihniyat al-Tahrīm: Salman Rushdie wa Haqīqat al-Adab [The Taboo Mentality: Salman Rushdie and the Truth about Literature]*. 1992. 5th edn. Damascus: Dār al-Madā, 2007.

Alexander, Edward. 'Professor of Terror.' *Commentary* 88, no. 2 (1989): 49–50.

Alloula, Malek. *The Colonial Harem*. Translated by Myrna Godzich and Wlad Godzich. Minneapolis, MN: University of Minnesota Press, 1986.

Almog, Oz. *The Sabra: The Creation of the New Jew*. Berkeley, CA and London: University of California Press, 2000.

Alter, Stephen G. *William Dwight Whitney and the Science of Language*. Baltimore, MD and London: Johns Hopkins University Press, 2005.

ʿĀmil, Mahdī. *Marks fī istishrāq Idwārd Said*. Beirut: Dār al-Farābī, 1985.

Amin, Camron. *The Making of the Modern Iranian Woman: Gender, State Policy, and Popular Culture, 1865–1946*. Gainesville, FL: University Press of Florida, 2002.

Amin, Samir. *Arab Nation*. London: Zed, 1978.

Anderson, Perry. 'On the Concatenation in the Arab World.' *New Left Review* 68 (2011): 5–15.

Apter, Emily. 'Saidian Humanism.' *boundary 2* 31, no. 2 (2004): 35–53.

Arat, Yeşim. 'Nation Building and Feminism in Early Republican Turkey.' In *Turkey's Engagement with Modernity: Conflict and Change in the Twentieth Century*, edited by Celia Kerslake, Kerem Öktem and Philip Robins. Basingstoke: Palgrave Macmillan, 2010.

Arat, Zehra, ed. *Deconstructing Images of the 'Turkish Woman.'* New York and Basingstoke: Palgrave Macmillan, 2000.

Arbel, Benjamin. *Trading Nations: Jews and Venetians in the Early Modern Eastern Mediterranean*. New York: E. V. Brill, 1995.

Association for the Study of Travel in Egypt and the Near East. http://www.astene.org.uk/ [accessed 1 May 2011].

Auerbach, Erich. *Literary Language and its Public in Late Latin Antiquity and the Middle Ages*. Translated by Ralph Manheim. London: Routledge, 1965.

———. *Mimesis: The Representation of Reality in Western Literature*. 1953. Translated by Willard R. Trask. Princeton, NJ: Princeton University Press, 1968.

———. 'Philology and *Weltliteratur*.' Translated by Maire and Edward Said. *The Centennial Review* 13 (1969): 1–17.

Avcioglu, Nabahat. *'Turquerie' and the Politics of Representation*. Farnham: Ashgate, 2011.

Badran, Margot. *Feminists, Islam, and Nation: Gender and the Making of Modern Egypt*. Princeton, NJ: Princeton University Press, 1991.

Ballaster, Ros. *Fabulous Orients: Fictions of the East in England 1662–1785*. Oxford: Oxford University Press, 2005.

Barnes, Julian. *Flaubert's Parrot*. London: Jonathan Cape, 1984.

Baron, Beth. *Egypt as a Woman: Nationalism, Gender and Politics*. Berkeley, CA and London: University of California Press, 2005.

———. *The Women's Awakening in Egypt*. New Haven, CT and London: Yale University Press, 1994.

Barr, James. *Setting the Desert on Fire: T. E. Lawrence and Britain's Secret War in Arabia, 1916–18*. London: Bloomsbury, 2006.

Bartolovich, Crystal and Neil Lazarus. *Marxism, Modernity and Postcolonial Studies*. Cambridge: Cambridge University Press, 2002.

Baudrillard, Jean. *The Spirit of Terrorism*. New York: Verso, 2002.

Bayat, Mangol. *Mysticism and Dissent: Socio-Religious Thought in Qajar Iran*. Syracuse, NY: Syracuse University Press, 1982.

Bean, Susan. *Yankee India: American Commercial and Cultural Encounters with India in the Age of Sail, 1784–1860*. Salem: Peabody Essex Museum, 2001.

Beaver, Dan. 'Flesh or Fantasy: Cannibalism and the Meanings of Violence.' *Ethnohistory* 49, no. 3 (2002): 671–85.

Beckford, William. *Vathek and Other Stories*, edited by Malcolm Jack. London: Penguin, 1995.

Beinin, Joel. *Workers and Peasants in the Modern Middle East*. Cambridge: Cambridge University Press, 2001.

Bell, Gertrude. *Safar Nameh, Persian Pictures: A Book of Travel*. London: R. Bentley and Son, 1894.

Benjamin, Roger. *Orientalist Aesthetics: Art Colonialism and French North Africa*. Berkeley, CA and London: University of California Press, 2003.

Berger, John and Jean Mohr. *Another Way of Telling*. 1981. Cambridge: Granta, 1989.

Berktay, Fatmagül. 'Looking from the "Other" Side: Is Cultural Relativism a Way Out?' In *Women's Studies in the 1990s: Doing Things Differently*, edited by Joanna de Groot and Mary Maynard, 110–31. Basingstoke and New York: Macmillan and St Martin's Press, 1993.

Bevis, Richard. 'Making the Desert Bloom: An Historical Picture of Pre-Zionist Palestine.' *The Middle East Newsletter* 5, no. 2 (February–March 1971): 1–15.

Birchwood, Matthew. *Staging Islam in England: Drama and Culture, 1640–1685.* Studies in Renaissance Literature. Cambridge: D. S. Brewer, 2007.

Black, Ian, and Benny Morris. *Israel's Secret Wars: A History of Israel's Intelligence Services.* New York: Grove Press, 2003.

Blackmur, R. P. *The Lion and the Honeycomb: Essays in Solicitude and Critique.* London: Methuen, 1956.

Blank, Diana R. 'A Veil of Controversy: the Construction of a "Tchador Affair" in the French Press.' *Interventions* 1, no. 4 (1999): 536–54.

Bloomfield, Maurice. 'Fifty Years of Comparative Philology in America.' *Proceedings of the American Philological Association* 50 (1919): 62–83.

———. 'Notes of Recent Publications, Investigations and Studies.' *JHU Circular* 11, no. 99 (1892): JHU Archives.

Blount, Henry. *A Voyage into the Levant: A Brief Relation of a Journey, Lately Performed by Master H. B. Gentleman, from England by the Way of Venice, into Dalmatia, Sclavonia, Bosnah, Hungary, Macedonia, Thessaly, Thrace, Rhodes and Egypt, unto Gran Cairo: With Particular Observations Concerning the Moderne Condition of the Turkes, and Other People Under the Empire.* London: Printed by I. L. [John Legatt] for Andrew Crooke, 1636.

Bové, Paul A. 'Continuing the Conversation.' *Critical Inquiry* 31, no. 2 (2005): 399–405.

———. 'Intellectuals at War: Michel Foucault and the Analytics of Power.' *SubStance* 11, no. 4 (1982–3): 36–55.

Brecht, Bertolt. *Poems: 1913–1956*, edited by John Willett and Ralph Manheim. London: Methuen, 1976.

Brennan, Timothy. *Wars of Position: The Cultural Politics of Left and Right.* New York: Columbia University Press, 2006.

Brown, Michelle. 'Setting the Conditions for Abu Ghraib: The Prison Nation Abroad.' *American Quarterly* 57, no. 3 (2005): 973–97.

Brown, Frederick. *Flaubert: A Life.* London: Pimlico, 2007.

Buck, C. D. 'Comparative Philology and the Classics.' *Transactions and Proceedings of the American Philological Association* 47 (1916): 65–83.

Bulliet, Richard W. *The Camel and the Wheel.* Cambridge, MA: Harvard University Press, 1975.

Burton, Antoinette. *Empire in Question: Reading, Writing and Teaching British Imperialism.* Durham, NC and London: Duke University Press, 2011.

Burton, Jonathan. *Traffic and Turning: Islam and English Drama, 1579–1624.* Newark, DE: University of Delaware Press, 2005.

Butler, Judith. *Bodies That Matter.* London: Routledge, 1993.

———. *Excitable Speech: A Politics of the Performative.* London: Routledge, 1997.

Canny, Nicholas. 'The Origins of Empire: An Introduction.' In *The Origins of Empire: British Overseas Enterprise to the Close of the Seventeenth Century. The Oxford History of the British Empire Volume I*, edited by Nicholas Canny, 1–33. Oxford and New York: Oxford University Press, 1998.

Casale, Giancarlo. *The Ottoman Age of Exploration.* Oxford and New York: Oxford University Press, 2010.

Çelik, Zeynep. 'Speaking Back to Orientalist Discourse.' In *Orientalism's Interlocutors: Painting, Architecture, Photography*, edited by Jill Beaulieu and Mary Roberts, 19–42. Durham, NC and London: Duke University Press, 2002.

———. 'Speaking Back to Orientalist Discourse at the World's Columbian Exposition.' In *Noble Dreams, Wicked Pleasures: Orientalism in America, 1870–1930*, edited by Holly Edwards, 77–97. Princeton, NJ: Princeton University Press, 2000.

Chandrasekaran, Rajiv. *Imperial Life in the Emerald City: Inside Iraq's Green Zone*. New York: Vintage, 2007.

Chaudhuri, Nupur and Margaret Strobel. *Western Women and Imperialism: Complicity and Resistance*. Bloomington, IN: Indiana University Press, 1992.

Chomsky, Noam. *The New Military Humanism: Lessons from Kosovo*. London: Pluto, 1999.

Cicek, Nazan. *The Young Ottomans: Turkish Critics of the Eastern Question in the Late Nineteenth Century*. London: Tauris Academic Studies, 2010.

Clifford, James. *The Predicament of Culture: Twentieth Century Ethnography, Literature, and Art*. Cambridge, MA: Harvard University Press, 1988.

Cohen, Gamliel. *The First Mistaʿaravim* [in Hebrew]. Tel Aviv: Israeli Ministry of Defence, 2002.

Cohen, Yeroham. *Palmach behind Enemy Lines in Syria* [in Hebrew]. Tel Aviv: Ha-Kibbutz ha-Meʾuḥad, 1973.

———. *By Light and in Darkness* [in Hebrew]. Tel Aviv: ʿAmikam, 1969.

Colley, Linda. *Britons: Forging the Nation, 1707–1837*. London and New Haven, CT: Yale University Press, 1992.

Conrad, Joseph. *The Nigger of the 'Narcissus'/ Youth*. London: Pan Classics, 1976.

Coulmas, Florian. 'Spies and Native Speakers.' In *A Festschrift for Native Speaker*, edited by Florian Coulmas, 355–67. The Hague: Mouton, 1981.

Crenshaw, Kim. 'Demarginalising the Intersection of Race and Sex: A Black Feminist Critique of Antidiscrimination Doctrine, Feminist Theory and Antiracist Policy.' In *Feminist Legal Theory*, edited by D. Kelly Weisberg, 383–95. Philadelphia, PA: Temple University Press, 1993.

———. 'Mapping the Margins: Intersectionality, Identity Politics and Violence against Women of Colour.' *Stanford Law Review* 43 (1991): 363–77.

Crenshaw, Kimberlè Williams, Richard Delgado, Charles R. Lawrence III and Mari J. Matsuda. *Words That Wound: Critical Race Theory, Assaultive Speech, and the First Amendment*. Boulder, CO: Westview Press, 1993.

Dahl, Robert. *Polyarchy*. New Haven, CT: Yale University Press, 1971.

Dalrymple, William. *White Mughals: Love and Betrayal in Eighteenth-Century India*. London: HarperCollins, 2002.

De Atkine, Norvell B. Foreword to *The Arab Mind*, by Raphael Patai, x–xviii. New York: Hatherleigh Press, 2002.

De Groot, Joanna. 'What Goes Around Comes Around: "Veiling," Women's Bodies, and Orientalisms Past and Present.' Paper presented at the *International Congress of Historical Sciences*, Sydney, 2005.

———. ' "Brothers of the Iranian Race": Manhood, Nationhood and Modernity in Iran 1870–1914.' In *Masculinities in Politics and War: Gendering Modern History*, edited by Stefan Dudink, Karen Hagemann and John Tosh, 137–56. Manchester: Manchester University Press, 2004.

———. 'Coexisting and Conflicting Identities: Women and Nationalisms in Twentieth Century Iran.' In *Nation, Empire, Colony: Historicizing Gender and Race*, edited by Ruth Roach Pierson and Nupur Chaudhur. Bloomington, IN: Indiana University Press, 1998.

————. ' "Sex" and "Race": The Construction of Image and Language in the Nineteenth Century.' In *Sexuality and Subordination: Interdisciplinary Studies of Gender in the Nineteenth Century*, edited by Susan Mendus and Jane Rendall, 89–108. London and New York: Routledge, 1989.

Deleuze, Gilles. *Foucault*. Paris: Éditions de Minuit, 1986.

Del Plato, Joan. *Multiple Wives, Multiple Pleasures: Representing the Harem, 1800–1875*. Madison and Teaneck, NJ: Farleigh Dickinson Press, 2002.

Demirdirek, Aynur. 'In Search of the Ottoman Women's Movement.' In *Deconstructing the Image of the 'Turkish Woman,'* edited by Zehra Arat. New York and Basingstoke: Palgrave Macmillan, 2000.

Deringil, Selim. *The Well Protected Domains: Ideology and the Legitimating of Power in the Ottoman Empire 1876–1908*. London: I. B. Tauris, 1997.

Derrida, Jacques. *L'Université sans condition*. Paris: Galilée, 2001.

————. *Mémoires: For Paul de Man*. Translated by Cecile Lindsay, Jonathan Culler, Eduardo Cadava and Peggy Kamuf, edited by Avital Ronell and Eduardo Cadava. New York: Columbia University Press, 1989.

Deutscher, Penelope. 'Mourning the Other, Cultural Cannibalism, and the Politics of Friendship (Jacques Derrida and Luce Irigaray).' *Differences: A Journal of Feminist Cultural Studies* 10, no. 3 (1998): 159–84.

Djait, Hichem. *L'Europe et l'Islam*. Paris: Seuil, 1978.

Douchin, Jacques-Louis. *La Vie érotique de Flaubert*. Paris: Pauvert, 1984.

Dror, Zvika. *The 'Arabists' of the Palmach* [in Hebrew]. Tel Aviv: Ha-Kibbutz ha-Meʾuḥad, 1986.

Du Camp, Maxime. *Literary Recollections*. London and Sydney: Remington: 1893.

Dyer, Geoff. 'The Goncourt Journals.' In *Working the Room*, edited by Geoff Dyer, 199–206. Edinburgh: Canongate Books, 2010.

Eisenstein, Zillah. *Against Empire: Feminisms, Racism, and the West*. London: Zed Press, 2004.

Eldem, Edhem. 'An Ottoman Traveller to the Orient: Osman Hamdi Bey.' In *The Poetics and Politics of Place: Ottoman Istanbul and British Orientalism*, edited by Zeynep Inankur, Reina Lewis and Mary Roberts, 63–82. Istanbul and Seattle, WA: University of Washington Press, 2011.

————, ed. *Un Ottoman en Orient: Osman Hamdi Bey en Irak*. Paris: Actes Sud, 2010.

Eliot, C. W. 'The Aims of Higher Education.' In *Educational Reform: Essays and Addresses*, edited by Charles W. Eliot, 223–52. New York: The Century Company, 1898.

————. ' "The New Education," Part II of II.' In *American Higher Education: A Documentary History*, edited by Richard Hofstadter and Wilson Smith, 632–47. Chicago: University of Chicago Press, 1961.

El Guindi, Fadwa. *Veil: Modesty, Privacy, and Resistance*. Oxford and New York: Berg, 1999.

El-Shakry, Omnia. *The Great Social Laboratory: Subjects of Knowledge in Colonial and Postcolonial Egypt*. Stanford, CA: Stanford University Press, 2007.

Erlich, Reuven. *The Lebanon Triangle: The Policy of the Zionist Movement and the State of Israel Towards Lebanon, 1918–1958* [in Hebrew]. Tel Aviv: Maʿarakhot, Israeli Ministry of Defence, 2000.

Eyal, Gil. *The Disenchantment of the Orient: Expertise in Arab Affairs*. Stanford, CA: Stanford University Press, 2006.

——. 'Dangerous Liaisons between Military Intelligence and Middle Eastern Studies in Israel.' *Theory and Society* 31, no. 5 (2002): 653–93.

Faroqhi, Suraiya N. *The Later Ottoman Empire.* Cambridge: Cambridge University Press, 2006.

Fazlur, Rahman. 'Islamic Modernism: Its Scope, Method and Alternatives.' *International Journal of Middle East Studies* 1, no. 4 (1970): 317–33.

Fernández-Armesto, Felipe. *Millennium: A History of Our Last Thousand Years.* 1995. London: Black Swan, 1996.

Findley, Carter Vaughn. *Turkey, Islam, Nationalism, and Modernity: A History, 1789–2007.* New Haven, CT and London: Yale University Press, 2011.

Finkel, Caroline. *Osman's Dream: The Story of the Ottoman Empire 1300–1923.* London: John Murray, 2005.

——. ' "The Treacherous Cleverness of Hindsight": Myths of Ottoman Decay.' In *Re-Orienting the Renaissance: Cultural Exchanges with the East,* edited by Gerald MacLean, 148–74. Basingstoke: Palgrave Macmillan, 2005.

Firth, Ann and Erika Martens. 'Transforming Supervisors? A Critique of Post-Liberal Approaches to Research Supervision.' *Teaching in Higher Education* 13, no. 3 (June 2008): 279–89.

Flaubert, Gustave. 'Correspondance, I (janvier 1830 à avril 1851).' In *Bibliothèque de la Pléiade,* edited by Jean Bruneau. Paris: Gallimard, 1973.

——. *Flaubert à l'Exposition de 1851.* Edited and translated by Jean Seznec. Oxford: Clarendon Press, 1951.

——. *Madame Bovary.* Translated by Geoffrey Wall. London: Penguin, 1992.

——. *Sentimental Education.* Translated by Robert Baldick. Harmondsworth: Penguin, 1964.

——. *La Tentation de Saint Antoine.* Edited by Emile Faguet. London: Dent & Sons; Paris: Crès et Cie, 1913.

——. *Three Tales.* Translated by A. J. Krailsheimer. Oxford: Oxford University Press, 1991.

——. *Voyage en Orient.* Edited by Claudine Gothot-Mersch. Paris: Gallimard, 2006.

Foucault, Michel. *The Archaeology of Knowledge.* London and New York: Routledge, 2003.

——. *Discipline and Punish: The Birth of the Prison.* London: Penguin, 1991.

——. *Dits et écrits,* vol. I–II. Paris: Gallimard, 2001.

——. *History of Sexuality, Vol. 1: The Will to Knowledge.* London: Penguin, 1998.

——. *Il faut défendre la société – Cours au Collège de France, 1975–1976.* Le Foucault Electronique v. 2001/Folio Editions, 1977.

——. 'Interview with Alessandro Fontana and Pasquale Pasquino.' In *The Foucault Reader,* edited by Paul Rabinow, 63–4. London: Penguin, 1991.

——. 'Of Other Spaces'. http://foucault.info/documents/heteroTopia/foucault.heteroTopia.en.html.

——. *The Order of Things: Archaeology of the Human Sciences.* London and New York: Routledge, 2007.

——. 'Truth and Power.' In *The Foucault Reader,* edited by Paul Rabinow, 157–75. London: Penguin, 1991.

Freud, Sigmund. *Totem and Taboo.* Translated by James Strachey. New York: Norton, 1950.

Gadamer, Hans-Georg. *Truth and Method*. 1960. Translated by Joel Weinsheimer and Donald G. Marshall. London: Continuum, 2004.

Games, Alison. *The Web of Empire: English Cosmopolitans in an Age of Expansion, 1560–1660*. Oxford and New York: Oxford University Press, 2008.

Gandhi, Leila. *Affective Communities: Anticolonial Thought, Fin de Siècle Radicalism and the Politics of Friendship*. Durham, NC and London: Duke University Press, 2006.

Gardner, Frank. *Blood and Sand*. London: Bantam, 2006.

Gelber, Yoav. *The Intelligence in the Yishuv: 1918–1947* [in Hebrew]. Tel Aviv: Israeli Ministry of Defence, 1992.

Gharieb, Samir. *Surrealism in Egypt and Plastic Arts*. Cairo: Prism, 1986.

Gibb, H. A. R. *Modern Trends in Islam*. Chicago: University of Chicago Press, 1947.

Göçek, Fatma Müge. *Rise of the Bourgeoisie, Demise of Empire: Ottoman Westernisation and Social Change*. New York and Oxford: Oxford University Press, 1996.

Goffman, Daniel. *The Ottoman Empire and Early Modern Europe*. Cambridge and New York: Cambridge University Press, 2002.

Göle, Nilüfer. *The Forbidden Modern: Civilisation and Veiling*. Ann Arbor, MI: University of Michigan Press, 1996.

De Goncourt, Edmond. *Pages from the Goncourt Journal*. Translated by Robert Baldick. London: Folio Society, 1980.

Gran, Peter. *Rise of the Rich: A New View of Modern World History*. Syracuse, NY: Syracuse University Press, 2010.

Green, Anne. *Flaubert and the Historical Novel*. Cambridge: Cambridge University Press, 1982.

Greenberg, Karen J. and Joshua L. Dratel, eds. *The Torture Papers: The Road to Abu Ghraib*. Cambridge: Cambridge University Press, 2005.

Gregory, Derek. *The Colonial Present: Afghanistan, Palestine, Iraq*. Oxford: Blackwell, 2004.

Hakim, Ophir. 'The Youngest of Them All: Havakuk Cohen' [in Hebrew]. *Hamanit: The Israeli Military Intelligence Journal* (April 1991).

———. 'To Be Afraid 26 Hours a Day: The Palmach Mistaʿaravim Unit' [in Hebrew]. *Hamanit: The Israeli Military Intelligence Journal* (April 1991).

Hanioğlu, M. Sÿuĺkruĺ. *A Brief History of the Late Ottoman Empire*. Princeton, NJ and Oxford: Princeton University Press, 2008.

Harkavy, Robert. *Strategic Basing and the Great Powers, 1200–2000*. London: Routledge, 2007.

Hassan, Fayza. 'Museums Across Egypt.' *Egypt Today*, April 2006.

Henry, Nancy. *George Eliot and the British Empire*. Cambridge: Cambridge University Press, 2002.

Hersh, Seymour. *Chain of Command: The Road from 9/11 to Abu Ghraib*. New York: Harper Collins, 2004.

———. 'The Coming Wars: What the Pentagon Can Now Do in Secret.' *The New Yorker*, 24 January 2005, http://www.newyorker.com/archive/2005/01/24/050124fa_fact.

Huntington, Samuel. 'The Clash of Civilizations?' *Foreign Affairs* 71 (1993): 222–49.

Hyde, Ralph. *Panoramania! The Art and Entertainment of the 'All-Embracing' View*. London: Barbican Art Gallery, 1988.

Ilan, Zvi. 'Ha-Ḥalutz in Syria and the Settlement in the Houran' [in Hebrew]. *Mi-Kan u-mi-Shaam: The Journal of the Damascus Jewry Organization in Israel* 13 (April 2011): 16–21.

Imber, Colin. *Ebu's-su'ud: The Islamic Legal Tradition*. Edinburgh: Edinburgh University Press, 1997.

İnalcık, Halil and Donald Quataert. *Economic and Social History of the Ottoman Empire 1300–1914*. Cambridge: Cambridge University Press, 1997.

'Iraqi "Ghost Detainees" Could Number 100,' *Guardian Unlimited*. http://www .guardian.co.uk/international/story/0,,1301712,00.html.

Irigaray, Luce. *I Love To You: Sketch for a Felicity Within History*. Translated by Alison Martin. New York: Routledge, 1996.

Irwin, Robert. *Camel*. London: Reaktion, 2010.

———. *For Lust of Knowing: The Orientalists and Their Enemies*. London: Allen Lane, 2006.

———. 'The Muslim World in British Fictions of the Nineteenth Century.' In *Britain and the Muslim World: Historical Perspectives*, edited by Gerald MacLean, 31–42. Newcastle upon Tyne: Cambridge Scholars Publishing, 2011.

Israel, Jonathan. 'The Emerging Empire: The Continental Perspective, 1650–1713.' In *The Origins of Empire: British Overseas Enterprise to the Close of the Seventeenth Century: The Oxford History of the British Empire, Volume I*, edited by Nicholas Canny, 423–44. Oxford and New York: Oxford University Press, 1998.

———. *European Jewry in the Age of Mercantilism*. Oxford: Clarendon Press, 1989.

Jackson, Ashley. *The British Empire and the Second World War*. London: Hambledon Continuum, 2006.

Jacob, Wilson Chacko. *Working Out Egypt: Effendi Masculinity and Subject Formation in Colonial Modernity*. Durham, NC and London: Duke University Press, 2011.

Jacoby, Russell. *The Last Intellectuals: American Culture in the Age of Academe*. New York: Basic Books, 1987.

Jahn, Beate. 'The Tragedy of Liberal Diplomacy: Democratization, Intervention, Statebuilding (Part I).' *Journal of Intervention and Statebuilding* 1, no. 1 (2007): 87–106.

Jay, Martin. *Downcast Eyes: The Denigration of Vision in Twentieth-Century French Thought*. Berkeley, CA and London: University of California Press, 1993.

Johnston, David and Mark Mazzetti, 'Interrogation Inc.: A Window into C.I.A.'s Embrace of Secret Jails,' *New York Times*. http://www.nytimes.com/2009/08/13/ world/13foggo.html?ref=us.

Kabbani, Rana. *Europe's Myths of the Orient: Devise and Rule*. London: Palgrave Macmillan, 1986.

Kandiyoti, Deniz. 'Contemporary Feminist Scholarship and Middle East Studies.' In *Gendering the Middle East*, edited by Deniz Kandiyoti. London: I. B. Tauris, 1996.

———, ed. *Women, Islam and the State*. Basingstoke: Macmillan, 1991.

———. 'Woman as Metaphor: The Turkish Novel from the Tanzimat to the Republic.' In *Urban Crises and Social Movements in the Middle East: Proceedings of the CNRS-ESRC Symposium Paris, May 23-27th, 1986*, edited by Kenneth Brown et al., 140–52. Paris: L'Harmattan, 1989.

Karam, Azza. 'Veiling, Unveiling and Meanings of the Veil: Challenging Static Symbols.' *Thamyris* 3, no. 2 (1996): 219–36.

254   *Bibliography*

Kashua, Sayed. 'How to Be an Arab.' *Haaretz*, 16 October 2009.

Katz, David S. *Jews in the History of England, 1485–1850.* Oxford: Clarendon Press, 1994.

Kedourie, Elie. *Democracy and Arab Political Culture.* Washington, DC: Washington Institute for Near East Policy, 1992.

Kilgour, Maggie. 'The Function of Cannibalism, at the Present Time.' In *Cannibalism and the Colonial World*, edited by Francis Barker, Peter Hulme and Margaret Iversen, 238–59. Cambridge: Cambridge University Press, 1998.

Krailsheimer, A. J. 'Introduction.' In *Salammbô*, edited and translated by A. J. Krailsheimer. Harmondsworth: Penguin, 1977.

Kramer, Martin. *Ivory Towers on Sand: The Failure of Middle Eastern Studies in America.* Washington, DC: The Washington Institute for Near East Policy, 2002.

Kurd ʿAlī, Muḥammad. *Khiṭaṭ al-Shām.* Beirut: Dār al-ʿIlm li-l-Malāyīn, 1969–71.

Kurtz, H. 'Correspondents Chafe over Curb on News.' *Washington Post*, 26 January 1991.

Kushnir, Shimʿon. *A Man in the ʿAravah: The Story of Yehudah Almog* [in Hebrew]. Tel Aviv: ʿAm ʿOved, 1973.

Lane, Edward William. *An Account of the Manners and Customs of the Modern Egyptians.* 1836. Revised edn. London: Minerva Library, 1890.

Lanman, Charles. *A Sanskrit Reader: Text, Vocabulary and Notes.* Cambridge, MA: Harvard University Press, 1884.

Laroui (al-ʿArawī), ʿAbd Allāh (Laroui). *The Crisis of the Arab Intellectual: Traditionalism or Historicism?* Berkeley, CA and London: University of California Press, 1976.

Larsen, Neil. *Determinations: Essays on Theory, Narrative and Nation in the Americas.* London: Verso, 2001.

———. *The Eloquence of Silence: Algerian Women in Question.* New York and London: Routledge, 1994.

Lazarus, Neil. *The Postcolonial Unconscious.* Cambridge: Cambridge University Press, 2011.

———. 'Representations of the Intellectual in *Representations of the Intellectual.*' *Research in African Literatures* 36, no. 3 (2005): 112–23.

———. *Nationalism and Cultural Practice in the Postcolonial World.* Cambridge: Cambridge University Press, 1999.

Lazreg, Marnia. *Questioning the Veil: Open Letters to Muslim Women.* Princeton, NJ and Oxford: Princeton University Press, 2008.

Le Strange, Guy. *Palestine under the Moslems: A Description of Syria and the Holy Land from A.D. 650 to 1500 Translated from the Works of the Medieval Arab Geographers.* 1890. Rpt. Beirut: Khayati, 1965.

Levell, Nicky. *Oriental Visions: Exhibitions, Travel and Collecting in the Victorian Age.* London: The Horniman Museum & Gardens, 2000.

Levy, Lital. 'Historicizing the Concept of Arab Jews in the Mashriq.' *Jewish Quarterly Review* 98, no. 4 (2008): 452–69.

Lewis, Bernard. 'The Roots of Muslim Rage.' *The Atlantic Online*, September 1990. http://altervsego.hypotheses.org/files/2009/12/The-Atlantic-Online-_-September-1990-_-The-Roots-of-Muslim-Rage-_-Bernard-Lewis.pdf.

Liebesny, Herbert J. 'Judicial Systems in the Near and Middle East: Evolutionary Development and Islamic Revival.' *Middle East Journal* 37, no. 2 (1983): 202–17.

Lockman, Zachary. 'Behind the Battles over US Middle East Studies.' http://www
.merip.org/mero/interventions/lockman_interv.html [accessed 10 July 2010].
———. *Comrades and Enemies: Arab and Jewish Workers in Palestine, 1906–1948.*
Berkeley, CA and London: University of California Press, 1996.
MacLean, Gerald. *Looking East: English Writing and the Ottoman Empire before 1800.*
Basingstoke and New York: Palgrave Macmillan, 2007.
———. *The Rise of Oriental Travel: English Visitors to the Ottoman Empire, 1580–
1720.* Basingstoke and New York: Palgrave Macmillan, 2004.
MacLean, Gerald and Nabil Matar. *Britain and the Islamic World, 1558–1713.*
Oxford and New York: Oxford University Press, 2011.
MacLeod, Arlene Elowe. *Accommodating Protest: Working Women, the New Veiling
and Change in Cairo.* New York: Columbia University Press, 1991.
Mahmood, Saba. *The Politics of Piety: The Islamic Revival and the Feminist Subject.*
Princeton, NJ: Princeton University Press, 2005.
Makdisi, George. *The Rise of Humanism in Classical Islam and the Christian West.*
Edinburgh: Edinburgh University Press, 1990.
Manning, Patrick. *Navigating World History: Historians Create a Global Past.*
New York: Palgrave Macmillan, 2003.
Mansel, Philip. 'The French Renaissance in Search of the Ottoman Empire.' In *Re-
Orienting the Renaissance: Cultural Exchanges with the East,* edited by Gerald
MacLean, 96–107. Basingstoke and New York: Palgrave Macmillan, 2005.
Mansour, Johnny. 'The Mistaʿaravim: Beginning, Crimes, Training and Tasks' [in
Arabic]. *Qaḍāyā Isrāʾīliyyā* 15 (2004): 6–20.
———. 'Behind the Shadow' [in Hebrew]. *Ba-Mahane: The weekly IDF Magazine* 42
(2010). http://dover.idf.il/IDF/News_Channels/bamahana/2010/42/15.htm.
Mardin, Şerif. *The Genesis of Young Ottoman Thought.* Syracuse, NY: Syracuse
University Press, 2000.
Mason, Carol. 'The Hillbilly Defense: Culturally Mediating U.S. Terror at Home
and Abroad.' *NWSA Journal* 17, no. 3 (2005): 39–63.
Massad, Joseph A. *Desiring Arabs.* Chicago: University of Chicago Press, 2007.
Masters, Bruce. *Christians and Jews in the Ottoman Arab World: The Roots
of Sectarianism.* Cambridge Studies in Islamic Civilization. Cambridge and
New York: Cambridge University Press, 2001.
Matar, Nabil. *Islam in Britain, 1558–1685.* Cambridge: Cambridge University
Press, 1998.
———. *Turks, Moors, and Englishmen in the Age of Discovery.* New York: Columbia
University Press, 1999.
McCall, Leslie. 'The Complexity of Intersectionality.' *Signs* 30, no. 3 (2005):
1771–800.
McClintock, Anne. *Dangerous Liaisons: Gender, Nation, and Postcolonial
Perspectives.* Minneapolis, MN: University of Minnesota Press, 1997.
———. *Imperial Leather: Race, Gender, and Sexuality in the Colonial Contest.*
New York: Routledge, 1995.
McGowan, Bruce. *Economic Life in Ottoman Europe: Taxation, Trade, and the Struggle
for Land, 1600–1800.* Cambridge: Cambridge University Press, 1981.
Melman, Billie. *Women's Orients: English Women and the Middle East, 1718–1918:
Sexuality, Religion and Work.* London: Macmillan, 1992.
Miles, Steven H. *Oath Betrayed.* New York: Random House, 2006.
Mishani, Dror. *The Ethnic Unconscious* [in Hebrew]. Tel Aviv: ʿAm ʿOved, 2006.

————. 'Gamliel Cohen Died: One of Israel's Most Senior Intelligence Agents' [in Hebrew]. *Arutz Sheva: Israel National News*. www.inn.co.il/News/News.aspx/30272.

Mitchell, Timothy. *Colonising Egypt*. Cambridge: Cambridge University Press, 1988.

Mitchell, W. J. T. 'The Imperial Landscape.' 1994. In *Landscape and Power*, edited by W. J. T. Mitchell, 5–34. Chicago: University of Chicago Press, 2002.

Mittelberg, David. *The Israel Connection and American Jews*. Westport, CT: Greenwood Publishing Group, 1999.

Mohanty, Chandra. *Feminism without Borders*. Durham, NC and London: Duke University Press, 2003.

Moore-Gilbert, Bart. *Postcolonial Theory: Contexts, Practices, Politics*. London: Verso, 1997.

Moors, Annelies. ' "Islamic Fashion" in Europe: Religious Conviction, Aesthetic Style, and Creative Consumption.' *Encounters* 1, no. 1 (2009): 182–9.

Nadelson, Theodore. *Trained to Kill: Soldiers at War*. Baltimore, MD: Johns Hopkins University Press, 2005.

Naipaul, V. S. 'Our Universal Civilization.' *Manhattan Institute*. http://www.manhattan-institute.org/html/wl1990.htm [accessed 11 January 2012].

Najmabadi, Afsaneh. *Women with Mustaches and Men without Beards*. Berkeley, CA and London: University of California Press, 2005.

————. 'Hazards of Modernity and Morality: Women, State, and Ideology in Contemporary Iran.' In *Women, Islam, and the State*, edited by Deniz Kandiyoti, 48–76. Basingstoke: Palgrave Macmillan, 1991.

Nash, Jennifer. 'Rethinking Intersectionality.' *Feminist Review* 89, no. 1 (2008): 1–15.

Nelson, Adam. 'Nationalism, Transnationalism, and the American Scholar in the Nineteenth-Century: Thoughts on the Career of William Dwight Whitney.' *The New England Quarterly* 78, no. 3 (2005): 347–76.

Newman, Gerald. *The Rise of English Nationalism: A Cultural History, 1740–1830*. London: Weidenfeld and Nicolson, 1987.

Nochlin, Linda. *The Body in Pieces: The Fragment as a Metaphor of Modernity*. London: Thames & Hudson, 1994.

————. 'The Imaginary Orient.' 1983. In *The Politics of Vision: Essays on Nineteenth-Century Art and Society*, 33–59. New York: Harper & Row, 1989.

Novak, Michael. *The Rise of the Unmeltable Ethnics: Politics and Culture in the Seventies*. New York: Macmillan, 1972.

Orr, Mary. 'Flaubert's Egypt: Crucible and Crux for Textual Identity.' In *Travellers in Egypt*, edited by Paul Starkey and Janet Starkey, 189–200. London: Garnet, 1998.

Ozdalga, Elizabeth. *The Veiling Issue: Official Secularism and Popular Islam in Modern Turkey*. Richmond, Surrey: Curzon, 1998.

Paidar, Parvin. *Women in the Political Process in Twentieth Century Iran*. Cambridge: Cambridge University Press, 1995.

Palmach Online Information Centre. 'The Blowing-Up of the Garage in Haifa.' http://www.palmach.org.il/show_item.asp?levelId=42858&itemId=8773&itemType=0.

————. 'The Castration Operation [in Hebrew]'. http://www.palmach.org.il/ show_item.asp?levelId= 38612&itemId= 5899&itemType= 0.

————. 'Departure of the 23 Yordei Hasira Boat'. http://www.palmach.org.il/ show_item.asp?levelId= 42858&itemId= 8607&itemType= 0.

————. 'Ha-Shaḥar Unit [in Hebrew]'. http://www.palmach.org.il/show_item .asp?levelId= 38612&itemId= 5533&itemType= 0.

————. 'The Villages Files' [in Hebrew]. http://www.palmach.org.il/show_item .asp?levelId= 38612&itemId= 5528&itemType= 0.

Patai, Rafael. *The Arab Mind*. New York: Scribner, 1973.

Pedahzur, Ami. *The Israeli Secret Services and the Struggle against Terrorism*. New York: Columbia University Press, 2010.

Peltre, Christine. *L'Atelier du Voyage: les Pentres en Orient au XIXe siècle*. Paris: Gallimard, 1995.

Phillips, Richard. *Sex, Politics, and Empire: A Postcolonial Geography*. Manchester: Manchester University Press, 2006.

Poirier, Richard. *The Performing Self: Compositions and Decompositions in the Languages of Contemporary Life*. Foreword by Edward W. Said. New Brunswick, NJ: Rutgers University Press, 1992.

Pollard, Lisa. *Nurturing the Nation: The Family Politics of Modernizing, Colonizing, and Liberating Egypt*. Berkeley, CA and London: University of California Press, 2005.

Prakash, Om and Manish Chakraborti. *Europeans in Bengal in the Pre-Colonial Period: A Brief History of Their Commercial and Cultural Legacy*. New Delhi: Embassy of the Netherlands, 2008.

Rajchman, John. *The Chomsky-Foucault Debate*. New York: The New Press, 2006.

Raz-Krakotzkin, Amnon. 'Exile within Sovereignty: A Critique of the "Negation of Exile" in Israeli Culture' [in Hebrew]. *Theory and Criticism* 4 (1993): 23–55.

Riepe, Dale. *The Philosophy of India and Its Impact on American Thought*. Springfield, IL: Charles C. Thomas, 1970.

Roberts, John. *The Art of Interruption: Realism, Photography and the Everyday*. Manchester: Manchester University Press, 1998.

Roberts, Mary. *Intimate Outsiders: The Harem in Ottoman and Orientalist Art and Travel Literature*. Durham, NC and London: Duke University Press, 2007.

Rodenbeck, John. *"Awalim;* or the Persistence of Error.' In *Historians in Cairo: Essays in Honor of George Scanlon*, edited by Jill Edwards, 107–22. Cairo and New York: American University in Cairo Press, 2002.

Rosenberg, Ralph R. 'The First American Doctor of Philosophy Degree: A Centennial Salute to Yale, 1861–1961.' *The Journal of Higher Education* 32, no. 7 (1961): 387–94.

Sacco, Joe. *Palestine*. Seattle, WA: Fantagraphics Books, 2001.

Sagnes, Guy. *L'Ennui dans la Littérature Française de Flaubert à Laforgue*. Paris: A. Colin, 1969.

Scarry, Elaine. *The Body in Pain*. Oxford: Oxford University Press, 1985.

Schiff, Judith Ann. 'Advice for the Language-lorn.' *Yale Alumni Publications*, March/April 2010.

Schwab, Raymond. *The Oriental Renaissance: Europe's Rediscovery of India and the East, 1680–1880*. Translated by Gene Patterson-Black and Victor Reinking. New York: Columbia University Press, 1984.

Scott, Joan Wallach. *The Politics of the Veil*. Princeton, NJ: Princeton University Press, 2007.

———. 'Gender: A Useful Category of Analysis.' *American Historical Review* 91, no. 5 (1986): 1056–61.

Shane, Scott. 'Interrogation Inc.: 2 U.S. Architects of Harsh Tactics in 9/11's Wake.' *New York Times*, 12 August 2009.

Shapira, Anita. *Yigal Allon, Native Son: A Biography*. Translated by Evelyn Abel. Philadelphia, PA: University of Pennsylvania Press, 2008.

Shaw, Wendy. *Ottoman Painting: Reflections of Western Art from the Ottoman Empire to the Turkish Republic*. London and New York: I. B. Tauris, 2011.

———. *Possessors and Possessed: Museums, Archaeology and the Visualization of History in the Late Ottoman Empire*. Berkeley, CA and London: University of California Press, 2003.

Shehadeh, Raja. *A Rift in Time: Travels with My Ottoman Uncle*. London: Profile, 2011.

Shenhav, Yehouda. *The Arab Jews: A Postcolonial Reading of Nationalism, Religion, and Ethnicity*. Stanford, CA: Stanford University Press, 2006.

———. 'Shimʿon Ḥoresh (Haroush) 1924–2006: A Legend in his Lifetime' [in Hebrew]. *Mabat Malam: Journal of the Israeli Intelligence, Heritage and Commemoration Centre* 40 (March 2005): 36–8.

Shirazi, Faegheh. *The Veil Unveiled: The Hijab in Modern Culture*. Gainesville, FL: University Press of Florida, 2001.

Shlaim, Avi. *The Iron Wall: Israel and the Arab World*. New York: W. W. Norton, 2001.

Shohat, Ella. 'Rupture and Return: Zionist Discourse and the Study of Arab Jews.' *Social Text* 75, no. 21 (2003): 49–74.

———. 'Sephardim in Israel: Zionism from the Standpoint of Its Jewish Victims.' *Social Text*, no. 19/20 (1988): 1–35.

———. 'The Invention of the Mizrahim.' *Journal of Palestine Studies* 29, no. 1 (1999): 5–20.

Singer, Amy. *Constructing Ottoman Beneficence: An Imperial Soup Kitchen in Jerusalem*. Albany, NY: State University Press of New York, 2002.

Sinha, Mirinalini. *Colonial Masculinity: The 'Manly' Englishman and the 'Effeminate' Bengali in the Late Nineteenth Century*. Manchester: Manchester University Press, 1995.

Sitton, Rafi and Yitzhak Shushan. *The People of Secrets* [in Hebrew]. Tel Aviv: Yediʿot Ahronot, 1990.

Smith, Tho., B. D. and Fellow of St Mary Magdalen College Oxon. *Remarks Upon the Manners, Religion and Government of the Turks. Together with a Survey of the Seven Churches of Asia, As they now lye in Their Ruines: And A Brief Description of Constantinople*. London: Printed for Moses Pitt, at the Angel in St Pauls Church-yard, 1678.

Snir, Reuven. ' "Ana min al-Yahud": The Demise of Arab-Jewish Culture in the Twentieth Century.' *Archiv Orientální* 74 (2006): 387–424.

———. ' "We Are Arabs Before We Are Jews": The Emergence and Demise of Arab-Jewish Culture in Modern Times.' *EJOS – Electronic Journal of Oriental Studies* VIII, no. 9 (2005): 1–47.

Sontag, Susan. 'Regarding the Torture of Others: Notes on What Has Been Done – and Why – to Prisoners, by Americans.' *New York Times Sunday Magazine*, 23 May 2004, 26–7.

Spacks, Patricia Meyer. *Boredom: The Literary History of a State of Mind*. Chicago: University of Chicago Press, 1995.

Spencer, Robert. *Cosmopolitan Criticism and Postcolonial Literature*. Basingstoke and New York: Palgrave Macmillan, 2011.

Spitzer, Leo. *Linguistics and Literary History: Essays in Stylistics*. Princeton, NJ: Princeton University Press, 1948.

Spurling, Hilary. *The Unknown Matisse: A Life of Henri Matisse; The Early Years, 1869–1908*. London: Hamish Hamilton, 1998.

Steegmuller, Francis, ed. and tr. *Flaubert in Egypt*. London: The Bodley Head, 1972.

Steiner, George. 'The Mandarin of the Hour–Michel Foucault.' *New York Times*, 'Books,' 18 February 1971.

Stoler, Ann Laura. *Carnal Knowledge and Imperial Power: Race and the Intimate in Colonial Rule*. Berkeley, CA and London: University of California Press, 2002.

Stuchtey, Benedikt and Eckhardt Fuchs, eds. *Writing World History 1800–2000*. Oxford: Oxford University Press, 2003.

Sugg, Richard. 'Eating Your Enemy: Richard Sugg Searches History to Explain the Phenomenon of Aggressive Cannibalism, Following Recent Allegations from Iraq.' *History Today* 58, no. 7 (2008). www.historytoday.com.

Tarlo, Emma. *Visibly Muslim: Fashion, Politics, Faith*. Oxford and New York: Berg, 2010.

Thompson, Jason. *Edward William Lane: The Life of the Pioneering Egyptologist and Orientalist*. London: Haus, 2010.

Tibebu, Teshale. *Hegel and the Third World: The Making of Eurocentrism in World History*. Syracuse, NY: Syracuse University Press, 2011.

Tilby, Michael. 'Flaubert's Place in Literary History.' In *The Cambridge Companion to Flaubert*, edited by Timothy Unwin, 14–33. Cambridge: Cambridge University Press, 2004.

Toohey, Peter. *Boredom: A Lively History*. New Haven, CT and London: Yale University Press, 2011.

Tromans, Nicholas. 'Palestine: Picture of Prophecy.' In *William Holman Hunt*, edited by Carol Jacobi and Katherine Lochnan, 135–60. Toronto, ON: Art Gallery of Ontario, 2008.

Usborne, David. 'John Currin: The Filth and the Fury.' *The Independent*, 16 March 2008.

Varisco, Daniel. *Islam Obscured: The Rhetoric of Anthropological Representation*. New York: Palgrave Macmillan, 2005.

Vico, Giambattista. *The New Science*. 1730. Translated by Thomas Goddard Bergin and Max Harold Fisch. Ithaca, NY: Cornell University Press, 1948.

Viswanathan, Gauri. *Masks of Conquest*. New York: Columbia, 1989.

Vitkus, Daniel J. *Turning Turk: English Theatre and the Multicultural Mediterranean*. Basingstoke and New York: Palgrave Macmillan, 2003.

Von Schlegel, Friedrich. *On the Language and Philosophy of the Indians* (1808), republished in *Aesthetic and Miscellaneous Works*. Translated by E. J. Millington. London: Henry G. Bohn, 1849.

Wall, Geoffrey. *Flaubert: A Life*. London: Faber and Faber, 2001.

Waters, Lindsay. 'In Responses Begins Responsibility: Music and Emotion.' In *Edward Said and the Work of the Critic: Speaking Truth to Power*, edited by Paul A. Bové. Durham, NC and London: Duke University Press, 2000.

Weeks, Emily. 'About Face: Sir David Wilkie's Portrait of Mehemet Ali, Pasha of Egypt.' In *Orientalism Transposed*, edited by Julie Codell and Dianne Sachko Macleod, 46–62. Aldershot: Ashgate, 1998.

White, Gabrielle D. V. *Jane Austen in the Context of Abolition: 'A Fling at the Slave Trade.'* London: Palgrave Macmillan, 2006.

Whitney, William Dwight. *Sanskrit Grammar*. Cambridge, MA: Harvard University Press, 1879.

Williams, Raymond. *Marxism and Literature*. Oxford and New York: Oxford University Press, 1977.

Wolfe, Cary. *Animal Rites*. Chicago: University of Chicago Press, 2003.

Yaʿari, ʿOdeda. *Contour Lines: The Story of Deni Agmon, Head of the Mistaʿaravim Unit* [in Hebrew]. Tel Aviv: Beit ha-Palmach, 2006.

Yeazell, Ruth Bernard. *Harems of the Mind: Passages of Western Art and Literature*. New Haven, CT: Yale University Press, 2000.

Yeğenoğlu, Meyda. *Islam, Migrancy and Hospitality in Europe*. Basingstoke and New York: Palgrave Macmillan, 2012.

Young, Robert. *White Mythologies: Writing History and the West*. London and New York: Routledge, 1990.

Žižek, Slavoj. *The Metastases of Enjoyment: Six Essays on Women and Causality*. London: Verso, 1994.

———. *Organs without Bodies*. London: Routledge, 2004.

Index

CPSIA information can be obtained
at www.ICGtesting.com
Printed in the USA
BVOW06*1201300817
493516BV00006B/33/P